19.95
68p

LEARNING
AND INDIVIDUAL DIFFERENCES

A Series of Books in Psychology

EDITORS: Richard C. Atkinson
Gardner Lindzey
Richard F. Thompson

LEARNING
AND INDIVIDUAL
DIFFERENCES

Advances in Theory and Research

ROBERT MANNING
STROZIER LIBRARY

SEP 8 1990

Tallahassee, Florida

Edited by

Phillip L. Ackerman, *University of Minnesota*
Robert J. Sternberg, *Yale University*
Robert Glaser, *University of Pittsburgh*

W. H. FREEMAN AND COMPANY   *New York*

BF
318
L385
1989

ROBERT MANNING
STROZIER LIBRARY

SEP 6 1990

Tallahassee, Florida

Library of Congress Cataloging-in-Publication Data
Learning and individual differences: Advances in theory
and research / edited by Phillip L. Ackerman,
  Robert J. Sternberg, Robert Glaser.
    p. cm.—(A Series of books in psychology)
  Bibliography: p.
  Includes index.
    ISBN 0-7167-1983-5. ISBN 0-7167-1985-1 (pbk.)
    1. Learning, Psychology of. 2. Difference (Psychology)
I. Ackerman, Phillip Lawrence, 1957– . II. Sternberg,
Robert J. III. Glaser, Robert, 1921– . IV. Series.
BF318.L385 1989
153.1'5—dc19

                                                88-16317
                                                CIP

Copyright © 1989 by W. H. Freeman and Company

No part of this book may be reproduced by any
mechanical, photographic, or electronic process,
or in the form of a phonographic recording, nor
may it be stored in a retrieval system, transmitted,
or otherwise copied for public or private use,
without written permission from the publisher.

Printed in the United States of America

1 2 3 4 5 6 7 8 9 VB 7 6 5 4 3 2 1 0 8 9

Contents

8   Inference and Discovery
in an Exploratory Laboratory   279
VALERIE J. SHUTE, ROBERT GLASER, AND
KALYANI RAGHAVEN

Contributors

PHILLIP L. ACKERMAN
Department of Psychology
University of Minnesota

JAMIE CAMPBELL
Department of Psychology
Western Ontario University

ROBERT M. GAGNÉ
Department of Educational Research
Florida State University

ROBERT GLASER
Learning Research and
  Development Center
University of Pittsburgh

JOHN L. HORN
Department of Psychology
University of Southern California

PATRICK C. KYLLONEN
Air Force Human Resources
  Laboratory
Brooks Air Force Base

KALYANI RAGHAVAN
Learning Research and
  Development Center
University of Pittsburgh

VALERIE J. SHUTE
Air Force Human Resources
  Laboratory
Brooks Air Force Base

ROBERT S. SIEGLER
Department of Psychology
Carnegie-Mellon University

RICHARD E. SNOW
School of Education
Stanford University

ROBERT J. STERNBERG
Department of Psychology
Yale University

RICHARD K. WAGNER
Department of Psychology
Florida State University

Preface

The topic of learning and individual differences is central to a wide range of research and applied programs, from basic research in acquisition of information-processing skills to the design of tailored instructional programs for increasing student achievement. Included are such theoretical and empirical issues as the relation between cognitive abilities and learning, individual differences in the acquisition of knowledge during child development, metacognitive strategies for learning in adults, and expression of abilities in both academic and everyday nonacademic environments. Results from basic research in this area will ultimately have an impact on instructional methods in schools and employment training methods.

An initial foray into this interdisciplinary topic was published in 1967, based on a conference held at the University of Pittsburgh in 1965. The edited volume based on that conference (R. M. Gagné, Editor, *Learning and Individual Differences*. Columbus, Ohio: Charles E. Merrill) provided an original and integrative consideration of the topic, mostly from the perspective of experimental psychology. Since the publication of the Gagné book, a great number of research programs in cognitive, developmental, differential, and instructional psychology have resulted in substantial changes in the character of inquiry in this area.

The editors of the present volume decided that, after twenty years, it was important to document the current work in the field and to provide in one place a description of the research that has appeared in many different contexts—experimental, cognitive, differential, educational and instructional, and developmental psychology.

The 1967 volume considered how state-of-the-art experimental psychology theory and empirical research could be related to individual differences research. *Learning and Individual Differences: Advances in Theory and Research* takes a different tack. It highlights research devoted to individual differences in learning that can facilitate exchange of ideas among people who take different approaches to the subject.

The aim of the current volume is to describe theoretical and empirical advances in the integration of approaches to learning and individual differences. Given the extent of such research, we have not attempted to be comprehensive in covering the subject. Rather, we have solicited in-depth treatments of research and theory on learning and individual differences from a sample of leading researchers in the field.

We view the inclusion of chapters in experimental psychology and differential psychology as crucial to the treatment of learning and individual differences. However, the progress of the past twenty years requires that we include other avenues of productive research, such as research concerning the integration of cognitive and differential approaches, the domain of developmental psychology, and the domain of instructional and educational psychology. We believe that this volume will provide students and researchers with an understanding of the efforts toward integration of the experimental and differential approaches to the study of behavior. The chapters describe the historical basis and justification for the study of learning and individual differences and review innovative approaches to varied issues in this field.

In Chapter 1, Robert M. Gagné describes the current state of research against a historical background. He reviews the state of the field twenty years ago and the numerous advances in the study of learning and individual differences since then, examining the transition from stimulus-response theory to information-processing conceptions of learning, developments in ability theory, and the emergent field of aptitude-treatment interactions.

The next four chapters present general frameworks for the study of individual differences in learning. Richard E. Snow presents in Chapter 2 a comprehensive and personal review of the development of aptitude-treatment interaction research. He describes the tactics and logic of this research and reports on ongoing empirical studies. Snow traces the changes in the nature of inquiry as the research emphasis has shifted from the study of the influence of cognitive variables to that of conative variables as determinants of individual differences in learning.

A fundamental issue of learning and individual differences has always been how a person's cognitive-intellectual abilities influence the learning situation. In Chapter 3 John L. Horn presents a framework of abilities that is important for learning, both for learning in specific domains and for knowledge acquisition and retention over the course of adult development and aging.

Chapter 4 by Patrick C. Kyllonen and Valerie J. Shute, provides a taxonomic description of learning that includes the learning environment, resulting knowledge type, content domain, and learning styles. This comprehensive taxonomy provides a framework that practitioners can use to determine methods for enhancing learning and that researchers can use to assess the measures employed to evaluate individual differences in learning. Kyllonen and Shute illustrate the workings of the taxonomy with a review of three computer-based intelligent tutors.

Phillip L. Ackerman (Chapter 5) presents a historical overview and a current theoretical perspective on individual differences in skill learning. He reviews how ability and information-processing perspectives can be integrated to provide a theory that predicts changing ability-performance correlations during task practice. Ackerman presents two empirical demonstrations of research in this area and discusses the implications of the theory for the study of individual differences in other domains of ability research.

The last three chapters describe empirical approaches to learning and individual differences. These approaches include innovative experimental paradigms along with traditional experimental procedures. Robert Siegler and Jamie Campbell (Chapter 6) describe a model of solution strategies and individual differences found in the acquisition of mathematics skills in children. They consider the implications of different styles of problem solving for individual differences in learning. Siegler and Campbell also place these discussions in the context of interactions between ability and process-level determinants of learning.

Robert J. Sternberg and Richard K. Wagner (Chapter 7) examine the distinctions between academic knowledge and practical knowledge. The authors discuss the nature and acquisition of practical knowledge, which is defined as knowledge that is procedural and relevant to everyday life. Sternberg and Wagner review empirical investigations that build a framework for characterizing practical knowledge and demonstrate the importance of such knowledge for both academic and everyday life situations.

Chapter 8, by Valerie J. Shute, Robert Glaser, and Kalyani Raghavan, considers individual differences in a complex learning environment—an intelligent tutor for economics principles. The authors examine the acquisition of knowledge and the demonstration of scientific hypothesis-testing skills in studies of college students. The intelligent-tutor paradigm provides a rich source of information about learning strategies and individual differences in situations where learners confront a relatively unstructured learning situation. The authors describe the tactics of this type of research and detail many manifestations of individual differences during acquisition of scientific knowledge.

In the 1967 book on learning and individual differences, Arthur Melton emphasized the importance of studying individual difference variables in terms of the process constructs of contemporary theory. Researchers have heeded Melton's advice; this volume provides evidence of advances along these lines of inquiry.

P. L. A.
R. J. S.
R. G.

LEARNING
AND INDIVIDUAL DIFFERENCES

1

Some Reflections on Learning and Individual Differences

ROBERT M. GAGNÉ *Florida State University*

The conference on learning and individual differences held twenty years ago at the Learning Research and Development Center, University of Pittsburgh (hereafter referred to as the LRDC Conference) brought together a number of investigators of human learning, particularly those whose work evidenced an awareness of the influence of differences in human characteristics. Many learning psychologists had been persuaded by Cronbach's influential article (1957) of the need for the development of rational connections between the streams of correlational psychology and experimental psychology. Cronbach had presented a challenge to his fellow investigators:

> Our job is to invent constructs and to form a network of laws which permits prediction. From observations we must infer a psychological description of the situation and of the present state of the organism. Our laws should permit us to predict, from this description, the behavior of organism-in-situation (p. 681).

The majority of contributors to the conference represented the experimental psychology stream, although there was due representation by those experienced in correlational research, including Cronbach, Glaser, and Carroll. The conference thus addressed the challenge to experimental psychologists: What have you discovered about individual differences lately? Its purpose was to explore what had been accomplished and what might be expected of research efforts resonating to this theme.

DIFFERENCES RELATED TO LEARNING — TWENTY YEARS AGO

The proceedings of the LRDC Conference are recorded in the book *Learning and Individual Differences* (Gagné, 1967). It is instructive to view the major themes discussed by the contributors in light of more recent research. Although I will not summarize articles by individual authors, I will refer to their chapters in that volume by the authors' names only.

In an opening chapter, Glaser reviews some of the prominent earlier work relating learning to individual differences. He cites the work of Woodrow (1946), who failed to find strong relationships between measures of intelligence and learning ability, and other efforts by Gulliksen (1942) and later by his students (Allison, 1960; Stake, 1961) to find such relationships. Glaser reviews other work that explored the relationship of measures of the initial state of the learner to rate of learning, and addressed the problem of selecting appropriate dependent measures of learning. Summing up this earlier work, Glaser points to the lack of a theoretical framework for both the selection of tests of individual abilities and the selection of learning measures.

Thus, despite a general recognition by 1965 of the problem of relating learning to human abilities and the need to develop both rational theory and methodology, we were not far from the starting gate. The research to date had done little to point the way toward clarification of the field, much less to arrive at well-verified generalizable conclusions.

CONCEPTIONS OF THE PROBLEM

Given this background to the conference, what were these investigators able to contribute to the articulation of the problem of relating individual differences to learning and to the lines of inquiry that might contribute to a better understanding of these relationships?

Essential to the understanding of their contributions is the recognition that the researchers attending the conference were enmeshed in the tradition of stimulus-response (S-R) and the paradigm of verbal paired associates. When they thought about theory, or the mediating role of learning processes, or the variation in stimulus conditions affecting the learner, most used language traditional to the study of paired-associate verbal learning. They made frequent references to such concepts as proactive and retroactive interference, stimulus and response generalization, strength of association, and others that have their most precise meanings in relation to pairs of verbal items in which one member is the stimulus and the other the response. Also, they tended to identify the independent variables of the learning situation as temporal rate of presentation, distribution of practice, amount of material, intratask similarity, and the like. I point out these qualities not to criticize the rationality of these contributions (which is indeed very good), but rather to indicate that their approach was bound by rather severe traditional restraints.

In his scholarly appraisal and interpretation of the conference, A. W. Melton noted the limiting effects of this experimental tradition. With unusual grasp of detail, Melton perceived that the most promising line of thought with which to attack the problem of relating individual differences to learning is one which identifies and measures the *processes* of learning. He made particular note of such examples of processes as intention to learn, discussed by Jenkins; attention, by Maltzman; consolidation and reactive inhibition, by Jensen; and discrimination learning set, by Zeaman and House. Melton (1967) stressed: *"what is necessary is that we frame our hypotheses about individual differences variables in terms of the process constructs of contemporary theories of learning and performance"* (p. 239).

This statement is an indication of the profound change that was taking place in the psychology of learning and memory: from conceptions of stimulus-response to those of information processing. Although most of his own experimental work on learning had been done within the S-R tradition, Melton nevertheless foresaw that the information-processing view would prevail. The *processes* that would be investigated in the future were the processes of what we now call cognitive psychology. Rather than examine the processes of associative bonds and their interactions, investigators would look at the processes of intake and transformation of forms of information — of encoding and rehearsal and storage and retrieval of information. And it is these processes that were to be related to individual differences.

SUBSEQUENT TRENDS IN RESEARCH

The ideas presented at the LRDC Conference precipitated the transition to a new era of research dominated by the paradigm of cognitive information processing. Contributors to the conference were able to come to a kind of agreement on the significance of learning processes for the individual differences problem; however their approach was cloaked within the familiar S-R research tradition. They were unable to formulate the problem with the use of the newer concepts of information processing. The influential article on human memory by Atkinson and Shiffrin, for example, was not to appear in print until 1968.

What has happened in the field of learning research since the 1965 conference? What efforts have been made to find links between individual differences and the process of learning? To what extent has research fulfilled the promise of the LRDC Conference? Although I will attempt a brief answer to this question, my effort is not a comprehensive review of the research literature. I will only touch upon the most prominent themes—the work that appears to indicate a trend, and a trend that is long-lasting enough to command attention.

Learning Processes

Surely one of the most prominent developments of the past twenty years has been the formulation of an information-processing view of learning and memory. This theory is still being developed, although most of its basic constructs are by now well known and widely accepted. Some of the main contributors to this cognitive theory have been Atkinson and Shiffrin (1968), Anderson and Bower (1973), Anderson (1976), Norman and Rumelhart (1975), Tulving (1972), and Newell and Simon (1972). A number of original contributions to theory have been collected in handbooks edited by Estes (1975–1978).

Cognitive theories of learning and memory borrow many of their processes from computer science, particularly the discipline of *artificial intelligence* (**AI**). From this source, in combination with the research of learning psychologists, have come ideas about processes such as pattern recognition, rehearsal, short-term storage, semantic encoding, memory search, retrieval, episodic memory, and the distinction of declarative and procedural knowledge stores. Obviously, then, if one investigates the relationship of learning to individual differences by way of learning processes, one has a long list of potential variables to consider. And the list is not complete—research continues to add new variations. Some of the more recent additions, for example, include the idea of memory organization called *schema* (Rumelhart, 1980) and the concepts of *composition* and *automatization* (Neves and Anderson, 1981).

Investigators are still developing these concepts of learning processes in another sense: There is no general agreement yet on the methods to be used to measure learning variables. We do not yet have great confidence in our methods of measuring when a pattern is recognized, what the outcomes of rehearsal are, what the nature of short-term storage is, how we know that a given memory is episodic rather than semantic, or how we assess the quality and extent of a schema. Thus, this new field of learning research needs not only an acceptable lexicon of operational definitions but valid and reliable techniques of measuring the variables of the learning process. It would appear that experimental psychology, if it is to pursue the investigation of learning processes, faces the challenge of an extended period of rigorous empirical investigation aimed particularly at establishing acceptable norms for many new concepts of learning and memory processes. For example, researchers must establish criteria for working-memory limits, encoding specificity, skill automaticity, and other cognitive constructs.

In general it appears that twenty years have made an enormous difference in the availability of conceptual weapons with which to tackle the problem of learning's relationship to human abilities. This change is particularly significant if one accepts the conclusion of the LRDC Conference that the search for likely variables from experimental psychology should focus upon learning processes. The basic framework of short-term and long-term memory and the distinction between declarative and procedural knowledge stores is widely accepted as a basis for research and theory building (Anderson, 1985). Within this framework, investigators have identified a number of processes relevant to learning and memory and given firm rational arguments for their relationships with each other. Investigators have given operational definitions to some processes that have been validated by empirical evidence; other processes appear likely to achieve such a status. In any case, the several processes that are now commonly under investigation (such as encoding, rehearsal, storage, retrieval) provide many opportunities for measurement as variables having differential implications as individual differences in learning and memory.

Human Abilities

The past twenty years have witnessed notable developments in the psychometric realm. Not until after the LRDC Conference was this field able to examine the results of a great surge of aptitude-treatment interaction (ATI) studies. Although Cronbach and R. C. Anderson were able to report on and interpret a few previous ATI studies at the conference, there were as yet few data. In more recent years, a number of reviews of ATI studies have appeared, including the classic work of Cronbach and Snow (1977).

Psychologists continue to vigorously pursue investigations to discover relationships between various human characteristics and instructional treatments. They tend to use traditional psychometric measures in their studies of the kinds of human qualities comprising the aptitude component of ATI. As summarized by Corno and Snow (1986), these qualities include crystallized and fluid intelligence, specific prior knowledge, achievement motivation, and several "cognitive styles." Corno and Snow propose that the problem of ATI divides into several questions, all under the general heading of *adaptive teaching.* One set of research problems focuses on the *circumvention of inaptitude,* as is accomplished by such techniques as cooperative learning among small groups of students (Johnson and Johnson, 1975; Slavin, 1983). Another set of problems centers upon *aptitude development,* of the sort which has been shown to occur for verbal analogies (Sternberg and Weil, 1980), spatial visualization (Kyllonen, Lohman, and Snow, 1981), and some metacognitive strategies (Corno, 1981). The development of positive personality characteristics favoring learning achievement is another area of active research (Goldfried, 1979; Schunk, 1984).

It is apparent that twenty years has seen the development of a great deal of empirically based knowledge of ATI—knowledge which was sought but was not yet available at the time of the LRDC Conference. Summaries of findings in this area have been made by Snow (1976), Messick (1984), Tobias (1987), and Peterson (1977), among others. Generally speaking, this kind of research begins with traditional psychometric measures, such as crystallized intelligence, spatial visualization, locus of control, field dependence-independence, and proceeds to relate these measures to some type of variation in instructional "treatment." Frequently, the novel aspects of such research have been evident in the invention of techniques of participant modeling, of metacognitive teaching, of anxiety reduction methods, or of modes of cooperative learning. One is led to speculate that a major reason for failure to discover interactive relationships in ATI in previous research may be a lack of ingenuity in the devising of variations in techniques of instruction. Notable in this regard is the lack of comparability of the two frameworks for aptitude and instructional treatment.

Learning Processes as Measurable Human Attributes

What has happened to the emergent theme of the LRDC Conference, that research should address the problem of relationships of learning to individual differences through examination of the processes of learning and memory? How have investigators answered Glaser's (1972) call for attention to the "new aptitudes"? although they have not entirely neglected the effort to identify and measure learning processes, their progress has been slow.

Extensive discussion of processes revealed by research on various aspects of intelligence is contained in a volume edited by Sternberg (1982). Psychologists are pursuing extensive research on cognitive processes from which one can foresee the emergence of well-understood and more-or-less standard operational meanings for many of these concepts. Examples of two process measures which appear to be of continuing usefulness are (1) the letter-matching task introduced by Posner and Mitchell (1967) and investigated in relationship to individual ability factors by Hunt, Lunneborg, and Lewis (1975); and (2) the sentence-picture–verification task introduced by Clark and Chase (1972), also employed in the research of Hunt and his colleagues.

The first of these tasks yields a measure of difference in reaction time between recognizing sameness or difference in letters that are physically identical (A,A) or identical in name only (A,a). The difference in reaction time provides a measure of *speed of access to concept names*. Hunt and his colleagues present evidence that this measure is substantially related to psychometric measures of verbal ability. A second task that appears to indicate the quality of a learning process involves the use of sentences describing pictures of the symbol combination + and *. The sentence types are "star above plus," "star not above plus," "star below plus," and "star not below plus." Following presentation of the sentence, a test picture is shown of one of the configurations of the symbols. The task requires the subject to indicate as rapidly as possible whether the sentence is true or false. As employed by Hunt and his colleagues (1975), this task yields the two process measures of *time to encode a sentence* and *time to verify sentence meaning*. A critical review of the evidence as well as some of the controversy regarding these measures is given by Cooper and Regan (1982). Both of these tasks are good examples of well-defined learning process measurement, holding promise for improved understanding of relationships of learning to individual differences. It is hoped that other learning processes derived from information-processing theories will be subjected to similar rational analysis and empirical study.

One notable contribution to the pursuit of a status of measurable attributes for learning processes is the book *Human Abilities: An Information Processing Approach,* edited by Robert Sternberg (1985). The book presents and evaluates evidence pertaining to such processes as speed of simple reaction time, speed of choice reaction, and speed of reasoning processes. Hunt's (1985) chapter identifies a number of processes making up the ability of verbal comprehension, and other chapters by various investigators give consideration to hypothetical processes involved in memory, imagery, mathematics, inductive reasoning, and problem solving. It is apparent that, in general, the authors of these chapters are better equipped to deal with cognitive processes related to learning than were the participants of the LRDC Conference. The difference is attributable primarily to the development of cognitive theory and related research, which has furnished investigators with a valuable set of conceptual "tools;" these tools include such concepts as *control process, working memory, rehearsal,* and *schema,* among others.

Studies of the processes that can be identified by analysis of various measures of ability have yielded interesting results. For example, Pellegrino and Glaser (1982) and Sternberg (1977) have analyzed solutions to tests of *analogies,* such as Raven's *Progressive Matrices.* Their investigations have shown three general classes of process to be involved in analogy solution (Pellegrino, 1985): (1) *attribute discovery,* (2) *attribute comparison,* and (3) evaluation, or *justification.* By suitable manipulation of the attributes of analogy items, the separate contributions of these processes to the total performance can be verified. Investigators have applied a similar kind of analysis to still another measure of general intellectual ability, the *series-completion* task. Here, according to Pellegrino, the kinds of processes identified are *relations detection, discovery of periodicity,* and *pattern completion.* Again, these processes have been separately verified by suitable manipulation of the attributes of the series-completion task.

It is significant that the types of intellectual processes identified in these analytic studies, while well defined, nevertheless appear to be relatively complex. Thus, processes like *lexical access* (in reading comprehension), *problem translation* (in mathematics problems), and *attribute comparison* (in analogies) seem likely to comprise even simpler mental operations and strategies. These more elementary processes may include pattern matching, response to similarity, and speed of retrieval. It seems clear, therefore, that the search for processes of learning that are elementary in nature, and distinctive as individual differences, poses many problems yet to be solved.

Suggestions for the measurement of elementary learning processes, and the possible relationships of these measures to variables from factor analyses of human abilities, are described in articles by Carroll (1976, 1980). For example, an ability such as *spatial orientation* can be conceived of as involving the process of mental image rotation, whereas an ability like *word fluency* appears to partake of cognitive strategies of memory search, including the use of the alphabet in a mnemonic technique. Carroll's analyses are particularly valuable in indicating the complex nature of ability measures when viewed as comprising cognitive operations and strategies. Obviously, were one to set out to measure the individual processes and strategies as separate abilities, one would need to proceed in a manner vastly different from the traditional method of psychometric testing.

A noteworthy attempt to examine specific information-processing operations as individual differences measures is the research of Project LAMP (Learning Abilities Measurement Program), under the direction of Dr. R. E. Christal at the Air Force Human Resources Laboratory. This group of investigators has attempted, among other approaches, to identify direct measures of speed of information processing in tasks involving such operations as encoding, comparison, decision, and response execution (Kyllonen, 1985). High reliabilities have been obtained for the tasks employed, and regularly increasing response latency was found for tasks representing simple reaction time, choice reaction time, physical identity, name identity, category identity, and meaning identity. These results are highly promising, and suggest the desirability of intensified research on speed of mental processing as a source of individual differences measures.

SUMMARY

In general, the research advances of the past twenty years have, at a minimum, reemphasized the problem of relating mental processes to individual differences, and provided some promising new approaches. We are capable of considerably more detailed and technically sophisticated analyses of information processing largely because of developments in information-processing theories of learning and memory (Anderson, 1985). The tradition of research in ATI, that of correlating aptitude measures with performance following different instructional "treatments," appears to be advancing toward a stage of well-informed rationality. Investigators approach problems within the framework of adaptive teaching, making distinctions between aptitude development and inaptitude circumvention (Corno and Snow, 1986). Analyses of various ability measures have succeeded in identifying intellectual processes that can be separately verified by experimental manipulation of task attributes. Studies of direct measures of elementary learning processes, such as those reported by Hunt (1985) and Kyllonen (1985), may point the way to procedures for the isolation and measurement of elementary intellectual processes of the sort that could appropriately be considered "new aptitudes."

REFERENCES

Allison, R. B. (1960). *Learning parameters and human abilities.* Princeton, N.J.: Educational Testing Service.

Anderson, J. R. (1976). *Language, memory, and thought.* Hillsdale, N.J.: Erlbaum.

Anderson, J. R. (1985). *Cognitive psychology and its implications,* 2d ed. New York: W. H. Freeman and Company.

Anderson, J. R., and Bower, G. H. (1973). *Human associative memory.* Washington, D.C.: V. H. Winston.

Atkinson, R. C., and Shiffrin, R. M. (1968). Human memory: A proposed system and its control processes. In K. W. Spence and J. T. Spence (Eds.), *The psychology of learning and motivation,* Vol. 2. New York: Academic Press.

Carroll, J. B. (1976). Psychometric tests as cognitive tasks: A new "structure of intellect." In L. B. Resnick (Ed.), *The nature of intelligence.* Hillsdale, N.J.: Erlbaum.

Carroll, J. B. (1980). *Individual difference relations in psychometric and experimental cognitive tasks.* Chapel Hill, N.C.: L. L. Thurstone Psychometric Laboratory, University of North Carolina.

Clark, H. H., and Chase, W. G. (1972). On the process of comparing sentences against pictures. *Cognitive Psychology,* 3:472–517.

Cooper, L. A., and Regan, D. T. (1982). Attention, perception, and intelligence. In R. J. Sternberg (Ed.), *Handbook of human intelligence.* Cambridge: Cambridge University Press.

Corno, L. (1981). Cognitive organizing in classrooms. *Curriculum Inquiry,* 11:359–377.

Corno, L., and Snow, R. E. (1986). Adapting teaching to individual differences among learners. In M. C. Wittrock (Ed.), *Handbook of research on teaching,* 3d ed. New York: Macmillan.

Cronbach, L. J. (1957). The two disciplines of scientific psychology. *American Psychologist,* 12:671–684.

Cronbach, L. J., and Snow, R. E. (1977). *Aptitudes and instructional methods: A handbook for research on interactions.* New York: Irvington.

Estes, W. K. (Ed.) (1975–1978). *Handbook of learning and cognitive processes,* Vols. 1–6. Hillsdale, N.J.: Erlbaum.

Gagné, R. M. (Ed.) (1967). *Learning and individual differences.* Columbus, Ohio: Merrill.

Glaser, R. (1972). Individuals and learning: The new aptitudes. *Educational Researcher,* 1 (6):5–13.

Goldfried, M. R. (1979). Anxiety reduction through cognitive–behavioral intervention. In P. C. Kendall and S. D. Hollon (Eds.), *Cognitive–behavioral interventions: Theory, research, and procedures.* New York: Academic Press.

Gulliksen, H. (1942). An analysis of learning data which distinguishes between initial preference and learning ability. *Psychometrika,* 7:171–194.

Hunt, E. (1985). Verbal ability. In R. J. Sternberg (Ed.), *Human abilities: An information-processing approach.* New York: W. H. Freeman and Company.

Hunt E., Lunneborg, C., and Lewis, J. (1975). What does it mean to be high verbal? *Cognitive Psychology,* 7:194–227.

Johnson, D. W., and Johnson, R. T. (1975). *Learning together and alone.* Englewood Cliffs, N.J.: Prentice-Hall.

Kyllonen, P. C. (1985). *Dimensions of information processing speed.* Interim Paper. Brooks AFB, Texas: Air Force Human Resources Laboratory. (AFHRL-TP84-56).

Kyllonen, P. C., Lohman, D. F., and Snow, R. E. (1981). *Effects of task facets and strategy training on spatial task performance* (Tech. Rep. No 14). Stanford, Calif.: Stanford University School of Education, Aptitude Research Project.

Melton, A. W. (1967). Individual differences and theoretical process variables: General comments on the conference. In R. M. Gagné (Ed.), *Learning and individual differences.* Columbus, Ohio: Merrill.

Messick, S. (1984). The nature of cognitive styles: Problems and promise in educational practice. *Educational Psychologist,* 19:59–75.

Neves, D. M., and Anderson, J. R. (1981). Knowledge compilation: Mechanisms for the automatization of cognitive skills. In J. R. Anderson (Ed.), *Cognitive skills and their acquisition.* Hillsdale, N.J.: Erlbaum.

Newell, A., and Simon, H. A. (1972). *Human problem solving.* Englewood Cliffs, N.J.: Prentice-Hall.

Norman, D. A., and Rumelhart, D. E. (Eds.) (1975). *Explorations in cognition.* New York: W. H. Freeman and Company.

Pellegrino, J. W. (1985). Inductive reasoning ability. In R. J. Sternberg (Ed.), *Human abilities: An information-processing approach.* New York: W. H. Freeman and Company.

Pellegrino, J. W., and Glaser, R. (1982). Analyzing aptitudes for learning: Inductive reasoning. In R. Glaser (Ed.), *Advances in instructional psychology,* Vol. 2. Hillsdale, N.J.: Erlbaum.

Peterson, P. L. (1977). Review of human characteristics and school learning. *American Educational Research Journal,* 14:73–79.

Posner, M., and Mitchell, R. (1967). Chronometric analysis of classification. *Psychological Review,* 74:392–409.

Rumelhart, D. E. (1980). Schemata: The building blocks of cognition. In R. J. Spiro, B. C. Bruce, and W. F. Brewer (Eds.), *Theoretical issues in reading comprehension.* Hillsdale, N.J.: Erlbaum.

Schunk, D. H. (1984). Self-efficacy perspective on achievement behavior. *Educational Psychologist,* 19:48–58.

Slavin, R. E. (1983). *Cooperative learning.* New York: Longman.

Snow, R. E. (1976). Research on aptitudes: A progress report. *Review of Research in Education,* 4:50–105.

Stake, R. E. (1961). Learning parameters, aptitudes, and achievements. *Psychometric Monographs,* 9.

Sternberg, R. J. (Ed.) (1982). *Handbook on human intelligence.* Cambridge: Cambridge University Press.

Sternberg, R. J. (1977). *Intelligence, information processing, and analogical reasoning: The componential analysis of human abilities.* Hillsdale, N.J.: Erlbaum.

Sternberg, R. J. (1985). *Human abilities: An information-processing approach.* New York: W. H. Freeman and Company.

Sternberg, R. J., and Weil, E. M. (1980). An aptitude-strategy interaction in linear syllogistic reasoning. *Journal of Educational Psychology,* 72:226–234.

Tobias, S. (1987). Learner characteristics. In R. M. Gagné (Ed.), *Instructional technology: Foundations.* Hillsdale, N.J.: Erlbaum.

Tulving, E. (1972). Episodic and semantic memory. In E. Tulving and W. Donaldson (Eds.), *Organization of memory.* New York: Academic Press.

Woodrow, H. A. (1946). The ability to learn. *Psychological Review,* 53:147–158.

2

Aptitude-Treatment Interaction as a Framework for Research on Individual Differences in Learning

RICHARD E. SNOW *Stanford University*

Learners differ profoundly in what they do in learning and in their success in any particular learning situation. This is an observable problem today, as it has been for centuries. A big part of the problem is understanding what different learners bring psychologically to the learning situation that confronts them. Over the past two decades a new start has been made on resolving this problem. The 1965 LRDC Conference, (see Gagné, 1967), was a key starting point.

In the first two chapters of the 1965 conference, Glaser and Cronbach, respectively, reached substantially the same conclusions regarding next steps for psychological research on learning and individual differences, despite their markedly different perspectives and emphases. Glaser (1967) traced the history of laboratory experimentation on learning and embraced a natural science perspective, recommending that individual differences be conceptualized as limiting or boundary conditions on the laws of learning. To study these limiting conditions: "the requirement for assessing initial state means . . . postulating *initial properties of the learner which interact with learning*" (p. 14, emphasis added). He doubted that the construct of general intelligence or other factor–analytically derived constructs would be useful in characterizing this initial state, since no theoretical framework existed to relate reference ability tests to learning measures. Cronbach (1967) described the educational side of the picture, emphasizing the adaptation of instruction to individual differences in learning by finding or designing alternative instructional methods to fit different students. This approach required:

> a new psychological theory of aptitude. An aptitude, in this context, is *a complex of personal characteristics that accounts for an individual's end state after a particular educational treatment* . . . [It] includes whatever promotes the pupil's survival in a particular educational environment, and it may have as much to do with styles of thought and personality variables as with the abilities covered in conventional tests. . . . *such a theory deals with aptitude-treatment interactions* (pp. 23–24, emphasis added).

To summarize these views, with some presumptive elaborations:

1. *Aptitude* refers to properties of the initial states of persons that account for the end states they reach through attempting to learn in particular ongoing situations; *treatment* refers to any one such situation.

2. Aptitude complexes, involving multiple personal properties, are expected to influence learning in particular treatments; conventionally defined abilities may not be the most important constituents of these aptitude constructs. Presumably, these initial-state complexes are not merely correlates of learning but are actually propaedeutic, that is, they are needed as preparation for successful response to learning conditions.

3. One can profitably study the interaction of such aptitudes and learning by experimentally manipulating treatment situations. Presumably, both between-person and within-person experiments can be informative in this regard; educational situations more likely afford the former, whereas laboratory situations allow either. In either case, aptitude-treatment interactions (ATI) are the focus.

4. A new psychological theory of aptitude is the goal. Such a theory would presumably identify the boundary states of aptitude and treatment variables within which generalizations about learning would be expected to hold. Such a theory would also presumably indicate ways in which instruction could be adapted to individual differences in aptitude.

This chapter traces the history of research from these starting points to the present day. It places ATI research on learning and instruction within the broader perspective of person-situation interactionism in psychology, of which it is a special case. It also attempts to bring some developments in research on cognition and motivation, and in the social psychology of education, into the ATI framework. Some empirical studies serve as examples, but this chapter is not an attempt at a comprehensive review of the literature. Some suggestions for future research, and some criticisms of past research, are also considered.

A BRIEF HISTORY OF ATI RESEARCH

The story of ATI research begins before 1965 to identify some origins, though the main concern is the period 1965 to 1985, in keeping with the plan of this volume. This recounting of developments in ATI research is a personal history of one participant. No claim is made that other researchers would necessarily single out the same milestones. I emphasize the research of the groups with which I worked at Purdue and then at Stanford. Particularly important were three team efforts. Seibert and I codirected a series of studies at Purdue, with United States Office of Education (USOE) support from 1958 to 1965. Cronbach and I then codirected the second team of researchers, under USOE sponsorship from 1966 to 1969; this work led to our 1977 book. The third team, which I codirected with David Lohman under Office of Naval Research (ONR) sponsorship, carried the project from 1975 to 1983.[1]

Early Developments

Origins Before 1965 Scholarly thinking about individual differences in learning, and even about adapting instructional treatments to student differences in aptitudes, stretches back to antiquity through a long line of philosophers (see Snow, 1982). There are old attempts to study persons and situations in consort in various fields of psychology (see Pervin and Lewis, 1978). And some experimentalists and some correlationists had conducted exploratory research on individual differences in learning well before 1965 (see Glaser, 1967, for a review).

---

[1]The following persons were a part of one or another of these efforts, and their work cited herein was, in many instances, supported by one of these projects: Ray Alvord, Katherin Baker, Charles Bethell-Fox, David Coffing, Janet Collins, Susan Crockenberg, Guy Fincke, Mike Friedman, Lita Furby, Lynn Gray, Jennifer Greene, Robert Heckman, Meg Korpi, Patrick Kyllonen, Suzanne Lajoie, Marcia Linn, Ellen Mandinach, Nancy Hamilton Markle, Brachia Marshalek, Akimichi Omura, Pearl Paulsen, Penelope Peterson, Tamarra Pickford, Ann Porteus, Gavriel Salomon, Enoch Sawin, Martin Smith, Nicholas Stayrook, John Swiney, Darlene Tullos, Dan Webb, Noreen Webb, Sia Wesson, Dan Woltz, Elanna Yalow. Many other persons also contributed.

But the systematic formulation of ATI as a general framework for research stems from Cronbach's work in the 1950s. A symposium debate on experimental design in research on psychotherapy was one spark (Edwards and Cronbach, 1952). Another was Cronbach's (1953) contrast of correlations between persons across tests, or situations, and correlations between such variables across persons. As Cronbach and Snow (1977) later summarized the argument, these two methods should be seen as:

> playing coordinate roles in sorting out interactions. The whole process of seeking order in behavioral or biological science is one of partitioning a grand matrix of organisms and situations into blocks in such a manner that a single generalization applies to all organisms and all situations classified within a block. The science of human behavior is built up by identifying a class of persons who respond similarly to some particular range of situation (p. 3).

The work of Cronbach and Gleser (1957; see the updated version, 1965) on test theory for personnel placement decisions posed the general question even more sharply; it became clear that to validate a test for job placement or educational classification, interaction between test scores and alternative job or treatment situations was the primary issue. The experimental question thus became central: How does one demonstrate the educational utility of a placement test? Cronbach (1957) then traced the history of the two disciplines of correlational and experimental psychology and described the interactional framework on which a unified science might be built. By 1965, Cronbach was ready to mount a programmatic effort on the ATI problem in instructional research, and his first conference paper (Cronbach, 1967) represents the initial steps of that project.

Prior to 1965, there had been isolated studies showing ATI results. Many investigators also had collected aptitude data in the context of instructional treatment comparisons but had not reported adequate analyses. There was, furthermore, no cumulation or systematic dissemination of this literature, and thus no integrated picture. My own isolated work as a graduate student in the period 1958 to 1963 serves as an example from this era that also introduces the generalized ATI matrix framework.

Seibert and I, and other colleagues at Purdue University, were engaged in evaluating instructional films for college-level physics. The films were specifically developed to capitalize on the power of cinematographic techniques for displaying physical phenomena (see Tendam, McLeod, and Snow, 1962). In my dissertation study (Snow, 1963a) and a companion analysis of film treatment characteristics (Snow, 1963b), we sought to show that learner characteristics and film characteristics jointly control learning. The dissertation design contrasted film versus live physics lecture demonstrations through a semester-long course, with immediate learning and retention criteria, but also a practice-stage analysis to reflect experience in learning from such treatments. Abilities, prior knowledge, attitudes, personality variables, and past film learning experience served as aptitudes, but were analyzed piecemeal, one or two at a time. Prior knowledge of physics showed no ATI when considered alone. However, when coupled with aptitude variables reflecting verbal and mathematical abilities, and also with measures of attitude toward and past use of instructional films, meaningful interactions were clear. Of particular interest was the finding that prior film learning experience seemed to aid new film learning, particularly in the absence of prior knowledge of physics; the effect seemed larger in later stages of the course. There were also marked ATI for two personality variables — responsibility and ascendancy — that did not depend on prior knowledge levels. The results, we thought, carried important implications despite what I now regard as a weak statistical analysis.

The details of these results need not be given space here (see Snow, Tiffin, and Seibert, 1965; Snow, 1988). The main point was that orderly ATI patterns could be obtained and explained, and that they involved prior knowledge, ability, and personality. If there were all these complex interactions to be found in a simple study, and if they varied in complex ways also as a function of experience in a particular course of instruction, then there ought to be a generalized multivariate framework for such research, as suggested by Cronbach's "grand matrix" conception noted earlier. There ought to be aptitude constructs that combined cognitive, conative, and affective individual characteristics. And these constructs should be studied, not just in grossly defined treatment contrasts such as "film versus live" but in more detailed multivariate analyses of instructional treatment variations, as well as person variations. Intermediate learning, or practice stage, measures should also be included.

Developing a Generalized Matrix Framework for ATI   Having demonstrated the presence of complex interactions among learner and treatment characteristics, Seibert and I sought to develop a generalized matrix framework for this research. We published a preliminary version in 1965. Later in 1965, David Wiley and I devised some methods of analysis for such data matrices; this became a technical appendix (Snow, 1966) to some later papers (Snow, 1968, 1974) but was never itself published. Parts of the scheme were applied by Smith (1965, 1967) and Heckman (1967), but a full-scale application has never been attempted.

The framework deserves further consideration, not for its minor historical interest but because it casts the problem in the generalized matrix form and suggests that most conventional ATI studies, and many other studies of individual differences in learning, problem solving, and cognitive performance, can be seen as special cases within this framework.

In Figure 2-1, three data matrices are arranged along their conformable edges. The A matrix contains scores of persons on aptitude variables. The T matrix contains scores of treatments on treatment variables. The O matrix contains outcome criterion scores of persons in treatments. Also shown are two vectors: $O_{p.}$ can be thought of as a particular column in O or as the mean of all columns—predictions of it from A yield the traditional main effects for aptitude variables regardless of treatment distinctions; this is the typical predictive validity study, as conducted by differential psychologists. $O_{.j}$ can be thought of as a particular row in O or as the mean of all rows—predictions of it from T yield main effects for treatment variables regardless of person differences, or in other words, predictions of average treatment difficulty based on treatment characteristics alone. Deriving these predictions is the traditional experimentalist's quest.

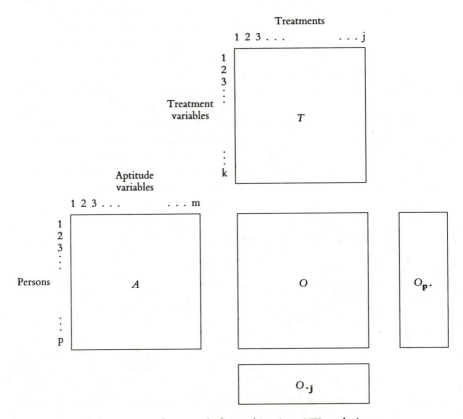

Figure 2-1 A three-matrix framework for multivariate ATI analysis.

The general aim of interaction research is to predict O from combinations of variables from A and T. Snow (1966) outlined the general statistical procedures, including the residualization of O based on predictions of O_p. and $O_{.j}$; residual O is the aptitude-treatment interaction variance after both main effects are extracted. Thus, in the grand scheme, interactions of A and T are used to partition O into regions that identify optimal person-situation matches. But the statistical and psychometric details would likely differ for the many special cases and alternative designs.

In the original design, treatments were defined as instructional message segments, such as films or film scenes in a series, paragraphs or sections in a continuing text, or frames in programmed instruction. The only limit on the definition of segments was that one or more criterion or outcome test items had to be associated with each treatment segment, to fill the O matrix. This is a within-person ATI design, where treatment variables might either be allowed to vary naturally across segments or be manipulated experimentally, or both. Part of the aim of this approach was to allow combinations of representative and systematic design, following the recommendations of Brunswik (1956; see Snow, 1968, 1974). Following the implications of my dissertation research, the concern also was to allow the study of differential adaptation to treatment over segments, or stages, of learning in a course of instruction.

Between-person experiments are special cases formed by adding dummy variables to A and T that partition O (preferably randomly). The conventional, between-person ATI study is one that chooses only a few global instructional treatments (as opposed to segments of an instructional sequence), defines them according to their profiles across treatment variables, and partitions the A matrix with a dummy variable to assign persons to treatments randomly. The analysis is then reduced to a comparison of regressions of an O column associated with each treatment onto the aptitude variables.

The treatments might also be experimental task conditions administered within-person to distinguish component processes in task performance, as in Sternberg's (1977) formulation. Contrast scores that reflect experimental manipulations (that is, cognitive components) are signifying ATI when they correlate with reference ability measures. O might contain reaction time as well as error data. Treatment segments might also be learning tasks, or trials or parts of a single learning task in series. The Stake (1961) and Allison (1960) correlational studies of abilities and learning fit this pattern, as do the controlled versus automatic task contrasts of Ackerman and Schneider (1985). Also, an L matrix might replace the O matrix, to represent intermediate learning process or activity measures associated with treatment trials or segments. The vector O_p. would then become an independent overall outcome measure, rather than a sum of L columns, in such studies. One can also imagine cubic matrices replacing A, T, and O to allow between-person comparisons of several molar treatments, each constructed as a series of treatment segments that also allows within-person analyses across task segments or practice stages. A variety of correlational analytic procedures might then be applied, following the sort of thinking represented by Cattell's (1946) covariation chart.

There is no space here for explication of all these possibilities, and there are as yet no good empirical examples of the full analysis anyway. The main point is that traditional correlational, experimental, and ATI studies of individual differences in learning are all special cases drawn from this framework, with resultant variations in how their data are analyzed. These special case variations can distort or make difficult attempts at integrated conceptualizations across these different kinds of studies. It should help (at least it helps me) to characterize each such study by the way it is drawn from the grand matrix. Furthermore, if aptitude is to be studied not only as a static description of the degree to which different persons are already adapted to performance in different treatment situations, but also as a within-person process of adaptation to progressive treatment situations, then the original matrix formulation with treatments as segments may be the most direct way to design such studies. Also, the items in an ability test are a progression of treatment segments, just as are the segments of an instructional treatment; one can thus study adaptation of individual differences across varying item characteristics within the same design. Keeping an eye on the general matrix, one is less likely to settle for simple views of ATI and simple designs by which to study them.

1965–1975

The Stanford Project   In 1965, Cronbach and I undertook a thorough review of the literature and a reexamination of methodology in ATI research; we also planned some new studies of our own. The task took on new dimensions and the literature blossomed as we studied it; the project took ten years to complete instead of the planned three. The end result was a book (Cronbach and Snow, 1977) that was less a summary of conclusions than a guide for future work.

The book summarized a huge volume of relevant research — ATI studies completed before and after 1965, plus related work on aptitude interrelationships, correlational analyses of individual differences in learning and transfer, and the problem of measuring learning rate. New ATI studies appeared frequently as the decade unfolded, and some of these were much improved in conception and design over past work. By and large, however, few of these studies penetrated beneath the molar labels for aptitude and instructional treatment variables that had driven educational research in earlier decades. Few studies escaped from the existing measures of aptitude constructs that had been devised for prediction rather than for interaction research, and few sought analyses of learning activities and processes within treatments.

The first wave of interest in ATI research was followed by rapid and, I believe, premature disaffection. Early reviews of the developing literature (Berliner and Cahen, 1973; Bracht, 1970; and Cronbach and Snow, 1969 — our own initial report hastily prepared to meet federal contract requirements) were unduly negative and, as it turned out, superficial. In time, statistical reasoning by itself was enough to show that ATI is indeed a likely outcome of properly done research (Cronbach and Snow, 1977). But both the substantive and the statistical issues were extremely complex; ATI research was thus extremely difficult to do properly. The problem would not yield to dissertation-size studies, nor to the quick series of journal articles that would support academic promotions. The zeitgeist seemed to move on to new, more tractable problems, or to parts of the ATI problem in other guises. (The disaffection provides an interesting case for the sociological study of educational psychology as well as of the negative influence of short-term federal funding.)

Nonetheless, it was possible to take a positive view of the decade's work. Much had been learned, and a range of conclusions and recommendations could be drawn, some reaching well beyond ATI research itself to touch the fundamental philosophy and methodology of behavioral science (see especially Cronbach, 1975, 1982a, 1982b).

The major conclusions of the Cronbach and Snow book (1977) for the purposes of this chapter are summarized below, without reciting again the justification for each; detailed substantive and methodological implications must be omitted here. The book remains the definitive record of the decade's work and ought to be consulted for details. (Another footnote to the sociology of our science is that the book has been cited as supporting a negative conclusion regarding the possibility of ATI — a thorough examination of it should lead the reader to quite the opposite conclusion.)

In brief, Cronbach and Snow (see also Snow, 1977b) concluded that:

1. Aptitude-treatment interactions exist. They are ubiquitous in educational learning. Many ability and personality variables have been identified in ATI as indicants of aptitude. Similarly, many instructional treatment variables have been identified within interactions.

2. There are many complex combinations, as predicted earlier. Indeed, such complexes push conventional theoretical thinking and statistical methodology to the limit. Some interactions can be statistically significant but be trivial when considered in the terms of variance accounted for. Some can account for more variance than the associated treatment main effects, and yet be compromised by further aptitude moderators. Conventional research design and statistical significance testing practices in instructional psychology are heavily biased against ATI hypotheses, and indeed against complex hypotheses of any sort.

3. No particular ATI hypothesis has been sufficiently confirmed or understood to serve as a basis for instructional practice. Investigators have obtained replications of results, but the subtle and shifting complexities of educational situations make all generalizations probabilistic. This is to be expected in educational research, and is no more a difficulty for ATI research, which is essentially a new scientific problem, that it is for other fields of instructional psychology.

4. In contrast to the earlier predictions of both Cronbach and Glaser, measures of general ability (G) enter interactions more frequently than other indicants of aptitude, despite the fact that measures of G also typically show strong aptitude main effects. Many different measures have been used to reach this conclusion, including measures designed to reflect "prior achievement" rather than "intelligence," or to distinguish fluid (G_f), crystallized (G_c), and spatial (G_v) abilities. The evidence does not allow assigning ATI predominantly to one of these closely related ability constructs, so G refers here to the general factor as a cognitive aptitude complex that combines these hypothesized constituents. The fluid-crystallized terminology is used without necessarily adopting the details of the Cattell-Horn theory of G_f and G_c. Given new evidence and a reconsideration of old evidence, G can indeed be interpreted as "ability to learn" as long as it is clear that these terms refer to a complex of processes and skills and that a somewhat different mix of these constituents may be required in different learning tasks and settings. The old view that mental tests and learning tasks measure distinctly different abilities should be discarded, even though we still lack a theory to integrate the two.

5. Perhaps the strongest $G \times T$ interaction involves treatments that differ in the structure and completeness of instruction. In *high structure* treatments, the teacher or instructional materials and arrangements maintain a high level of external control of learning activities, attention, pacing, feedback, and reinforcement; the instructional tasks are broken down into small units in clear sequence; and the contents and processes of learning are made more explicit and concrete. Such treatments help low G learners but seem to thwart high G learners, relative to *low structure* treatments where learners must act more independently and rely more on their own structuring to fill in gaps. In low structure environments, high G learners tend to do well while low G learners do poorly. An interpretation today of this evidence might focus on metacognitive and self-regulatory skills associated with high G. Instructional methods typically described as direct instruction, teacher-controlled, or drill and practice would be considered high structure treatments, whereas methods described as indirect, inductive, discovery-oriented, or learner-controlled would be considered low structure treatments. So-called conventional teaching would fall between these extremes, but closer to low than to high structure, in most cases.

However, many other classroom and learning task conditions can moderate these ATI effects, and they are not as yet describable at a process level.

6. Special ability constructs also enter into ATI, but less frequently and less consistently. No generalizations about ability distinctions, as between fluid and crystallized abilities or verbal and spatial abilities appear warranted, yet these distinctions clearly deserve further study in ATI research at a more detailed, process level. Specialized prior knowledge and prior experience relevant to the instructional treatments under consideration are also often important moderators of ATI effects, although again generalizations are hazardous. A key issue is the understanding of ability and prior knowledge as they integrate in learning processes.

7. Personality and motivational aptitudes enter a wide variety of ATI patterns. Perhaps the strongest $A \times T$ result here involves anxiety and aspects of achievement motivation called *achievement via independence* and *achievement via conformance,* in interaction with treatment variables quite similar to the high versus low structure contrast previously described. Anxious or conforming students do better with high structure; nonanxious or independent students do better with low structure. Ability and anxiety also often enter into higher-order interactions with this treatment variable.

8. Other specialized personality variables also interact but have not been studied sufficiently to yield generalizations. No single personality variable seems to be consistently important. Student perceptions of the teacher or treatment may also be important moderators of such ATI. It is clear that measurement problems and the absence of an organizing taxonomy for personality, motivational, attitudinal, and stylistic aptitude constructs hampers integration of this field.

Extensions and Reformulations   Beyond the above conclusions, which still are defensible today, it was clear from several related considerations that a host of new theoretical and methodological problems attended not only ATI research, but instructional psychology in general.

The two most important problems for further research seemed to require substantial reformulation of the attack. These two problems involved the twin needs for (1) more extensive examination of the real educational and social environments in which aptitudes and treatments interact, and (2) more intensive examination of the learning process differences that connect aptitude and treatment differences. Clearly, investigators had to recognize the tradeoffs. If one relied upon brief laboratory experiments where increased control and density of measurement afford detailed analyses of learning processes, strategies, and activities within treatments, then the small samples of persons and learning time, and the situational artificiality that necessarily attends such research, would make meaningful ATI difficult to detect, or to generalize once detected. The Cronbach and Snow (1977) review attested to that; the most potentially meaningful ATI came from broad aptitude and treatment variables in relatively long-duration, real-world instruction, and that was where ATI results would have to be understood and used. On the other hand, Cronbach and Snow also showed why detailed process analysis of aptitudes and treatments was badly needed. If one concentrated on broad field studies where large samples of persons and learning times, and naturally representative treatments, make meaningful ATI more detectable and generalizable, then multiple social contexts (such as, multiple classrooms or schools) must be included, treatment control and process tracing are sacrificed, and the statistical analysis must disentangle effects occurring at multiple levels of person and treatment aggregation.

To argue the last point first, education is to some degree a social enterprise, and social effects on learning are often to be expected. Students are only sometimes independent learners in classrooms; their learning may be influenced by their styles of transaction with others, and by their perceptions of others' treatment or performance. If these effects vary across classrooms or student groupings within classrooms, they may moderate aptitude or treatment effects and produce "failures to replicate"; no two classrooms can truly be considered replicates. More important, as one moves to multiple classrooms per treatment, ATI can be expected at the between-class as well as, or instead of, the within-class or individual level. Cronbach and Webb (1975) reanalyzed the old Anderson (1941) data, which was used in the first conference by Cronbach (1967) to demonstrate an ATI involving a difference between prior achievement and ability in interaction with drill and meaningful instruction in mathematics. The individual level interpretation comes easily to educational psychologists; meaningful instruction is best for able learners who have not done well previously in drill treatments, whereas less able but higher achieving learners do better in a continuation of drill. The reanalysis separated this within-class AT regression interpretation from the between-class AT regression, to show that if there were ATI effects at all in the Anderson data, they were between-class effects; that is, class average differences in aptitude pattern, rather than individual differences without regard to classroom, might have produced the result.

A study by Greene (1976) suggested other social effects as well. Here, random halves of classrooms were assigned to learner control versus teacher control of learning activities and time scheduling. At the individual level, there was no ATI using G measures as aptitude. The between-half-class trends, however, would suggest that learner control should be given to high G groups while teacher control should be imposed on low G groups. But the effect could well be due to perception of the treatment contrast; self-control may be beneficial to high G learners when they see some of their classmates denied it, whereas teacher control may be helpful to low G learners when some of *their* classmates are seen to be denied it!

Research by Webb (1977) took the social process question into still another avenue. In a study of small groups working on mathematics, she demonstrated that, to predict the learning outcome for an individual, one had to know the individual's prior ability, the mix of ability in that person's group, *and* the social role adopted by the person in that group. High G students did well when working alone, or in a heterogeneous-ability group where they took the role of tutor or explainer. Low G students did well in heterogeneous-ability groups if they asked questions and got high-ability explanations. Neither kind of student did well in uniform ability groups, therefore. Middle G students who actively interacted in solving problems benefited from group learning mainly in uniform- (that is, middle-) ability groups, not in heterogeneous-ability groups, where they tended to be left out of the high-low exchange.

It was clear from all this that one future arm of ATI research would have to reach improved substantive description of real educational environments, including their social character as well as their individual aptitudinal and treatment character, and would need to develop the methodology of distinguishing between-group and within-group regressions to do this. Educational understanding would progress by rich description of local educational environments, that is, by quantitative and qualitative evaluations or case studies of local experiments (Cronbach, 1975). All real-world educational experiments are indeed case studies, or collections of such studies, anyway. And, while generalized theory might be built up in the accumulation of evaluated cases, much could also be gained by the study of local theories designed to fit particular subject-matter and instructional conditions in one educational habitat, rather than all possible conditions; such theories could be prescriptive as well as descriptive if they were well geared to local conditions and made sensitive to those conditions through sequential monitoring of changes therein (Snow, 1977a).

The second problem was process analysis; it too was multifaceted. First of all, to understand ATI phenomena in more detail, one needed to know what it means to say that individuals differ in A and therefore differ in learning under conditions described by T—what are the constituent psychological content and process properties summarized by a given A score and how do they track through differences in learning activities and strategies under different T conditions to influence learning outcome? One needed to find a level of description for key aptitude and treatment variables that was more analytic than the molar labels used in the past, and yet was also theoretically useful for instructional design purposes [that is, that was *instructionally tractable,* to use Pellegrino and Glaser's (1980) term]. Furthermore, it was not just single A and T variables that needed such process interpretation; ultimately, aptitude and treatment *complexes* had to be analyzed and described because many of the ATI effects obtained previously were higher-order, multivariate interactions. Still another facet of the problem was that learning and achievement outcome from instruction had also to be considered multivariate. Although most previous studies had included only immediate learning criteria and ignored retention or transfer or affective outcomes, results often differed for different measures when multiple outcomes were studied. Under real instructional conditions, intermediate learning processes and activities were also inevitably multivariate.

Two studies, by Peterson (1976) and Porteus (1976), served to exemplify these problem facets, while also reinforcing two principal conclusions of the Cronbach and Snow (1977) review. Peterson (1976) studied high structure (HS) versus low structure (LS) treatments for two weeks in four high school social studies classrooms, using G plus anxiety (A_x), and also the two achievement motivational orientation measures mentioned previously as aptitudes. Porteus (1976) studied the same treatment and aptitude variables (although with somewhat different defining measures) in two high school classes in each of two year-long courses. Figure 2-2 gives comparable parts of the results for both studies, with G and A_x as aptitude predictors of a cognitive outcome measure taken after HS and LS treatments. Each square is a bivariate aptitude space with cross-cutting lines to divide the space into regions wherein either HS or LS was the superior treatment. The similarity of the two results constitutes a replication, and strongly reinforces the previous hypothesis that G and A_x jointly interact with treatment structure. The achievement orientation measures also

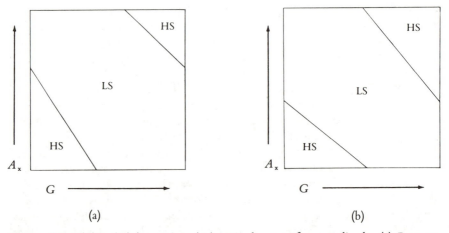

Figure 2-2 Ability (G) by anxiety (A_x) aptitude space from studies by (a) Peterson (1976) and (b) Porteus (1976), showing regions were high structure treatments (HS) and low structure treatments (LS) are superior.

interacted with treatment structure as predicted, but are not considered further here (see Snow, 1977b, 1987).

The process-analytic problem is to explain what it means in psychological content or process terms to say that persons in different regions of this bivariate aptitude space respond to the treatments differently. The Peterson and Porteus classroom studies could not penetrate to this level. Clearly, a deeper analysis of what people in these different regions say or do in learning is needed. Also needed is richer description of the multiple classroom climates and contexts. The problem is especially complicated because, as noted, the other aptitudes also interact with these same treatments, the methodology for partitioning the aptitude space rests on questionable assumptions about linearity, and the ATI results differ for different outcomes; Peterson got radically different results for an attitude outcome measure, and Porteus's ATI varied across learning stages in each course.

It was thus clear that another arm of further research had to find ways of analyzing the aptitude–learning outcome processes or (*aptitude processes* for short) that characterize learners who differ in complex ways in response to treatment demands. [See Snow (1980b, 1987) for further definition of aptitude processes and aptitude complexes in this regard.] It was also clear that achievement theories were needed to engage the multivariate criterion measurement aspect of the problem and to specify what facets of declarative and procedural knowledge and skill acquisition, and what attitudinal or motivational developments ought to be distinguished for instructional research of this sort.

Related Developments   Meanwhile, developments in other parts of the field were taking shapes that intersected with the ATI project. Research on aptitude thus had an integral place in more general efforts to build instructional theory, and even nomothetic psychological theory most broadly defined.

Glaser's (1976) conception of prescriptive theory for instruction, for example, had four parts: analysis of competent performance, description of initial state, fostering acquisition of competence, and assessment of instructional effects. His second part required a theory of aptitude. The methodology of ATI research was an important evaluative tool for his fourth part. And his first part, as noted above, requires an achievement theory. Research on adaptive instruction following Glaser's formulation (see also Glaser, 1977) resulted in the development of individually prescribed instruction (IPI) and eventually the adaptive learning environments model (ALEM; see Wang and Lindvall, 1984). These instructional systems incorporate ATI hypotheses implicitly, though at a microadaptive level rather than at the macroadaptive level that Cronbach and Snow (1977) had concentrated upon. When treated to field evaluations at a macro level, however, IPI as a treatment clearly produced ATI, and there was the further implication that IPI might relate differently to crystallized ability (G_c) than to fluid ability (G_f). One year-long study by Sharps (1973) suggested that IPI benefited lower G_c students relative to conventional instruction in elementary reading and mathematics, but that higher G_c students did better under conventional conditions than under IPI conditions; G_f related positively to learning in both treatments, but did not interact. In another year-long evaluation of IPI in elementary mathematics, Crist-Whitzel and Hawley-Winne (1976) obtained similar though more complex ATI. The IPI program appeared to serve lower G_c students well, relative to traditional teaching, particularly if they were also higher in G_f. Traditional teaching was better for students with the opposite aptitude pattern. Neither study analyzed the G_c-G_f distinction fully, but both implied that IPI is insufficiently adaptive for high G_c students, and perhaps also for low G_f students. And both reinforce the view that microadaptation and macroadaptation are complementary, as Cronbach and Snow (1977) had suggested, rather than competitive instructional strategies in the face of aptitude differences.

Developments in experimental psychology were also blending in. Underwood's (1975) conception of individual differences as a crucible in the construction of nomothetic theory broadened the earlier views of Glanzer (1967) and Melton (1967) from the LRDC Conference that individual differences should be studied in connection with theoretical process variables. Underwood argued that all psychological theories must deal with at least two intervening processes that have different functions in relation to at least one independent variable; that is, the intervening processes interact. If at least one such process can be measured reliably outside of the situation for which it serves theoretically, the correlation across individuals between this measure and the dependent variable must be nonzero in order for the theory to survive. This is an ATI; the differences between performance under (say) two experimental (treatment) conditions reflects a process and must correlate (interact) with an independent measure of that process (an aptitude measure). It is also a variation of the S-R-R paradigm advocated by Schoenfeld and Cumming (1963), although Underwood did not call it that.

Empirical work on what came to be called the *cognitive correlates* approach (Pellegrino and Glaser, 1979) had begun in Hunt's laboratory (see Hunt, Frost, and Lunneborg, 1973; Hunt and Lansman, 1975). The aim was to relate cognitive ability test scores to scores derived from paradigmatic laboratory tasks and thus to build process hypotheses about individual differences in ability. A *cognitive components* approach came from Sternberg's invention (in his 1975 dissertation) of a methodology for isolating experimentally some of the component processes in performance on testlike tasks (see Sternberg, 1977). Clearly a cognitive differential psychology was emerging aimed at the understanding of individual differences in information-processing terms. The Office of Naval Research (and in particular the leaders of its psychological sciences division, Glenn Bryan and Marshall Farr) deserves substantial credit for this development. Starting in 1975, ONR funded projects for Carroll, Hunt, Pellegrino and Glaser, Sternberg, Underwood, and me to work on process analysis of abilities, and eventually created a large circle of independent but communicative investigators. (Not coincidentally, ONR had earlier funded the Cronbach and Gleser work on the theory of classification tests, and also the 1965 LRDC Conference.)

Finally, an important start had been made, by Greeno and his colleagues, toward the characterization of the kinds of qualitative differences in knowledge structure that can arise from differences in instructional treatment (see Greeno and Mayer, 1975; Mayer and Greeno, 1972; Egan and Greeno, 1973; Mayer, Stiehl, and Greeno, 1975). Their work showed how both general cognitive aptitudes and specific prior experience could be brought together with faceted achievement post tests to study not only amounts of learning, but also different kinds of learning outcome; instruction that aims at discovery or general concepts evidently calls on different abilities in learning, produces different cognitive structures as outcome, and has different implications for transfer. They also showed that the study of aptitude – treatment – post test interactions (ATPI) could clearly contribute to improved achievement theories of instruction.

1975 – 1985

With these reformulations and related developments, the research program moved into its second decade. The ONR project started with an analysis of the new literature on the instructional and methodological issues that had come up since the Cronbach and Snow book (1977; see Snow, 1977b) and also the prospects for the analysis of aptitude processes in learning (see Snow, 1978b, 1980a). Because these two problem areas were then addressed separately, and for the most part by different people, they are summarized separately here.

School and Classroom Studies   Research on the methodological problems of large, multiple classroom, real school studies was pursued by Cronbach (1976, 1980, 1982a) in the context of educational program evaluation. The ATI problem became one important aspect, but only one, of the many kinds of contextual interactional problems to be faced in general evaluation research design. This work led to new views on the philosophy of social science research (for example, Cronbach 1982b), which called the conventional style of instructional psychology into serious question. Strings of simple experiments imposed on an instructional context without describing it and focused only on individual person interpretations were unlikely to yield the broad and neat generalizations typically expected. There were also empirical demonstrations of the value of an ATI perspective in large-scale instructional research (for example, Corno, 1979). And a sustained program of work developed concerning the statistics of multilevel regression analyses involving aptitude (Burstein, 1980a, 1980b,

1980c; Burstein, Linn, and Capell, 1978; and Burstein, Miller, and Linn, 1981). This fed, in turn, into research on the causal or structural modeling of school learning in large-scale studies (see Haertel, Walberg, and Weinstein, 1983). It was clear that aptitude variables should be routinely included in such models. School effectiveness research could thus benefit substantially from an ATI perspective (for example, see Frederiksen, 1980). Unfortunately, aptitude variables are still rarely considered in this work, except as univariate initial indicators.

Another view of the prospects for multilevel, classroom ATI research comes from studies by Schneider and Treiber (1984) and Schneider and Helmke (1985). They fitted a simple structural model of school learning involving measures of cognitive aptitudes, several aspects of classroom instructional quality, and several kinds of achievement outcome to their total sample data. But this fit masks important differences in the model's validity for different subgroups of classrooms. In one of their studies, for example, fifth-grade mathematics classrooms with high aptitude-outcome regression slopes were separated from classrooms with low within-class slopes. The instructional quality model accounted well for learning in classes with high aptitude-outcome relations but not in classes with low aptitude-outcome relations. The suggestion is that this particular model accounts for achievement in classrooms with a meritocratic climate or teacher style, but not in classrooms with a compensatory or remedial climate or teacher style. A different and to date unknown model of instructional quality effects on learning is needed for the latter situations.

Field instructional research at the level of the individual student, teacher, and classroom has rarely included an ATI perspective, despite the demonstrations of the previous decade. But some investigators have persisted, and there seems to be a slowly growing recognition of the benefit to be derived from inclusion of student aptitude analyses. There are some examples now of research on teaching from an ATI view (see Corno and Snow, 1986). Webb (1982, 1983) has continued the study of aptitude interactions in small groups. And particularly interesting findings have come from the work of Peterson and her colleagues, using student self reports of their cognitive activities during classroom learning, as well as experimental manipulations of teaching strategies and observations of teacher and student activities (see Peterson, 1987; Peterson, Swing, Braverman, and Buss, 1982; Peterson, Swing, Stark, and Waas, 1984; Peterson, Swing, and Steiber, 1986). The findings suggest that students differ substantially in the learning activities and strategies they employ. These differences seem to reflect prior aptitude differences and produce subsequent achievement differences. High G_c students are more likely than low G_c students to report employing strategies aimed at relating new information to prior knowledge or at using particular problem-solving steps in analyzing the new material; they also report more attention to and understanding of the lessons. When teachers were trained either to increase the amount of time students were engaged in mathematics learning or to promote student use of specified learning strategies, marked ATI resulted. Higher G_c students benefited more from the learning time than the learning strategy intervention, whereas lower G_c students benefited more from the strategy intervention than from the time intervention. Interview protocols showed clear qualitative differences in student learning strategies as a function of the teaching interventions. It was also the case, however, that ATI occurred at the class level; classes displaying a higher average G_c benefited more from learning strategy intervention, whereas lower G_c classes benefited more from learning time intervention. The implication seems to be that teachers implemented the strategy or time interventions differently as a function of class average ability level. At any rate, it is clear that the students' achievement, particularly of higher-order cognitive objectives, depended on their own aptitude and that of their classmates, as well as their teacher's use of one or the other intervention.

An Agenda for Process Analytic Studies   The aptitude processes (see Snow, 1980a) that Peterson and her group have been tracing in natural classroom teaching and learning activities can presumably be understood in more detail through laboratory analysis. At least there is the prospect that particular cognitive processing mechanisms identified in simulated instructional situations *may* have their counterparts in natural classroom learning. And the laboratory arrangements may guide the design of aptitude test revisions or "learning sample tests" which could be included in both laboratory and naturalistic research and which then might serve as vehicles to connect, at least correlationally, the results obtained in each environment (see Snow, 1978b; Snow and Peterson, 1985). This is one of the objectives of the process analysis arm of the continuing aptitude project at Stanford.

To advance toward a new theory of aptitude for learning, a process description is needed for both aptitude differences and learning differences that can identify *common* processes producing both. As noted above, this also requires measures capable of diagnosing individual differences in these processes in both laboratory and natural settings. This has been a primary objective of my own research in the past decade. A secondary objective has been to bring in conative (or motivational-volitional) and affective processes (Snow, 1980c).

The agenda for 1975 to 1985 in the process analytic arm of the aptitude research project was set as follows:

1. Formulate a priority list of the most important aptitude and instructional treatment constructs, judging from the ATI evidence of the previous decade. Since it is impossible to study in detail all of the potentially important individual difference variables that might serve as aptitudes for learning in some treatment situation somewhere, a process theory of aptitude has to be built up by

cycles of research; that is, A_1 in relation to T_1 has to be understood to some degree before A_2 and T_2 can be understood in relation to A_1 and T_1 and to each other. Similarly, A_3 and T_3 cannot be studied simultaneously with the other candidates, and should not be studied in isolation. The research strategy, however, should be sensitive from the start to the potential importance of *aptitude complexes* involving combinations of $A_1A_2A_3$ or their key parts as suggested, for example, by the combination of G and A_x in Figure 2-2. Certain *treatment complexes* may similarly be important.

2. Pursue process analysis of A_1 to identify its key aspects with respect to learning under T_1. Seek a level of description that is more analytic than the molar labels used in past ATI research, and yet is theoretically useful — or tractable — for instructional design and aptitude measurement design purposes. In doing this, use the theoretical and methodological tools emerging from developments in general cognitive psychology as well as cognitive differential psychology, but keep attention focused on the target of explaining the A_1T_1 interaction in learning. In other words, if general scholastic ability or intelligence (G) is to be the first aptitude studied, and the structuredness or completeness of instruction is to be the first treatment variable, then a theory of G as aptitude in high versus low structure (HS-LS) learning and transfer is the goal; a general theory of intelligence is not. Our theory should be focused on those aspects of intelligence that are operative in relation to treatment structure in instruction. Such a theory would thus be initially "smaller" or more limited than a general theory of intelligence, such as that sought by Sternberg (1977, 1985). Eventually, however, the theory would have to be "larger" than a theory of intelligence because it would have to incorporate A_2. If the second most important aptitude construct was to be achievement motivation (A_m), then the relation of G and A_m, or their parts, to HS-LS would have to be explained; theories of G would not ordinarily be expected to accommodate A_m.

3. Conduct studies that test the malleability of A_1 differences and the degree to which they can be removed or compensated for by direct training interventions. If direct training on some learning skills or strategies that are constituents of G can improve aptitude for learning, for example, then new instructional designs can incorporate such training. If not, then instructional design must seek alternative treatments that circumvent the persistent inaptitudes. Either direct training or alternative treatments will probably have to capitalize on other aptitude strengths in order to compensate for weaknesses, so the aptitude process theory will need to be accompanied by multivariate diagnostic measures of aptitude.

4. Finally, as noted initially, design such measures as learning sample tests that can be used to transport key aptitude process distinctions, specified in

the theory, between laboratory and field research. Using such measures for A_1 in relation to T_1, cycle back to study A_2, and so on, in this context.

Following the prescribed first step, the priority list depicted in Figure 2-3 was established. The figure also shows breakdowns of aptitude constructs into some hypothesized constituent parts and some hypothesized aptitude complexes, with their relations to treatment variables. The symbols used to identify aptitude constructs are identified further in the text below.

As shown in Figure 2-3, and as implied in the previous discussion, the first priority aptitude and treatment constructs were G and HS-LS. But it was clear that G was a complex of crystallized, fluid, and spatial visualization abilities (that is, $G_cG_fG_v$), and that these could be broken down further following a hierarchical factor model. G_c included both verbal comprehension (VC) ability

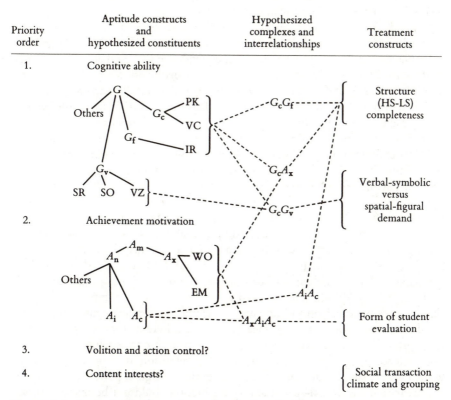

Figure 2-3 A priority list for analyses of aptitude and treatment constructs, with some hypothesized aptitude constituents and complexes.

and prior knowledge (PK) relevant to the subject matter of instruction. Our review and reanalysis of prior literature (by Lohman, 1979a) suggested that G_v consisted of separable spatial orientation (SO), spatial relations (SR), and visualization (VZ) abilities. And research by Gustafsson (1984) suggested that $G = G_f = $ IR (that is, Thurstone's inductive reasoning factor). These ability and knowledge factors thus became the starting points for process analysis.

On the other hand, it seemed that the first two treatment variables — the structuredness and completeness of instructional treatments — could not be easily disentangled; both would be interpreted as variation in the information-processing demands imposed upon or removed from the learner during instruction. The third priority treatment variable — verbal-symbolic versus figural-spatial demand — was also to be interpreted as relative information-processing burden in the contrasted media. Thus, the first cycle of process analytic research considered G in the interaction with the first two treatment variables, as aspects of high versus low structure (that is, HS-LS), and kept an eye also on verbal versus figural processing demands.

Based on research previously described, it also seemed clear that achievement motivation (A_m) and particularly its constituents in test anxiety (A_x), need for achievement (A_n), achievement via independence (A_i), and achievement via conformity (A_c) represented second and third priority aptitude complexes, connected also to HS-LS (see Snow, 1977b). A_x would especially need to be studied in interaction with G, and it could perhaps also be subdivided further into worry (WO) and emotionality (EM) components. The next treatment variable — form of student evaluation — might also be particularly important in relation to A_n and A_x. Beyond this point, Figure 2-3 suggests some other categories of aptitude and treatment variables deserving of further study, but discussion of these would go well beyond the purposes of this chapter.

Cognitive Aptitude Processes   The need for cognitive process analysis of the first aptitude complex in relation to similar analyses of learning and problem solving was the subject of an ONR-sponsored conference early in this second decade of ATI research (see Snow, Federico, and Montague, 1980a,b). The complexity of the problem was also shown by our continuing ATI studies. A study by Yalow (1980) demonstrated again the $G \times$ HS-LS interaction — less able learners were helped in immediate learning by more elaborated and structured instruction. But retention measures told a different story, suggesting that the more active mental work required in low structure treatments aided retention. Indeed, verbal elaboration resulted in less retention in verbal performance, while figural elaboration resulted in less retention in figural performance. It was also clear that the verbal-spatial ability distinction could not be made without more penetrating process analysis.

Our research through this period has been summarized in some detail elsewhere (see Snow and Lohman, 1984). Discussion here is confined to a brief overview of our evolving conceptualization and the results associated with it.

The laboratory research on G abilities ran in parallel with research by Hunt, Pellegrino, Sternberg, and others, as noted previously, but with some important differences. Whereas other investigators emphasized the identification of elementary information-processing components as the sources of individual differences in cognitive performance, using cognitive models not initially concerned with learning, we pursued the hypothesis that important aptitude differences are to be found in the adaptive organization and reorganization of component processes during cognitive test *and* learning task performance. These higher-order strategies, and flexible adaptation of them in the face of changing task demands, ought to be common to both the cognitive test performances typically used as indicants of aptitude and to the learning tasks typically presented by instruction. Adopting terminology used by Simon (1976), we called these sorts of aptitude differences *assembly and control* processes (see Snow, 1980a,b). Our early explorations using subjects' eye movements tracked during task performance, and also their retrospective reports, suggested that adaptive assembly and reassembly of processing, under some kind of control monitor that is sensitive to task changes, is a major feature of cognition and learning (Snow, 1978b, 1980a, 1981). Individual differences here, furthermore, suggested that human cognitive systems are in large part rather loosely coupled, idiosyncratic, and probabilistic, particularly in complex performance and among higher ability subjects; many different organizations of component processing might be assembled, according to task demands, and might vary within as well as between persons.

This view, coupled with the ATI perspective, led to a second difference between other conceptions and our own. The research in other laboratories tended to assume a common, stable process *within* the person *across* items, as though a given kind of task called forth one performance program that the person applied to each item in turn. Strategy differences between persons were recognized (Sternberg and Weil, 1980; MacLeod, Hunt, and Matthews, 1978) but not strategy shifting within persons. We developed a looser, dynamic sampling model of person-situation interaction, using ideas from Thomson (1919, 1939), Humphreys (1971), Simon (1969), and Gibson (1979); this allowed both within- and between-person variation in strategies. We see the person as a very large bank of process skill and knowledge components. As a result of the person's learning history, some of theses components are independent and unorganized; many are loosely connected, and some are tightly organized into conceptual or procedural assemblies, or algorithms, that can work as a unit automatically. These structures are highly idiosyncratic. The outer environment is the task situation at hand; it also can be described as a more or less structured and more or less complete collection of components and component assemblies that it provides, demands, or affords for human performance. It should be possible thus to describe persons, ability tests, and learning or instructional tasks in common terms (though not here; see Snow, in preparation; also Snow, 1983, 1986). The basic event at the interface of person and situation is a sampling, designed partly by the component assembly and control demands of and opportunities afforded by the performance situation, and partly by the component assembly and control possibilities of the performing person. Assembly and control processes thus operate at the interface, moderating this two-way sampling. Tasks differ in the components and assemblies they call forth; they differ also within themselves in this respect, from item to item, segment to segment, trial to trial, and so on. Persons differ in how well the components and assemblies they can produce match the demands and opportunities of the task. Aptitude differences appear as a result of sampling mismatch; they show through at the interface whenever the assembly and control processes of persons and tasks are mismatched, that is, whenever the person cannot adapt completely to the demands and opportunities of the outer environment. In short, the hypothesis is that cognitive aptitude differences in learning show in the organizational assembly and control activities learners use to adapt to new instruction, and these are the same activities learners use to adapt their performance in cognitive ability tests — hence, the correlation between G and learning in conventional instruction. This is not to say that *particular* components of prior knowledge or skill are not *also* common to ability test and learning task performance. It is rather to emphasize the adaptive organizational properties of both performances, because these have been underemphasized in past work.

Finally, in contrast to most other investigators, our work was guided by the factor analytic results. We recognize that factors based on correlations among cognitive ability tests, even though obtained many times in the past, are not necessarily fundamental unities. They may be regarded as task classification principles (Vernon, 1950) that place ability tests together according to the correlation of their component and assembly sampling characteristics. But we also recognize that any theory of cognitive aptitude has to account for the persistent pattern of correlations among ability tests — the positive manifold — and between them and learning tasks. To focus attention on the test and task intercorrelations themselves, as well as the most robust factors, we constructed a radex model of such correlations. The model is an inside-out version of that proposed by Guttman (1965, 1970; see Snow, Kyllonen, and Marshalek, 1984). It could serve as a provisional map of the topography of ability and learning correlations, as a guide to task analysis. The most important feature of this radex pattern to be explained by any theory is the gradient of apparent increases in processing complexity as one steps in along any array from the periphery of the radex toward its center where tests are highly loaded on G and where ability-learning correlations are highest (Marshalek, Lohman, and Snow, 1983). These are the ability tests, also, that typically enter into ATI with the HS-LS treatment variable in instructional research (Snow, 1980b, 1982). Our interpretation of this complexity continuum is that tasks in the periphery require relatively few component processes and relatively little reassembly of processing from item to item; processing is relatively automatic in such tasks. More complex tasks toward the center of the radex, however, not only require more components but also more flexible and adaptive, assembly and reassembly of processing from item to item. This is especially likely on novel complex tasks such as those regarded as measures of G_f and the visualization aspect of G_v, because these tests require persons to invent and adapt their strategies from item to item; prior knowledge, and even the growth of familiarity with task requirements from item to item, provide only a starting point as item difficulty increases. G_c tests also require adaptive reassembly during processing, but less so as task familiarity allows use of processing routines and knowledge previously assembled to be retrieved and applied to reach solutions. There is a limit, however, to the degree to which increases in complexity increase the correlation with G. Items can be made to differ so drastically from one another that each item becomes, in effect, a different new test. Then, correlations with G reach a threshold and perhaps even decline. Our results and those of others have so far supported this thinking. We cannot rule out other models, but we think this view fits much evidence from many sources.

Some studies have suggested that increasing complexity along the radex arrays results from both increases in the number of components involved and in their assembly requirements; some also suggest the limits in this progression. Lohman (1979b; see also Lohman and Kyllonen, 1983) manipulated three aspects of complexity in G_v tasks: the number of different component processes required, the amount or duration required for each process, and the physical complexity of the stimulus operated upon by each component process. Correlations with G were lowest for simple items and increased substantially as more spatial transformations were required. But correlations declined again with still further increases in task complexity. Swiney (1983), studying analogy tasks, demonstrated increasing correlation with G to a complexity threshold, and then a slight decline with further complexity. Marshalek (1981) studied verbal comprehension tasks. Again, correlations with G increased with task complexity. Here, no limit was reached.

Other studies have demonstrated the role of adaptive strategy shifting as a function of item difficulty and complexity, and experience across items in the task. Bethell-Fox, Lohman, and Snow (1984) identified two strategies in geometric analogy performance similar to those suggested earlier for visualization tasks by Snow (1978a). These strategies were called "constructive matching" and "feature comparison-response elimination," but they bear similarity also to componential models for analogical reasoning studied by Sternberg (1977) and Mulholland, Pellegrino, and Glaser (1980). The critical issue, however, was shown to be adaptation of strategy as a function of ability and difficulty level in the task. Constructive matching was used more for easier items and by subjects higher in G. Feature comparison-response elimination was used more on difficult items and by subjects lower in G. When and where strategies change cannot be predicted by item difficulty or subject ability alone. The eye track data also suggested important features of adaptive processing not captured in models of the Sternberg type. Kyllonen, Lohman, and Woltz (1984) demonstrated the same sort of adaptive shifting in spatial synthesis tasks. Within-task shifting of strategies involved changes in both the sequence of processing and in the components included in the sequence, and occurred differentially as experience accumulated in the task. Subjects invented strategies as they progressed that were suited to their ability profiles. Ability controlled strategy assembly as well as performance within a strategy. Thus, as one moves up the complexity gradient in the radex, increasing correlation of tasks with G and with other tasks may reflect increasing covariance due to these common adaptive functions.

Pellegrino (1984) has also reported componential analysis of several spatial ability tests that can be arrayed from periphery to center of the radex map. His results indicate that increasing numbers of components are required in each successive task model, but also that increasing strategy variance is evident as one moves to tasks nearer the radex center. This offers confirmation of our hypothesis from a different laboratory.

Studies of learning strategies in instruction have also shown that high and low G learners differ in adaptive strategy assembly. Less able learners need help in developing effective strategies, and direct instruction can be designed to provide this help. As instructional treatments are structured to control learner activities externally, and as they specify more completely the strategies or assemblies to be used, less able learners find learning less of a problem, and they do better. But external imposition of the structure and complete specification of the strategies to be used interferes with more able learners' free exercise of their own preferred assembly and control processes, and, as a result, they do less well in such treatments than they do when low structure – incomplete treatments leave them on their own. As instructional treatments become less structured and less complete, however, less able learners are cast adrift. A range of learning strategy and instructional studies, in our project and elsewhere, show this result. Some of these are summarized by Snow (1982) and Snow and Lohman (1984; see also Kyllonen, Lohman, and Snow, 1984). The Peterson studies noted earlier are also consistent. But research not conducted within the ATI tradition yields the same implication (see Resnick 1976; Greeno, 1978).

The next steps needed to tie process analyses of G-ability tests and instructional learning tasks together, however, must specify in more detail the adaptive assembly and control activities involved in both, and must trace their functioning over instructional segments in extended alternative treatments as suggested in the pattern of Figure 2-1. I hope that, in this pursuit, investigators can devise a more direct method of assessing this functioning in learning samples.

One of two small and preliminary studies in this direction (Snow, Wescourt, and Collins, 1979), dealt with 30 hours of instruction in basic programming language via computer. The single treatment was geared to provide adaptive help to students on demand. Correlations of G aptitude measures with learning outcome measures, and also with learning activity and strategy variations, were substantial. But it proved impossible to segment the instructional protocols for individual learners to bring out individual differences in strategic assembly and control functions. In the other (Gray, 1982), a learning, note-taking, and teach-back procedure was investigated. Treatment variation consisted of differing amounts of learning strategy intervention. The performance data showed again the ATI that results when less able learners are helped by the imposition of strategy training while more able learners are somehow hurt. More important, the note-taking and teach-back procedures allowed measurement of cognitive activities among the high school students that in turn correlated strongly with cognitive aptitude before instruction as well as achievement outcome following instruction. The aspects of cognitive activity measured included: number of errors, number of quotes, degree of elaboration and translation into idiosyncratic terms and personal reference, degree of subjective chunking and reordering of instructional content, and differences in chunk size. Higher G students elaborated and personalized the content, while lower G students tended to quote verbatim for rehearsal. More able learners were also much more likely than less able learners to have reorganized the material and formed larger, more coherent chunks, more comparable to those formed by expert learners (graduate students). Thus, the teach-back procedure deserves further study as an assessment of aptitude-related cognitive activities during learning.

Gray also studied a learning strategy intervention, and the results hark back to the Peterson work cited earlier. Directive strategies that are good for less able learners are not good for more able learners. The latter are better off given time to practice their own strategies. Negative effects of overdirection on able students have been noted before in ATI research and, clearly, such mathemathanic effects deserve further attention (see Snow, 1972; Cronbach and Snow, 1977; Lohman, 1986). Mathemagenic events for some students are mathemathanic events for others, and these are likely to be motivational as well as cognitive in origin. Hence, the next aptitude construct had to be brought into the picture.

To summarize, we cannot yet say that we possess an adequate process theory of cognitive aptitude. But the laboratory experiments, the correlational analyses, and the instructional studies do seem to converge on a common view. The adaptive, flexible, personalized assembly and control of strategies for information processing that characterize high G learners, and distinguish them from low G learners, also characterize the learning differences. And instructional treatment conditions that vary in structuredness and completeness moderate the degree to which these learning differences show through as aptitude or inaptitude.

Conative and Affective Aptitude Processes   As our project approached the mid-1980s, and understanding of the first aptitude complex advanced, attention turned to the incorporation of conative and affective aptitudes. In keeping with our priority list, the particular interest would be the constituents of achievement motivation and test anxiety in relation to high and low structure in instruction, as previously noted. But it was clearly important to take a broad view of the possibilities. Cognitive psychology in the United States had hardly considered the cognition-motivation interface at all. With ONR help, a conference was held to bring together examples from U.S. research of the possible roles of motivation, affect, personal style, interests, and self-regulatory behavior in learning from instruction (see Snow and Farr, 1987). Then I spent two years surveying relevant research in Europe as an ONR staff member.

The present writing finds the project only beginning to study the cognitive-conative-affective confluences, as a start to its third decade. There are as yet no new empirical findings to report, beyond those noted earlier. But it is clear that this problem poses a broad new challenge for research on learning and individual differences. Some examples of research from European laboratories can serve to show directions worth pursuing.

One way to bring the broad issue of goals, motives, and values into connection with the study of cognitive functioning is to examine longer range attitudes and perspectives of different individuals in relation to immediate performance. Another way is to study personal expectations about the details of immediate performance requirements. The work of d'Ydewalle and Lens (1981) and their colleagues at the University of Leuven uses these tacks as well as several others.

A study by Van Calster, Lens, and Nuttin (1987), for example, explored the possibility that some high school students might hold bleak attitudes about their own future, given today's economic conditions; this could influence their motivation for cognitive achievement more immediately. The main hypothesis tested was that motivation to perform cognitively (for example, to study in high school) is a function of interaction between the perceived instrumentality of such performance and attitudes about personal future. A related hypothesis predicted that future attitudes influence academic performance through the mediation of achievement motivation. Data were collected on a large sample of Flemish Belgian high school seniors using questionnaire measures of study motivation, perceived instrumentality of present academic performance for success in future life, and attitude toward the future. Ability and achievement measures were also collected.

The results showed striking interaction: the correlation of future attitude with study motivation was strongly positive among those students scoring high in perceived instrumentality and negative among those scoring low in perceived instrumentality. Also, the correlation between future attitude and cognitive achievement was positive for students high in perceived instrumentality but negative for those low in perceived instrumentality. Both correlation differences were statistically significant, and, as predicted, the second contrast was substantially reduced when study motivation was partialled out. The interactions were also demonstrated using contrasts between ability and achievement to reflect cognitive performance differences due to motivation differences.

The interpretation is that the motivational effects of perceived instrumentality depend on attitude toward the future: high perceived instrumentality will have a positive effect when attitude is positive, but a negative effect when attitude is negative. The implication follows that inducing a future time perspective about present cognitive performance will increase motivation for persons with positive attitudes toward the future. But reference to the future consequences of present cognitive performance may be dysfunctional for persons holding a negative outlook regarding their personal futures.

Lens's studies have also pursued implications of that part of Atkinson's theory of achievement motivation that distinguishes between performance on particular immediate cognitive tasks and cumulative achievement over long time spans: cumulative achievement is expected to be a linear function of performance in particular tasks and strength of motivation, but the relation between strength of motivation and immediate performance itself is expected to be curvilinear (that is, an inverted U). The curvilinearity results from inefficiency in performance caused by either under- or overmotivation; only optimal motivation for the task at hand will allow true ability to be expressed. Such a curvilinear hypothesis derives from the classical Yerkes-Dodson law and has been demonstrated in relatively pure forms. Its demonstration in any particular complex situation, however, depends on the difficulty of the task in relation to the ability of the persons studied, and also on the degree to which ego-involving conditions accompany the task (Lens and De Volder, 1980).

Lens (1983) has now considered the academic examination system in Belgium in this regard; his analysis suggests that the curvilinear relation should also be obtained here. This situation is complicated because academic performance over a semester or year is cumulative, whereas a particular final examina-

tion requires an immediate cognitive performance; there are few or no intermediate performance tasks in this system. The theory posits that achievement
motivation is the result of a combination of need for achievement and fear of
failure (test anxiety in this instance); if either is too high or too low, the
resultant achievement motivation will be nonoptimal. In this system, of course,
need for achievement might display more cumulative properties, whereas test
anxiety might be more connected to the immediate performance requirements
of examinations. Note that the examination system is thus part of the treatment;
its characteristics may also cause interactions with aptitudes.

The hypothesis was studied using standard measures of need for achievement and test anxiety, administered at the start of the year to a group of Flemish
Belgian first-year university students. Final examinations at the end of the year
provided the achievement data. The curvilinear prediction for both measures
was clear. The implication is that optimal performance comes from intermediate motivation; too much or too little need for achievement or fear of failure
apparently interferes with effective performance. The next step of course is to
analyze the kinds of inefficiencies in cognitive processing produced by persons
occupying different cells of the $A_n \times A_x$ matrix; they need not be the same in
each cell.

The research of d'Ydewalle (1984) examines motivation as an intervening
variable in the details of cognitive information processing during learning tasks.
The general hypothesis is that subjects in learning experiments construct, either
explicitly or implicitly, a complex mental representation about the task and its
requirements; this produces expectations that have motivational effects which
in turn will condition methods of processing, uses of cognitive resources, and
the learning and coping strategies of the subject.

To show how expectations of the subject interact with the presence-ab-
sence of details, the availability of a schema, and the nature of the experimental
materials to influence performance, d'Ydewalle presents a series of experiments
on free recall, recognition, text learning, and reproduction tasks. In one experiment, for example, free-recall test versus recognition test expectations were
induced by instructions for a word-list learning task. Then, half the subjects in
each group received a free-recall test whereas half received a recognition test. A
second list of words was then learned and followed again by either an expected
or an unexpected test. Marked effects of these expectancy variations appeared in
the order of the words learned and in primacy and recency effects, suggesting
that subjects with different expectations encode lists differently and use working memory differently in the task.

In other experiments, meaningful texts were used, with text scrambling
and study time varied experimentally along with test expectations. It was shown
that subjects expecting a reproduction test look more actively at the text struc-

ture, and their performance is particularly disrupted by scrambling of text sentences. But subjects expecting multiple-choice tests pay less attention to structure and are less influenced by scrambling. Unexpected reproduction tests cause the subject to try to reconstruct the text structure, but this is possible only with unscrambled texts. Interactions with ability also appear, because subjects differ in their ability to detect and reconstruct the structure of the text under different conditions.

Another study comes from De Leeuw (1983) in the Netherlands. In this work, computerized instructional programs that attempt to improve the problem-solving abilities of public school students have been evaluated; measures of ability and personality characteristics of the students have been used as moderator aptitude variables. One instructional program used a highly structured algorithmic approach, in which the necessary operations and their sequencing in problem solving are exhaustively prescribed to the student and then practiced. The comparison program used a less structured heuristic approach, in which students are guided toward discovery of the necessary operations and sequencing for themselves, with well-placed aids available in the course of instruction. The programs have been tried out on both inductive and deductive reasoning problems (number series extrapolations and syllogisms) representing two levels of complexity or difficulty.

Results suggest that student ability and anxiety interact with the instructional treatment contrast, particularly on more complex problems. Students characterized as low in debilitating anxiety, or high in critical thinking and related intellectual abilities, or both, performed better with heuristic instruction than with algorithmic instruction. The students high in debilitating anxiety, or low in relevant abilities, or both, did better with algorithmic instruction. Within the heuristic program, the anxious students asked for help more than others and benefited from it less, particularly on the complex problems.

Such results fit with the findings shown in Figure 2-2. But the Dutch work also indicates that the same patterns of interaction between student aptitudes and instructional methods occur when the aim of instruction is to develop problem-solving abilities directly. The implication is that problem-solving abilities may not be developed in the same way in all persons; in particular, precise teaching of algorithmic problem-solving procedures is good for anxious, less able beginners but bad for the more able and less anxious beginners, whose learning may be more heuristic and idiosyncratic.

Finally, research by Hagtvet (1986) in Norway has investigated ability-anxiety interaction in high school mathematics instruction, and further distinguished the G_f and G_c aspects of ability as well as the worry, emotionality, and fear of failure components of A_x. The substantial interactions obtained involved primarily G_c and the fear and emotionality components of anxiety. The most able learners were most negatively affected by anxiety. Low ability learners were not affected negatively and often did slightly better when anxious. This is also consistent with the results cited earlier.

All these studies, and a variety of others, argue strongly for an integration of cognitive, conative, and affective research on aptitude for learning. The integration, however, must combine information-processing analysis with a person-situation interactional perspective. The next section moves toward this goal.

A PERSPECTIVE FOR FUTURE RESEARCH

Interactional Psychology

Although lip service has long been paid to the observation that human behavior is a function of both person and situation, the broad and fundamental implications of a person-situation interaction perspective for psychology have not been widely recognized or pursued. After various fits and starts over the decades, however, there is now a movement called interactional psychology. Its center is in research on personality theory, but it is exhibited in and gathers strands from several other basic and applied fields, including physiological, clinical, instructional, developmental, and ecological psychology; industrial and ergonomic psychology; behavior genetics; and also ethology and cultural anthropology. Medical research is adopting interactional perspectives in the study and treatment of such complex problems as alcoholism. Still, however, there are relatively few programmatic efforts aimed at the basic issues, and even fewer are concerned with individual differences in learning. ATI research is the special case in this field that is primarily concerned with differential learning.

Interactional psychology as a program of new theory and research took shape in the mid-1970s. Magnusson and Endler (1977) began organizing international symposia on interactional approaches to the study of personality in 1975. They also brought together for the first time reprints of the many empirical and theoretical fragments scattered through the previous literature (see Endler and Magnusson, 1976), Pervin and Lewis (1978) also presented chapters reflecting the growing spectrum of interactional psychology. A particularly ambitious program of research by Hettema (1979, in press) has sought not only an improved theory of person-situation adaptation, a theme central to ATI research, but also assessment procedures specially designed for further study of these adaptational phenomena. Important work in particular theoretical domains such as achievement motivation, volition, and emotions has also become distinctly interactional in focus (see Heckhausen, Schmalt, and Schneider, 1985; Hoefert, 1982; Lantermann, 1980; Nygaard, 1977).

The interactional paradigm views human behavior as an aspect of the continuous reciprocal interaction between situation and person. This paradigm distinguishes sharply between the lawfulness of manifest behavior and the lawfulness of perceptions, cognition, motivations, and emotions; it assumes no one-to-one correspondence between these two levels but rather studies both. It further distinguishes between the main effects and the interaction variance observable in a person-situation matrix, as suggested in Figure 2-1. It assumes that persons will be best characterized by their unique patterns of stable and changing behavior across situations, or treatment segments, and that a taxonomy of persons and of situations can only be built on descriptions of these person-situation interactions.

Within this framework, advancing research addresses several critical issues, and these are directly relevant to future research on ATI, as well as on learning and individual differences generally. Perhaps the most important of these concern the conceptualization of the dynamic functions that reflect organismic change — adaptation, learning, development, inconsistency, and, in short, conation — and also the design of a measurement system that reflects this functioning of persons in situations, at both molar and molecular levels. But other related issues are also kept in sight. These concern the characterization of the types of situations being studied and the contrast between situations as perceived and situations as objectively described, and the roles played by goals, expectations, intentions, and prevailing attitudinal states. Only a brief view of this direction is possible here.

Figure 2-4 offers a schematic framework consistent with the previous discussion. There is a person-situation interface extending along a time line wherein particular observable behavior is connected to a momentary situation. On the person side, there is then an action control level wherein performance is assembled and reassembled from moment to moment; this adaptive functioning is under the control of situational demands and affordances in interaction with perceptions and prevailing cognitive-conative-affective states of the person. Perceptions of the situation and of prior behavioral effects (expectations) are distinguished from perceptions of goals and consequences (intentions). The situation at hand is one of a prevailing type with which a person may or may not have prior experience. The prevailing states or attitudes of a person about past and future situations and performance in them overarchs the bank or repertoire of cognitive knowledge and performance components available. Stimuli are situational cues processed through action control and higher levels and reflected back to behavioral responses. But particular stimuli and responses in momentary situations relate only probabilistically to the characteristics of the prevailing person states or situation types in which an observed moment occurs. A model of cognitive performance in learning and problem solving has to be geared to

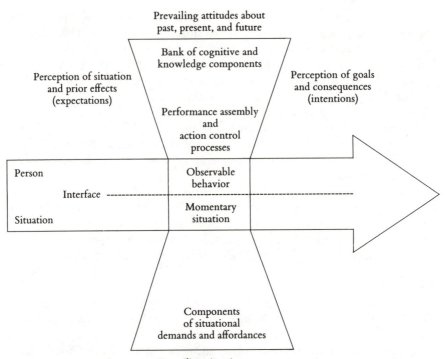

Prevailing situation type

Figure 2-4 A schematic organization of key aspects of person-situation interactions in learning from instruction.

reflect person and situation variation within this sort of person-situation interface.

Toward an Interactional Process Model

The traditional laboratory study of learning and problem solving usually assumed that a performance model could be built to represent a modal person performing a modal task. This generalized approach has always been limited by the dual problems of task and person variation, although these problems have not often been explicitly acknowledged. As cognitive psychological research has moved into the analysis of real instruction, the problems of task and person variation loom especially large; they no longer can be ignored. The definitions of learning and problem solving expand to include the definition of intelligence. But even more is implied by Figure 2-4. The person-situation interaction not only limits the generality of any particular cognitive performance model but also may introduce qualitative as well as quantitative moderating variables that reflect affective and conative, not just cognitive, process aspects of performance. Thus aspects of personality and motivation also come into the picture, and complex aptitude processes are suggested. These difficulties must now be confronted.

The big question now is: How do we build a theoretical model that accommodates the implications of all this? A closely related question is: How do we make this model instructionally tractable, so as to use and improve aptitude processes as well as understand them?

Individual Differences and Task Characteristics   In the earlier research aimed at performance models of paradigmatic laboratory tasks, and also of the sorts of tasks that appear on cognitive ability tests, it was first assumed that individual differences could be accounted for as quantitative parameter variations within the same uniform process model. The archetypical example is Hull's (1945) theory. This is not possible, because individual performances differ in strategic organization, not just in parameters associated with particular performance steps. There are also within-person variations across experience with a task, as well as between-person and between-task differences, that appear to be qualitative shifts and not just quantitative changes.

With cognitive psychology's increasing interest in instruction and other real-life activities, research attention has expanded from the study of knowledge-lean performance tasks and tests of earlier years to the study of knowledge-rich tasks. Here again, however, assumptions about individual differences have typically focused only on quantitative variations within a uniform process theory. Individuals may differ in their relevant knowledge base and the availability and accessibility of the knowledge specifically required for the task. They may differ also in the amount of experience already acquired in executing the task performance and its various components, and thus in automaticity of performance. Similarly, they may differ in speed and effectiveness of component processes. Just as with the knowledge-lean tasks, however, there is increasing evidence that knowledge-rich tasks often involve strategic variations within and between persons as a function of experience or variations in task difficulty. Strategy invention and strategy shifting seem particularly apparent in problem solving in mathematics and science, for example. Thus, a realistic model of either kind of task performance cannot be a uniform process model; it must provide for reorganizations of action flow in the process of learning and problem solving. Moreover, to have explanatory power the model must incorporate the person and task conditions that determine what particular form the flow of strategic activity over time will take, and it must account for individual differences in the successful adaptation of this flow across varying tasks. The problem in learning and in problem solving, particularly in instructional tasks, is dynamic adaptation.

A discussion by Elshout (1985) provides a particularly useful way to think about this in interaction terms. My discussion parallels his, with a mix of his and my terminology. In Elshout's view, a problem is a state of a certain person in a certain task situation such that, should the person succeed, any explanation of this event based only on the person's previous experience in this particular situation is excluded beforehand. And people certainly do succeed, often in ways exemplary of the best of intelligence. Cognitive theory posits that people first construct mental models of task environments and then choose whatever direction of further thinking this conception of the task suggests is most sensible. But a problem-solving situation is one in which the mental model constructed, presumably from past experience, is not adequate for directing a complete, successful, learning-thinking sequence. Some kind of improvising or heuristic processing must intervene. Heuristic processing and improvising are activities that have the direction of thought itself as the goal; when no stored strategy is available, the system must shift to processes aimed at finding or assembling a strategy. The assembly process must be conditioned by the person's expectations and intentions in this situation as well. On the task side, it is impossible to say what is an easy or a difficult task, or what is a well-structured or an ill-structured problem, in the abstract. It is not the task situation, per se, that indicates difficulty or complexity or lack of structure; it is the task characteristics in relation to the performances that a particular individual *can* assemble in this situation, or *typically does* assemble in this situation type. A problem is therefore a state in the interaction of a person and a task environment, and can only be identified and studied in that interaction. Individual and task *differences* in learning and problem solving can thus only be observed and understood in this interaction.

The Algorithmic-Heuristic Threshold   It is possible, however, to think of tasks as scaled along a continuum of difficulty or complexity within situation types for each individual. Such a scale, of course, would make sense only within types of situations, defined according to distinguishing task characteristics not yet identified. But Elshout imagines that there is a threshold for each person along such a continuum. Below the threshold, performance follows directly from the assembly the person already has in store for the task; the flow of activity is relatively automatic and algorithmic. Errors come mostly from cognitive slips rather than fundamental inadequacies in the system. Above the threshold, the person must increasingly operate in a heuristic, improvisational, controlled, and achievement-motivated mode. Here, errors occur because the previously stored cognitive components and knowledge base are inadequate, or poorly applied, the improvisational assembly and action-control devices are weak because they are not yet geared to the specific task type at hand, or achievement motivation flags prematurely. Furthermore, the farther above one's threshold one is forced to work, the more likely that heuristic processing and improvising degrade into helpless, perhaps anxious, muddling; errors become more conceptual and strategic. Novices are thus to be seen as persons who must work above their thresholds in most of a task type, whereas experts are those who can work below their thresholds in that task type. The goal of instruction is to move a person's threshold up, in each type of task that society and the person values. Raising the threshold means making more and more difficult or complex instances of the task type nonproblematical and automatic.

Ability and Treatment Structure Revisited   As argued earlier, the preponderance of ATI evidence suggests strong interaction between measures of individual differences in general ability (G) as aptitude and the contrast between highly structured, complete, or direct instructional treatments on the one hand, and relatively unstructured, incomplete, or indirect instructional treatments on the other; more able learners do better with less structure, and less able learners do better with more (Snow and Lohman, 1984). This finding is understandable as a threshold phenomenon; more able learners benefit from most of the instructional tasks presented by indirect, unstructured methods because task difficulty and complexity in these situations is either just below their threshold or only enough above threshold to be challenging or motivating. But the task in these situations is far above the threshold for less able learners; without explicitly structured teaching, they are left helpless, anxious, or unmotivated. Direct and complete instruction provides the extensive scaffolding needed to raise the thresholds of less able learners. But it makes the task far enough below threshold for the able learner that it becomes boring, and imposing its particular algorithmic structure may even interfere with the able learner's own preferred processing style.

Again, according to Elshout's (1985) evidence, rather little is learned by students working far above their thresholds. Close examination of their performance suggests that, while working style may improve slowly, serious misconceptions and erroneous beliefs may also be strengthened. Motivation is also decreased here. Learners working far below their thresholds may strengthen habitual automatic performance, but they are not challenged to extend their heuristic or improvisational abilities.

Elshout's threshold concept thus seems capable of accounting not only for G interaction with degree of structure and completeness in instruction, but also the interaction of achievement motivation and anxiety with this same treatment variable. For a given ability level, increased anxiety has the effect of lowering the threshold of tolerable complexity; increased need for achievement has the effect of raising it. But Lens's (1983) curvilinear trends for motivation and anxiety relations to achievement can also be described by the same threshold phenomenon; too much or too little arousal from either source pushes the threshold in the opposite direction, and performance is suppressed. And d'Ydewalle's (1984) research suggests, as noted previously, that expectations about some task characteristics (meaning the type of test to be faced) can set the person to performing above or below threshold (that is, in algorithmic versus heuristic modes). Much other evidence seems also to fall in line.

The important target for future research, then, is to understand for each person and each task situation, the *zone of tolerable problematicity*. This is Elshout's term, but similar conceptions have come from several other theorists (notably Vygotsky, 1978). It refers to the region around the threshold that is both sufficiently structured and sufficiently challenging. Such zones are probably only identifiable within substantive task types, so the identification of these situation types is a high priority for further research. Instruction within a substantive knowledge domain, aimed at this zone, appears to be the best way to improve learning and problem solving, and aptitude for both.

Higher-Order Person-Situation Interaction   Although research aimed at refining aptitude or task constructs needs to focus on particular variables, in the instructional context it is clear that higher-order interactions are the rule. There are few, if any, clear general relationships between particular person and task variables that hold across changes in population or subject matter or instructional context. This should be expected, because the effects of any one, or two, or three individual difference constructs will always be mediated by other differences in study methods and processes, personal styles, and perceptions of the instructional situation, including expectations about the formal evaluation or assessment aspect of this situation, as suggested above.

In much of the evidence on complex interactions, the crucial importance of learner's *intentions* is beginning to show through (Entwistle, 1985). Intentions seem also to shift the threshold and thus influence the role of other task and person characteristics. Learners intending to extract personal meaning from a particular instructional task or situation will process information deeply in it—they will seek a deeper structure, one that is more carefully, flexibly, and idiosyncratically organized. Learners intending to be ready to reproduce the knowledge anticipated in a subsequent test will adopt a more surface approach. Also identifiable is a pragmatic approach to learning involving attempts to organize time, effort, and study conditions but also to manipulate the assessment system to the learner's advantage. Independent attempts to identify these three learning styles or approaches have yielded consistent results; one study has also related the deep approach to intrinsic motivation and a perception of interest or relevance, the surface approach to fear of failure or test anxiety, and the strategic approach to achievement motivation and vocational motives (see Marton, Hounsell, and Entwistle, 1984).

Thus, such learning style differences can be linked to relatively stable person or aptitude variables, but they also vary within individuals as a function of task and situation variables. The study of problem solving in instructional situations cannot be limited to a cognitive processing model of problem solving especially because the instructional situation includes assessment procedures. Students' intentions for learning and their expectations about these procedures can induce a deep, surface, or pragmatic style regardless of instructional task variables. Even the most able, motivated, and interested learners sensibly marshal limited time to maximize payoff—they exhibit intelligent effort avoidance.

The suggestion is that research on problem solving, cognition-motivation interaction, and individual differences in instructional learning should concentrate on the *cognitive-motivational-intentional styles* induced in particular person-situation combinations as the central focus for modeling. The zone of tolerable problematicity around the threshold hypothesized earlier may be equivalent to the zone of deep processing hypothesized here. But this zone will be seen to shift and change as a function of person and situation factors as well as task type and difficulty. The person factors most certainly must include student perceptions and intentions. And the situation factors must certainly include the nature of the assessments expected. Following Entwistle (1985), it seems clear that the model sought must model the richness and variety of experience in this person-situation-problem nexus if it is to be an instructionally tractable as well as a theoretically useful construction.

To conclude, let us return to the language of Glaser and Cronbach quoted at the outset of this chapter. We need a theory of the initial properties of the learner which interact with learning—the complex of personal characteristics that accounts for an individual's end state after a particular educational treatment. We do not yet have such a theory. But we are now much closer. ATI research, coupled with new understanding of cognitive and motivational processes in learning and problem solving, has shown us what needs to be included in such a theory; it has also come a long way toward suggesting its possible form. The next two decades promise to be even more productive than the last two.

REFERENCES

Ackerman, P. L., and Schneider, W. (1985). Individual differences in automatic and controlled information processing. In R. F. Dillon (Ed.), *Individual differences in cognition, Vol. 2.* Orlando, Fla.: Academic Press.

Allison, R. B., Jr. (1960). Learning parameters and human abilities. Unpublished doctoral dissertation, Princeton University.

Anderson, G. L. (1941). A comparison of the outcomes of instruction under two theories of learning. Unpublished doctoral dissertation, University of Minnesota.

Berliner, D. C., and Cahen, L. S. (1973). Trait-treatment interaction and learning. In F. N. Kerlinger (Ed.), *Review of research in education,* Vol. 1. Itasca, Ill.: Peacock.

Bethell-Fox, C. E., Lohman, D. F., and Snow, R. E. (1984). Adaptive reasoning: Componential and eye movement analysis of geometric analogy performance. *Intelligence,* 8:205–238.

Bracht, G. H. (1970). Experimental factors related to aptitude-treatment interactions. *Review of Educational Research,* 40:627–645.

Brunswik, E. (1956). *Perception and the representative design of psychological experiments.* Berkeley, Calif.; University of California Press.

Burstein, L. (1980a). The role of levels of analysis in the specification of educational effects. In R. Dreeben, and J. A. Thomas (Eds.), *Analysis of educational productivity, Vol. I: Issues in microanalysis.* Cambridge, Mass.: Ballinger Press.

Burstein, L. (1980b). Analyzing multilevel educational data: The choice of an analytic model rather than a unit of analysis. In E. Baker and E. Quellmalz (Eds.), *Design, analysis, and policy in testing and evaluation.* Beverly Hills, Calif.: Sage Publications.

Burstein, L. (1980c). Analysis of multilevel data in educational research and evaluation. In D. Berliner (Ed.), *Review of research in education,* Vol. 8. Washington, D.C.: American Educational Research Association.

Burstein, L., Linn, R. L., and Capell, F. (1978). Analyzing multilevel data in the presence of heterogeneous within-class regressions. *Journal of Educational Statistics,* 3:347–383.

Burstein, L., Miller, M. D., and Linn, R. L. (1981). *The use of within-group slopes as indices of group outcomes.* CSE Report No. 171. Los Angeles: Center for the Study of Evaluation.

Cattell, R. B. (1946). *The description and measurement of personality.* New York: World Books.

Corno, L. (1979). A hierarchical analysis of selected naturally occurring aptitude-treatment interactions in the third grade. *American Educational Research Journal,* 16:391–410.

Corno, L., and Snow, R. E. (1986). Adapting teaching to individual differences among students. In M. Wittrock (Ed.), *Third handbook of research on teaching.* New York: Macmillan.

Crist-Whitzel, J. L., and Hawley-Winne, B. J. (1976). Individual differences and mathematics achievement: An investigation of aptitude-treatment interactions in an evaluation of three instructional approaches. Paper presented at the meeting of the American Educational Research Association, San Francisco.

Cronbach, L. J. (1953). Correlation between persons as a research tool. In O. H. Mowrer (Ed.), *Psychotherapy: Theory and research.* New York: Ronald.

Cronbach, L. J. (1957). The two disciplines of scientific psychology. *American Psychologist,* 12:671–684.

Cronbach, L. J. (1967). Instructional methods and individual differences. In R. Gagné. (Ed.), *Learning and individual differences.* Columbus, Ohio: Merrill.

Cronbach, L. J. (1975). Beyond the two disciplines of scientific psychology. *American Psychologist,* 30:116–127.

Cronbach, L. J. (1976). *Research on classrooms and schools: Formulation of questions, design, and analysis.* Stanford, Calif.: Stanford Evaluation Consortium.

Cronbach, L. J. (1982a). *Designing evaluations of educational and social programs.* San Francisco: Jossey-Bass.

Cronbach, L. J. (1982b). Prudent aspirations for social inquiry. In W. H. Kruskal (Ed.), *The social sciences: Their nature and uses.* Chicago: University of Chicago Press.

Cronbach, L. J., and associates (1980). *Toward reform of program evaluation.* San Francisco: Jossey-Bass.

Cronbach, L. J., and Gleser, G. C. (1965). *Psychological tests and personnel decisions.* Urbana: University of Illinois Press.

Cronbach, L. J., and Snow, R. E. (1969). *Individual differences in learning ability as a function of instructional variables.* Final Report to USOE (Contract OEC 4-6-061269-1217). Stanford University, School of Education, Stanford, Calif.

Cronbach, L. J., and Snow, R. E. (1977). *Aptitudes and instructional methods: A handbook for research on interactions.* New York: Irvington.

Cronbach, L. J., and Webb, N. (1975). Between-class and within-class effects in a reported aptitude × treatment interaction: Reanalysis of a study by G. L. Anderson. *Journal of Educational Psychology, 67:*717–724.

De Leeuw, L. (1983). Teaching problem solving: An ATI study of the effects of teaching algorithmic and heuristic solution methods. *Instructional Science, 12:*1–48.

d'Ydewalle, G. (1984). Motivational and information processing. Unpublished report, University of Leuven, Belgium.

d'Ydewalle, G., and Lens, W. (Eds.) (1981). *Cognition in human motivation and learning.* Leuven, Belgium, and Hillsdale, N.J.: Leuven University Press and Lawrence Erlbaum Associates.

Edwards, A. L., and Cronbach, L. J. (1952). Experimental design for research in psychotherapy. *Journal of Clinical Psychology, 8:*51–59.

Egan, D. E., and Greeno, J. G. (1973). Acquiring cognitive structure by discovery and rule learning. *Journal of Educational Psychology, 64:*85–97.

Elshout, J. J. (1985). Problem solving and education. Paper presented at the First Conference of the European Association for Research on Learning and Instruction, Leuven, Belgium.

Endler, N. S., and Magnusson, D. (Eds.) (1976). *Interactional psychology and personality.* Washington, D.C.: Hemisphere.

Entwistle, N. J. (1985). Explaining individual differences in school learning. Paper presented at the First Conference of the European Association for Research on Learning and Instruction, Leuven, Belgium.

Frederiksen, J. R. (1980). *Models for determining school effectiveness.* Boston, Mass.: Bolt, Beranek, and Newman.

Gagné, R. (Ed.) (1967) *Learning and individual differences.* Columbus, Ohio: Merrill.

Gibson, J. J. (1979). *The ecological approach to visual perception.* Boston: Houghton Mifflin.

Glanzer, M. (1967) Individual performance, R-R theory, and perception. In R. Gagné, (Ed.), *Learning and individual differences.* Columbus, Ohio: Merrill.

Glaser, R. (1967). Some implications of previous work on learning and individual differences. In R. Gagné (Ed.), *Learning and individual differences.* Columbus, Ohio: Merrill.

Glaser, R. (1976). Components of a psychology of instruction: Toward a science of design. *Review of Educational Research, 46*:1–24.

Glaser, R. (1977). *Adaptive education: Individual diversity and learning.* New York: Holt, Rinehart and Winston.

Gray, L. E. (1982). Aptitude constructs, learning processes, and achievement. Unpublished report. Stanford University.

Greene, J. C. (1976). Choice behavior and its consequences for learning: An ATI study. Unpublished doctoral dissertation, Stanford University.

Greeno, J. G. (1978). A study of problem solving. In R. Glaser (Ed.), *Advances in instructional psychology,* Vol. 1. Hillsdale, N.J.: Erlbaum.

Greeno, J. G., and Mayer, R. E. (1975). Structural and quantitative interaction among aptitudes and instructional treatments. Unpublished report, University of Michigan.

Gustafsson, J. E. (1984). A unifying model for the structure of intellectual abilities. *Intelligence, 8*:179–203.

Guttman, L. (1965). The structure of interrelations among intelligence tests. In *Proceedings of the 1964 invitational conference on testing problems.* Princeton, N.J.: Educational Testing Service.

Guttman, L. (1970). Integration of test design and analysis. In *Proceedings of the 1969 conference on testing problems.* Princeton, N.J.: Educational Testing Service.

Haertel, E. D., Walberg, H. J., and Weinstein, T. (1983). Psychological models of educational performance: A theoretical synthesis of constructs. *Review of Educational Research, 53*:75–91.

Hagtvet, K. A. (1986). Interaction of anxiety and ability on academic achievement: A simultaneous consideration of parameters. Paper presented at the American Educational Research Association, San Francisco.

Heckhausen, H., Schmalt, H-D., and Schneider, K. (1985). *Achievement motivation in perspective.* Orlando, Fla.: Academic Press.

Heckman, R. W. (1967). Aptitude-treatment interactions in learning from printed instruction: A correlational study. Unpublished doctoral dissertation, Purdue University.

Hettema, P. J. (1979). *Personality and adaptation.* Amsterdam: North-Holland.

Hettema, P. J. (Ed.) (in press). *The assessment of human adaptation.* Amsterdam: North-Holland.

Hoefert, H-W. (Ed.) (1982). *Person und situation: Interaktionpsychologische untersuchungen.* Göttingen: Verlag für Psychologie-Dr. C. J. Hogrefe.

Hull, C. L. (1945). The place of innate individual and species differences in a natural science theory of behavior. *Psychological Review, 52*:55–60.

Humphreys, L. G. (1971). Theory of intelligence. In R. Cancro (Ed.), *Intelligence: Genetic and environmental influences.* New York: Grune and Stratton.

Hunt, E. B., Frost, N., and Lunneborg, C. E. (1973). Individual differences in cognition: A new approach to intelligence. In G. Bower (Ed.), *The Psychology of Learning and Motivation,* Vol. 7. New York: Academic Press.

Hunt, E., and Lansman, M. (1975). Cognitive theory applied to individual differences. In W. K. Estes (Ed.), *Handbook of learning and cognitive processes,* Vol. 1. Hillsdale, N.J.: Erlbaum.

Kyllonen, P. C., Lohman, D. F., and Snow, R. E. (1984). Effects of aptitudes, strategy training, and task facets on spatial task performance. *Journal of Educational Psychology,* 76:130–145.

Kyllonen, P. C., Lohman, D. F., and Woltz, D. J. (1984). Componential modeling of alternative strategies for performing spatial tasks. *Journal of Educational Psychology,* 76:1325–1345.

Lantermann, E. D. (1980). *Interaktionen—person, situation und handlung.* München: Urban and Schwarzenberg.

Lens, W. (1983) Achievement motivation, test anxiety, and academic achievement. *University of Leuven Psychological Reports* No. 21. Leuven, Belgium: University of Leuven.

Lens, W., and de Volder, M. (1980) Achievement motivation and intelligence test scores: A test of the Yerkes-Dodson, hypothesis. *Psychologica Belgica,* 20:49–59.

Lohman, D. F. (1979a). *Spatial ability: A review and reanalysis of the correlational literature* (Tech. Rep. No. 8). Stanford, Calif.: Stanford University, Aptitude Research Project, School of Education.

Lohman, D. F. (1979b). *Spatial ability: Individual differences in speed and level* (Tech. Rep. No. 9). Stanford, Calif.: Stanford University, Aptitude Research Project, School of Education.

Lohman, D. F. (1986). Predicting mathemathanic effects in the teaching of higher-order thinking skills. *Educational Psychologist,* 21:191–208.

Lohman, D. F., and Kyllonen, P. C. (1983). Individual differences in solution strategy on spatial tasks. In R. F. Dillon and R. R. Schmeck (Eds.), *Individual differences in cognition,* Vol. 1. New York: Academic Press.

MacLeod, C. M., Hunt, E. B., and Mathews, N. N. (1978). Individual differences in the verification of sentence-picture relationships. *Journal of Verbal Learning and Verbal Behavior,* 17:493–508.

Magnusson, D., and Endler, N. S. (Eds.) (1977). *Personality at the crossroads: Current issue in interactional psychology.* Hillsdale, N.J.: Erlbaum.

Marshalek, B. (1981). *Trait and process aspects of vocabulary knowledge and verbal ability* (Tech. Rep. No. 15). Stanford Calif.: Stanford University, Aptitude Research Project, School of Education.

Marshalek, B., Lohman, D. F., and Snow, R. E. (1983). The complexity continuum in the radex and hierarchical models of intelligence. *Intelligence,* 7:107–128.

Marton, F., Hounsell, D. S., and Entwistle, N. J. (1984). *The experience of learning.* Edinburgh: Scottish Academic Press.

Mayer, R. E., and Greeno, J. G. (1972). Structural differences between outcomes produced by different instructional methods. *Journal of Educational Psychology,* 63:165–173.

Mayer, R. E., Stiehl, C. C., and Greeno, J. G. (1975). Acquisition of understanding and skill in relation to subjects' preparation and meaningfulness of instruction. *Journal of Educational Psychology,* 67:331–350.

Melton, A. W. (1967). Individual differences and theoretical process variables: General comments on the conference. In R. Gagné (Ed.), *Learning and individual differences.* Columbus, Ohio: Merrill.

Mulholland, T. M., Pellegrino, J. W., and Glaser, R. (1980). Components of geometric analogy solution. *Cognitive Psychology,* 12:252–284.

Nygaard, R. (1977). *Personality, situation, and persistence.* Oslo: Universitetsforlaget.

Pellegrino, J. W. (1984). Components of spatial ability. Paper presented at the NATO Advanced Study Institute on Advances in Measuring Cognition as Motivation, Athens, Greece.

Pellegrino, J. W., and Glaser, R. (1979). Cognitive correlates and components in the analysis of individual differences. *Intelligence,* 3:187–214.

Pellegrino, J. W., and Glaser, R. (1980). Components of inductive reasoning. In R. E. Snow, P-A. Federico, and W. E. Montague (Eds.), *Aptitude, learning, and instruction, Vol. 1: Cognitive process analyses of aptitude.* Hillsdale, N.J.: Erlbaum.

Pervin, L. A., and Lewis, M. (Eds.) (1978). *Perspective in interactional psychology.* New York: Plenum.

Peterson, P. L. (1976). Interactive effects of student anxiety, achievement orientation, and teacher behavior on student achievement and attitude. Unpublished doctoral dissertation, Stanford University.

Peterson, P. L. (1987). Selecting students and services for compensatory education. In B. I. Williams, P. A. Richmond, and B. J. Mason, (Eds.), *Designs for compensatory education: Conference proceedings and papers.* Washington, D.C.: Research and Evaluation Associates, Inc.

Peterson, P. L., Swing, S. R., Braverman, M. T., and Buss, R. (1982). Students' aptitudes and their reports of cognitive processes during direct instruction. *Journal of Educational Psychology,* 74:535–547.

Peterson, P. L., Swing, S. R., Stark, K. D., and Waas, G. A. (1984). Students' cognitions and time on task during mathematics instruction. *American Educational Research Journal,* 21:487–515.

Peterson, P. L., Swing, S. R., and Steiber, K. C. (1986). *Learning time vs. thinking skills: Alternative perspectives on the effects of two instructional interventions* (Program Report 86-6). Madison, Wis.: Wisconsin Center for Educational Research.

Porteus, A. (1976). Teacher-centered vs. student-centered instruction: Interactions with cognitive and motivational aptitudes. Unpublished doctoral dissertation, Stanford University.

Resnick, L. B. (1976). Task analysis in instructional design: Some cases from mathematics. In D. Klahr (Ed.), *Cognition and instruction.* Hillsdale, N.J.: Erlbaum.

Schneider, W., and Helmke, A. (1985). The role of classroom differences in achievement changes. Paper presented at the First European Conference for Research on Learning and Instruction, Leuven, Belgium.

Schneider, W., and Treiber, B. (1984). Classroom differences in the determination of achievement changes. *American Educational Research Journal,* 21:195–211.

Schoenfeld, W. N., and Cumming, W. W. (1963). Behavior and perception. In S. Koch (Ed.), *Psychology: A study of a science,* Vol. 5. New York: McGraw-Hill.

Seibert, W., and Snow, R. E. (1965). OASIS: A methodology for instructional and communications research. *Proceedings of the 73rd Annual Convention of American Psychological Association.* Washington, D.C.: American Psychological Association.

Sharps, R. (1973). A study of interactions between fluid and crystallized abilities and the methods of teaching reading and arithmetic. Unpublished doctoral dissertation. Pennsylvania State University.

Simon, H. A. (1969). *The sciences of the artificial.* Cambridge, Mass.: M.I.T. Press.

Simon, H. A. (1976). Identifying basic abilities underlying intelligent performance of complex tasks. In L. B. Resnick (Ed.), *The nature of human intelligence.* Hillsdale, N.J.: Erlbaum.

Smith, M.E. (1965). The prediction of learning effects from linear program characteristics. Unpublished master's thesis, Purdue University.

Smith, M. E. (1967). The correlational analysis of selected physical and content characteristics of programmed instruction. Unpublished doctoral dissertation, Purdue University.

Snow, R. E. (1963a). Effects of learner characteristics on learning from instructional films. Unpublished doctoral dissertation, Purdue University.

Snow, R. E. (1963b). *The importance of selected audience and film characteristics as determiners of the effectiveness of instructional films.* Final Report, USOE Grant No. 712142. Lafayette, Ind.: Audio Visual Center, Purdue University.

Snow, R. E. (1966). OASIS: Technical appendix. Unpublished report, Purdue University.

Snow, R. E. (1968). Brunswikian approaches to research on teaching. *American Educational Research Journal,* 5:475–489.

Snow, R. E. (1972). Individual differences in learning-related processes. Paper presented at American Educational Research Association, Chicago.

Snow, R. E. (1974). Representative and quasi-representative designs for research on teaching. *Review of Educational Research,* 44:265–292.

Snow, R. E. (1977a). Individual differences and instructional theory. *Educational Researcher,* 6:11–15.

Snow, R. E. (1977b). Research on aptitudes: A progress report. In L. S. Shulman (Ed.), *Review of research in education,* Vol. 4. Itasca, Ill.: Peacock.

Snow, R. E. (1978a). Eye fixation and strategy analysis of individual differences in cognitive aptitudes. In A. M. Lesgold, J. W. Pellegrino, S. D. Fokkema, and R. Glaser (Eds.), *Cognitive psychology and instruction.* New York: Plenum.

Snow, R. E. (1978b). Theory and method for research on aptitude processes. *Intelligence,* 2:225–278.

Snow, R. E. (1980a). Aptitude and achievement. *New Directions for Testing and Measurement,* 5:39–59.

Snow, R. E. (1980b). Aptitude processes. In R. E. Snow, P-A Federico, and W. E. Montague (Eds.), *Aptitude, learning and instruction, Vol. 1: Cognitive process analyses of aptitude.* Hillsdale, N.J.: Erlbaum.

Snow, R. E. (1980c). Intelligence for the year 2001. *Intelligence,* 4:185–199.

Snow, R. E. (1981). Toward a theory of aptitude for learning: Fluid and crystallized abilities and their correlates. In M. P. Friedman, J. P. Das, and N. O'Connor (Eds.), *Intelligence and learning.* New York: Plenum.

Snow, R. E. (1982). Education and intelligence. In R. J. Sternberg (Ed.), *Handbook of Human Intelligence.* New York: Cambridge University Press.

Snow, R. E. (1983). Aptitude theory. Presidential address to Division 15, American Psychological Association, Washington, D.C.

Snow, R. E. (1986). On intelligence. In R. J. Sternberg and D. K. Detterman (Eds.), *What is intelligence? Contemporary viewpoints on its nature and definition.* Norwood, N.J.: Ablex.

Snow, R. E. (1987). Aptitude complexes. In R. E. Snow and M. J. Farr (Eds.), *Aptitude, learning, and instruction, Vol. 3: Conative and affective process analyses.* Hillsdale, N.J.: Erlbaum.

Snow, R. E. (1988). Cognitive-conative aptitude interactions in learning. Paper presented at Minnesota Symposium on Learning and Individual Differences: Abilities, Motivation, and Methodology. Minneapolis, Minn.

Snow, R. E. (in preparation). The concept of aptitude. Aptitude Research Project, School of Education, Stanford University.

Snow, R. E., and Farr, M. J. (Eds.) (1987). *Aptitude, learning, and instruction, Vol. 3: Conative and affective process analyses.* Hillsdale, N.J.: Erlbaum.

Snow, R. E., Federico, P-A., and Montague, W. E. (Eds.) (1980a). *Aptitude, learning, and instruction, Vol. 1: Cognitive process analyses of aptitude.* Hillsdale, N.J.: Erlbaum.

Snow, R. E., Federico, P-A., and Montague, W. E. (Eds.) (1980b). *Aptitude, learning, and instruction, Vol. 2: Cognitive process analyses of learning and problem-solving.* Hillsdale, N.J.: Erlbaum.

Snow, R. E., Kyllonen, P. C., and Marshalek, B. (1984). The topography of ability and learning correlations. In R. J. Sternberg (Ed.), *Advances in the psychology of human intelligence,* Vol. 2. Hillsdale, N.J.: Erlbaum.

Snow, R. E., and Lohman, D. F. (1984). Toward a theory of cognitive aptitude for learning from instruction. *Journal of Educational Psychology,* 76:347–376.

Snow, R. E., and Peterson, P. L. (1985). Cognitive analyses of tests: Implications for redesign. In S. E. Embretson (Ed.), *Test design: Contributions from psychology, education, and psychometrics.* New York: Academic Press.

Snow, R. E., Tiffin, J., and Seibert, W. F. (1965). Individual differences and instructional film effects. *Journal of Educational Psychology,* 56:315–326.

Snow, R. E., Wescourt, K., and Collins, J. (1979). *Individual differences in aptitude and learning from interactive computer-based instruction* (Tech. Rep. No. 10). Stanford, Calif.: Stanford University, Aptitude Research Project, School of Education.

Stake, R. E. (1961). Learning parameters, aptitudes, and achievement. *Psychometric Monographs* (No. 9).

Sternberg, R. J. (1977). *Intelligence, information processing and analogical reasoning: The componential analysis of human abilities.* Hillsdale, N.J.: Erlbaum.

Sternberg, R. J. (1985). *Beyond IQ.* New York: Cambridge University Press.

Sternberg, R. J., and Weil, E. M. (1980). An aptitude-strategy interaction in linear syllogistic reasoning. *Journal of Educational Psychology,* 72:226–234.

Swiney, J. F., Jr. (1983). A study of executive processes in intelligence. Unpublished doctoral dissertation, Stanford University.

Tendam, D. J., McLeod, R. R., and Snow, R. E. (1962). An experimental evaluation of the use of instructional films in college physics. *American Journal of Physics,* 30:594–601.

Thomson, G. H. (1919). On the cause of hierarchical order among correlation coefficients. *Proceedings of the Royal Society,* A:95.

Thomson, G. H. (1939). *The factorial analysis of human ability.* London: University of London Press.

Underwood, B. J. (1975). Individual differences as a crucible in theory construction. *American Psychologist,* 30:128–140.

Van Calster, K., Lens, W., Nuttin, J. R. (1987). Affective attitude toward the personal future: Impact on motivation in high school boys. *American Journal of Psychology,* 100:1–13.

Vernon, P. E. (1950). *The structure of human abilities.* New York: Wiley.

Vygotsky, L. S. (1978). *Mind in Society.* Cambridge, Mass.: Harvard University Press.

Wang, M. C., and Lindvall, C. M. (1984). Individual differences and school learning environments. *Review of research in education,* Vol 11. Itasca, Ill.: Peacock.

Webb, N. M. (1977). *Learning in individual and small group settings* (Technical Report No. 7) Stanford, Calif.: Stanford University, Aptitude Research Project, School of Education.

Webb, N. M. (1982). Student interaction and learning in small groups. *Review of Educational Research,* 52:421–445.

Webb, N. (1983). Predicting learning from student interaction: Defining the interaction variables. *Educational Psychologist,* 18:33–41.

Yalow, E. S. (1980). *Individual differences in learning from verbal and figural materials* (Tech. Rep. No. 12). Stanford, Calif.: Stanford University, Aptitude Research Project, School of Education.

3

Cognitive Diversity: A Framework of Learning

JOHN L. HORN *University of Southern California*

Human abilities are simultaneously outcomes of learning and determinants of learning. It has proved difficult, however, to identify a system of abilities that satisfactorily and thoroughly represents these regularities. It is difficult to measure human cognitive capacities and to build a science and technology around such measurement. Controversy about fundamental features of cognitive functioning prevails among experts. The regard with which most individuals hold their abilities as reflections of their personalities generates ego involvement and emotional assertion. The result is much controversy about what can and cannot be measured and used in making educational decisions.

THE NATURE OF COGNITIVE ABILITIES

For many, the term "intelligence" is a synonym for cognitive abilities. Prominent psychologists argue that general intelligence represents most of what is meant by cognitive abilities and should be the basis for making most decisions in which evaluations of human differences in cognitive abilities are relevant (Eysenck, 1985; Jensen, 1984, 1985). Much evidence suggests, however, that for many scientific and practical purposes cognitive abilities are not well described in terms of any single capacity (Horn, 1985, 1986b). Also, there is widespread belief that cognitive abilities cannot be measured, or, even if they can, they cannot be assessed with sufficient reliability and validity to warrant using them in decision making (Hilliard, 1984; *Larry P.*, 1979; PASE, 1980). Substantial evidence exists, however, that calls this viewpoint into question (Anastasi, 1987; Cattell, 1971; 1980; Eysenck, 1985; Jensen, 1985; Matarazzo, 1972; Wolman, 1985). It is widely recognized that there are many, many cognitive abilities, but it is also recognized that this diversity has yet to be understood in terms of developmental and functional systems.

The brain is the wellspring for cognitive capacities. Today's evidence indicates that the brain maintains several separate functions, each located in particular centers and along separate pathways (Cowan, 1979; Bondareff, Mountjoy, and Roth, 1982; Eccles, 1977; Hubel, 1979; Iverson, 1979; Kety, 1979; Thompson, 1985). These functions underlie the expressions of different cognitive capacities and different abilities, but there is very little evidence of precise links between particular neurological functions and particular cognitive behaviors.

In a general way it is known that distinguishable neurotransmitter functions — the norepinephrine, dopamine, and serotonin systems — support distinct expressions of abilities. The norepinephrine system, centered around the locus coeruleus and branching largely into the hypothalamus and adjacent areas, is closely associated with concentration, attention, retrieval, and reasoning capacities. The dopamine system, centered around the substantia nigra and corpus striatum, is linked to motoric, language, and associational capacities of a kind that are notably affected in Parkinson's disease and schizophrenia. The serotonin system, operating largely along the raphe nuclei of the brain stem, is involved in arousal and inhibition of thinking. (See the references cited in the previous paragraph, plus Horn, 1982, 1985, and Iverson, 1979, for review.)

At a broader level of anatomical analysis, different sections of the brain are associated with different cognitive functions. For example, the left hemisphere of the brain is more closely associated with awareness of verbal stimuli than is the right hemisphere, which, in turn, is more closely linked to spatial abilities. Accumulated evidence suggests that top-to-bottom and front-to-back divisions of the brain are even more important indicators of distinct abilities than is the left-to-right division (Blackwood and Corsellis, 1976; Bourne, Ekstrand, and Dominowski, 1971; Prohovnik, 1980).

While analyses of brain functions point to distinctions among human cognitive capacities, the indivisibility of behavior presents major problems in distinguishing such capacities. There is no known way to definitively divide human performance into discrete categories of determinants, such as cognitive and motivational, or—breaking the cognitive category into subcategories—determinants of reasoning, retrieval, perception, and detection. Every expression of behavior involves cognition, motivation, temperament, and a large number of determinants that can be specified within each of these categories. Behavior is not divisible.

However, abstractions can represent divisions of behavior, and the abstractions can be objectified in operational definitions. This kind of division is required for scientific and practical purposes. It is necessary to divide behavior in this manner for the purposes of descriptive and inferential analyses, which are required for scientific understanding.

Cognitive abilities are not discrete traits, such as eye color or height; nor are they definitively identified elements, such as atoms or electrons or genes. They represent qualities abstracted from a continuous, homogeneous flow of behavior. The methods whereby the abstractions of abilities are effected—the operations of measurement—are essential features of ability definitions: the definitions do not correspond to any observation that the behavior, in nature, is partitioned into different categories.

There are infinite ways to slice a continuous flow of behavior; likewise, there are infinite ways in which the phenomena of cognition can be partitioned into abilities. These features of human cognition, and their implications, have been discussed by Commons (1985), Cronbach (1970), Thomson (1916), and Humphreys (1979a). A careful look at individuals discloses idiosyncratic combinations of capacities in each (Commons, 1985). People display a myriad of abilities. Humphreys observed that almost any cognitive psychologist can, virtually every day or two, make up a new test to measure a human ability; the list of abilities is neverending.

Comprehending Human Abilities

How can psychologists comprehend this myriad of abilities? The answer is, by building construct validity for each ability that can be separately measured. Cronbach (1988) has eloquently described the rules for such construction. Investigators must first approximately circumscribe the domain of the behavior of interest, then develop their theory about that domain. They must specify repeatable operations for objectively representing major concepts of the theory. Refutable hypotheses representing the assertions of the theory must be evaluated. The domain then can be comprehended in terms of the operational definitions of concepts and the evidence adduced to indicate support for particular hypotheses and lack of support for plausible alternative hypotheses. To the extent that the designated domain does indeed represent the infinity of interest

—and this can only be estimated in judgment—the infinity itself is comprehended. To thus build construct validity is not to trim an infinity into a finite, but to show that an infinity of adequate ideas about phenomena is small relative to a much larger infinity of inadequate ways to characterize observations.

Using Overlap

Analyses of overlap in measurement of different tests indicates how abilities can be comprehended in terms of a relatively small infinity. Such analyses demonstrate that most of the reliable measurements of large numbers of different cognitive tests can be accounted for with a relatively small number of common factors. Most of what is measured in a "new" ability test is already measured in other tests. Much of the infinity of cognitive capacities thus can be described in terms of a relatively small number of factor concepts. Any particular set of such concepts is only one from an infinity of possible sets of factor concepts, but evidence of relationships with other variables (outside the factor variables) further restricts the sets of factors that can provide adequate characterization of the phenomena.

Analysis based on common factors leaves reliable specific variance to be measured in particular tests, which means that each test still adds a small amount of reliable measurement to a neverending set of abilities, but this part of the phenomena can be small relative to the part that is described in terms of covariation. An infinity of ways of forming ideas about cognitive abilities thus can be reduced to a relatively few ways of understanding.

Circumscribing the Domain

A major problem in building construct validity by these rules is one of circumscribing the domain of behaviors that represent the infinite universe of human abilities. The sample domain of study should represent the universe. But how can the universe be designated? Without a good understanding of the universe, how can it be estimated that samples are or are not representative? Which among a myriad of human abilities are cognitive and which not? Which are indicative of truly basic capacities; which are merely derived from basic capacities or are of little consequence in human adaptation and adjustment? What basic capacities have yet to be represented by the tests investigators have constructed? Do the samples thus far researched contain abilities that are indicative of the truly important functions? It is difficult to answer such questions in nonarbitrary ways. It is difficult to specify boundaries for a domain that includes all truly important human abilities.

The difficulties to which I have just alluded are illustrated in a recent volume in which prominent cognitive researchers attempted to specify the nature of human intellect (Sternberg and Detterman, 1986). Much agreement can be found in these specifications, particularly if one makes allowances for use of different language to describe very similar behaviors and operational definitions, but the ponderings of these scientists revealed much variation in what experts conceive "intelligence" to be.

Using Breadth

Important differences in the descriptions of experts stem from different ideas about the breadth of the crucial abilities of human intellect (Detterman, 1986; Sternberg and Detterman, 1986). Many theorists aim to describe one such ability, a broad capacity identified with labels such as "IQ" or "general ability" or "intelligence." Other theorists seek to describe cognitive capacities less broad than G, identified with labels such as "attentive capacity," "encoding," "retrieval," "span of awareness." Between the narrow and the broad, definitions of abilities vary greatly.

At what level of breadth should cognitive abilities be described? The question is answered in different ways in the theories and practices of different researchers, but no system is known to be best for all purposes, and there is no agreement among experts that any one system is best for most purposes. Discussion concerning the proper level of analysis for cognitive abilities thus continues.

What constitutes breadth? There are only approximate answers to this question, but these answers are fundamental to understanding differences in expert viewpoints about the basic abilities of learning. Problems in clearly defining breadth come back to problems in defining basic capacities, specifying differences between capacities, showing how capacities combine to make abilities, and defining which abilities properly belong to the domain of intellect (cognition). There is no definitive listing of human cognitive capacities. There is no precise demarcation between different kinds of capacities. There are no precise rules for how capacities combine through development and in function. There is no certain way to distinguish between an ability that is intellectual and one that is not. Is musical ability (whatever one may mean by that) an intellectual ability, for example? Is span memory? Different experts argue cogently both "yes" and "no" to each of these questions, but no particular answer is accepted by most nor should be accepted in science without many qualifications.

In the face of these problems it has proved useful to distinguish between broad and narrow in terms of the average intercorrelation among components of an ability (Cronbach, 1970; Horn, 1972, 1986a; 1986b). *Intercorrelation* represents a coefficient of relationship for two arrays of numbers (usually measurements of individual differences). The analyses establish the degree of similarity for the orders of numbers of the different arrays. The numbers in the arrays 1, 2, 3, 4, 5 and 97, 98, 99, 100, 101 are ordered in precisely the same way; the correlation between these two arrays is 1.0 (one). The correlation of the following third array — 34, 38, 36, 37, 35 — with both the other arrays is 0.0 (zero), representing the fact that the order of the numbers (as stated) in this array is not at all similar to the order of the numbers in the other two arrays. The following fourth array — 105, 107, 106, 109, 108 — correlates .6 with the first two arrays and .4 with the third array; each of these correlations is intermediate between perfect agreement in order and no agreement. To establish the average intercorrelation among components of an ability is to determine if the average of the intercorrelations between different arrays of numbers — representing the orders of measurements on component 1, component 2, component 3, and so on — is near large or near small, large being the perfect agreement indicated by a correlation of 1, small being the lack of agreement represented by a correlation of 0. The question remains, what is a component? which leads back to the question, what are the basic capacities? But in a rough way these questions are answered, a priori, by the kinds of items and subtests — that is, components — investigators invent and put into tests.

Operationally, then, a broad ability can be defined as one for which the average among the intercorrelations of different components is small; a narrow ability is one for which the intercorrelations among the components of the ability are large.

Broad and Narrow Item Composites

Items of a test can represent components, and the items can be judged to be similar or to require different processes. But diversity need not be based on judgment alone; the extent of the intercorrelations among items is an indication. A broad ability, is one for which the item intercorrelations are small, whereas an ability measured with highly intercorrelated items is narrow.

The Stanford-Binet (SB) test that has been used throughout most of this century yields a broad measure of IQ. The intercorrelations among the different items of the SB test are small. However, small relative to what? We can compare the SB test with the Raven's matrices (RM) test, which is also regarded as a measure of IQ; however, relative to the SB test the intercorrelations among the different items of the RM test are large. The SB and RM tests do not measure the same thing, although they are said to measure IQ, and it is argued that IQ represents Spearman's (1927) concept of G (Jensen, 1984; 1987); the SB test is a diverse, broad measure based on many lowly correlated items representing several distinct cognitive components; the RM is a narrower measure, based on highly correlated items representing few cognitive capacities.

Broad and Narrow Subtest Composites

Abilities are often measured as combinations of subtest scores rather than as combinations of item scores. Subtests can be considerably more reliable than items. High reliability is desired when the aim is to define an ability in terms of identifiable, distinct processes—also called components of capacities. (This, however, has not always been the aim in research in which subtests have been used to define abilities.)

When an ability is defined in terms of subtests, a broad ability is one for which the intercorrelations among the subtest scores is small. The IQ measure of the Wechsler tests, such as the Wechsler Adult Intelligence Scale (WAIS) or Wechsler Intelligence Scale for Children (WISC) (Matarazzo, 1972), measured as a sum of scores on the subtests in Table 3-1, is an example of a broad measure. The intercorrelations among the subtests of the Wechsler range between .20 and .85; some of these correlations are found to be as low as .20. The correlation of SI with DS or with MZ characteristically is between .25 and .35.

The Wechsler definition of IQ is indeed broad, but it is considerably less broad than some other definitions. The sum of the subtest scores of the Woodcock and Johnson (1977), McCarthy (1972), or Kaufman and Kaufman (1983) tests (when the achievement tests are included in the latter) provide broader definitions, for example. There are still other batteries of tests designed to sure IQ, some of which involve more and some of which involve fewer subtests of different abilities (Horn, 1988; Horn and Goldsmith, 1981).

The average of the intercorrelations among the subtest components of popular measures of IQ is typically about .45, but the correlations among particular components, and the average over all components can drop below this figure, depending on the tests involved. For example, the correlation between two reasoning tests, induction and deduction, is usually somewhat smaller than .45. The correlation between attention and deduction tests is typically around .20 to .25. If measures of artistic abilities, musical abilities, or athletic abilities

Table 3-1 Wechsler Subtests Classified as Verbal and Performance

Verbal	Performance
IN: Information	PC: Picture completion
CO: Comprehension	PA: Picture arrangement
VO: Vocabulary	OA: Object assembly
SI: Similarities	BD: Block design
AR: Arithmetic	CD: Coding (digit symbol in the WAIS)
DS: Digit span	MZ: Mazes (not in the WAIS)

Note: There are new versions of the SB, WAIS, and WISC. The references throughout this chapter, however, are to the older versions of these tests; much more research information has been gathered on the older than on the newer tests.

are included among subtest measures that are said to indicate IQ, the average among the subtest correlations (still almost always positive) may well be below .20 — near .15 or even lower. The correlation between vocabulary and information, on the other hand, is usually greater than .50. The breadth of a measure of IQ varies greatly from one theorist to another, one measure to another, and one study to another.

MAJOR ABILITIES

Many multiple subtest measures are purported not to be measures of IQ, but to be measures of components of IQ. Examples of such measures are the well-replicated common-factor (WERCOF) abilities identified in the reviews of Ekstrom, French, and Harman (1979) and Hakstian and Cattell (1974). Table 3-2 provides summary descriptions of WERCOF abilities. The criteria used in identifying these abilities will be discussed in the next section.

Factor-Analytic Research

Common-factor analysis is a research approach aimed at reducing the arbitrariness that is represented in definitions of IQ. As the examples in the previous paragraphs have shown, IQ has been defined with all manner of different mixtures of subtests and corresponding capacities. Sound science cannot be built on such arbitrariness.

In addressing this problem, common-factor studies have aimed at identifying abilities not as mixtures designated a priori but as functional unities objectively located (Cattell, 1971). If in a context of many variables a particular set of variables "hang together" in an objectively rotated (Horn, 1967) simple-structure factor, this is evidence that the intercorrelated variables record processes that function together as a unit. For example, in the context of many manifestations of the functions of the heart, lungs, liver, and kidneys, measures of systolic and diastolic blood pressure in different parts of the body, pulse rate, and breathing rate intercorrelate to indicate the functional unity of the heart in distinction from the functional unity of the kidneys or liver. One must have ideas about how to sample variables that represent functional unities, and the sampling based on such ideas can be rather arbitrary unless good theory, backed by empirical evidence, dictates the sampling. With such provisos, the evidence of well-conceived and thorough factor analytic studies indicates regularities that likely represent a function of one kind or another.

A WERCOF ability is indicated by replication in at least three separate and technically adequate factor analytic studies, each based on variable and subject samples of sufficient size and diversity to provide a test of whether or not a common factor indicating the ability can be distinguished in company with similar factors. Replication is signalized by the presence of at least two, and

Table 3-2 First-Order (Primary) Mental Abilities

	Guilford Symbol	French Symbol	Replicated?
Acculturational knowledge abilities			
Verbal comprehension. Demonstrate understanding of words, sentences, and paragraphs.	CMU	V	Yes
Sensitivity to problems. Suggest ways to deal with problems — e.g., improvements for a toaster.	EMI	Sep	Yes
Syllogistic reasoning. Given stated premises, draw logically permissible conclusions even when these are nonsensical.	EMR	Rs	Yes
Number facility. Do basic operations of arithmetic quickly and accurately.	NSI	N	Yes
Verbal closure. Show comprehension of words and sentences when parts are omitted.			No
Estimation. Using incomplete information, estimate what is required for problem solution.	CMI		No
Behavioral relations. Judge interaction between people to estimate how one feels about a situation.	CBI		No
Semantic relations: Esoteric concepts. Demonstrate awareness of analogic relationships among abstruse bits of information.	CMR IMR		No
Mechanical knowledge. Demonstrate knowledge of industrial arts such as mechanics, electricity.		Mk	?
General information. Demonstrate knowledge in the areas of science, humanities, social sciences, business.		Vi	
Abilities of reasoning under novel conditions			
Induction. Indicate a principle of relationships among elements.	NSR	I	Yes

(continued)

Table 3-2 First-Order (Primary) Mental Abilities *(continued)*

	Guilford Symbol	French Symbol	Replicated?
General reasoning. — Find solutions for problems having an algebraic quality.	CMS	R	Yes
Figural relations. Demonstrate awareness of relationships among figures.	CFR		?
Semantic relations — common concepts. Demonstrate awareness of relationships among common pieces of information.	CMR IMR		No
Symbolic classifications. Show which symbol does not belong in a class of several symbols.	CSC		No
Concept formation. Given several examples of a concept, identity new instances.	CFC		No
Short-term apprehension and retrieval abilities			
Associative memory. When presented with one element of previously associated but otherwise unrelated elements, recall associated element.	MSR	Ma	Yes
Span memory. Immediately recall a set of elements after one presentation.	MSU	Ms	Yes
Meaningful memory. Immediately recall a set of items that are meaningfully related.	MSR	Mm	?
Chunking memory. Immediately recall elements by categories into which elements were classified.	MMC		No
Memory for order. Immediately recall the position of an element within a set of elements.	MSS		No
Long-term storage and retrieval abilities			
Associational fluency. Produce words similar in meaning to a given word.	DMR	Fa	Yes
Expressional fluency. Produce different ways of saying much the same thing.	DSS	Fe	Yes

	Guilford Symbol	French Symbol	Replicated?
Ideational fluency. Produce ideas about a stated condition or object — e.g., a lady holding a baby.	DMU	Fi	Yes
Word fluency. Produce words meeting particular structural requirementst — e.g., ending with a particular suffix.	DMR	Fw	Yes
Originality. Produce "clever" expressions or interpretations — e.g., titles for a story plot.	DMT	O	Yes
Spontaneous flexibility. Produce diverse functions and classifications — e.g., uses for a pencil.	DMC	Xs	Yes
Delayed retrieval. Recall material learned hours before.			No

Speed of thinking abilities

	Guilford Symbol	French Symbol	Replicated?
Perceptual speed. Under highly speeded conditions, distinguish similar visual patterns; find instances of a pattern.	ESU	P	Yes
Correct decision speed. Speed of finding correct answers to intellectual problems of intermediate difficulty.			No
Writing and printing speed. Quickly copy printed or cursive letters with words.			No

Visualization and spatial orientation abilities

	Guilford Symbol	French Symbol	Replicated?
Visualization. Mentally manipulate forms to visualize how they would look under altered conditions.	CFT	Vz	Yes
Spatial orientation. Visually imagine parts out of place and put them in place — e.g., solve jigsaw puzzles.	CFS	S	Yes
Speed of closure. Identify Gestalt when parts of whole are missing.	CFU	Cs	Yes
Flexibility of closure. Find a particular figure embedded within distracting figures.	NFT	Cs	Yes

(continued)

Table 3-2 First-Order (Primary) Mental Abilities *(continued)*

	Guilford Symbol	French Symbol	Replicated?
Spatial planning. Survey a spatial field and find a path through the field — e.g., pencil mazes.	CFI	Ss	Yes
Figural adaptive flexibility. Try out in possible arrangements of elements of visual pattern to find one arrangement that satisfies several conditions.	DFT	Xa	Yes
Length estimation. Estimate lengths or distances between points.		Le	Yes
Figural fluency. Produce different figures using the lines of a stimulus figure.	DFI		No
Seeing illusions. Report illusions in such tests as the Muller-Lyer, Sanders, and Poggenforff.	DFS		No
Abilities of listening and hearing			
Listening verbal comprehension. Show understanding of oral communications.			No
Temporal tracking. Demonstrate understanding of sequence of auditory information — e.g., reorder a set of tones.			No
Auditory relations. Show understanding of relations among tones — e.g., identify separate notes of a chord.			No
Discriminating patterns of sounds. Show awareness of differences in different arrangements of tones.			No
Judging rhythms. Identify and continue a beat.			No
Auditory span memory. Immediately recall a set of notes played once.			No
Perception of distorted speech. Demonstrate comprehension of language that has been distorted in several ways.			No

Note: After Ekstrom, French, and Harman (1979).

usually three or more, marker variables having salient (at least .30 or larger, often .40 or larger) loadings on the replicated factor in each study in which evidence of replication is sought. Ekstrom et al. (1979) provide a systematic accumulation and evaluation of evidence obtained not only from many separate studies but also from previous reviews of this domain of research. The work of Ekstrom et al. was to match, by inspection, similar factors across different studies. Factors that were not replicated in accordance with these criteria, but which came close to passing the replication test, are said to indicate "suggestions" of distinct primary abilities (or "not-so-WERCOF" abilities).

Factors as Conjunctive Concepts: Provisos

The evidence of simple-structure common factors among ability test performances is part of a larger body of evidence indicating how different capacities and different abilities intercorrelate and thus appear to be organized in function. Abilities indicated in this way represent conjunctive concepts: they are based on the conjunction of several indicators.

Most of the concepts of our culture are conjunctive (Bruner, Goodnow, and Austin, 1956). Race classifications are good examples of such concepts. The indicators in this case are such things as hair shape (indicating curliness), skin color, and shape of eyes. High "scores" on such indicators intercorrelate to indicate the distinctions we readily recognize as broad racial classifications (such as Caucasian or Asian) or, with more refined measures, narrower racial categories (such as American Indian or Eskimo). Similarly, different indicators of abilities intercorrelate to indicate distinctions between broad abilities, analogous to broad racial classifications, and conjunctions within the broad categories indicate narrower abilities.

Such conjunctive concepts represent lawful regularities, but they should not be regarded as indicating, necessarily, distinct entities analogous to the heart or liver or lobes of the brain; conjunctive concepts may indicate such entities, but they need not. To treat conjunctive evidence as indicating that an ability exists in the sense that a heart within a body exists (as in some assertions that G exists) is a logical error known as *reification* (Burt, 1941; Gould, 1981). Conjunctive evidence attests to either the repetitious workings of the same processes or the working together of different processes, but the processes may originate in different places. A conjunctive-ability concept can correspond to a function at another level of analysis, such as a neuroprocessor pathway in the brain, but the correlational evidence indicating the conjunction is not sufficient to support such an inference: the conjunctive evidence should be regarded as part of the basis for an hypothesis for which further evidence is needed.

There have been hundreds of studies of the conjunctions among indicators of individual differences in human abilities. Simple-structure, common-factor studies concisely, clearly, and objectively summarize much of this evidence.

Basic Features of Factoring

Whether or not an ability can be identified in a factor-analytic study depends on many features of the study design, particularly the design for selecting variables and subjects for analyses. If there are three or more subtests requiring similar processes (of reasoning, seriating, encoding, retaining, retrieving) an easily identified common factor usually can be found. It is more difficult to provide evidence for a common factor if subtests are designed to indicate quite different processes. Usually, more than three subtests will be needed to identify such a broad factor.

In general, the breadth of a factor, as well as the breadth of a measured ability based on a factor, depends on the number and diversity of different kinds of components of the factor, the evenness of the distribution of different components, the reliabilities of the component measures (items, subtests), the range of age of the subjects, subject differences in social and educational background, and a number of other such factors. Breadth is thus a complex dimension for characterizing abilities, even as it provides a useful starting point.

The covariance underlying the conjunctions of factors is not necessarily seen at the level of inspection of correlations. The covariance of a factor is intercorrelation remaining after intercorrelation associated with other factors has been partialled out. For many years, Cattell (1950) has referred to this as *source* covariation in contrast to *surface* covariance that can be seen by inspection of intercorrelations.

Better than most studies, common-factor, simple-structure studies indicate the distinctiveness of different patterns of covariation. The procedures for determining common factors and, more important, the procedures of objective rotation of factors in accordance with the principles of simple structure, work to ensure that results from factor-analytic studies are stable and can be replicated when patterns among correlations and unrotated principal components are not (Cattell, 1957; Horn, 1967; Horn, McArdle, and Mason, 1983; McArdle, 1984; Thurstone, 1947). A powerful theorem developed by Lawley (1943–44) and Meredith (1964) shows that even under conditions of nonrepresentative sampling from the universe of variables (which, as we have seen, always obtains), factors can indicate regularities that are reliable and can be replicated. Factor-analytic studies are particularly useful for these reasons.

Results from factor-analytic studies have been collated, summarized, and evaluated by a number of investigators (for example, Cattell, 1971; Ekstrom et al., 1979; French, 1951; French, Ekstrom, and Price, 1963; Guilford, 1967; Guilford and Hoepfner, 1971; Hakstian and Cattell, 1974, 1978; Horn, 1968, 1972, 1982, 1985, 1986a, 1986b; Horn and Donaldson, 1980; Pawlik, 1966, 1978). There is good agreement in the conclusions of these reviews. The Table 3-2 list of WERCOF abilities summarizes these conclusions.

The conclusions point to abilities at roughly two levels, a primary level and a second-order level. Factors at the primary level indicate composite abilities composed of capacities measured at the level of items and narrow subtests. Factors at the second-order indicate composite abilities composed of primary abilities.

Primary-Level WERCOF Abilities

In the work summarized by Ekstrom et al. (1976, 1979) and Hakstian and Cattell (1974), the tests used in the factoring studies were at a level that is roughly the same as the breadth of subtests used in mixture-measures of IQ. Common-factor studies of many kinds of such subtests indicated distinct WER-COF abilities, found repeatedly in separate studies. Each such ability was indicated by three or more somewhat different but covarying subtest measures.

In measuring WERCOF abilities, investigators usually select the most highly correlated subtests. The intercorrelations among the component subtests thus tend to be large. Such large intercorrelations define the abilities as narrow relative to the IQ measures discussed previously. Span memory (Ms), defined as the sum of subtest scores on the following tests, is an example of a WERCOF ability:

Digital span. Immediately after numbers are presented one at a time on a TV screen, reproduce (using a number pad or keyboard) the numbers in the order in which they were presented.

Tone span. Given that a high note is represented by one key, a low note by another key, press the keys in sequence to indicate an arbitrary sequence of high and low tones heard just moments before.

Location span. Immediately after a symbol (for example, a fly) appears sequentially in the squares of a three-by-three matrix of squares, reproduce the order by pressing keys corresponding to the nine squares of the matrix.

The intercorrelations among different measures of the Ms are typically in the .65 to .75 range when the reliabilities of the measures are of the order of .75 to .85.

Inspection of the list of established WERCOF abilities in Table 3-2 reveals that these abilities vary in breadth: not all are as narrow as Ms. In general, however, they are of roughly the same breadth and are narrow relative to most measures of IQ—although the ability measured with Raven's matrices, for example, is narrower than many of the WERCOF abilities.

We cannot confidently specify an optimum level or breadth on which to base studies of the abilities of learning. However, the list in Table 3-2 provides

—at roughly one level—a comprehensive indication of the different kinds of cognitive capabilities humans possess.

A major limitation in the study of primary abilities is that very little evidence-based theory has been developed to indicate the developmental and functional distinctiveness of the abilities. They represent separate patterns of covariation, but there is little firm evidence to indicate that these patterns correspond to distinct sets of genetic influences, distinct developmental histories, or distinct organizations within the brain. The covariational evidence establishes a prima facie case that separate WERCOF abilities are manifestations of distinct underlying processes. Guilford (1967) and his coworkers (Guilford and Hoepfner, 1971) have done a herculean job of bringing together such evidence as there is to support the prima facie case, but in the end that evidence is scant and not convincing (Carroll, 1972; Carroll and Horn, 1981; Horn, 1967, 1970; Horn and Knapp, 1973, 1974; Humphreys, 1971; Undheim, 1976).

The G_f-G_c System of Abilities

Difficulties in building evidence at the primary level have led investigators to move from WERCOF abilities to a broader level of common factors among these abilities. Here there is evidence, reviewed in several places (Brim and Kagan, 1980; Cattell, 1971; Gustafsson, 1984, 1985; Hakstian and Cattell, 1978; Horn, 1976, 1982, 1985, 1988; Horn and Donaldson, 1980; Undheim, 1976; Wolman, 1985), indicating that the factors are outcroppings of distinct influences operating through development, brain function, genetic determination, and the adjustments, adaptations, and achievements of school and work. An organization of this evidence has become known as G_f-G_c theory.

The factors of the G_f-G_c system are said to be second-order factors calculated on the basis of the primary factors indicating the WERCOF abilities. In most of the studies on which the G_f-G_c system is based, however, the factoring was based on a design in which scores on one subtest alone represented a primary factor, rather than a design in which primary factors were measured with several subtests. The factors of the G_f-G_c system thus usually have been identified among subtests, just as the factors of the WERCOF system were identified. But the samples of subtests in G_f-G_c studies were chosen to represent the domain of WERCOF abilities, rather than the broader domain of all capacities measured with subtests, as in the design for studies indicating the WERCOF abilities.

One consequence of these differences in sampling is that the intercorrelations among the subtests of G_f-G_c abilities are smaller than the intercorrelations among the subtests of WERCOF abilities. The G_f-G_c abilities are thus broad relative to WERCOF abilities. The measures of G_f-G_c abilities are in some cases as broad as measures of IQ.

Indeed, the G_f-G_c abilities are often described as different kinds of intelligence, and the system is referred to as one of multiple intelligences. Unlike different broad measures of IQ, however, the different intelligences of the G_f-G_c system correspond to distinctly separate patterns of covariation, found in several studies (Horn, 1968, 1972, 1976, 1986a; Horn and Cattell, 1966; Horn et al., 1981). Moreover, these distinctly different intelligences have different relationships with other variables, such as age, education, and brain damage: the different intelligences have different construct validities. We will first describe the G_f-G_c abilities, after which we will outline evidence indicating separate construct validities.

Knowledge or Crystallized Intelligence, G_c   A great variety of measures of knowledge will indicate a broad factor in almost any sampling of ability tests. Investigators regard this factor, G_c, as being highly indicative of intelligence (Humphreys, 1979a, 1979b; Sternberg et al., 1981). It represents knowledge needed to maintain and develop a culture. The factor is thus said to indicate the extent to which an individual has appropriated, for personal use, the intelligence of a culture. The following kinds of subtest measures are indicative of this broad form of intelligence.

General information. Measures knowledge about many areas of scholarship—the humanities, business, history, the social sciences, the physical sciences, and mathematics—as well as knowledge about avocational aspects of culture, including books, movies, music, sports.

Verbal knowledge. Measures understanding of the meanings of words, usually by means of vocabulary tests.

Common features (known as remote associations). Measures ability to determine a common feature in otherwise diverse elements. For example, indicate what is common to the following: bathtub, boxing, wedding, rosy.

Problem definition/representation. Measures ability to define and solve problems. Given a verbally developed problem and information of possible relevance for solving the problem, the individual must indicate which information is required, which is not required, which represents constraints, and which represents approaches.

Assessment of everyday arguments and evidence. Measures ability of an individual to decide, given an argument, if the conclusion is warranted or the reasoning is cogent.

Analogies reasoning, as measured with verbal analogies. Measures the ability to identify, given two words related in a particular way, a word that stands in the same relationship to a given word. For example, identify a word that represents the same relationship to "spade" as "ax" to "cut."

Syllogistic reasoning.   Often regarded as a measure of deductive reasoning, this test measures one's ability to determine whether or not conclusions logically follow from particular premises and arguments. For example, if some neurotransmitters are amino acids, and acetylcholine (ACh) is a neurotransmitter, is ACh an amino acid?

Story problem representation.   Measures ability to determine what serial operations are required to solve a problem. Given a verbally stated problem in which numerical calculations (addition, subtraction, multiplication, division) are needed, the individual must choose the series of calculations that can lead to a correct solution.

Most tests that aim to measure abilities of following instructions, either written or spoken, are well correlated with G_c. Since most tests, regardless of what they are designed to measure, require that subjects follow instructions, almost any test will correlate substantially with G_c unless care is taken to ensure that variance in understanding test instructions is not measured with the test. This is difficult to achieve.

Individual differences in understanding what is to be done in a novel learning task are likely to account for much of the variance among individuals in early performances on the task. Because readiness in understanding what is to be done rests in part on G_c comprehension, such as understanding instructions, measures of G_c are often good predictors of performance in the early stages of many kinds of learning, even learning of rather simple skills (Ackerman, 1987).

If individual differences in understanding instructions are measured with a particular test designed to measure a factor other than G_c, there will be spillover of G_c into the measure of the other factor. The largest (often unrotated) factor in ability test batteries often reflects such spillover of G_c into other factors.

Broad Reasoning or Fluid Intelligence, G_f An important and rather paradoxical finding represented by the G_f factor is that in almost any sampling of tests and subjects, the subtests that measure any form of reasoning in the immediate situation (as opposed to a history of reasoning) stand apart factorially from the many tests that measure knowledge and thus indicate G_c. The reasoning represented by G_f involves many mental operations — identifying relations, drawing inferences, formulating concepts, recognizing concepts, identifying conjunctions, recognizing disjunctions. The reasoning test that measures G_f will not depend heavily on knowledge that is available to some and not others, for in this case the test would measure G_c (or G_q, as explained later), but in other respects measures of G_f need not be highly similar. The following examples of subtest indicators of G_f illustrate this point.

Inductive reasoning, measured using letter series, number series, and/or figure series. In letter series, the task is to indicate the next letter in a series of the form: GHJMQV__?

Matrices reasoning with visual patterns. Given a set of figures that change in systematic ways across the columns and down the rows of a matrix, the individual must indicate what figure should appear in the lower right-hand cell of the matrix.

Interpreting verbal reasoning pertaining to visual patterns. Given a figure in which circles, squares, and triangles overlap in complex ways, the individual is asked to locate a dot in such a way that it is in, say, the circles and triangles, but not in the squares.

Classification. The individual must identify an element (figure, word, letter set) that does not belong with other elements. For example, which word in the following set of words does not belong with the others: rose, rock, carrion, perfume.

Conjunctive reasoning, as measured with set recognition. The individual must determine which items do and which do not belong together.

Analogies reasoning (described earlier as a measure of G_c). Verbal analogies can be a reasonably good measure of G_f, rather than G_c, only if the words of the analogies are equally familiar or equally esoteric for all examinees so that the relationships among the words, not knowledge, introduce variance in individual differences in correctly solving the problems.

To the extent that the items require reasoning rather than knowledge, the following tests, described previously as indicative of G_c, will measure G_f instead of, or as well as, G_c.

Story problem representation (often called general reasoning). If rather than emphasizing mathematical knowledge (measure G_q) or general knowledge (measure G_c), word problems require a reasoning with everyday information and concepts, they can provide a reasonably good measure of G_f.

Syllogistic reasoning (deduction). If the terms of syllogisms are equally common or obscure for all subjects, and the reasoning of the problems is difficult, the test will measure G_f rather than G_c.

Assessing everyday arguments and evidence. As in syllogistic reasoning, it is important that the main source of difficulty in the problems of this test be in reasoning if the test is to measure G_f.

Problem definition/representation. For this test to measure G_f (rather than G_c) the information of the problems must not be derived from advanced education and must be given in basic English (not requiring a big vocabulary).

Effectiveness in using problem-solving strategies. The strategies required must not be esoteric if this test is to measure G_f.

Broad Visual Intelligence, G_v Tasks that call for fluent visual scanning, Gestalt closure, mind's-eye rotations of figures, and ability to see reversals measure a kind of visual intelligence that is separate from G_f and G_c. This is indicated in the work of Kaufman and Kamphaus (1984) as well as in our studies (see Horn 1972; Horn and Cattell, 1966; Horn and Stankov, 1982). The following abilities are indicative of G_v:

Visual manipulation, as based on paper folding. The task is to perform mental operations that simulate the folding of a piece of paper, punching a hole through the folded paper, unfolding the paper, and identifying where the holes would appear.

Analytic perception, as measured in Gottschaldt figures (also known as hidden figures). The task is to identify whether or not a particular figure can be traced within a collection of many more lines than the lines of the figure.

In addition to being used to measure G_v, Gottschaldt figures has been used to indicate field independence (Witkin and Goodenough, 1981). Field independence was measured initially with rod-and-frame and tilting-room tests. These measures indicate inclination to use cues from one's own body, rather than environmental cues surrounding an object, as a basis for locating the object in space. Witkin and his coworkers presented evidence suggesting that measures obtained with the rod-and-frame and tilting-room tests covary with measures based on the hidden (Gottschaldt) figures test. Evidence is also presented to suggest that performance on these measures is associated with being male, not female. Work by Bock and Kolakowski (1973) suggests that some of the determination of individual differences G_v stems from a sex-linked major-gene influence. It is not known whether reaction time (RT) to correctly visualize rotational outcomes, as measured in the research of Shepard and Metzler (1971), is indicative of G_v. Studies of the visual abilities of pilot and navigator trainees in the U.S. Air Force (Guilford and Lacy, 1947) suggest that G_v is indicated less by the speed with which one visualizes than by the ability to visualize smoothly, easily, and fluently. Tests similar to the tests of this factor have been described as measuring simultaneous processing (Kaufman and Kamphaus, 1984). My view is that simultaneous processing (which I relate to temporal integration) is more characteristic of G_f, SAR, and G_a than of G_v, but simultaneous processing is an aspect of thinking that is not well defined by any broad factor; instead, it is likely to be isolated as one of the narrower WERCOF abilities. Research to support this view has yet to be done, however.

Gestalt closure. The task is one of filling gaps to complete a view that is obscure, as when parts of a figure have been erased or objects must be seen through a fog.

Design memory. Although usually designed to measure short-term memory, this test is often a good indicator of G_v because the task requires one to visualize steps in drawing a figure or visualize how lines must be put together to create a figure.

Visual constancy. The task is to visualize how a figure looks as it rotates in space. In most studies of G_v and its components, a count of correct responses provides the measure; this should be obtained under only moderately speeded conditions.

It is difficult to distinguish G_v from G_f if visual tests can be performed by reasoning. If tasks make few requirements for fluent visual thinking and primarily call for reasoning, they will be related mainly to G_f; if tasks require that one fluently "see" how figures change their appearance as they move in space or as one changes the perspective from which they are viewed, then they will mainly indicate G_v.

Short-Term Acquisition and Retrieval, SAR   The results from studies of information processing pertain most directly to the broad ability of short-term acquisition and retrieval, SAR. In the theory of Kaufman and his coworkers (Kaufman and Kamphaus, 1984) a concept of sequential (successive) processing is similar to the concept of SAR. Results from the correlational analyses of these researchers indeed suggest that the manifestations of sequential processing are similar to the behavioral indicants of SAR. One of the primary factors indicating this broad ability is the span memory (Ms) WERCOF ability described earlier as an example of a narrow ability. Tests such as digit span, tone span, and location span, as well as the following tasks, indicate the factor.

Word span. To the extent that this task measures individual differences in familiarity with words, it will indicate G_c rather than SAR. If the words are equally familiar or equally obscure to all respondents, the task will mainly indicate SAR.

Recency memory. After being presented with stimuli in a particular temporal order, most people recall the last few stimuli (most recently presented) better than they recall items that were at the beginning or in the middle of the string. Individual differences in recall of recently presented items are mainly associated with SAR. Primacy memory — memory for the first-presented items in a serial recall task — also measures SAR.

Design memory. Usually designed to measure G_v, this task can be expected to also indicate SAR because good performance requires immediate memory as well as visualization skills.

Long-Term Storage and Retrieval, TSR Existing evidence indicates that the manner in which information is organized at the time of encoding for memory storage is indicative of the manner by which the information is retrieved at a later date (Norman, 1979; Norman and Rumelhart, 1975). This is true even if there are long time intervals between acquisition and retrieval. Such results suggest that measures of SAR (immediate apprehension and retrieval over short periods of time) should be highly indicative of retrieval from storage in long-term memory. It is interesting — because it is counter-intuitive — that individual differences in SAR are independent of (although correlated with) individual differences in the facility with which information is consolidated for long-term memory storage and retrieved from this storage, TSR. This storage and retrieval can be measured with a variety of tasks. The following are representative.

Retention of learning after several minutes or hours. Tasks of short-term memory can be used to measure TSR if recall is measured after short-term memory has faded — that is, after at least several minutes, preferably after several hours. The measure best indicates TSR rather than SAR if the subject is not led to expect that recall will be requested after a long lapse of time.

Associational fluency. This task requires retrieving words that are connotatively similar to a given word. For example, subject is asked to say or write all the words he or she can think of that are similar to the word "warm." The subject lists words such as "teakettle" and "mother," which indicate relationships that are not so much logical as they are connotative. The task must not be highly speeded. There must be time enough to allow the subject to sample fully from memory storage. Writing or speaking speed should not produce substantial variance in the measure; otherwise, the task is mainly a measure of a broad speediness ability (or inclination), G_s. It is not clear how typing skill will affect measurement of TSR with this task. In previous work, typing skill was not involved.

Expressional fluency.   This task measures one's facility for coming up with (in writing or speaking) appropriate and different expressions for an idea.

Ideational fluency.   This task measures one's facility for finding different ways to interpret and write or talk about a particular event, for example, a woman boarding a bus.

Verbal production fluency.   The typical task is to write (or say) as many words as one can think of that begin with a particular letter.

Each of these preceding four fluency tasks should be measured with fairly liberal time limits in order to give subjects a chance to exhaust the elements of categories.

Memory acquisition.   The task is to retrieve material memorized verbatum, as, for example, a page of words. This task can call out the knowledge abilities of G_c. Indeed, the measure can be mainly indicative of G_c rather than TSR if the emphasis is on breadth of knowledge rather than fluent recall of knowledge. If the task mainly requires that one recite passages learned several minutes or hours previously, then performances will be mainly indicative of TSR. As with other measures of TSR, no part of the acquisition task should be highly speeded. It is not known whether or not time to reach a particular criterion in verbatum learning of verbal material better indicates TSR or G_c.

Intermodal transfer fluency.   The task is to indicate whether or not a given word provides a good description of a picture. This task seems to measure TSR because in judging whether or not a given word is a good descriptor one must search through one's store of concepts to find other words that might be better descriptors.

There can be difficulties in distinguishing TSR from SAR if the measures of TSR fail to tax ability to retrieve information stored at least several minutes or, preferably, several hours or days before.

Measures of TSR retrieval figured prominently in research on creativity (Cave, 1970; Cropley, 1972; Getzels and Jackson, 1962; Guilford, 1967; Mednick, 1956; Rossman and Horn, 1972; Torrance, 1972; Vernon, 1972a, 1972b). Such research seems to have gone out of vogue in recent years. Retrieval from quasi-permanent memory storage continues to be an interesting feature of human thinking, and investigators should carefully consider augmenting research batteries with good measures in the area of TSR.

Broad Speediness, G_s Speediness in intellectual tasks relates to carefulness, strategies (or metacognition), mood (such as depression), and persistence, as well as to features of physiological structure (neural, hormonal). One must be particularly cautious in interpreting findings in this area.

Almost any test can be made into a measure of G_s by decreasing the demands for knowledge and reasoning and increasing the demands for working quickly. Also, most speeded tests involve, to some extent, the G_s ability. Thus, measures such quantitative concepts, analogies, and dictation often correlate with G_s because they are administered under conditions that emphasis speed of performance. The following are illustrative of subtests that can be used to provide a fairly pure factor measure of speediness in intellectual performances.

Visual matching. Under constraints to respond quickly, the subject must find 1- to 5-digit numbers that are the same among a list of six such numbers.

Spatial relations. Under constraints to respond quickly, the subject must determine which two or three shapes among six choices (in a two-dimensional plane) fit together to form a displayed whole.

Visual scanning. Working as quickly as possible over a short period of time (for example, 2-minute trials), the subject must find, for example, as many letter ds as possible on a sheet of paper filled with the letters of the alphabet.

That which a test measures depends in part on the way it is administered. This can be seen with the spatial relations test. Given under conditions that do not emphasize speed, the spatial relations test measures G_v; given under speeded conditions, it measures G_s.

Auditory Intelligence, G_a Auditory intelligence, G_a, represents a facility for "chunking" streams of sounds, keeping these chunks in awareness, and anticipating an auditory form that can develop out of such streams. It is not heavily dependent on auditory acuity, which is a separate capacity (Horn and Stankov, 1982).

For centuries it has been recognized that auditory genius is not necessarily aligned with other forms of intelligent behavior; however, only recently did researchers make a clear operational distinction between G_a and other broad intellectual abilities (Horn, 1973; Horn and Stankov, 1982; Stankov, 1978; Stankov and Horn, 1980). In these studies first-order abilities were identified within a catholic sampling of auditory tasks. By factoring these primary abilities, along with first-order indicators of G_c, G_f, and G_v, investigators isolated G_a and a separate auditory acuity dimension. The primary factors that were found to indicate G_a involve detection, transformation, and retention of tonal patterns.

The following are some of the tasks of the primary factors that best indicate the G_a second-order factor.

Discrimination among sound patterns (DASP).   Detection of tonal patterns is a feature of this ability. In tonal classifications, one of the marker tests, the task is to identify which one of five chords does not belong with the others. Other markers require one to identify changes in patterns of notes. Dewar, Cuddy, and Mewhart (1977) interpreted an ability similar to DASP as "sensitivity to relational cues in sounds."

Maintaining and judging rhythms (MaJR).   The tasks that best indicate this ability require one to join in a beat, as provided by a metronome, and correctly continue the beat after the metronome has stopped. An incomplete words test in the Woodcock-Johnson (1989) test also indicates the ability. In this task one must identify a spoken word when particular sounds (phonemes) have been left out in the pronunciation. The suggestion is that the ability is important in understanding the rhythms of language (Robinson, 1977).

Temporal tracking of sounds (Tc).   The ability involved here seems to be one of holding sound patterns of past and present in mind while anticipating patterns of the future. Hearnshaw (1956) and Pollack (1969) labeled such an ability "temporal integration." In a prominent task measuring this ability one must retain nonsense syllables in awareness for several seconds, while a new pronunciation of nonsense syllables is going on, and identify just where in the newly pronounced set the first-pronounced syllables are located.

Auditory cognition of relations (ACoR).   This ability is analogous to visual Gestalt closure. In the chord decomposition task that helps define the ability one must identify separate notes that were heard in a chord. A factor indicating this ability had been identified in some of the early work of this century (French, 1951; Shuter, 1968).

Auditory immediate memory (Msa).   This is a weak indicator of the G_a ability. Msa represents a finding that span memory for sounds is distinct from (although well correlated with) span memory for visual patterns, including visually presented words and paralogs. It seems that Msa enables one to hold sound patterns in mind while performing cognitive manipulations of the kind expressed in the other abilities of G_a. This function of Msa in G_a is similar to the function of visual span memory (Ms) in G_f (Horn, 1970; Horn and Cattell, 1966).

From these examples we see that the abilities of G_a require, in different ways, holistic comprehension of patterns among sounds. As in the case of G_v, G_a is best indicated when the tasks do not emphasize the reasoning of G_f or the comprehension of G_c but instead require that one fluently perceive the flow of sounds.

Little has been done to show the importance of G_a to the understanding of development and achievement. The bits of evidence now in hand suggest that it is indeed important not only for understanding achievements in music, but also for understanding language development and academic achievement in the early years of schooling (Anastasi, 1986, 1987; Atkin et al., 1977a, 1977b; Minton and Schneider, 1980). In unpublished communication with me, Humphreys suggested that the listening measures of the STEP tests are probably more closely aligned with G_c than with G_a. This, he argues, probably accounts for the relatively high correlation the auditory tests have with school achievement in the Atkin et al. studies (1977a, 1977b). To facilitate tests of this supposition, measures of G_a and G_c should be included in test batteries designed for use in educational research.

Other Variance at the Broad Level in the Ability Domain

As developed thus far, G_f-G_c theory has mainly dealt with structural, developmental, and neurological distinctions between G_f and G_c. To a lesser degree, with emphasis on structural differences, the theory has taken account of distinctions between SAR, TSR, G_a, G_v, and G_s. However, other broad organizations among abilities have been identified and a few efforts have been made to bring concepts representing these abilities into the theory. The following are major examples of these efforts.

English Adeptness, ENG   In much research, as well as in common parlance, a concept of *verbal ability* is used instead of G_c or V (the verbal comprehension primary ability). This represents the fact that verbal linguistic organization of knowledge is a major determinant in behavior. The theory of G_c is an attempt to indicate organization that extends beyond verbal mediation (which mediation is best represented in G_f-G_c theory by the concept of V).

In educational practice one often is concerned to understand problems in the use of the dominant language that are in one sense more elementary than those that can be represented on the low end of G_c or V and yet in another sense are pervasively important in a child's development. The Woodcock-Johnson tests (Woodcock, 1978) represent efforts to provide diagnostic tools for dealing with such problems. Several subtests in these tests provide a basis for measuring skills that are confined to understanding the elements of English language. Although such skills are related to G_c, they represent a separate collection of abilities for which relationships with other variables are different from the corresponding relationships for G_c. It can be particularly important in the context of early school learning to take account of the differences between these abilities and G_c. Much learning depends on adequate use of these elementary aspects of the dominant language. The following tasks are indicative of English adeptness abilities.

Word parsing.   In sentences in which words have been run together, the task is to separate the words so sense can be made out of a statement that one must judge to be true or false.

Phonetic decoding.   Indicate awareness of homonyms for different letter combinations that, in conventional English, have the same pronunciation, for example, "threw" and "through."

Word meaning association.   Indicate very quickly whether or not pairs of words are approximate synonyms. The task could be mainly indicative of G_c or TSR, but if the words are not esoteric or mainly indicative of a wide range of knowledge, it might indicate, primarily, knowledge of English.

Quantitative Thinking, G_q   Also important in educational applications is the distinction between a broad quantitative ability, G_q, and both G_c and G_f. There is little doubt that by the time children enter high school G_q can be clearly distinguished from G_c and G_f. There is little doubt, too, that it is useful to draw this distinction in making educational guidance and placement decisions. The distinction also makes good theoretical sense; that is, it represents separation in function and development: the correlates of G_q are different from the correlates for G_c and G_f. For example, G_q is considerably more closely related to male-female differences in adolescence and adulthood than is G_f or G_c.

To clearly distinguish G_q from G_c it is important to use tests for G_q which probe knowledge about mathematics, per se, as distinct from knowledge about the culture in which understanding of mathematics developed. To distinguish G_q from G_f the tests for G_q should involve problems that are most readily solved only by application of previously worked methods and principles of mathematics, rather than by application of general skills of reasoning. For example, a problem requiring one to calculate a definite integral from zero to one for a quadratic usually (in most samples of individuals) will measure G_q rather than G_f because even a person who is very good at reasoning but knows little about mathematics probably will fail to arrive at a correct solution to the problem (unless the misleads give away the answer).

The following primary abilities and tests are among the best indicators of this G_q ability.

Numerical (N) computations.   The task requires solving addition, subtraction, multiplication, and division problems under somewhat (not highly) speeded conditions.

Computational fluency.   The subject must perform combinations of mathematical operations, such as multiplication before addition, which in turn must be done before doing division.

Math bugs.   The subject must indicate what is wrong with mathematical solutions. What is wrong may be in computation, definition (as in imaginary numbers), applications of algebra, or (among college-bound students) more advanced features of mathematics (such as use of integration).

Story problem representation.   Without actually doing calculations to arrive at numerical answers, the subject must indicate which steps in calculation must be made in order to arrive at a correct solution.

Qualifying Conclusion on Major Abilities   While the concepts outlined in this section represent much of what is presently known about individual differences in the organization of human abilities, it must not be assumed that these concepts represent the only, or best, way to talk about lawful regularities of cognition. There are broad organizations among abilities that are not well represented by ENG, G_q, and the basic concepts of G_f-G_c theory, and there are systems for describing these phenomena that are quite different from the G_f-G_c system. Anderson (1975), for example, organizes the phenomena of abilities in terms of an executive system in which major concepts identify principles of direction, controllability, automatization (open-loop, closed-loop, and modulation patterns), test-operate-test-exit (TOTE), short-term memory (STM), very short-term memory (VSTM), and propositional representation. Similarly, Rabbitt (1981) describes cognitive processing in terms of passive and active aspects of selective attention, associations, search and scanning strategies, awareness of contingencies, short-term memory, retrieval from storage, and temporal integration. Guttman (1970) uses broad concepts of retrieval from storage and reasoning to describe much of what is represented by the distinction between G_c and G_f. In the present volume still other systems are described for comprehending human thinking and individual differences in this thinking. The system of this chapter is not necessarily better than other systems. The system is useful, however, because in representing many lawful features of human cognition it also provides a basis for the construction of tests that can provide worthwhile diagnostic information in treatment and guidance, as in clinical and educational settings. The theory is also a useful refinement of theories of general intelligence.

Let us turn again to consideration of the phenomena to which G_f-G_c theory pertains, and indicate the nature of evidence beyond structural (factor analytic) evidence that points to the concept validity distinctions among the major concepts of the theory.

FURTHER REFINEMENT OF THE CONCEPT OF OVERLAP AMONG ABILITIES

As we stated previously, there is no sharp demarcation between abilities. The overlap among the broad abilities described in the previous section is extensive and complex. It is indicated in part by the variables (test indicators) that are notably correlated with two or more abilities. It is indicated also by the inter-correlations among the abilities.

Tasks are designed to indicate individual differences mainly in only one ability, or very few abilities. In such design, the sample of people for whom the test is designed must be kept clearly in mind. In a test that is well designed to measure G_c, for example, the demands for short-term memory should be reduced to a point where SAR produces only trivial variance in individual differences. This is rather easily accomplished in samples in which people are not severely limited in the capacities of SAR. If people are severely retarded in these capacities, however, as in advanced stages of Alzheimer's disease, (Katzman, 1986), it is very difficult to present test materials that can represent G_c as distinct from SAR or to distinguish between SAR and any ability: unless one is very careful to measure only the very limited capacity of the individual with Alzheimer's disease, all tests are likely to measure ability for holding information in immediate awareness.

The general principle illustrated by the example of someone with Alzheimer's disease is that distinctions among different abilities can be revealed only if, in measuring one ability, individual differences on other abilities are very much reduced (to suppose that such differences could be eliminated is unrealistic). This point is often overlooked, particularly in studies where strong claims are made about the "reality of G" (see Eysenck, 1939, 1982; Jensen, 1984). Research aimed at disclosing distinct human capacities requires that, in *proper samples of subjects,* tasks are as pure as one can make them in indicating one and only one cognitive process.

Often it is not possible to come very close to realization of this objective. For example, it is difficult to devise tasks that do not call out individual differences in knowledge (as in G_c) in the process of requiring expression of another ability (such as reasoning). Often tests are poorly designed to indicate one and only one ability. This is particularly true of tests that are sold for profit. Uncertain as to what a buyer may want in a test, the seller is likely to make it general—in other words, design it to measure many abilities—so that regardless of where it is used it will have some "validity."

Even in research aimed at distinguishing abilities, performances on a particular test are likely to measure individual differences in several abilities. It can be useful to see such measurement as indicating the exercise of alternative mechanisms: some individuals score well on the test because they have much of ability A; others score well because they have much of ability B. A test measuring alternative mechanisms will correlate to about the same extent with both A and B, if these can be distinguished factorially, and thus be an indicator of both abilities. To help illustrate the nature of cognitive processes, measurement devices can be designed to indicate alternative mechanisms (Horn and Cattell, 1966). Several alternative mechanisms can be at work in determining the individual differences measured with a particular device. Some tests are very complex in the sense that they require, or allow, expression of many different abilities.

Indeed, depending on sample variability, observed performances on different tests usually require exercise of several basic abilities: a good study design merely keeps variance on most of these abilities to a minimum to enable the measurement of one or two abilities. But in fact any expression of knowledge that can provide a measure of G_c also requires exercise of SAR and TSR, and reflects a history of exercise of G_f, G_v, and Ga. This kind of overlap is intrinsic: it is unavoidable in the measurement of abilities. In well-designed studies it is represented in the intercorrelations among abilities.

Figure 3-1 is a crude representation of overlap in the measurement of the broad abilities of the G_f-G_c theory. The distance between the vectors of the figure indicates, very roughly, the extent of overlap: vectors that are close together represent abilities that overlap quite a bit; vectors that are far apart represent abilities for which there is relatively little overlap. The figure indicates, for example, that G_c and SAR have less in common than G_c and G_f. The figure truly is crude, however, if not even a bit misleading. SAR, for example, should be closer to G_v than is depicted in the figure. A three-dimensional graphic is needed to represent this condition.

The figure does not indicate the complexity of particular tests of the ability domain. (Tests most highly related to factors are shown in Table 3-3.) For example, typically a verbal analogies test is complex, usually involving G_c, G_f and TSR, but sometimes bringing in SAR as well. On the other hand, typically a synonyms test is a fairly pure measure of G_c (with only relatively small involvement in TSR). An antonyms test, in contrast, is fairly complex: it requires considerably more reasoning (of G_f) than does the synonyms test. Many such comparisons of measures can be made. Mention of a few of these will help illustrate the basic point.

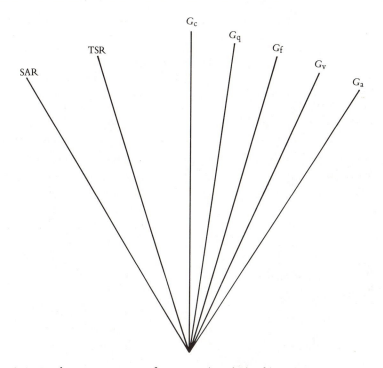

Figure 3-1 Crude representation of nearness (overlap) of broad abilities

The backward span memory test, requiring the subject to produce elements in the reverse of the order in which they were presented, is more complex than a test of forward span memory. It is a considerably better measure of G_f and consequently a poorer measure of SAR than is forward span memory.

Arithmetic tests are primarily indications of G_c or G_q if mainly speed and accuracy in calculation is required. They will indicate G_q rather than G_c if advanced (relative to the ages of the subjects) calculations are required. They will indicate G_f relatively more than G_c if rather complex applications are required in what are called word problems. If the word problems can be solved by reasoning that can be acquired outside courses in mathematics, the measure is likely to be more highly related to G_f than to G_c or G_q.

Virtually any test can be made into a measure of G_f by raising the requirements for exercising reasoning. Similarly, almost any test can be made into a measure of G_c by increasing the extent to which individual differences in knowledge are assessed. And, by increasing the requirements for speeded performance, almost any test can be made to measure G_s, at least in part.

Table 3-3 Some Tests Classified in Terms of the Primary Ability Best Measured with a Test

Test	French Symbol	Primary ability
Verbal: vocabulary	V	Verbal comprehension
Following written instructions	Ig	Integration
Following spoken instructions	CMS	Cognition of semantic systems
Reasoning: verbal analogies	CMR	Cognition of semantic relations
Problem definition	NMS	Convergence in semantic systems
Assessment everyday arguments	Sp	Sensitivity to problems
Deduction	Rs	Syllogistic reasoning
Story problem representation	Es	Estimation
Numerical: computations	R	General reasoning
Math bugs	ESS	Evaluation of symbolic systems
Computational skill: fluency	N	Number facility
Inductive reasoning	I	Induction
Set recognition	ESC	Evaluation of symbolic classes
Set relationships	ESR	Evaluation of symbolic relations
Visual conceptualization	S	Spatial orientation
Visual manipulation	Vz	Visualization
Visual constancy	Sc	Spatial scanning
Analytic perception	Cf	Flexibility of closure
Perception: moving windows	Cs	Speed of closure
Digit span	Ms	Span (nonsense) memory
Tone span	Md	Auditory span
Location span	Mv	Visual memory
Memory: word span	Mm	Meaningful memory
Memory acquisition	Ma	Associative memory
Design memory	Mo	Memory for order
Spatial organization	Mv	Visual memory
Memory retention and learning	MMR	Memory for semantic relations
Verbal productive fluency	Fw	Word fluency
Intermodal transfer fluency	Sr	Semantic redefinition
Effective problem-solving strategy	EMI	Evaluate semantic implications
Word parsing	NMC	Converge semantic classes
Phonetic decoding	NMI	Converge semantic implications
Word-meaning association	CMC	Cognition of semantic classes
Attention	P	Perceptual speed

We must understand, then, that the fact of overlap among abilities is a major feature of intellectual performances. Several years ago, in attempting to make sense out of evidence showing that quite different tests measuring logically separate abilities are nevertheless positively intercorrelated, Godfrey Thomson (1916) developed a sampling theory of bonds of the mind. This theory is still useful in envisioning overlap among abilities.

Thomson's basic idea is that the performances of different individuals on a particular test represent samples from among a very large set of basic interrelated capacities, rather as if one were to repeatedly flash a spotlight on sections of smoke in a large smoke-filled room. The extent of correlation among different tests is then seen to be a function of the extent of overlap of spotlighted samples identified with different flashes or, in other words, the overlap of different capacities identified with the different tests. Figure 3-2 is a schematic representation of this phenomenon. The overlap of ovals A and B represents tests that sample many of the same interrelated capacities (dots, particles) and thus are highly correlated, whereas the small overlap of ovals C and D represents tests that sample few of the same capacities and thus are only lowly correlated. If one visualizes a page of dots over which many ovals might be drawn, a factor can represent several overlapping ovals on this page; distinctions between factors can be seen as sets of such overlapping ovals that are separated on the page. Seen in this way, common factors may be regarded as little more than scoops of smoke one might draw from a smoke-filled room. Each such scoop represents particles found together at a particular time and place, but no scoop represents a reality apart from the fact that all the particles drift together as part of the same smoke-filled room.

This notion that tests measure only rather arbitrary samples of many interrelated cognitive capacities repr_sents Thompson's concept of general intelligence—the smoke-filled room itself—and is not unlike the theory of Humphreys (1979a, 1979b, 1984), a highly respected present-day researcher of human abilities. It is well established that in almost any sample of subjects one

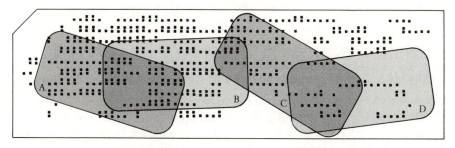

Figure 3-2 Schematic representation of overlapping cognitive abilities

might draw, almost all tests of cognitive abilities are positively intercorrelated. In any battery of such tests, a single factor can be defined at the highest order of factoring. These facts often give rise to the idea that all cognitive tests measure, to a greater or lesser extent, one general ability: all the particles of smoke are in one room. This is the position championed by Humphreys (1962, 1979b). Different tests, then, are viewed as merely samples of this general ability — that is, different scoops of smoke.

It is difficult to refute such a theory. Ability tests do have the quality of being particular, arbitrary inventions, created at particular times and places, rather like scoops of smoke. Without a good rationale for claiming that existing tests truly do circumscribe a domain of human cognitive capacities, it is difficult to argue that any observed factor among test performances is any more than a particular sample of performances that could be just as well drawn in any of an infinite number of other ways.

The arguments against this position are mainly appeals to plausibility and to the scientific and applied efficacy of the multiple-factor alternative. It is plausible to suppose that the many tests used in WERCOF research do, in a rough way, circumscribe much of the domain of human cognitive capacities. Replicated ability factors indicate that if one accepts this view and samples from the (assumed) domain, not necessarily in a representative manner but in a reasonable manner, then the domain can be described in terms of multiple regions that are not entirely arbitrary — rather as if investigators were to agree about the location of a smoke-filled room and agree to sample sections of the room in accordance with the coordinates of three dimensional space. Added information on separate construct validities then for the separate sections bulwark arguments to the effect that, indeed, the "smoke" is one part and not another part of the room, and it is useful to partition smoke in the manner indicated.

Such arguments do not refute a scoops-of-smoke theory, but they do put the ball in the other court, so to speak, by requiring advocates of such theories to show why scoops-of-smoke theory better represents the evidence of separate construct validities for separate abilities than do theories in which this evidence is rationalized. (Anastasi, 1986). The sections that follow will outline this evidence.

EVIDENCE INDICATING DISTINCT CONSTRUCT VALIDITIES FOR SEPARATE FACTORS

Factor-analytic (structural) evidence thus provides a basis for an empirically founded, analytic, hierarchically organized, multidimensional system of describing and, in that sense, understanding human abilities. Each of the "intelligences" of this system is a broad set of capacities, skills, and learning sets. Each is indicative of what is called intelligence (Humphreys, 1979a, 1979b, 1984). Yet each is psychometrically distinct from the others. The earliest indications of the system came from research on the adult development of intellectual abilities (Cattell, 1941) and studies of intellectual correlates of neurological damage (Hebb, 1941, 1949). These lines of evidence continue to provide the main empirical justification for the theory, but limited sets of evidence suggest that the system makes sense in terms of genetic determinants (Bock and Kolakowski, 1973; Cattell, 1971; Nichols, 1978; Vandenberg, 1971). Early work by Ferguson (1956, 1964), on which the theory is partially based, and evidence adduced by Cronbach and Snow (1977) suggest that the system is useful in educational applications. Whether or not the system makes good sense in occupational decision making has yet to be convincingly demonstrated (Ghiselli, 1966; Hunter, in press; Hunter, Schmidt, and Jackson, 1982; McNemar, 1964).

To see the developmental relevance of the theory one need only recognize a wealth of evidence indicating that the abilities of G_f and SAR, on the one hand, and the abilities of G_c and TSR, on the other, have different relations to age over the lifespan. The abilities of G_f decline (on an average over many adults) with age in adulthood. These abilities also reflect irreversible outcomes of injury to particular parts or functions of the central nervous system (CNS). Research has not pinned down precisely where these parts and functions are in the CNS, but growing evidence suggests that a section of brain function referred to as the Ht (which will be described more fully in the next section) is intimately related to the behaviors of G_f.

Several investigators have hypothesized that laterality differences in brain function are major features of G_f. For example, the block design of the Wechsler tests is often regarded as a measure of G_f (although it measures a specific factor and G_v as well as G_f) and, also, as a measure of right cerebral hemisphere function. In fact, performances on block design indicate left hemisphere function, too, and although it appears to be more affected by lesions in the right hemisphere than by seemingly comparable lesions in the left hemisphere. It is not clear whether this correlation mainly represents a relationship for the specific factor, G_v, G_f, or a combination of the three.

The abilities of SAR also decline (on the average) with age in adulthood and injury to the CNS. SAR abilities correlate less with academic achievement than do G_f abilities, and several other lines of evidence indicate that the construct validity of SAR is different from the construct validity of G_f.

The abilities of G_c improve with age in adulthood (or at least do not decline as early or as markedly as the G_f or SAR abilities). The G_c abilities also tend to "spring back" and be maintained following CNS damage. Similarly, and contrary to what is expected from consideration of how memory declines with age in adulthood, the memory abilities of TSR (fluency of retrieval of concepts from long-term storage) increases with age over much of the adulthood period of development. Different correlates for TSR and G_c indicate a need to recognize a distinction between these two broad sets of abilities.

The abilities that decline with brain damage and with age in adulthood, G_f and SAR, are referred to as *vulnerable abilities* (Beeson, 1920; Botwinick, 1977; Horn, 1982, 1985; Matarazzo, 1972). Abilities that do not decline with age in adulthood and return to nearly pre-injury levels following brain damage — G_c and TSR — are classified as *maintained abilities*. Maintained abilities are more highly related to measures of educational attainment and elevated social class than are vulnerable abilities. The variance for maintained abilities increases with age in adulthood, at least through the period from about age 30 to age 65; the variance for vulnerable abilities is nearly constant throughout this period (Horn, 1986a,b). These generalizations are based largely on cross-sectional studies, but are supported by results from longitudinal and mixed designs (Baltes and Schaie, 1976; Horn, 1986a, 1986b; Horn and Donaldson, 1976, 1977, 1980; McArdle, Aber, and Horn, 1987; Schaie and Baltes, 1977; Schaie and Gribbin, 1975).

The distinction between maintained and vulnerable cognitive capacities is not well described as distinction between verbal and nonverbal abilities. This conclusion is indicated by the presence of verbal abilities in the G_f factor and nonverbal abilities in G_c. It is indicated also by findings, such as those of Bromley (1974), Sharp et al. (1977), and Ryan and Butters (1979), showing that alcoholics perform poorly on verbal tasks if these are designed to require complex reasoning with novel relations — that is, tasks that measure G_f.

It is tempting to believe that a distinction between *automatic processing abilities* and *controlled information processing* capacities, as described in the theory of Ackerman (1986, 1987; Ackerman and Schneider, 1985), represents the difference between maintained and vulnerable abilities — or least indicates an important aspect of this difference. Ackerman (1987) points out that when one encounters an intellectual task for the first time there is great need to bring all capacities to bear for "educing relations, deriving strategies, [and] memorizing critical information." The abilities thus marshaled are the vulnerable capacities, G_f and SAR. As one continues to cope with the demands of particular classes of intellectual problems, one automatizes many features of the problem. Also, as illustrated in Cronbach and Snow (1977), one classifies complex problems (sometimes inappropriately) in ways that enable one to use general, worked-out strategies for arriving at solutions; one uses experience to guess about task requirements and in other such ways structures the problem so that it can be attacked with solution strategies worked out and deposited in the maintained abilities (G_c and TSR). These reactions to problem situations thus call in the maintained abilities and are, in a sense, almost automatized. For example, one jumps to conclusions that skills in G_c can be applied in attempting to solve new problems.

The automatization involved in calling on maintained abilities in problem situations is not the same, however, as the process that develops with increasing practice as one learns a skill such typing or playing the piano (Shiffren and Schneider, 1977). In learning typing, one progresses to a point where, without conscious awareness, one's fingers press appropriate keys to quickly spin out words and sentences. One does not so quickly or at such a low level of consciousness apply the conceptualization abilities of G_c in solving a financial problem. The automatization of skill learning is analogous to some applications of maintained abilities, however. For example, rigidities in adult thinking are not unlike the fingering errors that result when one's unconscious thinking processes refuse to make the transition from typing on a typewriter to typing on a word processor, the keyboard of which is slightly different from the key system of a typewriter.

As Anderson (1975) emphasizes, rather elementary (automated) processes exercise executive power over parts of our most exalted thinking. For example, in searching through a number of items for the presence of a particular item adults exhaustively scan all items even though directed search and termination of search after finding the item are sensible, efficient ways of thinking in such situations. To say that elementary processes govern our most exalted thinking is not to argue that such processes are to be equated with abilities, such as G_c and G_f, that more nearly represent this thinking. The details of how automated skills, as in language, enter into the high-level thinking of G_c and G_f are, as yet, only dimly understood.

LIFE EVENTS RELATED TO CHANGES IN VULNERABLE ABILITIES

Research indicates that what is often called "loss of memory" in discussions of aging and brain damage is best understood as loss of the reasoning capacities of G_f (Horn, Donaldson, and Engstrom, 1981). In studies designed to show, analytically, the particular kinds of cognitive capabilities that are associated with individual differences and aging differences in G_f, the results indicate that organization at the stage of encoding novel information (Hultsch, 1971; Mandler, 1967) declines as G_f declines. This is particularly the case for encoding done spontaneously, as in measures of incidental memory, but it is true also for forced encoding directed by explicitly activated metamemory and depth of processing procedures (Botwinick, 1977; Craik, 1977). Broad G_f ability accounts for much of the aging decline of each of several narrower abilities, but the simpler processes account for only part of the aging decline of G_f. Collectively, the simple processes account for roughly one-half the aging decline variation of G_f.

The important point here is a new interpretation of a body of findings pertaining to aging, brain damage, and memory: what is seen as memory loss, as in SAR, is mainly an outcome of failure to organize information for encoding; this failure reflects an inability to (spontaneously) perceive relationships and draw conclusions, and this inability is the low side of fluid general reasoning, G_f. There is failure to spontaneously perform what Craik and Lockhart (1972) have referred to as depth of processing. Fluid general reasoning also involves capacities for dividing attention, maintaining close attention, and avoiding preoccupation with irrelevancies (Horn, 1980, 1982, 1985, 1986a; Horn and Donaldson, 1980; Horn et al., 1981, based largely on the work of Rabbitt, 1979, 1981; see also McDowd, in press; Walsh, 1986). Loss of speed in cognitive processing also appears to reflect, primarily, loss of G_f capacities, such as the ability to immediately see relationships and make inferences.

To better understand abilities, it is useful to describe them in terms of influences with which they are associated. In particular, it is useful to describe vulnerable abilities in terms of the influences that appear to produce the changes that indicate vulnerability. Consumption of alcohol, for example, both in the short run and after prolonged use, generally has been found to be negatively related to performances that reflect the actions of vulnerable abilities — G_f or SAR (Kish and Cheney, 1969; Parker and Noble, 1980; Parsons, 1975, 1977; Tarter, 1975). On the other hand, it appears that use of alcohol does not produce substantial, persistent loss of the maintained abilities. An early study in this area illustrates the point.

Wechsler (1941) described a pattern of deterioration in chronic alcoholic patients that was characterized by "loss of abilities calling for synthesis, new learning, and the organization and manipulation of novel situations, . . . [but] relatively small loss in simple stimulus-response reactions, reproduction of simple ideas and tests involving established habits." Kleinknicht and Goldstein (1972) reviewed other studies that also indicate this pattern. Scores on the information, vocabulary, and comprehension subscales of the Wechsler Adult Intelligence Scale (WAIS indicators of G_c) have near-zero correlations with alcoholic versus not classifications when, in the same samples of subjects, such classifications have negative correlations with scores on the object assembly, block designs, and digit symbol subtests — indicators of G_f and SAR (Goldstein and Shelley, 1971; Grant et al., 1978; Sanchez-Craig, 1980). Similarly, measures of TSR are largely unrelated to the extent of persistent heavy use of alcohol, but performances on trail making (an indicator of G_f) are related to such use (Matarazzo, 1972).

The capacities of G_f and SAR are notably affected by lesions and malfunctions in an area of the brain we will refer to as Ht, representing the hippocampus, amygdala, upper parts of the temporal lobe, the fornix, thalamus, mammillary bodies, and other nearby structures. Extended and heavy use of alcohol is associated with loss of function in the Ht area, perhaps particularly in the mammillary bodies (Butters and Cermak, 1975; Drachman and Arbit, 1966; Parsons, 1975, 1977; Sweet, Talland, and Ervin, 1959; Turner, 1969). Injuries to the Ht that notably and permanently affect the capacities of G_f and SAR can leave G_c and TSR relatively unimpaired.

It seems, then, that mechanisms that produce malfunctions in the Ht are implicated in processes that selectively bring about aging the alcohol-related declines in G_f and SAR, but do not directly affect G_c and TSR. Research suggests that these mechanisms are linked to blood-flow processes that supply oxygen and nutrients to the neural structures of the brain.

Many checks and balances work to ensure that all areas of the brain receive an adequate supply of blood. Nevertheless, fluctuations in blood flow can occur. The Ht area of the brain is particularly vulnerable to diminutions in this flow (Hachinski, 1980). The arteries that supply the Ht region are different from the arteries that supply many other regions of the brain. Instead of Y-branching with continuation, the arteries of this area branch at right angles from the main trunks and terminate in the area as end-arteries. This means that a drop in blood pressure can result in dimunition in blood supply to this area. Blood pressure decline could become critical in the Ht region before it became critical — or even if it never became critical — in other regions of the brain. The Ht region is also a notable distance away from main arteries of the brain, the carotid and vertebral. For this reason, too, it can be expected to be more affected by fluctuations in blood pressure than other sections of the brain. Under any condition of diminution of blood flow, the flow would cease earliest at the branches that are most distant from the primary suppliers. The result would be loss of oxygen and nutrients to these areas, and resulting loss of neurons.

If the Ht region is more susceptible to diminution of blood supply than are other sections of the brain, then it should be more susceptible to damage that accompanies drop in blood pressure. Infarcts, for example, might be more common (probabilistically) in the Ht area than elsewhere in the brain. Corsellis (1976) found, indeed, that infarcts occur more frequently in the hippocampus than in comparison structures.

Several kinds of life events can produce a decrease in blood supply to the head. Inebriation is one cause, particularly if it is severe enough to produce loss of consciousness. Blows to the head and loss of consciousness for any of several reasons can be associated with substantial changes in the distribution of blood to the head. The consequence can be loss of neural tissue in areas of the brain that are particularly vulnerable to loss of blood supply. Such factors are linked to aging decline of intellectual abilities (Heikkinen, 1975; Hertzog, Schaie, and Gribbin, 1978).

Almost anyone can experience the kinds of life events that produce diminution in blood supply to the head. They are more likely to have occurred in older than in younger people for several reasons, over the course of many years in adulthood, the blood supply to vulnerable areas of the brain can be expected probabilistically to drop below critical levels and result in loss of the neurological basis for some intellectual capacities.

Thus factors producing diminution of blood supply to the head can account for an expected aging decline of G_f or SAR or both. Viewed either longitudinally or in cross-section, this decline is shown in averages over many individuals. What is seen as "normal aging" decline of one or the other or both vulnerable abilities may reflect this kind of environmentally induced decline. The implication is that while such aging decline is relentless when seen in the averages over samples of individuals, it may nevertheless mainly represent loss that occurs to some, but not all, of the many people on which the averages are based. The declines thus may mainly reflect individual differences in lifestyles.

Although many factors of lifestyle might induce probabilistic decline of vulnerabilities, the use of alcohol presents a particularly interesting possible example. Alcohol is used by roughly 80 percent of the adults in the United States, and there are large individual differences in the amounts of such use. It is conceivable that such use accounts for most "normal aging" decline of either SAR or G_f or both of these abilities (Leber and Parsons, 1982).

Studies suggest that use of even very small amounts of alcohol, perhaps over short periods of time, can produce some loss of vulnerable abilities — although this loss may be small and reversible (Hartford and Samorajski, 1982; MacVane et al., 1981; Parker et al., 1983; Parker and Noble, 1977). Heavy use of alcohol over several years in adulthood is associated with cognitive deficits on G_f measures such as the block design, object assembly, picture completion, and picture arrangements tests of the WAIS, and on such SAR measures as digit span and paired associates memory (Leber and Parsons, 1982; Overall and Gorham, 1972; Overall, Hoffman, and Levine, 1978; Schear and Nebes, 1978). On the other hand, there are suggestions that moderate use of alcohol, even over extended periods of life, does not produce deterioration of vulnerable abilities and may promote development of maintained abilities (Goodwin et al., 1987); Hill, 1983; Wood and Elias, 1982).

What is "heavy" or "light" use of alcohol? Is drinking 14 ounces of whiskey every Saturday night for five years equivalent in its effect on G_f to drinking 2 ounces every night of the week for thirty years? Probably not. Results in the literature fail to provide clear answers for questions of this kind, however.

An effect produced by alcohol consumption can occur through direct influence, as in producing anoxia, but it can occur indirectly as well. Heavy alcohol use may be accompanied by events such as blows to the head (in fights), loss of consciousness resulting from falls, and respiratory malfunctions associated with exposure.

Patterns of loss of abilities associated with heavy use of alcohol are similar to the patterns of loss and maintenance of abilities associated with adulthood aging. The neurological losses that accompany alcohol use also appear to be similar to neurological losses associated with aging. Basic questions follow from such observations: (1) Are the aging declines of vulnerable abilities (as seen in averages based on many people) entirely, mainly, partly, or not at all a reflection of declines associated with the lifestyle components of alcohol use of some of the people in these samples? (2) Are the aging declines that can be linked to components of alcohol use mainly associated with the abilities of G_f or the abilities of SAR or both?

This suggestion that aging decline of G_f and SAR is caused by patterns of use of alcohol in adulthood should not be interpreted as support for popular ideas that aging is nothing more than alcoholism or alcoholism is premature aging. A major problem with these ideas, and the evidence from which they derive, is that the category "alcoholism" is a ragbag of several distinct patterns of use of alcohol any one of which could be, and several of which would not be expected to be, mainly associated with declines in G_f and SAR (Horn, Wanberg, and Foster, 1987). Also, many people who use alcohol in ways that appear to cause declines in G_f and SAR are not classified as alcoholics. Alcoholism probably is not premature aging, but particular patterns of use of alcohol over long periods of adulthood seem to result in brain damage which registers in deficits in cognitive ability performances (Cermak and Ryback, 1975; Clark and Haughton, 1975; Goldstein and Shelly, 1971; Kinsbourne, 1974; Jenkins and Parsons, 1981). My reading of this evidence leads to a hypothesis that these performance deficits represent declines in processes underlying G_f and SAR.

LIFE EVENTS RELATED TO CHANGES IN MAINTAINED ABILITIES

Existing evidence suggests that G_c is a vast array of abilities organized in a meshlike interwoven knowledge system. If one imagines that each node of this mesh is an element of knowledge of the system, and threads leading to a node are pathways that enable a person to access the element, then it seems that many, many strands lead to, and are woven into, each node. This produces a condition of overdetermination: because there are many, many strands leading to each node, one can lose some of the strands and still have enough left to easily access the information. In the terms of this analogy, G_c is the mesh itself and TSR represents ease of movement along the strands leading to nodes of knowledge.

Psychological overdetermination of knowledge systems is supported by neurological overdetermination. The strands leading to nodes of knowledge correspond, in the brain, to many, many neurons and many, many neurotransmitter connections, interwoven into functional organizations. Up to a point, if aging or brain injury reduces the number of neural strands, this need not show up in loss of maintained abilities because many neural strands remain to give access to stored information. However, after a critical amount of neural loss, there can be notable and irreversible decline in maintained abilities (Schaie, 1983).

Knowledge systems are not static: they are repreatedly restructured within each waking day of adulthood (Broadbent, 1958, 1966; Norman, 1979, 1982).

Contrary to popular belief, maintained abilities can involve speediness and indicate flexibility and creativity (Horn, 1978, 1980). Material learned months or years before testing and well stored in a person's knowledge system, is on the average more rapidly retrieved by older adults than by younger ones, provided the measurement task does not emphasize motor speed, as in the physical act of writing, to the detriment of thinking speed. This occurs, it seems, because in repeated restructurings of one's knowledge system, there is not only an increase in overdetermination, permitting shortcuts to access some items and more pathways to access, but also some improvement in the organization of the system itself, which also makes items more accessible (Norman, 1979; also the Baltes, Reese, and Lipsitt 1980 review). Broadbent (1966) likens the knowledge system to a library in which each day one rearranges the books to make it easier to find any particular book.

How do lifestyle factors, operating over adulthood, produce enhancement, overdetermination, and maintenance of G_c knowledge and TSR access? Very little is known about the restructuring of a knowledge system over the course of adult development.

SOME IMPLICATIONS

Enough has been said, perhaps, to illustrate in general how one might strategically sample ability measures to study outcomes and predictors of learning. Such a sample of ability measures, obtained through a battery of tests and subtests, provides a framework for studying learning. The following are some specific suggestions for forming such batteries.

It is well established that learning is related to the abilities of the WER-COF and G_f-G_c systems. There are virtually no exceptions to findings showing that any reliable and valid criterion measure of learning is predicted by several (among many) well-measured intellectual ability tests (Fleishman, 1960; Fleishman and Hempel, 1955; Hunter, in press; Pintrich et al., 1986). The correlations typically are of the order of .50 over periods of a year, but there is large variance around this "typical" value. In many cases predictive and postdictive correlations are substantially larger or smaller than .50.

The meta-analyses of Hunter (in press, and the work he reviews) caution against expecting large differences in the predictabilities obtainable with distinct tests. One should be aware that in the work on which meta-analyses have been based, the criteria often were poorly distinguished. When educational criteria are distinct, distinctly different tests best predict outcomes.

G_c abilities are closely similar to educational achievements; not suprisingly, therefore, G_c abilities are usually the best predictors of educational achievements. Educational outcomes that are highly verbal, as so measured, are best predicted by verbal abilities; outcomes involving understandings of numbers and figures, if well measured, are best predicted by tests of G_q. Prediction is often particularly good over short periods of time — less than five years. As the span between prediction and outcome increases, correlations between a predictor ability and a performance outcome often decrease systematically (Henry and Hulin, 1987; Humphreys, 1960, 1962, 1979a; Humphreys, Davey, and Park, 1985). This is not necessarily the case, however, as Ackerman (1987) has emphasized.

The extent to which we can generalize about the predictive validity of an ability measure depends on the variance (on the ability) in the samples in which validity coefficients are obtained. In a highly selected sample, such as a group of graduate students in mathematics, measures (of G_q, say) that very well predict in more heterogeneous samples may not predict very well at all.

Predictability is also conditional on the opportunities provided to the measured individuals. For example, if students are shut out of the opportunities of advanced education programs on the basis of low G_c scores, we cannot discover that those who scored high on G_f but low on G_c are among the top graduates of the programs. If opportunities are restricted because of the educational system's failure to obtain and use test information, the result can be serious failure to realize value for the society, as well as attenuation of validity coefficients for some abilities. This, incidentally, is one reason I uphold testing in opposition to critics who seek policies that allow only grades, teacher references, or interview information, not test scores, to be used in selection for educational programs. Such policies not only exclude independent thinkers who do not conform well to the sometimes arbitrary and silly demands of educational systems and teachers, they also systematically exclude some individuals who score high on abilities such as G_f and G_v that are not accurately represented in grades and ratings (or measures of G_c) but which can predict high performance in the long run.

There is considerable controversy surrounding the question of whether predictor relationships usually decrease as the span of time between prediction and outcome increases. Ackerman's answer is that the decrease is not ubiquitous; rather, it depends. On the one hand, there is the frequent finding of a quasi-simplex pattern of correlations between successive measures of the same, or nearly the same, ability: as the span of time between measures increases, the correlation decreases. Ackerman reminds us that this pattern exists not only for ability measures, or even only for psychological data; it is found for repeated measures of almost any dynamic process (Humphreys, Davey, and Park, 1985). But this finding tells us little more than that change is occurring; individuals change in their rank order on almost any measure of individual differences. This occurs even when there is high correlation between measures obtained at widely separated intervals of time, as in measures of height, for example. But, Ackerman emphasizes, it occurs even when there is relatively high correlation between a predictor measure obtained early in a process of change (learning) and a performance measure obtained late in such a process — for example, near a time when performance is asymptotic. The predictor-performance correlation can be substantially larger than some of the performance-performance correlations of the quasi-simplex. Performance at different points in learning a skill are predicted by different abilities measured before learning is commenced.

Ackerman cites evidence from Fleishman and Hempel (1954) to illustrate these points. In the acquisition of perceptual and motor skills, early-trial performances are predicted by general intellectual abilities. These predictions decrease for subsequent trials, but predictions from measures of complex coordination and perceptual speed, which in early trials were quite small, increase systematically: as asymptotic levels of performance of the skill are reached, complex coordination and perceptual speed measures, obtained before learning began, predict with higher correlations than performance measures, as such, obtained in trials preceding the near-asymptotic performance of the final trials of learning.

In relatively early accounts of the way in which broad abilities such as those of G_f-G_c theory might develop, Ferguson (1956, 1964) argued that the process may be much like the processes indicated in skill acquisition. This theory suggests that predictor measures obtained early in development might be found to have relatively high correlations with near-asymptotic ability manifestations measured late in development, even when quasi-simplex analysis indicated relatively little prediction from early learning to late learning of the same ability. A charge to search for such simplex-breaker predictors has been given to knights of the orders of developmental education and psychology, but as yet no Percival, Galahad, or Bors has succeeded in the quest. Ferguson's theory, amplified in the recent work of Ackerman (1987), remains a compelling heuristic for guiding studies of the developmental distinctions identified in G_f-G_c theory.

The intercorrelations among repeated measures with tests that represent G_f and G_c (Cattell, 1971; McArdle, Aber, and Horn, 1987) mainly indicate the quasi-simplex pattern. Correlations between early (in development) measures of G_c decrease monotonically with increase in time between the measures, and this is true also of the correlations for measures of G_f. It seems, therefore, that measures at different points in development for these abilities can be regarded as within-task performances for which the ubiquitous quasi-simplex pattern obtains over the life course of development. It appears that the simplex decrease is larger for G_c than for G_f (Cattell, 1971). In part this represents the fact that variance on G_c increases substantially with age, whereas variance on G_f remains relatively stable over the same span of age (McArdle et al., 1987). The evidence also suggests that variance on the abilities of SAR increases with age in adulthood (Rabbitt, 1981). Thus, simplex decrease in repeated-measures correlations for these abilities can be anticipated and, indeed, is suggested by the reviews of Humpreys (1960, 1962), Humpreys et al. (1985), and Jones (1970).

Cattell (1971), particularly, has suggested that early measures of G_f may be simplex-breaker predictors of later measures of G_c, and some of the evidence is supportive of this hypothesis (Cattell, 1971; Crano, 1977). For example, measures of G_f obtained with Cattell's culture-fair test correlate to approximately the same extent with vocabulary measures obtained one and three years apart when the retest correlations for the vocabulary measures decrease in accordance with the simplex pattern. More research is needed to verify such findings. Such research requires large samples of subjects and tests: large N is needed, for example, to attain power for statistical tests of equality and differences of covariances. Gathering data in accordance with these requirements is expensive. Unfortunately, money for research in the behavioral sciences is still very, very limited: the funding rate for approved research proposals in the behavioral science sections of the National Institutes of Health is still far below 50 percent.

A major implication of the research reviewed in this chapter is that, instead of continuing the near-reflex study of IQ or G, investigators should focus on exploring the distinctions among different abilities. The evidence suggests that IQ is not a very useful scientific concept. Similarly, the evidence fails to support any hypothesis of a general learning factor (Fleishman, 1960). Several different ability factors are involved in most learning, and different abilities vary in importance and relationship to each other at different stages of learning.

In future work, tests selected from different broad factors can provide a good system for measuring abilities that in predictive and post-dictive studies are likely to yield new understandings of educational achievements. Relatively small test batteries can be formed by using one test from each of the broad abilities. Although small, such batteries will cover a broad spectrum of intellect. For several of the tests of these batteries investigators could establish reliably different beta-weights for the prediction of educational outcomes — provided, of course, that the outcomes themselves are measured with good precision, and along distinct dimensions. (Often criterion measurement is the weakest link in a chain of arguments aimed at indicating distinct construct validities for distinct ability tests.)

Some of the tests of both primary and second-order abilities are more complex than others. Tests that are distinct in studies based on homogeneous samples of subjects often are not distinct in samples in which gross differences characterize subsamples. Under such conditions, tests that are distinct in factoring studies are found to measure much that is common, and distinct beta-weights in prediction studies will not be found for measures of abilities that have been shown to be distinct in factor-analytic studies.

Although the WERCOF system of replicated primary abilities contains many ambiguities, it is the best indication we currently have of the nature and number of narrow abilities that can be independently measured. A battery defined by one test representing each of the WERCOF factors "covers the waterfront" of major abilities that can be relevant for understanding learning precursors and outcomes.

"Independence" in this context refers to Gramian independence — that is, a true rank of m for a system of m variables — rather than to stochastic independence — expected intercorrelations of zero for a system of m variables. A practical measure of Gramian independence can be made operational by requiring that the squared multiple correlation (SMR) of a measure with all other measures (of a set) be significantly smaller than the squared correlation of a variable with its own true-score component — that is, its internal reliability. The variable thus must have more in common with itself than with all the variables with respect to which it is expected to be independent.

It is not known that all the WERCOF abilities will pass a reasonable test for Gramian independence, but a good guess is that this will be true for twenty or more (Hakstian and Cattell, 1974). This means that many of these measures could, in principle, have reliably distinct beta-weights in multiple predictions of educational achievement and background (Humphreys, 1978). Again one must realize that this is realistic only if criterion measures are finely differentiated.

In these ways, then — using an understanding of the WERCOF and G_f-G_c systems — investigators can derive a comprehensive framework for studying learning. Within this framework future researchers can build a detailed theory showing how the abilities of the systems are involved in each of many different kinds of learning and learning situations (Cronbach and Snow, 1977). With such a theory in hand, future educators will be able to make much better guidance decisions and program plans than they make today. For this to happen, however, our society's commitment to scientific study of human behavior must be maintained; indeed, relative to our current commitments to other pursuits (such as military build up), our commitments to research in psychology and education probably should increase.

ACKNOWLEDGMENTS

I thank the following people for suggested corrections and other improvements to an earlier draft of this chapter. These contributions helped me to improve the chapter substantially. For this help, I am grateful the following friendly critics (listed in alphabetical order): Anne Anastasi, Jack Carroll, David Epstein, Lloyd Humphreys, Arthur Jensen, Alan Kaufman, Jack McArdle, and Lazar Stankov. I am also indebted to Phillip Ackerman for some very good advice.

REFERENCES

Ackerman, P. L. (1986). Individual differences in information processing: An investigation of intellectual abilities and task performance during practice. *Intelligence,* 10:109–139.

Ackerman, P. L. (1987). Individual differences in skill learning: An integration of psychometric and information processing perspectives. *Psychological Bulletin,* 102:3–27.

Ackerman, P. L., and Schneider, W. (1985). Individual differences in automatic and controlled information processing. In R. F. Dillon (Ed.), *Individual differences in cognition,* vol. 2. New York: Academic Press.

Anastasi, A. (1987). *Psychological testing,* 6th ed. New York: Macmillan.

Anastasi, A. (1986). Experiential structuring of psychological traits. *Developmental Review,* 6:181–202.

Anderson, B. F. (1975). *Cognitive Psychology.* New York: Academic Press.

Atkin, R., Bray, R., Davidson, M., Herzberger, S., Humphreys, L. C., and Selzer, V. (1977a). Cross-lagged panel analysis of sixteen cognitive measures at four grade levels. *Child Development,* 21:78–81.

Atkin, R., Bray, R., Davidson, M., Herzberger, S., Humphreys, L. C., and Selzer, V. (1977b). Ability factor differentiation, grades 5–11. *Applied Psychological Measurement,* 1:65–66.

Baltes, P. B., Reese, H. W., and Lipsitt, L. P. (1980). Life-span developmental psychology. *Annual Reviews of Psychology,* 30:65–110.

Baltes, P. B., and Schaie, K. W. (1976). On the plasticity of intelligence in adulthood and old age. Where Horn and Donaldson fail. *American Psychologist,* 31:720–723.

Beeson, M. F. (1920). Intelligence of senescence. *Journal of Applied Psychology,* 4:219–234.

Blackwood, W., and Corsellis, J. A. (Eds.) (1976). *Greenfield's neuropathology.* London: Arnold.

Bock, R. D., and Kolakowski, D. (1973). Further evidence of sex-linked major-gene influence on human spatial visualizing ability. *The American Journal of Human Genetics,* 25:1–14.

Bondareff, W., Mountjoy, C., and Roth, M. (1982). Loss of neuronas of origin of the adrenergic projections to cerebral cortex (nucleus locus coeruleus) in senile dementia. *Neurology,* 32:164–168.

Botwinick, J. (1977). Aging and intelligence. In J. E. Birren and K. W. Schaie (Eds.), *Handbook of the psychology of aging*. New York: Van Nostrand Reinhold.

Bourne, L. F., Ekstrand, B. R., and Dominowski, R. L. (1971). *The psychology of thinking*. Englewood Cliffs, N.J.: Prentice-Hall.

Brim, O. G., and Kagan, J. (Eds.). (1980). *Constancy and change in human development*. Cambridge, Mass.: Harvard University Press.

Broadbent, D. E. (1958). *Perception and communication*. London: Pergamon Press.

Broadbent, D. E. (1966). The well-ordered mind. *American Educational Research Journal*, 3:281–295.

Bromley, D. B. (1974). *The psychology of human aging*, 2d ed. London: Penguin.

Bruner, J. S., Goodnow, J. J., and Austin, G. A. (1956). *A study of thinking*. New York: Wiley.

Burt, C. (1941). *Factors of the mind*. London: University of London Press.

Butters, N., and Cermak, L. (1975). Some analyses of amnesic syndromes in brain-damaged patients. *The Hippocampus*, 2:377–409.

Carroll, J. B. (1972). Stalking the wayward factors. *Contemporary Psychology*, 17:321–324.

Carroll, J. B. (Forthcoming). *Human cognitive abilities*.

Carroll, J. B., and Horn, J. L. (1981). On the scientific basis of ability testing. *American Psychologist*, 36:1012–1020.

Cattell, R. B. (1941). Some theoretical issues in adult intelligence testing. *Psychological Bulletin*, 38:592.

Cattell, R. B. (1950). *Personality*. New York: McGraw-Hill.

Cattell, R. B. (1957). *Personality and motivation structure and measurement*. New York: World Book.

Cattell, R. B. (1971). *Abilities: Their structure, growth and action*. Boston: Houghton-Mifflin.

Cave, R. L. (1970). A combined factor analysis of creativity and intelligence. *Multivariate Behavioral Research*, 5:177–191.

Cermak, L. S., and Ryback, R. S. (1975). Recovery of verbal short term memory in alcoholics. *Journal of Studies of Alcohol*, 37:46–52.

Clark, J., and Haughton, H. (1975). A study of intellectual impairment and recovery rates in heavy drinkers in Ireland. *British Journal of Psychiatry*, 126:170–184.

Commons, M. (1985, April). *How novelty produces continuity in cognitive development within a domain and accounts for unequal development across domains*. Toronto: Society for Research on Child Development.

Corsellis, J. A. N. (1976). Aging and the dementias. In W. Blackwood and J. A. N. Corsellis (Eds.), *Greenfield's neuropathology*. London: Arnold.

Cowan, W. M. (1979). The development of the brain. *Scientific American*, 241:112–133.

Craik, F. I. M. (1977). Age differences in human memory. In J. E. Birren and K. W. Schaie (Eds.), *Handbook of the psychology of aging*. New York: Van Nostrand-Reinhold.

Craik, F. I. M., and Lockhart, R. S. (1972). Levels of processing: A framework for memory research. *Journal of Verbal Learning and Verbal Behavior*, 11:671–684.

Crano, W. D. (1977). What do infant mental tests test? A cross-lagged panel analysis of selected data from the Berkeley Growth Study. *Child Development*, 48:144–151.

Cronbach, L. J. (1970). *Essentials of psychological testing,* 3d ed. New York: Harper and Row.

Cronbach, L. J. (1988). Construct validation after thirty years. In R. Linn (Ed.), *Intelligence: Measurement, theory and public policy.* Urbana, Ill.: University of Illinois Press.

Cronbach, L. J., and Snow, R. E. (1977). *Aptitudes and instructional methods.* New York: Irvington.

Cropley, A. J. (1972). A five-year longitudinal study of the validity of creativity tests. *Developmental Psychology,* 6:119–124.

Detterman, D. K. (1986). Quantitative integration: The last word. In R. J. Sternberg and D. K. Detterman (Eds.), *What is intelligence?* Norwood, N.J.: Ablex.

Dewar, K. M., Cuddy, L. L., and Mewhart, D. J. K. (1977). Recognition memory for single tones with and without context. *Journal of Experimental Psychology: Human Learning and Memory,* 3(1):60–67.

Drachman, D. A., and Arbit, J. (1966). Memory and the hippocampal complex. II. Is memory a multiple process? *Archives of Neurology,* 15:52–61.

Eccles, J. C. (1977). *The understanding of the brain.* New York: McGraw Hill. 1977.

Ekstrom, R. B., French, J. W., and Harman, H. H. (1976). *Manual for kit of factor-referenced cognitive tests.* Princeton: Educational Testing Service.

Ekstrom, R. B., French, J. W., and Harman, H. H. (1979). Cognitive factors: Their identification and replication. *Multivariate Behavior Research Monographs* (2):79.

Eysenck, H. J. (1939). Review of "Primary mental abilities" by L. L. Thurstone. *British Journal of Psychology,* 9:270–275.

Eysenck, H. J. (Ed.) (1982). *A model for intelligence.* New York: Springer-Verlag.

Eysenck, H. J. (1985). The theory of intelligence and the psychophysiology of cognition. In R. J. Sternberg (Ed.), *Advances in the psychology of human intelligence,* vol. 3. Hillsdale, N.J.: Erlbaum.

Ferguson, G. A. (1956). On transfer and the abilities of man. *Canadian Journal of Psychology,* 10:121–131.

Ferguson, G. A. (1964) On learning and human ability. *Canadian Journal of Psychology,* 8:95–112.

Fleishman, E. A. (1960). Abilities at different stages of practice in rotary pursuit performance. *Journal of Experimental Psychology,* 60:162–172.

Fleishman, E. A., and Hempel, W. E., Jr. (1954). Changes in factor structure of a complex psychomotor test as a function of practice. *Psychometrika,* 19:239–252.

Fleishman, E. A., and Hempel, W. E., Jr. (1955). The relation between abilities and improvement with practice in a visual discrimination reaction task. *Journal of Experimental Psychology,* 49:301–316.

French, J. W. (1951). The description of aptitude and achievement tests in terms of rotated factors. *Psychometric Monographs,* No. 5.

French, J. W., Ekstrom, R. B., and Price, L. A. (1963). *Manual and kit of reference tests for cognitive factors.* Princeton, N.J.: Educational Testing Services.

Getzels, J. W., and Jackson, P. W. (1962). *Creativity and intelligence.* New York: Wiley.

Ghiselli, E. E. (1966). *The validation of occupational aptitude tests.* New York: Wiley.

Goldstein, G., and Shelley, C. H. (1971). Field dependence and cognitive perceptual and motor skills in alcoholics: A factor analytic study. *Quarterly Journal Studies for Alcoholism,* 32:29.

Goodwin, J. S., Sanchez, C. J., Thomas, P., Hunt, M. S., Garry, P. J., and Goodwin, J. M. (1987). Alcohol intake in a healthy elderly population. *American Journal of Public Health,* 77:173–176.

Gould, S. J. (1981). *The mismeasure of man.* New York: Norton.

Grant, I., Adam, K. M., Carlin, A. S., Rennick, P. M., Judd, L. L., Schoof, K., and Reed, R. (1978). Organic impairment in polydrug users. *American Journal of Psychiatry,* 135:178–197.

Guilford, J. P. (1967). *The nature of human intelligence.* New York: McGraw-Hill.

Guilford, J. P., and Hoepfner, R. (1971). *The analysis of intelligence.* New York: McGraw-Hill.

Guilford, J. P., and Lacy, J. I. (Eds.) (1947). *Printed classification tests.* Research Report No. 5. Army Air Forces Aviation Psychology Program.

Gustafsson, J. E. (1984). A unifying model for the structure of intellectual abilities. *Intelligence,* 8:179–203.

Gustafsson, J. E. (1985). Measuring and interpreting g. *The Behavioral and Brain Sciences,* 8:231–232.

Guttman, L. (1970). Integration of test design and analysis. In *Proceedings of the 1969 Invitational Conference on Testing Problems.* Princeton, N.J.: Educational Testing Service.

Hachinski, V. (1980). Relevance of cerebrovascular changes in mental function. *Mechanisms of Aging and Development,* 10:1–11.

Hakstian, A. R., and Cattell, R. B. (1974). The checking of primary ability structure on a broader basis of performances. *British Journal of Educational Psychology,* 44:140–154.

Hakstian, A. R., and Cattell, R. B. (1978). Higher stratum ability structure on a basis of twenty primary abilities. *Journal of Educational Psychology,* 70:657–659.

Hartford, J. T., and Samorajski, T. (1982). Alcoholism in the geriatric population. *Journal of American Geriatric Society,* 30:18–32.

Hearnshaw, L. S. (1956). Temporal integration and behavior. *Bulletin of British Psychological Society,* 9:1–20.

Hebb, D. O. (1941). The clinical evidence concerning the nature of normal adult test performance. *Psychological Bulletin,* 38:593.

Hebb, D. O. (1949). *The organization of behavior: A neuropsychological theory.* New York: Wiley.

Heikkinen, E. (1975). Health and socio-economic factors related to physical activity among the aged. In *Physical activity/exercise for the aging.* International Seminar. Wingate Institute, Israel.

Henry, R. A., and Hulin, C. L. (1987). Stability of skilled performance across time: Some generalizations and limitations on utilities. *Journal of Applied Psychology,* 72:457–462.

Hertzog, C., Schaie, K. W., and Gribbin, K. (1978). Cardiovascular disease and changes in intellectual functioning from middle to old age. *Journal of Gerontology,* 33:872–883.

Hill, S. Y. (1983). Alcohol and brain damage: Cause or association? *American Journal of Public Health,* 73:487–489.

Hilliard, A. G. (1984). IQ testing as the emperor's new clothes: A critique of Jensen's bias in mental testing. In C. R. Reynolds and R. T. Brown (Eds.), *Perspectives on bias in mental testing.* New York: Plenum.

Horn, J. L. (1967). On subjectivity in factor analysis. *Educational and Psychological Measurement,* 27:811–820.

Horn, J. L. (1968). Organization of abilities and the development of intelligence. *Psychological Review,* 75:242–259.

Horn, J. L. (1970). Review of "The nature of human intelligence" by J. P. Guilford. *Psychometrika,* 35:273–277.

Horn, J. L. (1972). State, trait and change dimensions of intelligence. *British Journal of Educational Psychology,* 42:159–185.

Horn, J. L. (1973). Theory of functions represented among auditory and visual test performances. In J. R. Royce (Ed.), *Contributions of multivariate analysis to psychological theory.* New York: Academic Press.

Horn, J. L. (1976). Human abilities: A review of research and theory in the early 1970's. *Annual Review of Psychology,* 27:437–485.

Horn, J. L. (1978). Human ability systems. In P. B. Baltes (Ed.), *Life-span development and behavior.* New York: Academic Press.

Horn, J. L. (1980). Intelligence and age. In R. Tissot (Ed.), *Etats deficitaires cerebraux liés à L'Age. Tiré à part du volume Symposium Bel-Air VI.* Geneva, Switzerland: George et Cie S. A. Librairie de l'Université.

Horn, J. L. (1982). The aging of human abilities. In B. B. Wolman (Ed.), *Handbook of developmental psychology.* New York: Prentice Hall.

Horn, J. L. (1985). Remodeling old models of intelligence. In B. B. Wolman (Ed.), *Handbook of intelligence.* New York: Wiley.

Horn, J. L. (1986a). Intellectual ability concepts. In R. L. Sternberg (Ed.), *Advances in the psychology of human intelligence,* vol. 3. Hillsdale, N.J.: Erlbaum.

Horn, J. L. (1986b). Some thoughts about intelligence. In R. J. Sternberg and D. K. Detterman (Eds.), *What is intelligence? Contemporary viewpoints on its nature and definition.* Norwood, N.J.: Ablex.

Horn, J. L. (In press). A context for understanding information processing studies of human abilities. In P. A. Vernon (Ed.), *Speed of information-processing and intelligence.* Norwood, N.J.: Ablex.

Horn, J. L., and Cattell, R. B. (1966). Refinement and test of the theory of fluid and crystallized intelligence. *Journal of Educational Psychology,* 57:253–270.

Horn, J. L., and Donaldson, G. (1976). On the myth of intellectual decline in adulthood. *American Psychologist,* 31:701–719.

Horn, J. L., and Donaldson, G. (1977). Faith is not enough: A response to the Baltes-Schaie claim that intelligence will not wane. *American Psychologist,* 32:369–373.

Horn, J. L., and Donaldson, G. (1980). Cognitive development in adulthood. In O. S. Brim and J. Kagan (Eds.), *Constancy and change in human development.* Cambridge, Mass.: Harvard University Press.

Horn, J. L., Donaldson, G., and Engstrom, R. (1981). Apprehension, memory and fluid intelligence decline in adulthood. *Research on Aging,* 3:33–84.

Horn, J. L., and Goldsmith, H. (1981). Reader be cautious: "Bias in Mental Testing" by Arthur Jensen. *American Journal of Education,* 89:305–329.

Horn, J. L., and Knapp, J. R. (1973). On the subjective character of the empirical base of Guilford's structure-of-intellect model. *Psychological Bulletin,* 80:33–43.

Horn, J. L., and Knapp, J. R. (1974). Thirty wrongs do not make a right: Reply to Guilford. *Psychological Bulletin,* 81:502–504.

Horn, J. L., McArdle, J. J., and Mason, R. C. (1983). When is invariance not invariant: A practical scientist's look at the ethereal concept of factor invariance. *Southern Psychologist,* 1:179–188.

Horn, J. L., and Stankov, L. (1982). Auditory and visual factors of intelligence. *Intelligence,* 6:165–185.

Horn, J. L., Wanberg, K. W., and Foster, F. M. (1987). *Guide to the Alcohol Use Inventory (AUI).* Minneapolis, MN: National Computer Systems.

Hubel, D. H. (1979). The brain. *Scientific American,* 241:44–53.

Hultsch, D. F. (1971). Organization and memory in adulthood. *Human Development,* 14:16–29.

Humphreys, L. G. (1960). Investigations of the simplex. *Psychometrika,* 25:313–323.

Humphreys, L. G. (1962). The organization of human abilities. *American Psychologist,* 17:475–483.

Humphreys, L. G. (1971). Theory of intelligence. In R. Cancro (Ed.), *Intelligence: Genetic and environmental influences.* New York: Grune and Stratton.

Humphreys, L. G. (1978). Doing research the hard way: Substituting analysis of variance for a problem in correlational analysis. *Journal of Educational Psychology,* 70(6):873–876.

Humphreys, L. G. (1979a). The construct of general intelligence. *Intelligence,* 3:105–120.

Humphreys, L. G. (1979b). A factor model for research on intelligence and problem solving. In L. B. Resnick (Ed.), *The nature of intelligence.* Hillsdale, N.J.: Erlbaum.

Humphreys, L. G. (1984). General intelligence. In C. R. Reynolds and R. T. Brown (Eds.), *Perspectives on bias in mental testing.* New York: Plenum.

Humphreys, L. G., Davey, T. C., and Park, R. K. (1985). Longitudinal correlation analysis of standing height and intelligence. *Child Development,* 56:1465–1478.

Hunter, J. E. (In press). Cognitive ability, cognitive aptitudes, job knowledge, and job performance. *Journal of Vocational Behavior.*

Hunter, J. E., Schmidt, F. L., and Jackson, G. B. (1982). *Meta-analysis: Cumulating research findings across studies.* Beverly Hills, Calif.: Sage Press.

Iverson, L. L. (1979). The chemistry of the brain. *Scientific American,* 241:134–149.

Jenkins, R. L., and Parsons, O. A. (1981). Neuropsychological effects of chronic alcoholism on tactual performance. *Alcoholism: Clinical Experimental Research,* 5:26–33.

Jensen, A. R. (1984). Test validity: g versus the specificity doctrine. *Journal of Social and Biological Sciences,* 7:93–118.

Jensen, A. R. (1985). Race differences and type II errors: A comment on Borkowski and Krause. *Intelligence,* 9:33–39.

Jensen, A. R. (1987). The g beyond factor analysis. In J. C. Conoley, J. A. Glover, and R. R. Ronning (Eds.), *The influence of cognitive psychology on testing and measurement.* Hillsdale, N.J.: Erlbaum.

Jones, M. B. (1970). A two process theory of individual differences in motor learning. *Psychological Review,* 77:353–360.

Katzman, R. (1986). Alzheimer's disease. *The New England Journal of Medicine,* 314:964–973.

Kaufman, A. S., and Kamphaus, R. W. (1984). Factor analysis of the K-ABC for ages 2½ through 12½ years. *Journal of Educational Psychology,* 76:623–637.

Kaufman, A. S., and Kaufman, N. L. (1983). *Kaufman Assessment Battery for Children: Interpretative manual.* Circle Pines, Minn.: American Guidance Service.

Kety, S. S. (1979). Disorders of the human brain. *Scientific American,* 241:202–218.

Kinsbourne, M. (1974). Cognitive deficit and the aging brain: A behavioral analysis. *International Journal of Aging and Human Development,* 5:41–49.

Kish, G. B., and Cheney, T. M. (1969). Impaired abilities in alcoholism; measured by the General Aptitude Test Battery. *Quarterly Journal of Studies of Alcohol,* 30:384–388.

Kleinknecht, R. A., and Goldstein, S. G. (1972). Neuropsychological defects associated with alcoholism — a review and discussion. *Quarterly Journal Studies of Alcohol,* 33:999–1021.

Larry P. et al. vs. Riles et al. (1979) United States District Court for the Northern District of California, C-71-2270RFP, slip opinion.

Lawley, D. N. (1943–1944). A note on Karl Pearson's selection formula. *Proceedings of the Royal Society of Edinburgh* (Section A), 62:28–30.

Leber, W. R., and Parsons, O. A. (1982). Premature aging and alcoholism. *The International Journal of the Addictions,* 17:61–88.

MacVane, J., Butters, N., Montgomery, K., and Farber, J. (1981). Cognitive functioning in men social drinkers: A replication study. *Journal Studies in Alcohol,* 43:181–95.

Mandler, G. (1967). Organization and memory. In K. W. Spence and J. T. Spence (Eds.), *The Psychology of learning and motivation: Advances in research and theory,* vol. 1. New York: Academic Press.

Matarazzo, J. D. (1972). *Wechsler's measurement and appraisal of adult intelligence,* 5th ed. Baltimore, Md.: Williams and Wilkins.

McArdle, J. J., Aber, M. S., and Horn, J. L. (1987). Adult abilities and aging: A repeated measures meta-analysis of the WAIS. Unpublished Report. Psychology Department, University of Virginia.

McCarthy, D. (1972). *McCarthy scale of children's abilities.* New York: The Psychological Corporation.

McDowd, J. M. (In press). The effects of age and extended practice on divided attention performance. *Journal of Gerontology.*

McNemar, Q. (1964). Lost: Our intelligence. Why? *American Psychologist,* 19:871–882.

Mednick, S. A. (1956). The associative basis of the creative process. *Psychological Review,* 63:81–97.

Meredith, W. (1964). Notes on factorial invariance. *Psychometrika,* 29:177–185.

Minton, H. L., and Schneider, F. W. (1980). *Differential psychology.* Prospect Heights, Ill.: Waveland.

Nichols, R. C. (1978). Twin studies of ability, personality and interests. *Homo,* 29:158–173.

Norman, D. A. (1979). Perception, memory and mental processes. In L. G. Nilsson (Ed.), *Perspectives on memory research.* Hillsdale, N.J.: Erlbaum.

Norman, D. A. (1982). Learning and memory. New York: W. H. Freeman and Company.

Norman, D. A., and Rummelhart, D. E. (1975). *Explorations in cognition.* New York: W. H. Freeman and Company.

Overall, J., and Gorham, D. (1972). Organicity vs. old age in objective and projective test performance. *Journal of Consulting Psychology,* 39:98–105.

Overall, J. E., Hoffman, N. G., and Levine, H. (1978). Effects of aging, organicity, alcoholism, and functional psychopathology on WAIS subtest profiles. *Journal of Consulting Clinical Psychology,* 46:1315–1322.

Parker, D. A., Parker, E. S., Brady, J. A., and Schoenberg, R. (1983). Alcohol use and cognitive loss among employed men and women. *American Journal of Public Health,* 73:521–523.

Parker, E. S., and Noble, E. P. (1977). Alcohol consumption and cognitive functioning in social drinkers. *Journal of Studies in Alcohol,* 38:1224–1232.

Parker, E. S., and Noble, E. P. (1980). Alcohol and the aging process in social drinkers. *Journal of Studies on Alcohol,* 41:170–178.

Parsons, O. A. (1975). Brain damage in alcoholics: Altered states of unconscious. In M. M. Gross (Ed.), *Alcoholic intoxication and withdrawal.* New York: Plenum.

Parsons, O. A. (1977). Permanent brain damage in alcoholism. Neuropsychological defects in alcoholics. *Alcoholism: Clinical and Experimental Research,* 1:51.

PASE: Parents in action on special education et al. vs. Hannon et al. (1980). United States District Court for the Northern District of Illinois, Eastern Division, C-74-3586RFP, slip opinion.

Pawlik, K. (1966). Concepts and calculations in human abilities. In R. B. Cattell (Ed.), *Handbook of multivariate experimental psychology.* Chicago: Rand McNally.

Pawlik, K. (1978). Faktoranalytische personlichkeits-forschung. In G. Strube (Ed.), *Die Psychologie des 20 Jahrhunderts.* Zurich: Kindler.

Pintrich, P. R., Cross, D. R., Kozma, R. B., and McKeachie, W. J. (1986). Instructional psychology. *Annual Review of Psychology,* 37:611–651.

Pollack, R. H. (1969). Ontogentic changes in perception. In D. E. Elkind and J. H. Flavell (Eds.), *Studies in cognitive development.* New York: Oxford University Press.

Prohovnik, I. (1980). *Mapping brainwork.* Malmo, Sweden: CWK Gleerup.

Rabbitt, P. M. A. (1979). How old and young subjects monitor and control responses for accuracy and speed. *British Journal of Psychology,:* 305–311.

Rabbitt, P. M. A. (1981). Cognitive psychology needs models for changes in performance with old age. In J. Long and A. Baddeley (Eds.), *Attention and performance.* Hillsdale, N.J.: Erlbaum.

Robinson, G. M. (1977). Rhythmic organization in speech processing. *Journal of Experimental Psychology: Human Learning and Memory,* 3:83–91.

Rossman, B. B., and Horn, J. L. (1972). Cognitive, motivational and temperamental indicants of creativity and intelligence. *Journal of Educational Measurement,* 9:265–286.

Ryan, C., and Butters, N. (1979). Memory deficits in chronic alcoholics: Continuities between the "intact" alcoholic and the alcoholic Korsakoff patient. In H. Begleiter and B. Kissin (Eds.), *Alcohol intoxication and withdrawal.* New York: Plenum Press.

Sanchez-Craig, M. (1980). Random assignment to abstinence or controlled drinking in a cognitive-behavior program: Short-term effects on drinking behavior. *Addictive Behaviors,* 5:35–39.

Schaie, K. W. (Ed.), (1983). *Longitudinal studies of adult psychological development.* New York: Guilford.

Schaie, K. W., and Baltes, P. B. (1977). Some faith helps see the forest: A final comment on the Horn and Donaldson myth of the Baltes-Schaie position on adult intelligence. *American Psychologist,* 32:1118–1120.

Schaie, K. W., and Gribbin, K. (1975). Adult development and aging. *Annual Review of Psychology,* 26:65–96.

Schear, J. M., and Nebes, R. D. (1978). Memory for verbal and spatial information as a function of age. Paper presented at symposium on neuropsychological assessment in the elderly. Annual meeting of the Gerontological Society, Dallas, Texas.

Sharp, J. R., Rosenbaum, G., Goldman, M. S., and Whitman, R. D. (1977). Recoverability of psychological functioning following alcohol abuse: Acquisition of meaningful synonyms. *Journal of Consulting Psychology,* 45:1023.

Shepard, R. N., and Metzler, J. (1971). Mental rotation of three-dimensional objects. *Science,* 171:701–703.

Shiffrin, R. M., and Schneider, W. (1977). Controlled and automatic human information processing. II. Perceptual learning, automatic attending and a general theory. *Psychological Review,* 84:127–190.

Shuter, R. (1968). *The psychology of musical ability.* London: Methuen.

Spearman, C. (1927). *The abilities of man: Their nature and measurement.* New York: Macmillan.

Stankov, L. (1978). Fluid and crystallized and broad perceptual factors among the 11 to 12 year olds. *Journal of Educational Psychology,* 70:324.

Stankov, L., and Horn, J. L. (1980). Human abilities revealed through auditory tests. *Journal of Educational Psychology,* 72:21–44.

Sternberg, R. J., Conway, B. E., Ketron, J. L., and Bernstein, M. (1981). *People's conceptions of intelligence.* Technical Report. New Haven, Conn.: Yale University, Department of Psychology.

Sternberg, R. J., and Detterman, D. K. (Eds.) (1986). *What is intelligence: Contemporary viewpoints on its nature and definition.* Norwood, N.J.: Ablex.

Sweet, W. H., Talland, G. A., and Ervin, F. R. (1959). Loss of recent memory following section of fornix. *Transactions of the American Neurological Association,* 84:76–79.

Tarter, R. (1975) Psychological deficit in chronic alcoholics: A review. *International Journal of the Addictions,* 10:327–368.

Thompson, R. F. (1985). *The brain: An introduction to Neuroscience.* New York: W. H. Freeman and Company.

Thomson, G. H. (1916). A hierarchy without a general factor. *British Journal of Psychology,* 8:271–281.

Thurstone, L. L. (1947). *Multiple factor analysis.* Chicago: University of Chicago Press.

Torrance, E. P. (1972). Predictive validity of the Torrance tests of creative thinking. *The Journal of Creative Behavior,* 6:236–252.

Turner, E. (1969). Hippocampus and memory. *Lancet,* 2:1123–1126.

Undheim, J. O. (1976). Ability structure in 10- to 11-year-old children and the theory of fluid and crystallized intelligence. *Journal of Educational Psychology,* 68:411–423.

Vandenberg, S. G. (1971). What do we know today about the inheritance of intelligence and how do we know it? In R. Cancro (Ed.), *Intelligence: Genetic and environmental influences*. New York: Grune and Stratton.

Vernon, P. E. (1972a). The usefulness of "creativity tests." *The School Guidance Worker*, 27:30–35.

Vernon, P. E. (1972b). The validity of divergent thinking tests. *The Alberta Journal of Educational Research*, 18:249–258.

Walsh, D. A. (1986). Aging and human visual information processing. *Geriatric Opthamology*, 2:29–35.

Wechsler, D. (1941). *The measurement of adult intelligence*, 2d ed., Baltimore: Williams and Wilkins.

Witkin, H. A., and Goodenough, D. R. (1981). *Cognitive studies: Essence and origins*. New York: International Universities Press.

Wolman, B. B. (Ed.) (1985). *Handbook of intelligence*. New York: Wiley.

Wood, W. E., and Elias, M. E. (Eds.) (1982). *Alcoholism and aging: Advances in research*. Boca Raton: CRC Press.

Woodcock, R. W. (1978). *Development and standardization of the Woodcock-Johnson psycho-educational battery*. Allen, Tx.: DLM Teaching Resources.

Woodcock, R. W., and Johnson, M. B. (1977). *Woodcock-Johnson psycho-educational battery*. Allen, Tx.: DLM Teaching Resources Corp.

Woodcock, R. W. (1989) Woodcock-Johnson psycho-educational battery—revised.

4

A Taxonomy
of Learning Skills

PATRICK C. KYLLONEN[1] *Institute for Behavioral Research, University of Georgia*

VALERIE J. SHUTE *Air Force Human Resources Laboratory*

What is the relationship between intelligence and learning ability? This question engaged contributors to the 1965 conference on *learning and individual differences,* and, we believe, the sophistication of the answer to this question, perhaps as clearly as to any other, highlights exactly how far our theories have come over the last twenty years.

Certainly the prevalent position among the contributors to the 1965 conference, and indeed the general opinion until recently, was that there is no relationship between intelligence and the ability to learn or, perhaps, that the relationship is weak at best. This position reflects conclusions drawn from the widely cited series of studies by Woodrow (1946), who found that with extended practice on a variety of learning tests (such as canceling tasks, analogies, addition), the performance of brighter students did not improve at a rate substantially greater than that shown by poorer students. Woodrow's studies are no longer viewed as incontrovertible in addressing the intelligence-learning

---

[1] Currently at Air Force Human Resources Laboratory, Brooks Air Force Base, Texas.

issue, primarily because of problems with the measures of learning ability he employed: his learning tasks may have been too simple (Humphreys, 1979; Campione, Brown, and Bryant, 1985), and his conception of learning as improvement due to practice was too simplistic. Had he selected other kinds of learning tasks and measured learning with other performance indices, his results might have been quite different, as subsequent investigation has shown (Snow, Kyllonen, and Marshalek, 1984).

We may draw a general conclusion here: to address questions regarding learning ability, such as the question of its correlates and its dimensionality, it is important to have a clear idea of exactly what is meant by learning ability to the extent that one can specify learning indicators. Problems and confusions such as those introduced by Woodrow could have been resolved by selecting learning indicators from an agreed-upon taxonomy of learning skills. To clarify this point, for the purposes of this paper we distinguish learning *abilities* from learning *skills*. We define *abilities* as individual-difference dimensions in a factor analysis of learning tasks. We define *skills* as candidate individual-difference dimensions which are presently only conceptually distinct. In this way, we believe that proposing learning skills logically precedes establishing the individual differences dimensions underlying learning. Proposing a taxonomy of learning skills should assist in determining the dimensions of learning ability. (We realize that our use of the terms *abilities* and *skills* may be somewhat idiosyncratic.)

There are many potential benefits to having a widely accepted taxonomy of learning skills. Consider Bloom's *Taxonomy of Educational Objectives* (1956). Its primary purpose was to serve as an aid, especially to teachers, for considering a wider range of potential instructional goals and for considering means of evaluating student achievement consistent with those goals. Although the taxonomy has been criticized for vagueness (what exactly is analysis anyway?) (Ennis, 1986), it has served teachers well over the last thirty years, at least as demonstrated by its continued inclusion in teacher training curricula. Its main effect has probably been to encourage instructing and testing of higher-order thinking skills (analysis, synthesis, evaluation). A taxonomy of learning skills could have a parallel effect in encouraging the development of instructional objectives concerned with teaching higher-order learning skills.

Fleishman and Quaintance (1984) have outlined a number of ways, both scientifically and practically, in which a performance taxonomy in psychology would be beneficial. The main scientific benefit would be that results from different studies using different methods could more easily be compared and synthesized. Study A finds that some manipulation drastically affects performance on task X whereas study B finds that the same manipulation has no effect on performance of task Y. Are the studies contradictory or compatible? A taxonomy could help decide.

The main practical benefit of having a taxonomy of learning skills is that consumers of research findings could more easily determine the limits of generalizability from current research findings to an immediate practical problem. For example, it would be convenient to be able to produce learnability metrics for any kind of learning task, either in the classroom (for example, a particular algebra curriculum) or outside the classroom (such as a new word-processing system). A taxonomy of learning skills would be an important first step toward achieving a generally useful learnability metric system.

There are also more specific motivations for the immediate development of a taxonomy of learning skills. The National Assessment of Educational Progress (NAEP, "The Nation's Report Card") is a biennial survey of student achievement in areas such as mathematics, science, and computer science designed to provide information to Congress, school officials, and other policy makers regarding the state of American education. In recent years there has been increasing attention given to the assessment of higher-order skills in these subject matters (Murnane and Raizen, 1988). It is likely that because of political pressures this effort will continue with or without a taxonomy, but a taxonomy of learning skills could assist in the development of new, more refined test items to measure learning skills relevant to math and science.

Perhaps the most conspicuous benefits of having a viable taxonomy of learning skills, however, would be realized in the burgeoning domain of intelligent computerized tutoring systems (ITS). A number of such systems have been developed (Yazdani, 1986), and the potential for generalizing and synthesizing results across the different systems is being seen as increasingly critical (Soloway and Littman, 1986). Too often, researchers caught up in the excitement of developing powerful, innovative instructional systems have neither the interest nor the expertise for systematically evaluating those systems. There have been a few small-scale evaluation studies of global outcomes (Anderson, Boyle, and Reiser, 1985), but the field could obviously benefit from an accepted taxonomy. System developers could state what kinds of learning skills were being developed, and evaluators could determine the degree of success achieved. In this way, a taxonomy could provide a useful metric by which to compare and evaluate tutors as to their relative effectiveness not only in teaching the stipulated subject matter, but also in promoting more general learning skills.

Intelligent tutoring systems would benefit from a learning taxonomy in a second way. Because of the precision with which instructional objectives may be stated, the degree of tutorial control over how these objectives guide instructional decisions, and the precision with which student learning may be assessed, the ITS environment enables the examination of issues on the nature of learning that investigators simply were unable to address in the past. Educational research has been notoriously plagued with noisy data due to the very nature of field research and the inherent lack of control over the way instructional treatments are administered and learning outcomes measured. The controlled ITS environment thus offers new promise as the ideal testbed for evaluating fundamental issues in learning. With these systems we now have the capability of generating rich descriptions of an individual learner's progress during instruction. A taxonomy should help in determining exactly what indicators of learning progress and learner status we ought to be producing and examining. The acid test of the utility of any learning taxonomy is whether it could actually be used to assist in such an endeavor. The goal of this chapter is to propose such a taxonomy. We begin by looking at what has been done thus far.

A TAXONOMY OF LEARNING TAXONOMIES

Investigators have adopted various approaches to the development of learning taxonomies. One way of organizing these approaches, which we will apply here, is by the categories of (a) *rational*, based on a conditions-of-learning analysis, (b) *correlational*, based on an individual-differences analysis, and (c) *model-based*, from formal computer simulations of learning processes.

Rational Taxonomies

Rational taxonomies are by far the most common. Examples of this type are taxonomies proposed by Bloom (1956), Gagné (1985), Jensen (1967), and Melton (1964). Proposed taxonomies are based on a speculative, rational analysis of the domain, and frequently the analysis applied is of a conditions-of-learning nature. That is, the proposer defines task categories in terms of characteristics that will foster or inhibit learning or performance.

One of the first attempts to organize the varieties of learning was Melton's (1964) proposal of a simple taxonomy based primarily on clusters of tasks investigated by groups of researchers. The categories, roughly ordered by the complexity of the learning act, were *conditioning, rote learning, probability learning, skill learning, concept learning,* and *problem solving*. This general scheme has been given an updated treatment by Estes (1982) who examined conditions that facilitated and inhibited these and related classes of learning, and looked for evidence of individual differences in each class.

A task-based scheme was also the basis for learning taxonomies proposed by Jensen (1967) and Gagné (1965, 1985). Jensen proposed a three-faceted taxonomy (similar in some ways to Guilford's structure of intellect model): a *learning type* facet incorporated Melton's seven categories; a *procedures* facet indicated variables such as the pacing of the task, whether the task consisted of spaced or massed practice, stage of learning, and the like; and a *content* facet indicated whether the task consisted of verbal, numerical, or spatial stimuli. Jensen proposed that his taxonomy could be used as an aid in interpreting some research findings, such as why arbitrarily selected learning tasks do not inter-correlate very highly (answer: because they do not share any facet values). He hoped that his taxonomy would suggest a more systematic approach to selecting learning tasks for future studies, but there is not much evidence that researchers have subsequently followed his suggestions.

Gagné's taxonomy (1965, 1985), on the other hand, has been widely taught and put to use in the area of instructional design (Gagné and Briggs, 1979). Gagné proposes five major categories of learned capabilities based on a rational analysis of common performances characteristics. *Intellectual skills* (procedural knowledge) reflect the ability to use rules; this capability in turn depends on the ability to make discriminations and to use concepts, and rules themselves combine to form higher-order rules and procedures. *Cognitive strategies* (executive control processes) reflect the ability to govern one's own learning and performance processes. *Verbal information* reflects the ability to recall and use labels, facts, and whole bodies of knowledge. *Motor skills* and *attitudes* are two additional learned capabilities Gagné includes to round out the list.

These categories serve various purposes. During task analysis, they assist the investigator in defining and analyzing instructional objectives and in evaluating an instructional system to determine whether its objectives have been met. For example, if the goal is to have the student acquire a conceptual skill, then the objective that the student be able to *discriminate* one thing from another may be indicated. In the design phase, the categories suggest different approaches for delivering instruction, since, according to Gagné, the five capabilities differ in the conditions most favorable for their learning. For example, with verbal information, order is not important but providing a meaningful context is, whereas for motor skills, providing intensive practice on part skills is critical.

All these taxonomic systems, Gagné's in particular, are beneficial, but it is important to acknowledge their limitations. One problem inherent in this approach is the degree to which it is subject to imprecision, which makes for communication difficulties and violates one of the main motivations for developing the taxonomy in the first place. Without a strong model of learning requirements in a task, and without a foundation of empirical relationships, task analysis is still primarily an art rather than a technology.

A second major problem with the rational approach was apparent to Melton (1964, 1967), who, in fact, argued that it be abandoned. The problem is that a taxonomic scheme based primarily on a rational analysis of task characteristics will only incidentally include actual psychological process dimensions. And presumably the process dimensions are what govern the most important aspect of the taxonomy: information regarding predicted task-to-task generality. Melton suggested that while the task-based approach might be initially useful, it was preferable ultimately to base the taxonomy on process characteristics rather than "a mish-mash of procedural and topographic (i.e., perceptual, motor, verbal, 'central') criteria" (p. 336). Although it was preliminary at that time to have actually suggested replacements to the task-based categories, we will show later how cognitive science now provides suggestions for what they might be.[1]

Correlational Taxonomies

A second approach, one less commonly used in the domain of learning skills, has been primarily empirical. The history of individual-differences research can be seen largely as an attempt to develop taxonomies of intelligence tests based on performance correlations (Thurstone, 1938), and there have been some attempts to develop similar taxonomies of learning tasks (Allison, 1960; Malmi, Underwood, and Carroll, 1979; Stake, 1961; Underwood, Boruch, and Malmi, 1978).

The correlational approach has one critical advantage over the rational approach as a means for taxonomy development: it directly addresses the issue of the transferability of skills among tasks. That is, if we know that performance on learning task X is highly correlated with performance on task Y, then a natural proposal is that a high proportion of the skills required by task X are also required by task Y. Further, training on task X should transfer at least somewhat to task Y. Thus patterns of correlations among performances on learning tasks could in principle be the basis for the construction of a taxonomy of learning skills.

A very closely related idea — that individual differences investigations could serve as acid tests in constructing general theories of learning — was developed by Underwood (1975). His proposal was that if a theory assumed some mechanism, and the mechanism could be measured in a context outside that in which it was initially developed, then the viability of the mechanism could be tested by correlational analysis.

These ideas were applied in an ambitious investigation that examined the intercorrelations among a wide variety of verbal memory tests (Underwood, Boruch, and Malmi, 1978). The purpose was to determine whether theoretical notions developed in the general (nomothetic) learning literature, such as the idea that memories have imaginal and acoustic attributes, or that recognition processes are distinct from recall processes, could be verified with an individual-differences analysis.

Memory-task stimuli were primarily words. In some tasks words were randomly selected, but in others words were chosen to elicit particular psycho-

---

[1] It is historically interesting that it was at Melton's 1963 conference that Fitts (1963) proposed a highly process-oriented taxonomy of psychomotor skills which was only much later adapted by Anderson (1983) as the basis for a cognitive learning theory.

logical processes. For example, concrete and abstract words were mixed, under the assumption that recall differences would reflect the degree of imagery involvement. Words were embedded in various kinds of memory tasks (paired associates, free recall, serial recall, memory span, frequency judgment). It was expected that clear word-attribute factors would emerge, thus supporting certain theoretical notions regarding properties of memory; however Underwood and colleagues discovered two somewhat unanticipated results. First, most of the variance was due to general individual differences in associative learning; only a small percentage was due to any subject-task interaction. Second, the two factors that did emerge were not associated with word attributes, as might have been expected, but with type of task (free recall versus paired associates and serial learning); but even this apparently is not a robust task division. A follow-up study (Malmi, Underwood, and Carroll, 1979) found the same evidence for a general associative-learning factor, but the two extracted factors split tasks in a slightly different way (free recall and serial learning versus paired associates).

What is the implication for a taxonomy of learning skills? Association formation rate apparently is a general and perhaps fundamental learning parameter. It may be that further subtle distinctions could be made among types of association formation, but the evidence in both these studies suggests little practical payoff in searching for such distinctions.

Underwood and colleagues were primarily interested in memory per se, and thus their tasks represent a fairly narrow range of learning. A useful complement to their analysis would be a study that more systematically sampled learning tasks from something like Melton's or Gagné's taxonomy. In this regard we consider a pair of studies by Stake (1961) and Allison (1960), who administered a diverse variety of learning tasks to large samples of seventh graders and Navy recruits, respectively. Allison's learning tasks were four paired-associates tasks (verbal, spatial, auditory, and haptic stimuli); four concept-formation tasks (spatial and verbal stimuli); two mechanical assembly tasks consisting of a short study film followed by an assembly test; a maze-tracing task; a standard rotary-pursuit task; and a task that involved learning how to plot quickly on a polar coordinates grid. Stake's learning tasks were listening comprehension (repeated study-test trials of the same story), free recall (words, numbers), paired associates (words, dot patterns, shapes, numbers), verbal concept formation, and maze learning. In both studies a variety of aptitude tests were also administered.

The original analyses of these data were somewhat problematic (see Cronbach and Snow, 1977), but a reanalysis conducted by Snow, Kyllonen, and Marshalek (1984) using multidimensional scaling (MDS) revealed a number of dimensions by which the learning tasks could be organized. First, in both studies, *learning tasks varied systematically in complexity*. This was indicated by two findings: the learning tasks varied substantially (a) in the degree to which performance on them correlated with measures of general intellectual ability, and (b) in how close to the center of the multidimensional scaling configuration they appeared. Centrality reflects the average correlation of a test with other tests in the battery and may be taken as a measure of complexity (Marshalek, Lohman, and Snow, 1983; Tversky and Hutchins, 1986). Snow and colleagues suggested that the complexity relationship could be due either to some tasks subsuming others in terms of process requirements or to increased involvement of executive control processes such as goal monitoring.

Second, in both analyses there was evidence for a *novel* versus *familiar* learning task dimension, which Snow and associates interpreted as supporting the classical distinction between fluid and crystallized intelligence (Cattell, 1971), but which might also be seen as supporting a distinction between inductive and rote learning. In the Allison analysis, the paired-associates tasks and some of the concept-formation tasks appeared on one side of the scaling configuration. The concept formation tasks so positioned were those which repeatedly used the same stimuli, thus enabling the successful use of a purely rote strategy. On the other hand, the assembly tasks and the novel plotting task, which required subjects to assemble a new solution procedure essentially from scratch, appeared on the opposite side of the configuration.

The MDS analysis of the Stake (1961) data (learning rate scores) similarly suggested a fluid-inductive versus crystallized-rote dimension. Listening comprehension, verbal paired-associates, and verbal free-recall tasks appeared on the crystallized side of the configuration. The verbal concept-formation task along with the spatial and number pattern paired-associates tasks, which were partially amenable to an inductive learning strategy (response patterns could, but did not have to be induced), fell on the fluid-inductive learning end.

The reanalysis by Snow and colleagues thus provides a number of ideas that could facilitate taxonomy development. In particular it suggests task complexity and learning environment (inductive-novel task versus rote-familiar task) dimensions. Does this suggest we ought to continue along these lines to develop a full taxonomy? Unfortunately, we see two problems with the approach. One is simply practicality. Because of the time and expense involved in collecting data on performance of learning tasks, which typically require many more subject hours than do other cognitive measures, there have not been the same kind of large scale empirical analyses of learning-task batteries as there have been of intelligence-test batteries (although data sets reviewed in Glaser, 1967, and Cronbach and Snow, 1977, could be reanalyzed along the lines of the Snow et al. approach). Even with the well-designed studies Snow and colleagues reanalyzed, there is considerable underdetermination of process dimensions because not enough varieties of learning tasks were administered by Stake and Allison. Thus, although the dimensions that are revealed in the reanalysis by Snow and colleagues are suggestive, they certainly do not seem a sufficient basis for proposing a taxonomy of learning skills. It might take more like a few hundred diverse learning tasks to be able to see something that might serve as the basis for a true full-blown taxonomy. Obviously, such a study would be prohibitively expensive.

A second problem with the correlational approach to taxonomy building is one inherent in a purely bottom-up approach to theory development. That is, on what basis should learning tasks be selected for inclusion in a battery that is to be analyzed? Factor-correlational structures or categories directly reflect the nature of the tasks included in the analysis and only those tasks, and thus the empirical approach is inherently analytic and in some sense conservative. Correlational analyses certainly may be useful for initial forays or purely exploratory work in suggesting underlying relationships among tasks that might not have been anticipated at the outset. But it cannot be complete in any sense. One cannot simply be careful to "sample a broad range of tasks." A sampling scheme for choosing tasks already implies a taxonomy. Clearly, some means for generating original taxonomic categories is required.

Information-processing Model-based Taxonomies

The two classes of learning taxonomies thus far discussed have their roots in two different schools of thought—behaviorism in the case of rational taxonomies, psychometrics in the case of the empirical-correlational taxonomies—that historically precede modern cognitive psychology. One unfortunate side effect of the cognitive revolution had been a decline of interest in learning phenomena. Until the mid 1960s, when behaviorism was still largely predominant, learning issues held center stage. With the subsequent rise of cognitive psychology and the information-processing perspective, theories of memory and performance came to dominate. Only recently has there been a rather sudden and dramatic upsurge of interest in learning from an information-processing perspective. Although many of the same issues remain, these second looks at learning through newer theories (Anderson, 1983; Rosenbloom and Newell, 1986; Rumelhart and Norman, 1981) have resulted in a richer theoretical picture of learning phenomena.

Corresponding to this rise of interest in learning, there have been proposals for model-based categories or taxonomies of learning types. These attempts differ from the correlational taxonomies in that they have not yet been completely validated, at least not as taxonomies of learning skills. However, we do see correspondences between some of the dimensions that have emerged in the correlational analyses and some of the proposed learning mechanisms and categories, which we will point out as we go along. The model-based taxonomies differ also from the rational taxonomies in that they arise not simply from speculation and rational task analysis (although they certainly incorporate such methods) but from systematic information-processing models of learning that have been demonstrated to be specified to a degree of precision sufficient for implementation as running computer programs. Thus taxonomies in this category are those investigations that have entailed the use of computer simulation of learning processes as a means of developing learning theory.

One model-based taxonomy is suggested by Anderson's (1983) ACT* (Adaptive Control of Thought) theory. The theory proposes two fundamental forms of knowledge. *Procedural knowledge* (knowledge how) is represented in the form of a production system, a set of if-then rules presumed to control the flow of thought. *Declarative knowledge* (knowledge that) is represented in the form of a node-link network of propositions, which are presumed to embody the content of thought.

The ACT* theory, in its most recent formulation (Anderson, 1983; 1987a), specifies three basic types of learning, one to accommodate declarative (fact) learning, one specific to procedural learning, and one applicable to both types. Learning in declarative memory is accomplished solely by the probabilistic *transfer* to long-term memory of any new proposition (that is, a set of related nodes and links) that happens to be active in working memory. It is worth noting that the finding of Underwood and colleagues (1978) of a broad and general associative-learning factor lends empirical support to Anderson's claim for a single declarative-learning mechanism.

A second learning mechanism, *knowledge compilation,* accounts for procedural learning. Knowledge compilation actually consists of two related processes. Learning by *composition* is the collapsing of sequentially applied productions into one larger production. This corresponds to the transition from step-by-step execution of some skill to one-pass (all-at-once) execution. Learning by *proceduralization* is a related process in which a production becomes specialized for use in a particular task. This corresponds to the transition from the use of general problem-solving skills to tackle novel problems to the employment of task-specific skills, tuned to the particular problem at hand. Anderson's third learning mechanism, *strengthening,* operates somewhat analogously to the traditional learning principle of reinforcement. Both facts and procedures are presumed to get stronger and hence more easily and more reliably retrieved, as a function of repeated practice.

To appreciate Anderson's theory, it is important to note that it models the dynamics of skill transition, and is not simply a list of the different ways in which learning can occur or a categorization of learning tasks. The basic idea is that upon initial exposure to novel material, such as a geometry or computer-programming lesson, the learner first engages in declarative learning, forming traces of the various ideas presented. Then, when given problems to solve later in the lesson, the learner employs very general methods such as analogy, random search, or means-ends analysis, which operate on the declarative traces to achieve solution. Employing these very general methods is cognitively taxing in that it severely strains working memory (to keep track of goals and the relevant traces), and thus initial problem solving is slow and halting. But portions of the process of using these general methods and achieving particular outcomes (some of which actually lead closer to solution) are automatically *compiled* while they are being executed. This is the procedural learning component. The learner essentially remembers the sequence of steps associated with solving a particular problem, or at least parts of the problem. Then when confronted with the problem again at some point in the future, the learner can simply recall that sequence from memory, rather than have to rethink the steps from scratch. With practice on similar problems, the compiled procedure is *strengthened,* which produces more reliable and faster problem solving. With continued practice, the skill ultimately is automatized in that it becomes possible to execute the skill without conscious awareness and without drawing on working memory resources.

Again there may be a correspondence between an individual-difference dimension and a distinction implicit in the model-based taxonomy. Snow and colleagues' novel learning tasks, presumed to tap fluid intelligence, may be likened to the novel learning situations that Anderson studies, which presumably tap very general problem-solving skills. On the other side, Snow and colleagues' familiar learning tasks, which call on crystallized skills, can be characterized in ACT* terms as engaging the declarative learning mechanism or involving the retrieval of already compiled procedures. It is noteworthy that despite rather major differences in methodology inherent in the individual-differences versus model-based approach, there is some convergence in the categories of learning skill. Although Anderson (1983, 1987a) views the emergence of the learning dimension as the result of the transition of skill, rather than perhaps as an array of fundamentally different kinds of learning tasks, there is a basic compatibility between the conclusions of the research approaches.

A second approach to building a model-based taxonomy is based on an integration of the literature from the artificial intelligence subspecialty of machine learning. Investigators have proposed taxonomies of research in machine learning (Carbonell, Michalski, and Mitchell, 1983; Michalski, 1986; Langley, 1986; Self, 1986), and there even exists something of a consensus in the field regarding the categories in the taxonomy.

One dimension of machine-learning research particularly relevant to our concerns here is *learning strategy,* which Michalski (1986) defines as the *type of inference* employed during learning, and which he characterizes as follows:

> In every learning situation, the learner transforms information provided by a teacher (or environment) into some new form in which it is stored for future use. The nature of this transformation determines the type of learning strategy

used. . . . These strategies are ordered by the increasing complexity of the transformation (inference) from the information initially provided to the knowledge ultimately required. Their order thus reflects increasing effort on the part of the student and correspondingly decreasing effort on the part of the teacher (p. 14).

It is interesting that the classification of machine-learning research yields such a nice process classification and thereby seems promising as a realization of Melton's ultimate hopes for a taxonomy of learning. The kinds of inferencing strategies Carbonell and colleagues and Michalski suggest are listed in Table 4-1. (We have added an additional category, "learning by drill and practice," to the list because we use the list as the basis for one of the proposed taxonomy categories, and it is convenient to denote that here.) Note that while there may be some similarity between the categories of Carbonell et al. and Michalski and those proposed by Melton, Gagné, and others, the basic difference is that in the Carbonell-Michalski system the underlying motivation for distinctions is necessarily the existence of differences in cognitive processing requirements. We will return to a more thorough discussion of these categories in the next section.

We believe that Anderson's and Carbonell-Michalski's model-based attempts to propose varieties of learning represent a considerable advance beyond either the rational or correlational taxonomies and go a long way in abating some of the most severe criticisms of earlier taxonomies. Yet all three approaches yield ideas on the varieties of learning skills that might be fruitfully synthesized. The remainder of the chapter will represent our initial attempt to integrate these ideas.

A PROPOSED TAXONOMY OF LEARNING

Thus far we have discussed why a taxonomy of learning is important, and what others have done in the way of proposing taxonomies. We now proceed to propose a taxonomy based on a synthesis of some of the ideas just reviewed, with an eye toward two major objectives. First, the taxonomy should be useful as a learning task–analysis system. That is, it should be useful in answering questions like what are the component skills involved in learning to disassemble a jet engine, operate a camera, program a computer, or make economic forecasts? Second, the taxonomy should serve to focus our research. Specifying the ways people learn may suggest where we ought to be expending more research energy. We do not see this as dictating research directions, as some critics of psychological taxonomies have suggested (Martin, 1986), but as suggesting potentially high-payoff research directions. For example, we already know much about declarative learning, such as what kinds of individual differences to expect and the relation of declarative learning to other cognitive skills. We know considerably less about procedural learning skills. The taxonomy may

Table 4–1 Learning Strategies from a Taxonomy of Machine-Learning Research

Rote learning. Learning by direct memorization of facts without generalization.

Learning from instruction (advice taking; learning by being told). The process of transforming and integrating instructions from an external source (such as a teacher) into an internally usable form.

Learning by deduction

  Knowledge compilation. Translating knowledge from a declarative form that cannot be used directly into an effective procedural form; for example, converting the advice "Don't get wet" into specific instructions that recommend *how* to avoid getting wet in a given situation.

  Caching. Storing the answer to frequently occurring questions (problems) in order to avoid a replication of past efforts.

  Chunking. Grouping lower-level descriptions (patterns, operators, goals) into higher-level descriptions.

  Creating macro-operators (*composition*). An operator composed of a sequence of more primitive operators. Appropriate macro-operators can simplify problem solving by allowing a more "course-grained" problem-solving search.

Learning by drill and practice. Refining or tuning knowledge (or skill) by repeatedly using it in various contexts and allowing it to strengthen and become more reliable through generalization and specialization.

Inductive learning. Learning by drawing inductive inferences (a mode of reasoning that starts out with some assertions, e.g., specific observations, and concludes with more general and plausible assertions, i.e., hypotheses explaining the initial assertions) from facts and observations obtained from a teacher or an environment.

Learning by analogy. Mapping information from a known object or process to less known but similar one.

Learning from examples. Inferring a general concept description from examples and (optionally) counterexamples of that concept.

Learning from observation and discovery (learning without a teacher; unsupervised learning). Constructing descriptions, hypotheses, or theories about a given collection of facts or observations. In this form of learning there is no a priori classification of observations into sets exemplifying desired concepts.

Note: All categories except *"learning by deduction"* are from Carbonell et al. (1983); *"learning by deduction"* is from Michalski (1986). The definitions are taken from the glossary in Michalski et al. (1986). Note that *"learning by drill and practice"* was not a category included by Carbonell et al. (1983) or Michalski (1986), but we included it in the taxonomy, and thus for economy we describe it here.

pinpoint other learning skills on which research attention may productively be focused.

We have selected four dimensions, illustrated in Figure 4-1, as particularly important in classifying learning skills. The two dimensions shown in Figure 4-1a — *knowledge type* and *instructional environment* — are motivated primarily by

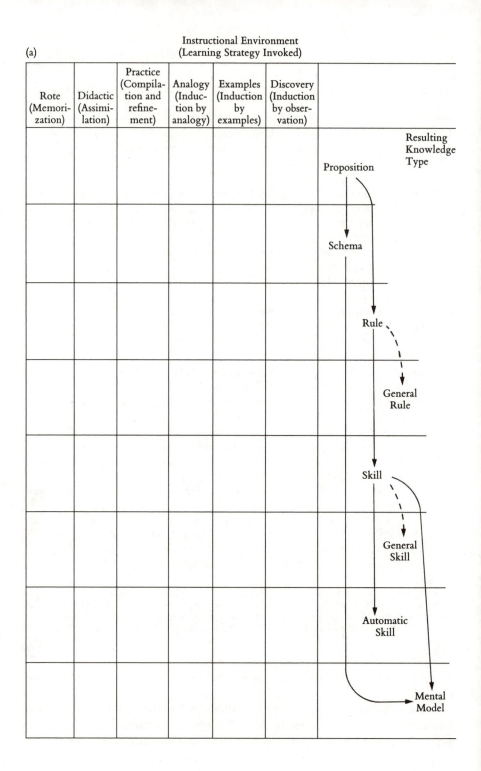

(b)

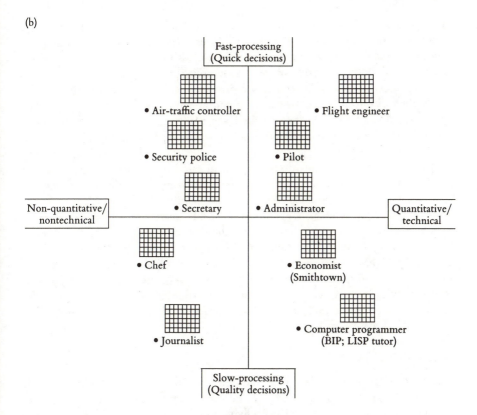

(c)

Holistic processing ⟷ Serial processing

Active/impulsive orientation ⟷ Passive/reflective orientation

Systematic/punctilious approach ⟷ Haphazard/exploratory approach

Theory-driven (top-down) ⟷ Data-driven (bottom-up)

Spatial representation ⟷ Verbal representation

Deep processing ⟷ Superficial processing

Low internal motivation ⟷ High internal motivation

Figure 4-1 Learning skills taxonomy. a. Environment-by-knowledge type matrix: cell entries would be various learning tasks. b. Environment-by-knowledge type matrices plotted in a hypothetical two-dimensional domain-space: proximal matrices should show relatively greater transfer among parallel learning skills. c. Suggested learning styles that might interact with other taxonomy dimensions in determining what learning skill a particular learning task measures.

our discussion of Anderson's and Carbonell-Michalski's systems, respectively, although Gagné's ideas on learned capabilities served to broaden the range of categories included in knowledge type. The crossing of these two dimensions (Figure 4-1a) defines a space of general learning tasks.

The motivation for the other two dimensions, illustrated in Figure 4-1b,c —*domain* and *learning style*—became apparent when we began examining applications of the taxonomy, which we discuss in the next section of the paper. Figure 4-1b illustrates a hypothetical *domain-space* as the crossing of the degree of quantitativeness and the importance of quality versus speed in decision making. The idea is that any domain can be located in such a space, and that the set of learning skills defined by the first two taxonomy dimensions (Figure 4-1a) may prove to be empirically distinct from parallel learning skills in other domains. We represent this idea in Figure 4-1b by scattering knowledge type by instructional environment matrices over the domain space, for various occupational-training domains. The two dimensions portrayed in the domain space are only suggestive, and are meant only to express how domain interacts with the first two taxonomy dimensions. Finally, Figure 4-1c lists a variety of possible learning styles, which, we propose, must be considered in conjunction with the first three taxonomy dimensions in determining what skills are being tapped by a particular learning task.

Knowledge Type

The distinction between declarative and procedural knowledge is fundamental. Further refinements are possible: declarative knowledge can be arrayed by complexity, from propositional knowledge to schemas (packets of related propositions). Similarly, procedural knowledge can be arrayed from simple productions, to skills (packets of productions that go together), to automatic skills (skills executed with minimal cognitive attention). Productions and skills can also be arrayed by generality, from a narrow (specific) to a broad (general) range of applicability. A final knowledge type is the mental model, which requires the concerted exercise of multiple skills applied to elaborate schemata. Knowledge types are dynamically linked: acquisition of a set of propositions may be prerequisite to acquisition of a related schema or to a procedural skill; both in turn may be prerequisite to acquisition of some mental model.

In cognitive science circles, the declarative-procedural distinction is sometimes said to be formally problematic in that declarative knowledge can be mimicked by procedures (Winograd, 1975). One can declaratively know that "Washington was the first president", alternatively, one can have the procedure to respond "Washington" when asked "who was the first president?" We finesse the problem here by keeping close to an operational definition of knowledge type: we define knowledge in terms of how it is tested. Declarative knowledge can be probed with a fact recognition test (sentence recognition, word matching), or, in the case of schemata, with clustering and sorting tasks (Chi, Feltovich, and Glaser, 1981). Procedural knowledge requires a demonstration of the ability to apply the knowledge to predict the output of some operator (operator tracing) or to generate a set of operators to yield some output (operator selection). Possession of skills and automatic procedures may be operationally determined by examining the degree of performance decrement under imposition of secondary tasks (Wickens, Sandry, and Vidulich, 1983) or through other methods of increasing processing demands (Spelke, Hirst, and Neisser, 1976; Schneider and Shiffrin, 1977; Shiffrin and Schneider, 1977). Possession of an appropriate mental model might require testing performance on a complex simulation of some target task. Table 4-2 gives an illustrative (not exhaustive) list of tests for the various knowledge types.

Instructional Environment

Instruction delivered in a classroom setting or even on a computer will inevitably provide the student with opportunities to incorporate the material in multiple ways. Real instruction occurs in a diverse environment from the standpoint of student control versus teacher control and consequently in the kinds of inferences students are required to make. Nevertheless, it is useful to differentiate instructional environments in a local sense: it should be possible to tag a specific instruction segment as to the form in which it is delivered and the kinds of inference processes or learning strategies it is likely to invoke. Following Carbonell et al. and Michalski (Table 4-1) we propose to characterize local instructional environments according to the amount of student control in the learning process. At one end, rote learning (such as, memorizing the multiplication table) involves full teacher control, little student control. Didactic learning (by textbook or lecture), learning by doing through practice and knowledge compilation, learning by analogy, learning from examples, and learning by observation and discovery offer successively more student control and less teacher control.

Note that we modify the Carbonell-Michalski list slightly by combining their learning-by-deduction (compilation) category with a learning-by-refinement category (suggested to us by W. Regian, personal communication, May 4, 1987). What we are pinpointing is the ability to refine one's skill (by strengthening, generalization, and discrimination) based on feedback following performance. Before one is engaged in this kind of learning, we assume the skill has already been acquired (perhaps in a rote fashion) and compiled, and is now at the phase of being refined. But because compilation and refinement are probably hopelessly intertwined in actual learning contexts, we combine them into a single learning-by-doing (practice environment) category.

Table 4-2 Sample Tests for the Various Knowledge Types

Knowledge type	Type of test	Sample item
Proposition	*Sentence verification*	"AND yields High if all inputs are high, Low otherwise — True or False?"
	Stimulus matching	"AND D—Match or Mismatch?"
	Paired associates	"Which symbol is associated with AND?"
	Free recall (components)	"What are the different types of logic gates?"
Schema	*Free recall (structure)*	"Reproduce the circuits you just studied"
	Sorting	"Sort the circuits into categories"
	Classification	"Pair circuit diagrams with these devices"
	Sentence completion/cloze	"AND yields ___ if all ___ are ___"
	Lexical decision	"XAND is a legal logic gate — True or False?"
Rule	*Operator tracing*	Determine output of logic gate (AND, HIGH, LOW) = ?
	Operator selection	Choose an operator to achieve a result (?, HIGH, LOW) = HIGH
General rule	*Transfer of training*	Learn and be tested on other kinds of logical relations such as those introduced in symbolic logic
Skill	*Multiple operator tracing/selection*	Trace through (or select) a series of linked logic gates in a circuit [could also use hierarchical menus methodology]
General skill	*Transfer of training*	Learn and be tested on constructing or verifying logical proofs
Automatic skill	*Dual task*	Trace logic gates while monitoring a secondary signal

Knowledge type	Type of test	Sample item
	Complexity increase	Trace logic gates that become increasingly complex
Mental model	*Process outcome prediction*	Troubleshoot a simulated target task; "walk-through" performance test

Note: Sample items are tests that might be administered to a student finishing a lesson on logic gates as part of a course in electronics troubleshooting (see, for example, Gitomer, 1984).

Domain (Subject Matter)

The inclusion of subject matter as a taxonomy dimension reflects the fact that much of learning has a strong domain-specific character. One can be an expert learner in one domain and a poor learner in another. Certainly there is some generality in learning skills over domains. Glaser, Lesgold, and Lajoie (in press) suggest that metacognitive skills might be fairly general. But even here, there is little evidence that metacognitive skill in mathematics (Schoenfeld, 1985) predicts metacognitive skill in writing (Hayes and Flower, 1980).

It is appropriate to ask the question of the topic range over which some general learning skill is likely to be useful. It may be that the degree to which a subject matter taps quantitative or technical knowledge, and the degree to which it taps verbal knowledge captures some of the transfer relations among academic subjects. The degree of social involvement may also play a role, especially when considering the universe of occupational training courses rather than simply academic training. As is suggested in Figure 4-1b, it may be that the relative importance of speed versus quality in decision making is a critical domain dimension. But again, the dimensions portrayed in Figure 4-1b are only meant to be suggestive.

More generally, we envision a complete *domain-space*. The underlying dimensionality of such a space could be discovered through a study of the similarity (either judged or as shown in transfer of performance relations) among all jobs, courses, or learning experiences in any specifiable universe of interest, and could be represented as a multidimensional scaling of the jobs or courses so rated. An empirically determined domain-space would specify the likelihood that (or the degree to which) a particular taxonomic skill, defined by the environment and the knowledge type, would transfer to or be predictive of a parallel skill (that is, one defined by the same environment and knowledge type) in another domain. Proximal domains, in the multidimensional space, would yield high transfer among parallel skills; distal domains might yield only minimal transfer. For example, assuming the importance of the quantitative dimension, skill in learning mathematics propositions through didactic instruction might predict skill in learning physics propositions through instruction; but neither may be related to the ability to learn history propositions through instruction.

Learning Style

All sorts of subject characteristics — aptitudes, personality traits, background experiences — affect what is learned in an instructional setting. But we focus on characteristics of the learner's preferred mode of processing, or learning style, because our primary concern is characteristics over which the instructional designer may exercise control. Because style implies a choice by subjects as to how to orient themselves toward the learning experience, it should be manipulable through instruction.

A considerable literature on cognitive style exists (Messick, 1986). Among those that have received the most attention are field dependence-independence (Goodenough, 1976) and cognitive complexity (Linville, 1982), but these are now presumed to primarily reflect ability (Cronbach and Snow, 1977; Linn and Kyllonen, 1981). Impulsivity-reflectivity (Baron, Badgio, and Gaskins, 1986; Meichenbaum, 1977) more clearly fits our criteria for inclusion in the taxonomy, in that it is malleable: subjects can be trained to be more reflective in problem solving, and this improves performance. Other styles we consider in our analyses of learning environments are holistic versus serial processing, activity level, systematicity and exploratoriness, theory-driven versus data-driven approaches, spatial versus verbal representation of relations (Perrig and Kintsch, 1984), superficial versus deep processing, and low versus high internal motivation. Some dimensions may affect learning outcomes quantitatively: active students may learn more. Others may affect outcomes qualitatively: spatial versus verbal representations will result in different relationships learned.

Cognitive style may interact with other taxonomy dimensions in determining what learning skill is being tapped in instruction. A study by Pask and Scott (1972) which identified holist versus serialist processing styles illustrates this interaction. In this study, serialists, those who focus on low-order relations and remembering information in lists, were contrasted with holists, who focus on high-order relations and remembering the overall organization among items to be learned. Pask and Scott showed that presenting a learning task (that is, learning an artificial taxonomic structure) in a way that matched the learner's style resulted in better overall learning. A critical point for this discussion is that the presentation of material should tap different skills for subjects who differ on this style dimension. Presenting a long list of principles may be a difficult memory task for serialists, who attempt to memorize each relationship presented. For holists, the same task may tap conceptual reorganization skill rather than memorization skill.

Summary

The first three dimensions of the taxonomy define a space of learning tasks (Figure 4-1a set in the domain-space of Figure 4-1b). Each cell represents a task that teaches a particular subject matter (such as physics principles: Newton's second law), by a particular means (for example, by analogy), resulting in a particular kind of knowledge outcome (for example, a schema). A particular taxonomic learning skill then may be defined by performance on a particular taxonomic learning task. There will be interactions among dimensions: some subject matters lend themselves more readily to certain kinds of knowledge outcomes. For example, propositions are emphasized in nonquantitative fields; procedures are the focus in quantitative fields. And knowledge outcomes covary with instructional method: we more commonly learn propositions than procedures by rote.

As an illustration of some of these ideas, consider the instructional goal of teaching the concept of *electric field* (Glynn et al., in press). A *rote* approach might be to have students simply memorize the definition: "an electric field is a kind of aura that extends through space." A *didactic* approach might specify that students read the definition embedded in the context of a larger lesson, then to have the student demonstrate understanding by having him or her paraphrase the definition. The difference between the two approaches could be reflected in the way in which the knowledge was tested. The appropriate rote test would be verbatim recognition or recall; the appropriate instruction test would be paraphrased recognition or recall.

The electric field concept could be taught by having students *practice* using it: following a discussion of properties of force such as how an electrical force holds an electron in orbit around a proton, students would be given an opportunity to solve problems that made use of the concept. One could also lead students to *induce* the concept, by pointing out how it is *analogous* to a gravitational field, by providing them with *examples* and counterexamples, or by having them *discover* it with a simulator, or in a laboratory.

Unlike the first three dimensions, the fourth dimension—learning style—refers to characteristics of the person rather than the environment. Inclusion of the learning style dimension is an admission that providing a particular kind of environment guarantees neither the kind of learning experience that will result nor the kind of learning skill being tapped. Interactions exist between person characteristic and instructional treatment (Cronbach and Snow, 1977, especially Chapter 11), and thus, as we tried to illustrate in the example on holist versus serialist processing, the style engaged at the time of learning and testing will partly determine what learning skill is being measured.

APPLYING THE TAXONOMY: THREE CASE STUDIES

In this section of the chapter we want to consider how the learning taxonomy might facilitate the development of indicators of learning skill in actual practice. We consider this a kind of test run for the taxonomy. Having proposed a taxonomy, we will now demonstrate how it might be applied. We discuss three computerized instructional programs, each of which includes some capability for determining what and how students are learning. We suggest ways in which additional learning indicators might be generated in light of our taxonomy.

We see the taxonomy playing two roles here. One, although not the focus of the chapter, is to help us classify instructional programs. By our taxonomy, similar programs are ones that teach the same type of knowledge (propositions, skills, and so on), provide the same instructional environment (rote, discovery), teach the same domain material such as computer programming, economics), and encourage the same kind (style) of learner interaction (reflectivity, holistic processing, and so on). Programs are dissimilar to the degree that they mismatch on these dimensions. An important part of our discussion of the three tutoring systems then is to indicate at least informally what learning skills are being exercised, and to what degree.

The second and, for current purposes, more important role for the taxonomy is to assist us in thinking more broadly about learning skills and outcomes. The taxonomy with its specified methods and tests can pinpoint what potentially important learning events are simply not being measured by existing instructional programs. We can imagine generating alternative instructional programs by varying the degree to which different kinds of learning skills are exercised.

The three programs we discuss in this section are intelligent tutoring systems, and so we begin by providing a few preliminary remarks on their general organization.

General Comments on Intelligent Tutoring Systems

Figure 4-2 illustrates the components of a hypothetical and somewhat generic intelligent tutoring system. In this system, the student learns by solving problems, and a key system task is to generate or select problems that will serve as good learning experiences.

The system begins by considering what the student already knows—the *student model*—what the student needs to know—the *curriculum*—and what curriculum element (lesson or skill) ought to be instructed next—the *teaching strategy*. From these considerations the system selects (or generates) a problem, then either works out a solution to the problem (with its *domain expert*), or simply retrieves a prepared solution. The program then compares its solution to

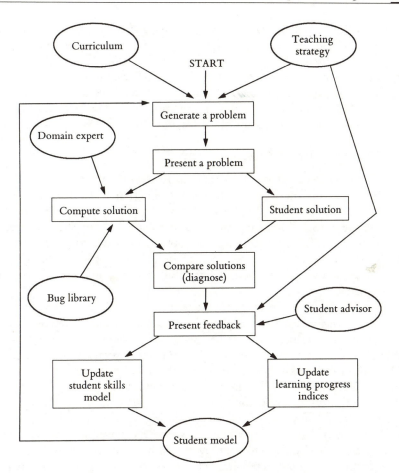

Figure 4-2 Components of a generic intelligent tutoring system. (Boxes represent decisions the program makes; ellipses represent knowledge bases the program consults.)

one the student has prepared and performs a diagnosis based on the differences between the solutions.

The program provides feedback based on student-advisor considerations such as how long it has been since feedback was last provided, whether the student was already given a particular bit of advice, and so forth. After this, the program updates both the student skills model (a record of what the student knows and does not know) and increments learning progress index counters. These updating activities modify the student model, and the entire cycle is repeated, starting with selecting or generating a new problem.

Not all ITSs include all these components, and the problem-test-feedback cycle does not adequately characterize all systems. But this system fairly describes many existing ITSs and perhaps most interactions with human tutors. Thus an examination of the components of the generic tutor should yield some ideas on how learning progress and the current status of the learner may be indicated. Note that much of this information is contained in the dynamic student model. We now discuss three instantiations of this generic tutor.

BIP: Tutoring Basic Programming

General System Description   The Basic Instruction Program (BIP) was one of the first operational intelligent tutoring systems (Barr, Beard, and Atkinson, 1976; Wescourt et al. 1977).[2] BIP teaches students how to write programs in the language BASIC by having the student solve problems that get progressively more difficult. The system selects problems according to what the student already knows (based on past performance), which skills it believes ought to be taught next, and its understanding of the skills required by the problems in its problem bank.

The BIP architecture is consistent with the generic tutor. Its *Curriculum Information Network* represents all the skills to be taught and the relations among them. Skills are represented quite narrowly, for example, "initialize a counter variable" or "print a literal string." The relations specify whether skills are analogous to other skills, whether they are easier or harder or at the same difficulty level as other skills, and whether there are any prerequisite skills. As examples, (a) printing a numeric literal (or constant) is considered conceptually analogous to, (b) but also easier than, printing a string literal; (c) both are considered easier than printing a numeric variable; (d) printing a numeric literal is considered a prerequisite to printing the sum of two numbers.

A programming *task* is represented in terms of its component skill requirements. For example, a BIP task might ask the student to compute and print out the number of gifts sent on the twelfth day of Christmas, given that on the first day 1 gift was sent, on the second day 1 + 2 gifts were sent, on the third day, 1 + 2 + 3 were sent, and so on. The student is expected to write a program that computes the sum of $1 + 2 + \ldots + 12$. Based on a task analysis conducted by BIP's authors, BIP knows that the component skills required for solving this particular problem are *initialize numeric variable, use for-next loop with literal as final value,* and so forth. Each task is assumed to tap a number of skills.

The BIP student model is a list of the student's status with respect to each of ninety-three skills in the curriculum. There are five discrete status levels: *unseen* (not yet seen a problem that required the skill), *trouble* (seen but has not

---

[2]Barr et al. developed BIP-I; Wescourt et al. developed its successor BIP-II. The two systems are fairly similar, but we assume the newer system where there are discrepancies.

solved a problem that required the skill), *marginal* (learned to a marginal degree), *easy* (not yet seen but an easy skill to learn), and *learned* (to a sufficient degree). After each problem, skill status is updated as a result of the student's self-evaluation and through two domain-expert–like components to BIP: a BASIC interpreter that catches syntax errors, and a solution evaluator that determines whether the program is producing correct output. Finally, BIP also provides a number of aids to the student. The student may request help (suggestions as to how to solve the problem), a model solution (such as, a flowchart), or a series of partial hints.

BIP selects problems by first identifying skills the student is ready for (ones that do not have any unlearned prerequisites) but that need work, which means (in order of priority) (a) skills students have had trouble with (from tasks they have quit), (b) skills analogous to learned skills, or (c) skills postrequisite to learned skills. It calls skills so identified *needed* skills. BIP then identifies a *task* with needed skills but no unlearned prerequisites.

If the student successfully solves the selected task, BIP updates the student model by crediting the associated task skills. If the student fails the problem or gives up (that is, requests a new task), BIP determines which skills to blame according to criteria such as the student's self-evaluation, whether the student already learned some of the skills or analogous ones, and whether any task skills or analogous ones are in an unlearned state.

There are a number of ways in which aptitude information guides problem selection. For the fast learner, if two skills are linked by difficulty (one is harder than the other), the system assumes that the easier one is not a needed skill; BIP also will select tasks with multiple needed skills. If the student is consistently having trouble, BIP opts for a slow moving approach and minimizes the number of needed skills introduced in a single task.

Learning Indicators   Snow, Wescourt, and Collins (1986) collected aptitude and other personal data from twenty-nine subjects who had used BIP and performed a number of analyses on the relationships between those data and BIP variables. Table 4-3 shows the list of learning indicators used by Snow et al. We have divided the list into three categories: learning summary indices, learning activity variables, and time allocation variables.

The sample was too small to draw definitive conclusions about relationships, but there were some suggestive findings worthy of further pursuit. First, the *best* learning progress index seemed to be the slope of the number of skills acquired over the number of skills possible — that is, skills slope. Determination of best is based on two considerations: skills slope was most representative of other learning progress indices in that it had higher average intercorrelations with those indices (centrality), and it had higher average correlations with the learning activity variables (a validity of sorts). Particularly intriguing was that skills slope, along with a global achievement posttest, was more highly related

Table 4-3 Learning Indicators from BIP, the Programming Tutor

Learning summary indices
1. Number of problems seen
2. Mean time per problem
3. Number of skills acquired
4. Skills acquired per problem (slope, intercept, standard error)
5. Skills acquired per time on task (slope, intercept, standard error)
6. Skills acquired per skills possible (slope, intercept, standard error)

Learning activity variables
(counts of activities, to be divided by number of problems seen)
1. Student produces correct solution
2. Student has difficulty on the task (according to BIP)
3. Student admits not understanding the task
4. Student disagrees with solution evaluator
5. Student requests solution model
6. Student requests solution flow chart
7. Student requests model program
8. Student starts problem over
9. Student requests at least 1 hint before starting
10. Student requests at least 1 but not all hints
11. Student requests all hints (0-5 on a problem)
12. Student quits the problem
13. Student quits the problem after seeing all the hints
14. Student quits the problem without seeing any hints
15. Student tests different input cases after successful solution
16. Student tests different input cases after failed solution
17. Student uses BIP input data after failed solution
18. Student runs program parts rather than complete program
19. Student requests aid (model, help, hint) after an error

Time allocation variables*
21. Planning: Proportion of time spent before coding
22. Implementing: Proportion of time spent writing code
23. Debugging: Proportion of time spent debugging code

*Time on the tutor must fall into one and only one of the three time allocation portions.

to the activity variables than was the raw number of skills acquired. Snow and colleagues suggested this may have been due to skills slope capturing more about the progress of learning over time.

The second major finding concerned the role of the activity variables in predicting learning outcome. As it turned out, most of the tool-use indicators, such as requests for demonstrations, hints, and model solutions, were associated with poor posttest performance. Poor performers also spent more time debugging and less time planning than did others, and were more likely to quit the task or start over. In contrast, good performers requested fewer hints, spent more time implementing rather than debugging, and were more likely to test different cases after a successful run of their program (indicator 15). This may have reflected good students' desire to perform additional tests of their knowledge, perhaps to probe the boundaries of their understanding, even after passing the test.

Applying the Taxonomy In evaluating the BIP tutor with respect to the taxonomy, we ask two questions: (a) what learning skills does BIP exercise (that is, how can BIP be classified), and (b) how comprehensive are the indicators used by Wescourt et al. and Snow et al. in measuring students' learning skills and their learning progress?

To address the first question, consider a distinction between what is tested for and what is taught. BIP primarily tests for fairly specific skills in that virtually all its tests are of the multiple operator selection variety, meaning that students write programs. The posttest also undoubtedly taps some propositional schematic knowledge, but not extensively. Other knowledge outcomes could be tested for but they are not. BIP teaches skills by having students first read a text (*learning from instruction,* in taxonomy terminology), then apply the studied skills in a problem-solving context (*learning through compilation and learning by drill and practice*). Some students also request help and thereby engage in *learning from examples.* The good students also tend to invoke *observational learning* when they perform additional tests of their programs.

Figure 4-3a summarizes our assessment of (a) what skills are being exercised by BIP, indicated as the solid bar, and (b) what skills are being tested for, indicated as the striped bar. Bar size represents the proportion of time spent either engaging the learning skill (solid) or having the ability tested (striped), relative to engaging or testing other skills. It is important to keep in mind that this analysis is rather informal. We made some rough computations of the times engaged in the various activities, based on a review of the data on the learning indicators of Snow et al., and on the report of Wescourt et al. of some other summary statistics. Our analysis is meant to be merely suggestive. A more rigorous, systematic analysis of BIP could produce a precise breakdown, separately for each student, of the time spent exercising and testing various learning skills. Also note that Figure 4-3 indicates only the knowledge type and instructional environment dimensions. Domain is indicated in Figure 4-1b (computer programming is highly quantitative and technical, and the quality of decisions is emphasized). Learning style is not directly assessed in BIP.

An approach to the second question, concerning indicator comprehensiveness, is suggested by Figure 4-3a: which skills are being exercised and not tested? First, we can see that although students are learning rules, they are not tested for them. This could be remedied by including operator tracing or

Instructional Environment (Learning Strategy Invoked)

(a) BIP

Rote	Didactic	Practice	Analogy	Examples	Discovery	

Resulting Knowledge Type

Proposition

Schema

Rule

General Rule

Skill

General Skill

Automatic Skill

Mental Model

(b) the LISP tutor

Rote	Didactic	Practice	Analogy	Examples	Discovery	

Resulting Knowledge Type

Proposition

Schema

Rule

General Rule

Skill

General Skill

Automatic Skill

Mental Model

(c) Smithtown

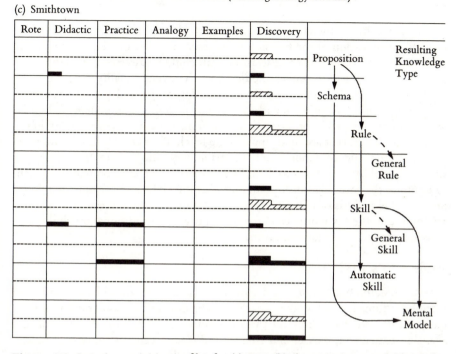

Figure 4-3 Learning activities profiles for (a) BIP, (b) the LISP tutor, and (c) Smithtown; solid bars represent the proportion of time the particular skill (defined by the environment-by-knowledge type cell task) is *exercised* by the tutor, relative to other skills; striped bars represent the proportion of time the skill is *tested*, relative to other skills.

selection tests. Second, students also are probably acquiring some general rules and skills regarding program-writing strategies, but BIP does not directly test for these. Transfer of training tests inserted into the program (as part of the curriculum) would help determine the generality of the skills learned in BIP. Third, students read text, and get tested on their knowledge during the posttest, but it would be possible to more directly test the propositional and schematic knowledge resulting from reading the text by administering sentence verification tests, sorting tasks, and the like (see Table 4-2). Finally, the task of writing programs is an operator selection task and thus is more difficult than a task that would require students merely to understand the workings of a program (an operator tracing task). Students may understand a program they are unable to write. The inclusion of a program understanding task would tap knowledge that would be missed otherwise and thus should enhance the accuracy of the student model.

In sum, BIP generates many indicators of student status and learning progress. Application of the taxonomy suggests a number of additional ways in which students' knowledge and learning skill could be assessed. Expanding the breadth of learning-skill probes should affect the overall quality of any intelligent tutoring system both in its role as a training device and as a research tool. The performance of an ITS with a student-modeling component is highly dependent on the quality of the student model insofar as the system's main job is to select problems that are of an appropriate level. Thus an ITS should improve with a better student model, and we made suggestions here for refining a student model. As a research tool, an ITS can serve as an environment in which to examine the interrelationships among learning skills and learning activities. Snow et al.'s analysis of BIP relied on a rich set of learning indicators. However we think that the taxonomy can be used to provide an additional psychological basis for expressing those indicators.

Anderson's LISP Tutor

General System Description   Anderson and his research group have developed intelligent tutoring systems for geometry, algebra, and the programming language LISP. We focus here on the LISP tutor. Descriptions of the tutor are available (Anderson, Boyle, and Reiser, 1985), and thus we only summarize some of the main features of the system especially as they contrast with BIP.

The LISP tutor follows the generic architecture fairly closely. Students read some material in a textbook, but then go on to spend most of their time interacting with the program. The program selects problems, gives the student help or advice when asked, and interrupts if the student is floundering.

An innovation of the LISP tutor is its use of what Reiser, Anderson, and Farrell (1985) call the *model-tracing* methodology, the process by which the tutor understands what the student is trying to do while the student attempts to solve a problem. Whenever the student types in an expression (as part of a solution attempt) the tutor evaluates the expression as to whether it is the same as what the ideal student would type in, or whether it indicates a misconception (or *bug*). If a misconception is indicated, the tutor intervenes with advice.

For a tutor to analyze the student's response so microscopically, it has to know essentially every correct step and every plausible wrong step in every problem. The LISP tutor does not incorporate enough domain knowledge to be able to interpret *every* action a student might take, but it does have enough knowledge to be able to interpret all correct solutions and approximately 45 to 80 percent of students' errors (Reiser et al., 1985). (In cases where the tutor cannot interpret a student's behavior it typically probes the student with a multiple choice question.) When the LISP tutor poses a problem, it goes about trying to solve the problem itself, simultaneously with the student. It solves the posed problem with its own production system, which consists of approximately 400 production rules for correctly writing programs (Anderson, 1987b). It also solves the problem in various plausible incorrect ways, through the action of about 600 incorrect ("buggy") production rules. Determining what the student is doing is a matter of comparing student input with its internal production system results.

Learning Indicators   The LISP tutor keeps a record of the student's status with respect to each skill being taught, where skills are the 400 correct production rules. An indicator of how well the student knows a rule is incremented when the student uses the rule correctly, and decremented when the student makes an error. Remedial problems may be selected to give a student experience in using a troublesome rule.

Unfortunately, studies have not been done on the relationships among learning indicators and outcomes. Most of the evaluation studies have simply compared LISP-tutored students with classroom or human-tutored students on a standard achievement test administered at the end of the course. However, one study did investigate individual differences in acquisition and retention of individual productions over a series of ten lesson sessions (reported by Anderson, in press). In this analysis, each production was scored for the number of times it was used incorrectly in problem solving, separately for each session. A series of factor analyses were performed on these data to determine whether production factors would emerge. For example, it could be that productions associated with one *kind* of learning (such as learning to trace functions or planning) would form a factor separate from some other *kind* of learning (such as learning to select functions or coding). Or lesson-specific factors could have emerged. In fact, Anderson found evidence for two broad factors: an *acquisition factor* captured individual differences in speed of production acquisition and a *retention factor* captured individual differences in the likelihood that acquired productions were retained in a later session.

Applying the Taxonomy   Consider first how we might classify the LISP tutor. Students spend most of their time learning specific production rules and skills and are continually tested for their ability to apply them in writing LISP functions. Every student action can be viewed as a test response because the system is interpreting that response as an indication of whether the student knows a particular production rule. Thus, learning and testing activities in the LISP tutor are almost completely integrated.

Although students are learning *skills*, insofar as writing functions is a multiple operator selection task, the LISP tutor is testing for students' knowledge of the *rules* underlying those skills. But this merely reflects the fact that skills in the LISP tutor are defined precisely in terms of their constituent rules. Interestingly, the fact that the LISP tutor can represent students' skill without directly evaluating that skill (in other words, the system never evaluates whether the function works, per se) is evidence against the taxonomy's supposition of skill as a separate knowledge type. However, this presumes a rule-level understanding of skill. In domains for which such a detailed understanding is not yet available (most domains imaginable at this time), skill probably ought to be considered a functionally distinct category even if only for pragmatic reasons.

The instructional environment is one in which students learn initially through brief instruction (a pamphlet or a textbook), but then go on to compile and refine that knowledge by engaging in extended problem solving. Figure 4-3b summarizes our assessment of what learning skills are being exercised and tested in the LISP tutor.

Note that in addition to indicating that students are learning declarative knowledge by instruction, and procedural knowledge by compiling and practicing it, we have indicated other learning products and sources. The other products are the general rules and skills probably being taught by the LISP tutor, even though that is not a goal for the tutor. The other sources have to do with the LISP tutor's capability of delivering context-sensitive tutorial advice, and through its coaching capabilities can readily change the nature of the instructional environment. On one occasion it might correct a student's attempt through direct instruction, but then it might later suggest an analogy to a student, or provide examples of a concept.

Now consider the testing comprehensiveness issue. As can be seen in Figure 4-3b, we consider all of the LISP tutor's testing to be for rule knowledge either in the compilation or the drill and practice environments. (We could also consider automatic skills to be tested, but that would require a rather detailed analysis of the LISP tutor's entire production collection of how big, compiled productions subsume their smaller precursors.) Note that first, as with BIP, students' success at propositional learning and their ability to acquire general rules and skills is not tested. This situation could be remedied with the insertion of sentence verification and transfer-of-training tests. But a more intriguing suggestion from the standpoint of research arises from the LISP tutor's multifaceted coaching capability, which offers various kinds of tutorial remediation, to greatly expand the range of learning events that may be investigated. For example, it would be possible (and interesting) to keep track of production strength modification separately for each of the various instructional environments. That is, one could trace the growth in rule indicators over time as a function of whether those rules were taught (or remediated) with instructional advice, analogies, examples, and so on. One could ask, for example, whether instruction using analogies results in greater subsequent ability to use the rule(s) so instructed.

In summary, because of the way in which it models students' knowledge as production rules, and carefully controls the learning environment, the LISP tutor is ideally suited for measuring learning skills such as the rate at which productions are composed, or the probability of compiling a sequence of productions as a function of exposure to that sequence. Augmented with the additional tests and performance records suggested by the application of the taxonomy, the LISP tutor could serve as an excellent research tool for investigating the time course of learning and individual differences therein.

Smithtown: Discovery World for Economic Principles

General System Description   Unlike the other two systems, Smithtown's main goal is to enhance students' general problem-solving and inductive-learning skills. It does this in the substantive context of microeconomics in teaching the laws of supply and demand (Shute and Glaser, in press). Smithtown is highly interactive. Students pose questions and conduct experiments within the computer environment, testing and enriching their knowledge of functional relationships by manipulating various economic factors.

As a discovery environment, Smithtown is quite different from BIP and the LISP tutor in that there is no fixed curriculum. The student — not the system — generates problems and hypotheses. After generating a hypothesis such as "Does increasing the price of coffee affect the supply or demand of tea?" the student tests it by executing a series of actions, such as changing the values of two variables and observing the bivariate plot. This series of actions, or *behaviors,* for creating, executing, and following up a given experiment, define a *student solution.*

Despite having no curriculum, Smithtown does have the instructional goal of teaching general problem-solving rules and skills (called *good critics*) such as "collect baseline data before altering a variable" or "generalize a concept across two unrelated goods." Instead of a curriculum guiding instructional decisions, Smithtown relies on a process of constantly monitoring student actions, looking for evidence of good and poor behavior, then coaching students to become more effective problem solvers. The system keeps a detailed history list of all student actions, grouping them into (that is, interpreting them as) behaviors and solutions. Smithtown diagnoses solution quality in two ways. It looks for overt errors by comparing student solutions with its *buggy critics,* which are sets of actions (or nonactions) that constitute nonoptimal behaviors (for example, "fail to record relevant data in the online notebook"). It also compares student solutions with its own *good critics* (expert solutions). Discrepancies between the two are collected into a list of potential problem areas and passed on to the coach for possible remediation. To illustrate, if the student had failed to enter data into the online notebook for several time frames and had made some changes to variables, the system would recognize this as a deficient pattern and prompt the student to start using the notebook more consistently.

Smithtown's *student model* is based on two statistics: (a) the number of times the student demonstrates a buggy critic (errors of commission), and (b) the ratio of the number of times the student uses a good critic over the number of times it was applicable (errors of omission). Coaching is based on the heuristic of first advising about buggy behaviors, then advising on any blatant errors of omission. Advice is always given in the context of a particular experiment, so, like the LISP tutor, it is context sensitive. For example, the coach might say, "You haven't graphed any data yet and I think you should try it out. This is often a good way of viewing data. It lets you plot variables together and some surprising relationships may become apparent." However, the coach is fairly unobtrusive: after advice is given, there is no further coaching for some time.

Smithtown also knows about variable relationships that constitute economics principles, such as "Price is inversely related to quantity demanded." If a student uses the system's hypothesis menu and states this relationship (for example, "As price increases, quantity demanded decreases"), the student is congratulated and told the name of the law just discovered ("Congratulations! You have just discovered what economists refer to as the *Law of Demand*").

Learning Indicators   Shute, Glaser, and Raghavan (Chapter 8 of this volume) conducted an extensive evaluation of differences among students in what they learned and how they interacted with Smithtown. Two data sources were used: a list of all student actions and a set of verbal protocols in which students justified their actions and predicted outcomes of the actions.

Table 4-4 shows a set of twenty-nine learning indicators constructed for analyzing individuals' performance. Indicators are clustered into three general behavior categories: (a) *activity exploratory level* (indicators relating to activity level and exploratory behaviors), (b) *data management level* (indicators for data recording, efficient tool use, and use of evidence), and (c) *thinking and planning level* (indicators for consistent behaviors, effective generalization, and effective experimental behaviors).

Shute et al.'s sample ($N = 10$) was too small to analyze formally, but the indicators were examined to determine which ones discriminated successful from unsuccessful learners. Two subjects, one who performed poorly on the pretest but well on the posttest (a successful learner) and one who who did poorly on both tests (an unsuccessful learner) were selected for more careful scrutiny.

The two subjects differed mostly on indicators of thinking and planning skills, in other words, effective experimental behaviors. In particular, the better subject collected and organized data from a more theory-driven perspective, which contrasted with a more superficial and less theory-driven approach used by the poorer subject. The better subject generalized concepts across multiple markets (which the poorer subject did not do), engaged in more investigations

Table 4-4 Learning Indicators from Smithtown, the Economics Tutor

Activity and exploratory level skills

I. Activity level
1. Total number of actions
2. Total number of experiments
3. Number of changes to the price of the goods

II. Exploratory behaviors (counts; i.e., number of . . .)
4. Markets investigated
5. Independent variables changed
6. Computer-adjusted prices
7. Times market sales information was viewed
8. Baseline data observations of market in equilibrium

Data-management level skills

III. Data recording
9. Total number of notebook entries
10. Number of baseline data entries of market in equilibrium
11. Entry of changed independent variables

IV. Efficient tool usage (ratios of number of effective uses over number of uses)
12. Number of relevant notebook entries ÷ total number of notebook entries
13. Number of correct uses of table package ÷ number of times table used
14. Number of correct uses of graph package ÷ number of times graph used

V. Use of evidence
15. Number of specific predictions ÷ number of general hypotheses
16. Number of correct hypotheses ÷ number of hypotheses

Thinking and planning level skills

VI. Consistent behaviors (counts; i.e., number of . . .)
17. Notebook entries of planning menu items
18. Notebook entries of planning menu items ÷ planning opportunities
19. Number of times variables were changed that had been specified beforehand in the planning menu

VII. Effective generalization (event counts; i.e., number of times . . .)
20. An experiment was replicated
21. A concept was generalized across unrelated goods
22. A concept was generalized across related goods
23. The student had sufficient data for a generalization

VIII. Effective experimental behaviors (event counts; i.e., number of times . . .)
24. A change to an independent variable was sufficiently large
25. One of the experimental frames was selected
26. The prediction menu was used to specify an event outcome
27. A variable was changed (per experiment)
28. An action was taken (per experiment)
29. An economic concept was learned (per session)

poorer subject. The better subject also made large changes to variables so that any repercussions could be detected. This contrasted with typically small changes made by the poorer subject, who justified these choices by claiming they were more "realistic." Replicating experiments to test the validity of results is an important scientific behavior and similar to BIP's indicator 15. The better subject conscientiously replicated experiments whereas the poorer subject did not. One other indicator, data management skills, distinguished the two subjects. The better subject recorded more notebook entries, and the ones that were recorded consistently included relevant variables from the planning menu. The poorer subject used the notebook sporadically and often failed to record important information.

Applying the Taxonomy   Again, we first consider the classification of Smithtown. *Knowledge types* taught are primarily general skills (that is, effective inquiry strategies for a new domain), domain-specific skills pertaining to economics knowledge, and domain-specific mental models of the functional relationships among microeconomic factors. Students also are presumed to acquire some declarative knowledge and rules about economics while interacting with the environment. The *instructional environment* is a discovery microworld, and thus most of the learning that occurs results from students inducing knowledge and skills through observation and discovery, then perhaps compiling those skills by practicing them in the conduct of experiments. There is tutorial assistance if a student is judged to be floundering in discovery mode, however; we indicate this in Figure 4-3c as learning propositions and skills by direct instruction. Figure 4-3c shows that in overall emphasis, Smithtown is quite distinct in both goals and approach from BIP and the LISP tutor.

Regarding the issue of testing comprehensiveness in Smithtown, we consider two kinds of tests: (a) the on-line indicators used by the system in diagnosis, and (b) the separate posttest that measured economics knowledge gained during the tutorial. For the purpose of filling out Figure 4-3c, we considered half the total testing to be on-line and the other half to be the posttest; the striped bars are marked as to the testing source. Figure 4-3c shows that as in the LISP tutor, the on-line indicators primarily reflect rule and skill knowledge, but in Smithtown the testing context is the discovery environment. Another key difference is that the rule and skill knowledge is not related to the economics domain, but rather to the subject's ability to manipulate the environment and use its tools to test hypotheses. The posttest did tap domain knowledge. One part of the posttest battery was a multiple choice test that measured declarative knowledge. A second part was a scenarios test that had subjects reason through various economics scenarios. The scenarios test illustrates a means for assessing mental models: it was designed to get at students' ability to run mental simulations of complex economics scenarios (see Shute and Glaser, in press, for a detailed discussion of the test).

Figure 4-3c suggests that perhaps the greatest mismatch between learning skills that were exercised and those that were tested occurs in the general rule and skill cells. A shortcoming of the Smithtown evaluation is that one of its stated primary goals is to help students become more effective in conducting experiments in a microworld environment, acquiring general skills as a result of their investigations. But this instructional goal was measured only indirectly on the posttest, which relied on declarative tests of economics knowledge. A more direct assessment of the degree to which the stated goals could be reached would require a transfer of skills in a system structured similarly to Smithtown but containing different domain knowledge. (Interestingly, there is such a system, but the transfer experiment has not yet been conducted.) Truly general inquiry skills developed in Smithtown would presumably transfer to the new environment.

Another smaller mismatch is that declarative knowledge of basic economic principles was tested at posttest, but not while students were interacting with the tutor. It seems reasonable from both a research standpoint and the standpoint of enhancing the student model to integrate declarative knowledge tests with tutoring.

A major factor missing here and throughout our discussion of the three tutors is the style dimension. Inspection of Table 4-4 shows that the set of indicators Smithtown collects and monitors are really not direct indicators of learning skill per se, but rather are style indicators in the sense that they reveal how an individual organizes his or her learning environment. From this perspective, key questions addressed in the Shute et al. analysis had to do with style interrelationships (the question of dimensionality of style) and the relationship between style and learning outcome (the question of validity). In one sense, this is exactly the study needed to understand learning skills in the most natural, ecologically valid context. It is also a preliminary question to one of the goals we are pushing for here: to be able to assess basic learning skills, controlling for learning style. Smithtown may be best suited for analysis of the style issue. But before style variables are better understood, more structured environments such as BIP and the LISP tutor, which by forcibly directing learning activities designate a less important role for individual variability in learning style, may be more conducive to research on basic learning skills.

LEARNING INDICATORS FOR VALIDATION STUDIES

To this point, we have discussed how the taxonomy might be applied so as to enable a more thorough evaluation of student learning skills and outcomes. The applications discussed above might have the flavor of suggestions for improving the tutors. That is not the intention. We see the main function of the taxonomy as primarily a research one. By more thoroughly examining what students learn in instruction, it should be possible to conduct more refined studies on individual differences in learning. Snow et al. generated and analyzed a set of learning indicators, Anderson did a similar analysis, and a similar analysis is underway for Smithtown. Our claim is that the taxonomy should suggest additional ways in which to record learning skills, and this should result in a psychologically rich and principled set of additional learning indicators. Each cell in the full four-dimensional taxonomy defines a proposed learning skill. An important next question, open to empirical investigation, concerns the true reduced-space dimensionality of learning skills. From an individual differences perspective, how many learning *abilities* must we posit, and at what level of detail, to characterize *skill* differences among learners over all taxonomy cell tasks?

There is also a second, related application. The taxonomy should help us develop learning indicators for instructional programs that can serve as criteria against which other individual difference measures, such as aptitude and basic abilities tests, might be validated. That is, our taxonomy-derived indicators can serve as supplements or even replacements for the conventional criteria of post-course achievement tests, course grade point average, on-the-job performance tests, and supervisor or teacher ratings in the conduct of construct validation studies. Indeed, it was this goal of creating more extensive criteria against which new aptitude tests might be validated that led us into the taxonomy project in the first place.

Learning Abilities Measurement Program (LAMP)

Over the past several years, the Air Force has supported a basic program of research designed to explore the possibility of using contemporary cognitive theory as the basis for a new system of ability measurement (Kyllonen, 1986; Kyllonen and Christal, in press). Currently, the Air Force, as well as the other services, selects and assigns applicants at least partly on the basis of their performance on a conventional aptitude battery, which includes tests of reading comprehension, arithmetic reasoning, numerical operations, and so forth. The goal of the Learning Abilities Measurement Program (LAMP) is to provide the research base that might lead to supplementing or even replacing those conventional tests with new measures more closely aligned with an information-processing perspective.

What might these new tests be? The project has thus far investigated measures of working-memory capacity, information-processing speed, breadth and depth of declarative knowledge, availability of strategic knowledge, and other such abilities. It would go beyond the scope of this chapter to review the project's research (see Kyllonen, 1986; Kyllonen and Christal, in press, for current reviews), but the prototypical study investigates the relationship between various kinds of cognitive measures (such as working-memory capacity) and learning-outcome measures (list recall) under various instructional conditions (such as variations in study time).

A major focus of the research is examining the relationships between ability measures and learning outcomes. But the range of learning outcomes investigated thus far, not only on our project but on others as well, has been quite limited in two ways. First, the range of learning skills examined has been rather narrow: this is especially apparent given the breadth of potential learning skills suggested by the taxonomy. But second, and perhaps even more important, learning tasks employed have not been truly representative of real-world learning activities. Tasks tend to be short-term laboratory tasks, which afford more control, but also leave bigger validity gaps with the kind of operational learning to which we eventually wish to generalize. This inhibits the transition of research to application, insofar as generalization from narrow laboratory tasks to real-world learning tasks is tenuous. And as Greeno (1980) has argued, use of ecologically valid learning tasks is defensible from the standpoint of leading to better basic research as well.

Thus, for both applied and theoretical reasons, a decision was made recently to expand the range of learning criteria employed. A recently completed laboratory at Lackland Air Force Base accommodates thirty work stations capable of administering intelligent computerized instruction like that reviewed previously. Intelligent tutoring systems in the domains of computer programming, electronic troubleshooting, and flight engineering have been developed or are currently underway. Over the next several years we will investigate learning on these tutors and conduct studies that examine the relationship between basic cognitive abilities and various learning skills and outcomes. We expect the taxonomy as described here to assist us in developing learning indicators for the tutorial environments.

Applying the Taxonomy: A Practical Guide

Thus, we are employing a two-pronged approach in generating learning skill indicators for LAMP validation studies. We design instructional programs capable of producing rich traces of learner activities, then we intend to analyze and categorize those activities so as produce psychologically meaningful learning indicators. Tables 4-5 and 4-6 present the general outline for our approach. Note that we have written the design and analysis steps in such a way as to be broadly useful. Although our application is in the design and (especially) analysis of intelligent tutoring systems, the steps suggested could be adapted to any kind of instructional system, computerized or even classroom.

Table 4-5 Applications of the Taxonomy: Instructional System Design Steps

1. Determine desired *knowledge outcomes*
   a. State the instructional goals (e.g., acquisition of a mental model, a set of propositions, a set of skills).
   b. Specify the particular facts, skills, or mental models to be taught.
   c. Determine tests to be used for assessing particular knowledge outcomes (Table 4-2).
2. Determine *environment* for achieving knowledge outcomes
   a. Consider the kind of learning strategy desirable to invoke (Table 4-1).
   b. Consider alternative means for achieving knowledge outcome (could be used as a remediation strategy, or simply as a variation to avoid instructional monotony).
   c. Record student learning success with respect to the knowledge-outcome-by-instructional-environment matrix. This allows more precise statements of the effectiveness of the instruction.
3. Consider *learning style* issues
   a. Consider whether to encourage particular types (styles) of interaction.
   b. If learning style is left free, make provisions to record the manner in which the student interacts with the instructional environment (for suggestions see Tables 4-3 and 4-4). This also allows more precise statements of the effectiveness of the instruction.
   c. If particular learning styles are encouraged through feedback and suggestions, consider varying the kinds of styles encouraged so as to allow experimental comparisons of the relative effectiveness of various styles.

SUMMARY AND DISCUSSION

We have presented a taxonomy of learning based on previous research and on contemporary cognitive theory. We have also proposed how the taxonomy can be applied to generate indicators of what a student in an instructional situation is learning, and how well he or she is learning it. But just how well does our proposed taxonomy-indicator system work?

Consider four major uses for the system (these and a fifth research application are listed in Table 4-7). First, the taxonomy can suggest what kinds of skills are being exercised and tested in an instructional setting. In this capacity the taxonomy serves in much the same way Bloom's or Gagné's taxonomies do. The advantage of our proposal is that it is more closely tied to current cognitive theory, which we hope will enable us to apply the system more easily in analyzing learning in somewhat naturalistic instructional settings. A second use for the system concerns primarily the environment dimension. The specification of multiple instructional environments provides a way to think about a range of means for achieving particular knowledge outcomes. If an instructor's

Table 4-6 Applications of the Taxonomy: Learning Task Analysis Steps

1. Determine the *knowledge outcome* goals for the instruction
   a. Determine the nature of the stated instructional goals (e.g., acquisition of a mental model, a set of propositions, a set of skills).
   b. Determine what kinds of tests are embedded within the instruction (consulting Table 4-2).
   c. Determine the match between the tests used and the knowledge outcomes intended (as in Figure 4-3).
2. Determine the nature of the *instructional environment*
   a. For every instructional exchange (every student-instructor interaction episode), consider what learning strategy is invoked (consulting Table 4-1) during the exchange. Generate learning activities profiles for the entire instructional program (as in Figure 4-3).
   b. Organize records of student learning success with respect to the knowledge-outcome-by-instructional-environment (KO × IE) matrix. That is, devise a means for assigning each student a separate learning success score for each cell in the KO × IE matrix. Scores would be based on tests following particular instructional exchanges.
3. Consider *learning style* issues
   a. Consider whether particular types (styles) of interaction are encouraged.
   b. If learning style is left free, and there is between-student style variability, but no within-student style variability, then separate students by style before conducting any analyses of the KO × IE matrix.
   c. If learning style is left free, and there is within-student style variability (e.g., students engage in holistic processing some times, serial processing at others), create separate KO × IE profiles for the various style orientations.
4. Considerations for transfer studies
   a. Degree of transfer should be a function of the similarity of the learning activities profiles for two learning tasks.
   b. Similarity is computed over the KO × IE matrices (possibly for separate styles) and *domain.*
5. Considerations for optimizing or predicting global outcomes
   a. Expected global outcome for a particular student will depend on the match between the student's personal learning-skill profile and the learning skills the instruction exercises (the learning activies profile, Figure 4-3).
   b. Optimizing global outcomes for a particular student can be seen as a linear programming problem. Instruction should maximize exercising the student's strongest skills subject to the cost (e.g., in time) for exercising those skills.

goal is to teach a mental model of some system, the instructor can simply instruct it, use an analogy, have the student discover the model through observation of the system, or employ another instructional approach. A third use for the system is to make predictions about transfer relations among learning experiences. We would predict that the closer, taxonomically, two learning

Table 4–7 Applications of the Taxonomy: What It Can Be Used For

Instructional system evaluators (teachers and administrators)
1. Facilitates analysis of the kinds of learning skills that are being exercised and tested in an instructional setting (see Figure 4-3)

Instructional system designers
2. Suggests a range of possible instructional environments for achieving particular knowledge outcomes (see Table 4-1/Figure 4-1)
3. Specifies techniques (tests) for probing a wide range of knowledge and learning skill outcomes (see Table 4-2)

Cognitive researchers
4. Suggests predictions about transfer relations among learning experiences (see Figure 4-1/Table 4-6)
5. Suggests indicators (dependent variables) of what and how well a student is learning (see Figure 4-3/Tables 4-2, 4-6)

situations are, the more likely that whatever is learned in one will transfer to the other. Of course this is an open empirical question. A benefit of the taxonomy is that it suggests a straightforward research program for addressing this kind of question.

While all three of these applications may be useful, we believe that the most important role of the taxonomy is in establishing the means for probing a much wider range of knowledge and learning-skill outcomes. This capability is obviously important for research purposes, but it also is important for evaluating educational systems. Consider a general problem in evaluating innovative educational programs (discussed by Nickerson, Perkins, and Smith, 1985). Over the years many such programs, such as ones for teaching creative thinking or ones for teaching general thinking skills, have been developed. All too often, casual observation suggests that such programs are having desirable effects on students, but such effects do not show up under the scrutiny of carefully conducted evaluation studies. Creators of such programs typically complain that the scientific model of evaluation is inappropriate because the true gains students experience are somehow missed. One role for the taxonomy might be to suggest how additional learning outcomes and skills can be assessed in order to enable a more thorough evaluation.

Even among the three instructional programs we reviewed here, a rather conservative approach to assessing the impact of the tutoring system was taken. To some extent, the LISP tutor, BIP, and Smithtown all depended on standard achievement outcome tests as a means for their validation. While it is important to establish that these tutors do affect overall achievement, it is not sufficient. While interacting with a tutor, or in any instructional environment, students can be learning many different things. A major role for the taxonomy is to suggest a richer testing system for evaluating a broader range of student outcomes.

Finally, the taxonomy-indicator system should facilitate pursuit of both applied and basic research questions. Our major practical application for the taxonomy is to have it assist in the specification of variables that indicate what and how well a subject is learning as the subject interacts with a tutor over a lengthy series of lessons. These variables then will serve as criteria against which newly developed measures of cognitive ability will be validated. In addition, a wide range of basic research issues is opened up. Are the different knowledge types affected by the same variables? Are fast propositional learners also fast production-rule learners? Are there interactions between knowledge type and the instructional environment? Are individual differences in learning more dependent on the knowledge type or the environment? Our research programs are only at the very beginning stages in addressing these kinds of fundamental questions about the nature of learning and individual differences therein.

ACKNOWLEDGMENTS

Support was provided by the Air Force Human Resources Laboratory and the Air Force Office of Scientific Research, through Universal Energy Systems, under Contract No. F41689-84-D-0002/58420360, Subcontract No. S-744-031-001. We thank Raymond Christal, Wesley Regian, Dan Woltz, William Alley, Stephanie Rude, Bruce Britton, and Shawn Glynn for their valuable comments on the taxonomy.

REFERENCES

Allison, R. B., Jr. (1960). *Learning parameters and human abilities.* Unpublished doctoral dissertation, Educational Testing Service and Princeton University.

Anderson, J. R. (1983). *The architecture of cognition.* Cambridge, Mass.: Harvard University Press.

Anderson, J. R. (1987a). Skill acquisition: Compilation of weak-method problem solutions. *Psychological Review,* 94:192–210.

Anderson, J. R. (1987b). Production systems, learning, and tutoring. In D. Klahr, P. Langley, and R. Neches (Eds.), *Production system models of learning and development.* Cambridge, Mass.: MIT Press.

Anderson, J. R. (In press). Analysis of student performance with the LISP tutor. In N. Frederiksen (Ed.), *Diagnostic monitoring of skill and knowledge acquisition.* Hillsdale, N.J.: Erlbaum.

Anderson, J. R., Boyle, F., and Reiser, B. (1985). Intelligent tutoring systems. *Science,* 228:456–462.

Baron, J. Badgio, P. C., and Gaskins, I. W. (1986). Cognitive style and its improvement:

A normative approach. In R. J. Sternberg (Ed.), *Advances in the psychology of human intelligence,* Vol. 3. Hillsdale, N.J.: Erlbaum.

Barr, A., Beard, M., and Atkinson, R. C. (1976). The computer as a tutorial laboratory: The Stanford BIP project. *International Journal of Man-Machine Studies,* 8:567–596.

Bloom, B. S. (1956). *Taxonomy of educational objectives: Cognitive domain (Handbook I).* New York: McKay.

Campione, J. C., Brown, A. L., and Bryant, N. R. (1985). Individual differences in learning and memory. In R. J. Sternberg (Ed.), *Human abilities: An information processing approach.* New York: W. H. Freeman and Company.

Carbonell, J. G., Michalski, R. S., and Mitchell, T. M. (1983). An overview of machine learning. In R. S. Michalski, J. G. Carbonell, and T. M. Mitchell (Eds.), *Machine learning: An artificial intelligence approach.* Los Altos, Calif.: Morgan Kaufmann.

Cattell, R. B. (1971). *Abilities: Their structure, growth, and action.* Boston: Houghton Mifflin.

Chi, M. T. H., Feltovich, P. J., and Glaser, R. (1981). Categorization and representation of physics problems by experts and novices. *Cognitive Science,* 5:121–152.

Cronbach, L. J., and Snow, R. E. (1977). *Aptitudes and instructional methods: A handbook for research on interactions.* New York: Irvington.

Ennis, R. H. (1986). A taxonomy of critical thinking dispositions and abilities. In J. B. Baron and R. J. Sternberg (Eds.), *Teaching thinking skills: Theory and practice* New York: W. H. Freeman and Company.

Estes, W. K. (1982). Learning, memory, and intelligence. In R. J. Sternberg (Ed.), *Handbook of human intelligence.* Cambridge: Cambridge University Press.

Fitts, P. M. (1963). Perceptual-motor skill learning. In A. W. Melton (Ed.), *Categories of human learning* New York: Academic Press.

Fleishman, E. A., and Quaintance, M. K. (1984). *Taxonomies of human performance: The description of human tasks.* Orlando, Fla.: Academic Press.

Fredericksen, N., and Pine, J. (In press). Assessment of learning in science and mathematics. *Report on indicators of quality of education in science and math.* Washington, D.C.: National Academy of Sciences/National Research Council.

Gagné, R. M. (1965). Problem solving. In A. W. Melton (Ed.), *Categories of human learning.* New York: Academic Press.

Gagné, R. M. (1985). *The conditions of learning and theory of instruction.* New York: Holt, Rinehart & Winston.

Gagné, R. M., and Briggs, L. J. (1979). *Principles of instructional design,* 2d ed. New York: Holt, Rinehart & Winston.

Gitomer, D. (1984). A cognitive analysis of a complex troubleshooting task. Unpublished doctoral dissertation. University of Pittsburgh.

Glaser, R. (1967). Some implications of previous work on learning and individual differences. In R. M. Gagné (Ed.), *Learning and individual differences.* Columbus, Ohio: Merrill.

Glaser, R., Lesgold, A., and Lajoie, S. (In press). Toward a cognitive theory for the measurement of achievement. In R. R. Ronning, J. Glover, J. C. Conoley, and J. C. Witt (Eds.), *The influence of cognitive psychology on testing, Buros/Nebraska symposium on testing,* Vol. 3. Hillsdale, N.J.: Erlbaum.

Glynn, S. M., Britton, B. K., Semrud-Clikeman, and Muth, D. K. (In press). Analogical reasoning and problem solving in science textbooks. In J. A. Glover, R. R. Ronning, and C. R. Reynolds (Eds.), *Handbook of creativity: Assessment, research, and theory.* New York: Plenum.

Goodenough, D. R. (1976). The role of individual differences in field dependence as a factor in learning and memory. *Psychological Bulletin,* 83:675–694

Greeno, J. G. (1980). Psychology of learning, 1960–1980: One participant's observations. *American Psychologist,* 35:713–728.

Hayes, J. R., and Flower, L. S. (1980). Identifying the organization of writing processes. In L. W. Gregg and E. R. Steinberg (Eds.), *Cognitive processes in writing.* Hillsdale, N.J.: Erlbaum.

Humphreys, L. G. (1979). The construct of general intelligence. *Intelligence,* 3:105–120.

Jensen, A. R. (1967). Varieties of individual differences in learning. In R. M. Gagne (Ed.), *Learning and individual differences.* Columbus, Ohio: Merrill.

Kyllonen, P. C. (1986). Theory based cognitive assessment. In J. Zeidner (Ed.), *Human productivity enhancement,* Vol. 2: *Acquisition and development of personnel.* New York: Praeger.

Kyllonen, P. C., and Christal, R. E. (In press). Cognitive modeling of learning abilities: A status report of LAMP. In R. Dillon and J. W. Pellegrino, *Advances in testing and training.* New York: Academic Press.

Langley, P. (1986). Editorial: On machine learning. *Machine Learning,* 1:5–10.

Linn, M. C., and Kyllonen, P. C. (1981). The field dependence-independence construct: Some, one, or none. *Journal of Educational Psychology,* 73:261–273.

Linville, P. A. (1982). Affective consequences of complexity regarding the self and others. In M. S. Clark and S. T. Fiske (Eds.), *Affect and cognition: The seventeenth annual Carnegie symposium on cognition.* Hillsdale, N.J.: Erlbaum.

Malmi, R. A., Underwood, B. J., and Carroll, J. B. (1979). The interrelationships among some associative learning tasks. *Bulletin of the Psychonomic Society,* 13:121–123.

Marshalek, B., Lohman, D. F., and Snow, R. E. (1983). The complexity continuum in the radex and hierarchical models of intelligence. *Intelligence,* 7:107–127.

Martin, D. W. (1986). Turning research art into science. *Contemporary Psychology,* 31:211–212.

Meichenbaum, D. (1977). *Cognitive behavior modification: An integrative approach.* New York: Plenum.

Melton, A. W. (1964). The taxonomy of human learning: Overview. In A. W. Melton (Ed.), *Categories of human learning.* New York: Academic Press.

Melton, A. W. (1967). Individual differences and theoretical variables: General comments on the conference. In R. M. Gagne (Ed.), *Learning and individual differences.* Columbus, Ohio: Merrill.

Messick, S. (1986). Cognitive style. In R. E. Snow and M. J. Farr (Eds.), *Aptitude, learning, and instruction,* Vol. 3: *Conative and affective process analysis.* Hillsdale, N.J.: Erlbaum.

Michalski, R. S. (1986). Understanding the nature of learning: Issues and research directions. In R. S. Michalski, J. G. Carbonell, and T. M. Mitchell (Eds.), *Machine learning: An artificial intelligence approach,* Vol. II. Los Altos, Calif.: Morgan Kaufmann.

Murnane, R. J., and Raizen, S. A. (1988). *Improving indicators of the quality of science and mathematics education in grades K–12.* Washington, D.C.: National Academy Press.

Nickerson, R. S., Perkins, D. N., and Smith, E. E. (1985). *The teaching of thinking.* Hillsdale, N.J.: Erlbaum.

Pask, G., and Scott, B. C. E. (1972). Learning strategies and individual competence. *International Journal of Man-Machine Studies,* 4:217–253.

Perrig, W., and Kintsch, W. (1984). *Propositional and nonpropositional representations of text* (Tech. Rep. No. 131). Boulder, Colo.: Institute of Cognitive Science, University of Colorado.

Reiser, B. J., Anderson, J. R., and Farrell, R. G. (1985). *Dynamic student modeling in an intelligent tutor for LISP programming.* Proceedings of the Ninth International Joint Conference on Artificial Intelligence, Vol. 1. Los Altos, Calif.: Morgan Kaufmann.

Rosenbloom, R. S., and Newell, A. (1986). The chunking of goal hierarchies: A generalized model of practice. In R. S. Michalski, J. G. Carbonell, and T. M. Mitchell (Eds.) *Machine learning: An artificial intelligence approach,* Vol. II. Los Altos, Calif.: Morgan Kaufmann.

Rumelhart, D. E., and Norman, D. A. (1981). Analogical processes in learning. In J. R. Anderson (Ed.), *Cognitive skills and their acquisition.* Hillsdale, N.J.: Erlbaum.

Schneider, W., and Shiffrin, R. M. (1977). Controlled and automatic human information processing: I. Detection, search, and attention. *Psychological Review,* 84:1–66.

Schoenfeld, A. H. (1985). *Mathematical problem solving.* New York: Academic Press.

Self, J. (1986). The application of machine learning to student modelling. *Instructional Science,* 14:327–338.

Shiffrin, R. M., and Schneider, W. (1977). Controlled and automatic human information processing: II. Perceptual learning, automatic attending, and a general theory. *Psychological Review,* 84:127–190.

Shute, V. J., and Glaser, R. (In press). An intelligent tutoring system for exploring principles of economics. In R. E. Snow and D. Wiley (Eds.), *Straight thinking.* San Francisco: Jossey Bass.

Snow, R. E., Kyllonen, P. C., and Marshalek, B. (1984). The topography of learning and ability correlations. In R. J. Sternberg (Ed.), *Advances in the psychology of human intelligence,* Vol. 2. Hillsdale, N.J.: Erlbaum.

Snow, R. E., Wescourt K., and Collins, J. (1986). *Individual differences in aptitude and learning from interactive computer-based instruction* (Tech. Rep. No. 10). Stanford, Calif.: Standford University School of Education.

Soloway, E., and Littman, D. (1986). *Evaluating ITSs: The cognitive science perspective.* Proceedings of the Research Planning Forum for Intelligent Tutoring Systems. San Antonio, Tex.: Air Force Human Resources Laboratory.

Spelke, E., Hirst, W., and Neisser, U. (1976). Skills of divided attention. *Cognition,* 4:215–230.

Stake, R. E. (1961). Learning parameters, aptitudes, and achievement. *Psychometric monographs,* No. 9.

Thurstone, L. L. (1938). Primary mental abilities. *Psychometric monographs,* No. 1.

Tversky, A., and Hutchins, J. W. (1986). Nearest neighbor analysis of psychological spaces. *Psychological Review,* 93:3–22.

Underwood, B. J. (1975). Individual differences as a crucible in theory construction. *American Psychologist,* 30:128–134.

Underwood, B. J., Boruch, R. F., and Malmi, R. A. (1978). Composition of episodic memory. *Journal of Experimental Psychology: General,* 107:393–419.

Wescourt, K. T., Beard, M., Gould, L., and Barr A. (October, 1977). *Knowledge-based CAI: CINS for individualized curriculum sequencing* (Tech. Rep. No. 290). Stanford, Calif.: Institute for Mathematical Studies in the Social Sciences, Stanford University.

Wickens, C. D., Sandry, D., and Vidulich, M. (1983). Compatibility and resource competition between modalities of input, central processing, and output: Testing a model of complex task performance. *Human Factors,* 25:227–248.

Winograd, T. (1975). Frame representations and the declarative-procedural controversy. In D. G. Bobrow and A. Collins (Eds.), *Representation and understanding.* New York: Academic Press.

Woodrow, H. (1946). The ability to learn. *Psychological Review,* 53:147–158.

Yazdani, M. (1986). Intelligent tutoring systems survey. *Artificial Intelligence Review,* 1:43–52.

5

Individual Differences
and Skill Acquisition

PHILLIP L. ACKERMAN *University of Minnesota*

The past twenty years have brought numerous advances in learning theories and individual differences theories. However, because of a lack of integration of these predominantly independent domains, the issues of skill acquisition examined at the 1965 conference greatly overlap those discussed in this chapter. Many of the participants in the 1965 conference on learning and individual differences discussed individual differences in skill acquisition (Gagné, 1967). Fleishman (1967a, 1967b) paid particular attention to correlations between ability and performance during task practice. Other authors discussed this and other concerns related to skill acquisition such as changes in interindividual variability (Glaser, 1967; see also Anderson, 1967; Glanzer, 1967).

This chapter begins with definitions of terms and descriptions of a few limiting conditions. The rest of the chapter is divided into four main sections. The first section reviews approaches to individual differences in skill acquisition that were under consideration in 1965. The discussion will be coupled with a description of developments in the intervening twenty years. The second section is devoted to brief reviews of (a) a modern, general approach to skill acquisition, (b) a recently developed structure of abilities for skill acquisition, and (c) a proposed theory of individual differences in skill acquisition that unifies these two paradigms. The third section of the chapter contains a review of empirical studies that focus on the proposed theory of individual differences in skill acquisition. Finally, the fourth section of the chapter discusses the implications of the theory and data for future research in individual differences in learning, and for other, related research areas.

Because the area of memory and knowledge structures has become so diverse during the rise of cognitive psychology, it is currently impractical to consider at once individual differences in all types of knowledge acquisition. It is thus necessary in this chapter to limit the domain of skills under consideration. First of all, recent theories of learning and the structure of knowledge (Anderson, 1982, 1983) have convincingly pointed to a distinction between knowledge *about* something — declarative knowledge — and knowledge of *how to do* something — procedural knowledge. For present purposes, it is important to limit the skill domain to procedural knowledge, or knowledge which may be *proceduralized* (Anderson, 1983). Thus, this chapter will be predominantly concerned with the latter type of knowledge — here termed "skills."

In a recent review of human motor skills research Adams (1987) emphasized the need for establishing a working definition of skills. For the treatment of skill acquisition in this chapter, the skeleton of Adams's three defining criteria has been borrowed. Thus: "(1) Skill is a wide behavioral domain. (2) Skill is learned. (3) Goal attainment is importantly dependent upon motor behavior" (Adams, 1987, p. 7).

More details are provided in the Adams article, but these three criteria subsume the domain to be considered. In sum, the sphere of coverage here includes knowledge of how to perform tasks which depend to a strong degree on motor behavior.

This specification of skills includes aspects of behaviors such as riding a bicycle, typing or word processing, using hand tools, and, presumably, cooking a meal from a recipe. An important consideration for the present approach is that each of these skills is subsumed in a finite domain of behaviors. These skill specifications necessarily exclude a variety of *nonmotor* learned behaviors that are not as easily tractable, such as chess mastery, solving physics problems, and analogical reasoning. (Of course, several such nonmotor behaviors will be covered in other chapters in this volume; e.g., see Shute, Glaser, and Raghavan, Chapter 8.)

Consequently, this chapter is concerned with the learning of skills that require motor responses (often speeded) to well-defined stimulus classes. Most prominent among the issues in this chapter will be the relations between cognitive-intellectual abilities and individual differences in task performance during skill acquisition.

A SHORT REVIEW OF HISTORICAL
AND CURRENT ISSUES

Up to 1965 the major sources of research pertaining to individual differences and learning fell into four domains: (1) *gain* as an index of learning during practice, (2) trial-by-trial intercorrelations of performance measures, (3) practice and variability, and (4) ability-performance associations. In years subsequent to 1967, a number of findings and discussions have shed light on the meaning of these sources of data. Each of these domains will be considered in turn.

Gain as an Index of Learning During Practice

Woodrow and his colleagues conducted several studies of individual differences in learning during the 1930s and 1940s. In these studies learning was defined as the gain in performance from before practice to after practice. When individual differences early and late in practice were evaluated, no substantial correlations were found between intelligence measures and learning. Woodrow and others concluded from this research program that neither global measures of intelligence (Woodrow, 1946), nor specific measures of so-called primary abilities (Simrall, 1946) could be identified with an ability to learn, interpreted as gain scores (compare Glaser, 1967; Anderson, 1967).

In 1965 it was noted that for the tests used by Woodrow et al., substantial individual differences were present at both early and late measurement occasions. These discussions indicated that when individual differences exist at the first measurement occasion (and measures are not perfectly reliable), gain scores suffer from serious regression problems (Anderson, 1967; see also Lord, 1963). More recent treatment (Cronbach and Furby, 1970) has demonstrated that use of gain scores to correlate learning with abilities encounters serious statistical artifacts. The main problem is that regression-to-the-mean effects (in comparing repeated measures on the same individuals) have the result of artifactually indicating that early high performers tend to show low (or negative) gain scores, while low performers tend to show large positive gain scores — *even if there is no net change in group performance.* These artifacts, among other estimation difficulties, preclude equating amount of learning with gain from one trial to the next. Because partial correlation techniques destroy the importance of initial performance on later proficiency, regressed gain scores fail to offer a solution to the regression-to-the-mean problem (Cronbach and Furby, 1970). As a result, even today it is impossible to objectively evaluate the arguments put forth by

Woodrow and his colleagues (Woodrow, 1946; Simrall, 1946) concerning the association of intelligence with the ability to learn.

It is important to qualify these results, though. Performance on the first trial of some concept attainment or discrimination learning tasks cannot be considered to be right or wrong in a sense that the subject knows the answer. For all intents and purposes, each subject starts off with the same random-guessing initial performance. As such, initial scores have zero (or near zero) variability. When zero variance is present in initial scores, regression-to-the-mean effects do not occur. Under these conditions gain scores can indeed be productively employed. One measure of learning under these conditions is the number of trials to some performance criterion (such as 95 percent correct). Studies by Zeaman and House (1967; House and Zeaman, 1960) indicated that when all subjects begin a task at equal performance levels, general intelligence does indeed positively correlate with skill acquisition measures.

Trial-by-trial Intercorrelations of Performance Measures

Examination of a different aspect of individual differences, that is, intercorrelations between successive performance scores during practice, has revealed a pattern which is ubiquitous to skill acquisition data, known as the simplex (Humphreys, 1960).

The characteristic simplex pattern of correlations is that the largest values occur in the diagonal entries (that is, adjacent task trials) and correlations decline as the trials become more distant from one another; in other words, the lowest value will correspond to the correlation between the first and last trial. Generally, these correlations are found to decline in a smooth fashion, although the correlations are nearly always positive. An example of a simplex-like intercorrelation matrix (over skill acquisition trials) is presented in Table 5-1.

Given this decline in the magnitude of correlations over practice, one can infer that the underlying determinants of individual differences in task performance undergo substantial changes during the course of skill acquisition. This simplex-like pattern of trial intercorrelations supports the notion that whatever abilities determine novel task performance, such abilities no longer determine performance after task practice (compare Anderson, 1967; Dubois, Manning, and Spies, 1959; Humphreys, 1960; Jones, 1962; Reynolds, 1952a, 1952b).

The clear inference from this pattern of intercorrelations is that individuals continuously change their rank order on performance over practice. These changes indicate that the underlying determinants of performance cannot be identical from one trial to the next. So far, hypotheses about the *specific* causes of these changes have not successfully identified the ability determinants of performance. Much theoretical discussion has been accorded to this topic (Corballis, 1965; Jones, 1962, 1970a, 1970b, Alvares and Hulin, 1972). Jones (1962) initially hypothesized that practice is a process of simplification; the ability

Table 5-1 Example of Simplex-like Within-task Correlation Matrix

Session of Practice	1	2	3	4	5	6	7	8	9	10	11
2	.77										
3	.66	.82									
4	.52	.65	.74								
5	.44	.55	.68	.67							
6	.35	.41	.54	.57	.81						
7	.36	.43	.54	.67	.77	.77					
8	.25	.29	.38	.54	.64	.68	.79				
9	.28	.31	.38	.53	.61	.66	.78	.78			
10	.26	.32	.41	.51	.63	.70	.78	.71	.78		
11	.26	.35	.39	.41	.53	.57	.64	.56	.66	.77	
12	.22	.28	.38	.46	.50	.55	.53	.51	.59	.64	.72

Note: Practice data for category search task (memory set size = 2 items).

factors that determine individual differences during initial task performance reduce in influence or drop out as skills are acquired. Jones (1970a, 1970b) later argued that a two-process model could also explain the basic simplex phenomenon. Jones suggested that rate of improvement and terminal (final asymptotic performance) factors may underlie the data.

Analysis of patterns of trial-by-trial intercorrelations has been used (if not extensively) in identification of two particular skill acquisition characteristics. As has been discussed elsewhere (Ackerman, 1987; Jones, 1970b; Reynolds, 1952a, 1952b), these two characteristics relate to the rate of correlation attenuation (meaning the rate of decline between initial or early task performance and each additional set of trials), and the rate of change in adjacent correlations with practice (meaning changes in stability of individual differences in performance). Both of these characteristics presumably provide crude measures of the amount of change in the underlying determinants of task performance. By manipulating the information-processing requirements of tasks, one might identify task characteristics that produce (a) greater or lesser changes in ability requirements from initial to final performance, or (b) increases or decreases in the stability of individual differences in performance as skills are acquired.

A few examples where false performance feedback was used have indicated that parameters of trial-by-trial correlations can be altered (Jones, 1970b). However, as a result of dynamic changes in the array of other determinants of task performance (such as fatigue and motivation), it appears that such measures are otherwise less sensitive to changes in task information-processing demands, as compared to correlations between ability and performance.

Corballis (1965) has pointed out, though, that the simplex structure can be equally well resolved mathematically by an infinite number of different models, including a factor accretion model (new factors being added over practice), and a random walk model (changes in performance determinants occurring randomly with practice). Given this nonuniqueness problem, it is evident that analysis of only trial-by-trial intercorrelations fails to yield a sufficient method for determining the causes of changes in individual differences during skill acquisition. Thus, current claims to the contrary (Henry and Hulin, 1987), external referents must be used in order to determine the causes of the simplex pattern of trial intercorrelations (Ackerman, in press).

Two approaches to using external referents have been undertaken in the literature. One method is to examine the distribution characteristics of performance measures, to discover interactions between individual differences in performance, changes with practice, and the influence of task information-processing requirements on these measures. The other method is to directly compare correlations between reference cognitive abilities and individual differences in task performance during skill acquisition. Both of these methods will be discussed in turn.

Practice and Variability

As Glaser pointed out in 1967, study of inter-individual variability can be traced at least as far back as the early part of this century. E. L. Thorndike (1908) posed the question as to whether individuals converge in level of performance (that is, demonstrate a decrease in variability) or diverge (that is, demonstrate an increase in variability) with task training. The issue was an important one at the time to various participants in the heredity versus environment debate (Glaser, 1967, p. 2). If individuals converged in performance during training, so the argument went, then differences between individuals were environmentally determined so that additional task experience reduced the magnitude of individual differences. Conversely, if divergence in performance was found, then heredity was the determinant of individual differences in intellectual performance.

Over the three decades that followed Thorndike's paper, this controversy was accorded much empirical research and discussion. Reviews of the literature indicated that findings favoring convergence were about as frequent as findings favoring divergence with task practice (Anastasi, 1934; Kincaid, 1922, 1925; Reed, 1931). Even though no final conclusions were reached in the literature, interest in the topic of practice and variability generally wanted after the 1930s (see Woodrow, 1938).

Recent attention has been devoted to a review of this particular controversy. Spurred by the desire to link information-processing theories of skill acquisition and individual differences, Ackerman (1987) performed a limited reanalysis of the previous practice and variability data. Two major difficulties were found to obscure the otherwise decisive data of the period. The first difficulty was that the common measure of variability used today, the standard deviation, is a relatively recently adopted statistical tool in psychology. Researchers used many different variability measures well into the 1930s that were confounded to varying degrees with mean performance level with mean performance level (for example, mean variability or mean/variance). The second difficulty was that some investigators used measures of performance that assessed performance in terms of *attainment* (the number of items completed in a fixed period of time), while other investigators assessed performance in terms of *reaction time,* RT—the time taken to complete one item. These measures of performance are reciprocals of one another, and thus reflect nonlinear transformations. Changes in mean performance levels due to learning for one type of measure will bring about different effects to the associated variabilities for the other type of measure.

Investigations of RT performance tended to indicate reduced inter-individual variability with practice whereas measures of attainment performance yielded mixed results, partly because a uniform decrease in RT yields wider and wider interindividual differences (increased variability) as the length of time increases. For example, assume two individuals initially complete one math problem in 8 seconds and 10 seconds, respectively, at the beginning of training. At the end of training, the time to complete one math problem is 6 seconds and 8 seconds, respectively. Over a 1-hour time period, pretraining attainment performance would be 450 and 360 problems, and post-training performance would be 600 and 450. For RT measures, the range of individual differences would stay constant; but for attainment measures, the range of individual differences would increase. A more dramatic variability increase would be found if the time period were increased from 1 hour to 8 hours.

Recent theories of skill acquisition and information processing (Anderson, 1982, 1983; Newell and Rosenbloom, 1981) provide a theoretical and empirical framework that depends on RT measures. This approach is reasonable given the general concern of current psychological theory with the speed of information processing (Sternberg, 1969), rather than directly with the long-term productivity of individuals (for example, number of math problems completed in 8 hours). Reexamination of the literature with this information-processing approach clears up the confusion about practice and variability. When the previous data are transformed to an RT metric and variability is assessed with the now typical estimate of the standard deviation, the results of practice and variability are conclusive. When initial tasks are within the abilities of the respondents (that is, successful performance is possible, although more time consuming for some subjects), *variability of performance decreases with practice.* A sampling of the historical data is reviewed and reanalyzed in Ackerman (1987).

Current investigations of information-processing determinants of skill acquisition, however, indicate that the this finding is *not* a universal product of task practice (Ackerman, 1986a). Specifically, information-processing parameters of task complexity and transfer of training moderate the effects of practice on interindividual variability. Manipulations of task complexity and transfer affect both the initial level of variability and the rate of attenuation with practice.

In addition, the degree of information-processing consistency also moderates the effects of practice and variability. A *consistent* task is defined as one for which the learner can deal with inputs and outputs in an unvarying or consistent manner from one instance to another (Schneider and Shiffrin, 1977). A task that lacks consistency will require that the learner change how he or she deals with information, so that the learner must be constantly attentive to changes in information-processing demands. It has been stated that consistency is a necessary condition for the development of skilled performance (see Shiffrin and Schneider, 1977, and discussion later in this chapter under "Empirical Evaluation of the Theory").

When a learner cannot handle system inputs in a consistent fashion, as is characteristic in situations like threshold detection (for example, radar monitoring), or in highly complex tasks where the consistency of input and output may not be grasped by the learner, skilled performance is not ordinarily achieved. Compatible with this interpretation, study of the manipulation of task consistency has demonstrated that performance variability decreases *only* when the information-processing requirements are predominantly consistent. That is, when the task configuration precludes the development of skilled performance, RT variability remains constant (or increases) over practice, even when some overall performance improvement occurs.

It can be said that during the normal course of skill acquisition, individuals converge in performance; the magnitude of between-subject variability decreases during skill acquisition. While factors such as task complexity and previous learning (transfer) affect the parameters of this convergence, a lack of task consistency can preclude convergence altogether. When tasks are predominantly inconsistent, the initial spread of high and low performers is likely to be maintained, even over long practice or training periods.

Such factors, while obviously important in describing the general patterns of individual differences during skill acquisition, do not *directly* address the causes of such patterns. The next section describes attempts to ascertain the role of cognitive abilities in the acquisition and maintenance of skilled performance.

Ability-Performance Correlations

In 1967 Fleishman (1967b) summarized findings from a series of ability-performance studies. He concluded that when examining the relations between abilities and perceptual/motor task performance over practice, (a) ability-performance correlations *changed* as a function of practice, (b) broad intellectual abilities were more highly correlated with early task performance, whereas narrow (e.g., perceptual/motor) abilities tended to correlate more highly with performance late in practice, and (c) an ability factor specific to the task becomes increasingly important as practice proceeds. Note, though, even in the late 1950s and 1960s, there was considerable controversy over this final finding (see Dubois, Manning, and Spies, 1959; Ferguson, 1956; Fleishman, 1967a, 1967b; Humphreys, 1960).

Basically, the controversy revolved around whether the factor analytic procedures used by Fleishman et al. were conducted in a way that avoided the ubiquitous early and late task factors found in factor analysis of any data collected longitudinally — such as would be found with outdoor temperature measures (Humphreys, 1960). Such objections resulted in a degree of skepticism towards any hypothesis of *task-specific* factors emerging from learning data. Briefly, there is only a scarce set of studies that examine the association between performance levels during task practice and reference cognitive abilities. The older psychometric literature has been reviewed several times in the past twenty years (see Fleishman, 1972; Fleishman and Quaintance, 1984). Some of this research also has been reviewed and reanalyzed elsewhere (Ackerman, 1987; Cronbach and Snow, 1977; Snow, Kyllonen, and Marshalek, 1984).

To review the recent studies, however, it will be necessary to provide a context of advances in general principles of skill acquisition and of advances in ability theory. As a preview, some of the Fleishman et al. claims are generally supported. Some abilities decline in correlation with performance, while others increase in correlation with performance over practice. Specific exceptions and more definitive principles will be outlined in the course of this chapter.

Summary

Thus, to summarize briefly in the context of current study of individual differences in skill acquisition:

1. Except for discovery tasks that require all learners to begin at the same level of performance (such as chance guessing or zero performance), gain from initial to practiced performance is a measure that is not suitable to estimating individual differences in learning. For discovery tasks, there appears to be a

moderate association between intellectual abilities and the time taken to acquire skilled performance.

2. The ubiquitous simplex-like patterning of trial-by-trial intercorrelations during skill acquisition implies that the ability determinants of individual differences in initial performance are not the same as the determinants of final, skilled performance.

3. For tasks that are consistent, and where performance can be assessed with RT measures, the magnitude of individual differences decreases with task practice; that is, individuals converge in performance. For tasks that do not have this fundamental property of consistency, interindividual variability stays constant (or increases). Measures of interindividual variability are also influenced by other information-processing parameters, such as task complexity and transfer of training.

4. Consistent with item 2 but from more direct assessments, ability-performance correlations change as tasks are acquired. Some ability measures increase in association with performance variables, some are stable, and other ability measures decrease in correlation.

This set represents the foundation of empirical phenomena that must be successfully dealt with by any theory of individual differences in skill acquisition. What follows is the development and exposition of a theoretical approach to these phenomena. The next section will identify the information-processing determinants of skill acquisition, as well as the intellectual abilities that are important in skill acquisition. The review begins with an overview of skill acquisition theory.

SKILL ACQUISITION, ABILITIES, AND AN INTEGRATIVE THEORY

Skill Acquisition

A comprehensive review of the skill acquisition literature lies beyond the scope of this chapter (although see Adams, 1987; Anderson, 1982, 1983; Fitts and Posner, 1967; Schneider and Shiffrin, 1977). However, from the early discussions by Bryan and Harter (1899), James (1890), Thorndike (1914) and others, commonality has been established for the fundamental characteristics of skill acquisition. Converging depictions of skill acquisition have been offered from several perspectives over the last few decades.

In contrast to the hierarchical plateau description provided by Bryan and Harter, more recent researchers have stressed that skill acquisition is ordinarily a continuous process, without breaks or discontinuities in performance improvements. Several theorists have found it parsimonious to incorporate stage or phase designations to delineate different aspects of the learning process (Adams, 1987). Fitts, for example (Fitts, 1964; Fitts and Posner, 1967) suggested that from the perspective of information processing, skill acquisition can be segmented into three phases: *cognitive* (phase 1), followed by *associative* (phase 2), and finally, *autonomous* (phase 3).

These three phases have been analogously represented in production system models of learning, such as that of Anderson (1982, 1983) as (1) declarative stage, (2) knowledge compilation, and (3) procedural stage. In addition, these skill acquisition phases have been identified from a more empirical framework, for example, by Shiffrin and Schneider (1977; Schneider and Shiffrin, 1977; Schneider, 1985), as (1) controlled processing, (2) mixed controlled and automatic processing, and (3) automatic processing. Across the Fitts, Anderson, and Schneider and Shiffrin models the underlying processes at each skill acquisition phase or stage are qualitatively identical (and for the Anderson and Shiffrin and Schneider approaches are, by and large, quantitatively identical; see Anderson, 1982, 1983).

Phase 1 The *cognitive* phase of skill acquisition appears to involve all of the requisite memory and reasoning processes that allow the learner to attain an understanding of the task requirements. The content of a task at this point often consists of the specification of task goals (that is, some end result of proficiency or task completion) and frequently includes instruction of declarative knowledge about the task, as, for example, an overview of the mechanical system or general principles of equipment operation. During this phase the learner may examine the proximal and distal goals of the training program, may observe demonstrations of the task, may encode and store task rules, and may derive strategies for the task. Learners performing at this level of skill acquisition devote most, if not all, of their attention to understanding and performing the task in question. That is, when confronted with additional information-processing requirements, as with the inclusion of a secondary task, learners are unable to adequately devote attention to the secondary task *and* to the learning of the criterion task simultaneously (Nissen and Bullemer, 1987). In the cognitive phase, performance is slow and error prone. Once the learner has come to an adequate cognitive representation of the task, he or she can proceed to the second stage, that is, the *associative* phase.

Phase 2 For *consistent* tasks (see earlier definition of consistency), performance speed and accuracy markedly improve over the course of practice. During the *associative* phase of skill acquisition, learners put together (compile) the sequences of cognitive and motor processes required to perform the task. As various methods for simplifying or streamlining the task are tried and evaluated, performance generally becomes faster and less error prone than in the cognitive phase. Historically, association was meant to reflect the building of connections between stimulus (or system) inputs and the requisite outputs performed by the learner (Woodworth, 1938). In modern terms, the *associative* label is given to this phase of skill acquisition to reflect the process of building sequences of efficient associations between stimulus inputs and response operations. At the more generic level of production systems, the associative phase of skill acquisition means that productions needed to accurately perform the task become fully formulated after consistent practice. During this phase 2 of skill acquisition, then, the stimulus-response connections of the skill are refined and strengthened. Furthermore, the cognitive load on the learner is reduced as the goals and procedures are moved from short-term or working memory to long-term memory (Fisk and Schneider, 1983). When a secondary task is added during the associative phase, criterion task performance may not improve to the same degree as under single task conditions, but the criterion skill is less susceptible to interference from external attention demands (Yeh and Schneider, 1985).

Phase 3   The final, *autonomous* phase of skill acquisition is reached when the learner has essentially automatized the skill and the task can be efficiently performed with little attention. During phase 3, the skill has been internalized such that once a stimulus is presented, the responses can often be prepared and executed without conscious mediation by the learner. After a substantial amount of consistent task practice, skilled performance becomes fast and accurate, and the task can often be performed with minimal impairment while attention is also being devoted to a secondary task (see Schneider and Fisk, 1982a). Although improvements in performance during practice are still found at this final level of skill acquisition, practice functions at this stage are well described in terms of diminishing returns, in keeping with the power law of practice (Newell and Rosenbloom, 1981).

This three-phase skill acquisition framework, along with a consideration of major constraints of learning tasks, can be incorporated into an individual differences perspective. The following discussion develops this framework.

Task Constraints and Skill Acquisition

Skill acquisition research has identified numerous limiting constraints on the learner, characteristics of tasks, and conditions of learning that moderate whether or not, or how, learning takes place over practice. In order to reasonably limit discussion, only three fundamental task-learner characteristics have been included within the present framework. These broad characteristics are generically referred to as (a) transfer, (b) complexity, and (c) consistency.

Transfer Increasing the degree of positive transfer of training from previous experience is hypothesized to allow learners to begin a task with performance that is superior to novice learners. Under optimal transfer circumstances, learners may have little in the way of phase 1 cognitive demands and so may start at phase 2 (or even at phase 3 if an identical or highly similar task has been previously acquired). It follows that increases in positive transfer of training can be depicted by a positive shift along the practice continuum. Initial performance on the task may change as a result of positive transfer, although asymptotic levels of association are not expected to be affected. Negative transfer of training, on the other hand, not only leads to depressed early performance, but may also affect the speed of skill acquisition and possibly the ultimate asymptote of performance.

Complexity In contrast to the facilitative effects of positive transfer of training, increasing task complexity places a greater load on the cognitive-attentional apparatus. As such, an increase in task complexity (for example, by raising the number of items that must be held in memory, the number of and types of processing — such as the difference between 3-digit mental addition and 3-digit mental multiplication) increases the demand for phase 1 processing. From the production system perspective, more complex tasks require a greater number of productions (or more complex productions) for successful skilled performance. As a byproduct, initial phase 1 RTs of complex tasks are slower than RTs of a task of moderate complexity.

By definition, increased task complexity is associated with an increase in the nonredundant productions necessary for task completion. If these productions can be performed in parallel with practice, asymptotic performance levels are identical for tasks differing in complexity (such as for memory search; see Shiffrin and Schneider, 1977). Phase 3 demands may be identical for two tasks that differ only in complexity.

Consistency The effects of consistency are somewhat more complicated, given that the degree of consistency can be defined as either *within*-task components or *between*-task components. For a novel task, phase 1 demands are identical for various degrees of consistency. Tasks with predominant proportions of inconsistent components do not progress beyond phase 1 even with practice, given that consistency is necessary for the development of skilled performance. Tasks with mixtures of consistent and inconsistent components fall in between consistent and inconsistent tasks, with the amount of skill development contingent on the proportion of consistent components.

When individual task components are only partly consistent, development of phase 2 and phase 3 is slowed since inconsistent events will decrement the strength of the consistent production system under development. Depending on the nature of the task component in question, as the level of within-component consistency is lowered, the transition to later skill phases slows, and ultimately halts (to remain in phase 1). Evidence for such trends can be found in the experimental psychology literature. For example, Schneider and Fisk (1982b) found that there is essentially a decreasing degree of autonomous skill development as the amount of task consistency decreases. The initial results indicate that autonomous processing can be thought of as a continuum. Pure autonomous information processing can be attained only when both stimulus inputs and responses are entirely consistent. When consistency is absent, the task must be performed with phase 1 controlled information processing.

Although this discussion is a simplification of skill acquisition, the concepts provide the first half of the foundation for unifying experimental and differential approaches to skill acquisition. The next section concentrates on the second half of the foundation, a specification of abilities for skill acquisition.

Abilities for Skill Acquisition

Defining cognitive-intellectual abilities is a task no less difficult than defining such concepts as short-term memory or attention. Theoretical (stipulative) and operational definitions of abilities abound (Robinson, 1950; Miles, 1957). However, there is enough commonality among most definitions to allow for a reasonable working description of the constructs.

General Intelligence (General Ability) Early theories of intelligence occasionally involved operational definitions; intelligence was variously defined as "education of relations" and "the education of correlates" (Spearman, 1927), "the power to think abstractly" (Terman, 1921), and "the ability to undertake activities that are characterized by (1) difficulty, (2) complexity, (3) abstractness, (4) economy, (5) adaptiveness to a goal, (6) social value, and (7) the emergence of originals, and to maintain such activities under conditions that demand a concentration of energy and resistance to emotional forces" (Stoddard, 1943).

In more recent literature, a general cognitive-intellectual ability is commonly defined from an indirect procedure. From this viewpoint, a general ability is implied by the variance common to the universe of all psychological ability tests. Such an ability is often found to account for about 50 percent of the individual differences variance in large batteries of ability tests (Vernon, 1961). One inference is that the general ability represents a broad construct that underlies nonspecific information-processing efficacy. The ubiquitous finding that ability tests reveal positive intercorrelations provides one major justification for the construct of general intelligence (Humphreys, 1979). One way of formalizing the ability construct is the broad definition of intelligence offered by Humphreys (1979). He states that "[general] intelligence is the resultant of the processes of acquiring, storing in memory, retrieving, combining, comparing, and using in new contexts information and conceptual skills."

In this view, general intelligence *must* be a determinant of individual differences in the processes that are described by Fitts, Anderson, and Shiffrin and Schneider as underlying phase 1 of skill acquisition.

Perceptual Speed Ability   The construct of perceptual speed has been accorded less research, discussion, and controversy than has the general ability. However, as with a general ability, the traditional views of perceptual speed abilities are derived via review of test intercorrelations and clusterings.

The general finding from empirical studies is that perceptual speed is an ability class that can be separated from other ability classes, including numerical, verbal, and spatial abilities (see Thurstone, 1944; Ekstrom et al., 1976; Lohman, 1979). Demonstrations that perceptual speed can be separated from spatial abilities are especially important, given that many prototypical perceptual speed tests contain spatial content. Across the content domain, in general, a derived perceptual speed factor represents individual differences in the speed with which cognitive test items can be completed when the domain includes only simple items that can be easily answered by all or most members of the subject population.

Many tests have been posited to load on a perceptual speed factor. Marker tests include "finding a's" (Ekstrom et al., 1976), which entails searching through a list of words and marking any word containing the letter *a*, or "scattered x's," where the examinee searches for *x*'s in fields of random letters (Thurstone and Thurstone, 1941). Another test is the digit-symbol test (Wechsler, 1955), which involves a paired-associates type of information processing—that is, memorization (or rapid reference to a list) of a set of digit-symbol pairs and transcribing symbols on a list of digit probes. Other tests include comparisons of identical items—proofreading with numerical, verbal, or figural content, with a requirement to indicate mismatches. Many of these tests appear to involve the generation and strengthening of very simple production systems (or associations) that can be used to effectively solve the test items.

In the language of skill acquisition, individual differences found on perceptual speed tests are directly attributable to the speed with which these small sets of productions can be implemented and compiled or proceduralized. Therefore, this ability class captures the information-processing operations characteristic of skill acquisition phase 2, the associative phase.

A definition that illustrates this view has been provided by Werdelin and Stjernberg (1969). They state that "the perceptual speed factor is a measure of the capacity to automatize, by means of practice, the solution of perceptual problems, which have originally depended on the visual-perceptual factors" (p. 192).

Psychomotor Ability   As with the preceding abilities, the psychomotor domain represents an amalgamation of identifiable but related subabilities. A general psychomotor ability represents individual differences predominantly in the speed of responses to test items with few or minimal cognitive processing demands. Whereas perceptual speed ability represents cognitive processing of generally simple (but cognitively involving) items, psychomotor ability represents processing speed (and accuracy to a certain degree), mostly independent of information processing.

Prototypical measures of psychomotor abilities include simple reaction time, rotary pursuit, tapping speed, rate of manipulation, finger dexterity, and so on (Fleishman, 1954). While some of these tests require a degree of information processing (mostly in terms of sensory feedback), the underlying characteristic of these tests is *the examinee knows, ahead of time, exactly what responses need to be made.* Reasoning (as with the general ability), memory, and the formation of new associations (as with perceptual speed) are all minimized in tests that tap these abilities.

A stipulative, but nonetheless operational, definition of psychomotor ability is as follows: psychomotor ability represents individual differences in the speed (and accuracy) of motor responding that are characteristic of psychophysical limitations of the human subject. The differentiating processes of psychomotor ability are those that underlie *asymptotically* compiled and tuned perceptual/motor production systems. Psychomotor abilities are therefore identified as characteristic of phase 3 of skill acquisition.

These three ability classes — general, perceptual speed, and psychomotor — do not exist in a vacuum. By building on previous models for the structure of intelligence, it is possible to diagram the interrelations among these abilities and the associations between these abilities and a wide range of other cognitive-intellectual abilities. The next section considers the issue of representation.

A Structure of Abilities for Skill Acquisition

Several representations of abilities linked with types of information processing have been offered in the literature subsequent to 1965. Some are essentially piecemeal mappings of abilities with information-processing paradigms (for example, Carroll, 1980), while others are general, all-encompassing theories of abilities and information processing (for example, Sternberg, 1985). In order to allow for an empirically based mapping of abilities to information-processing skills, an intermediate approach is required.

Modern ability theories are often categorized as hierarchical in nature, with the general ability defining the highest level node in the hierarchy. Major group factors (such as verbal, figural, numerical) are located at lower nodes in the hierarchy, and specific abilities at still lower nodes (Vernon, 1961). For present purposes, a functionally equivalent and more parsimonious representation of the major components of intellectual abilities is the radex (Guttman, 1954; Marshalek, Lohman, and Snow, 1983; Snow, Kyllonen, and Marshalek, 1984).

A spatial representation of the structure of intelligence from this framework is illustrated in Figure 5-1 (from Marshalek et al., 1983). Here, general intelligence is represented as the centroid, with different major content abilities as slices of the ability circle. *Complexity* of processing is reflected in the distance from the centroid, the most complex test requirements located close to G. As one moves to the periphery, less complex abilities are located. It should be noted that such a two-dimensional representation is an approximation to the relations between the major components of intelligence.

In the Marshalek et al. (1983) model, tests that tap speeded abilities appear in the periphery of the relevant content slices. A broad perceptual speed ability is not represented as a single ability in this model, but rather represents a family of abilities specific to particular content domains, such as speed of lexical access, speed of figural comparison, and so on (however, see Snow, Kyllonen, and Marshalek, 1984 for some alternative solutions). For this to be a veridical

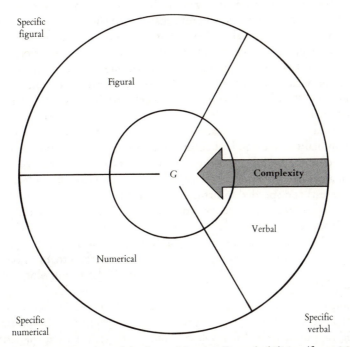

Figure 5-1 A radex-based model of cognitive-intellectual abilities (from Marshalek, Lohman, and Snow, 1983). The construct of complexity-specificity is represented as the proximity to the center of the circle. Content abilities are represented as different slices of the circle. In the Marshalek et al. model, perceptual speed is represented as content domain specific. Copyright 1983 by Ablex Publishing Corporation. Reprinted by permission.

representation, a random sample of tests assessing perceptual speed with different test content (letters, numbers, figures) will demonstrate little common variance. However, earlier psychometric studies indicate that perceptual speed tests do reveal greater common variance than would be expected from the Marshalek et al. perspective (see, for example, Thurstone, 1944; Roff, 1952; Fleishman, 1954; Ekstrom et al., 1976; Lord, 1956).

The problem of representation can be rectified by dividing the Marshalek et al. complexity continuum into *two* continua, namely *complexity* and *speed*. That is, the modification is to explicitly distinguish between the complexity of cognitive demands and the speededness of cognitive demands. Although highly speeded abilities are less frequently of interest to differential psychologists, these are emphasized (perhaps overly so) by cognitive experimental psychologists. The essential point from the cognitive approach is that task demands can be both speeded *and* complex (aspects of piloting an aircraft would be one obvious example).

An inherent limitation of any multidimensional scaling representation of abilities is that any test with low communality will show up on the periphery of the solution. In the Marshalek representation, both speeded *and* specific ability tests are represented on the periphery of the structure. Thus, the complexity continuum equates speeded processes with simple or specific processes. The additional provision of a speed continuum allows not only for complex speeded processes, but also for a distinction between specific processes and speeded processes, such as a distinction between a test of architecture knowledge on the one hand and a test of visual reaction time on the other hand. If both tests had low communality in a standard ability test battery, they would presumably be represented on the periphery of the figural part of the Marshalek et al. structure. The fundamental differences between specific declarative knowledge (the architecture test) and speeded information processing of figural stimuli (the visual RT test) missed by the Marshalek structure would be revealed with a modified structure that separated speededness of processing from complexity.

With this modification, the three ability classes of interest for the study of skill acquisition (general, perceptual speed, and psychomotor) can be incorporated into a single spatial model. In keeping with the terminology offered by Lohman (1979), the dimension added to the structure is called *level-speed* (level tests beings generally equivalent to power tests). The level-speed dimension allows representation of both perceptual speed and psychomotor abilities. Using the basic two-dimensional (complexity and content) surface at the extreme on the level-speed dimension (that is, zero speededness of information-processing demands), and an arbitrary value representing the extreme in speededness (with the absence of cognitive processing—in other words, noncognitive motor speed), the structure of human abilities can be represented as a cylinder, as idealized in Figure 5-2. Theoretically, as one moves down the cylinder, con-

Level

Phase 1

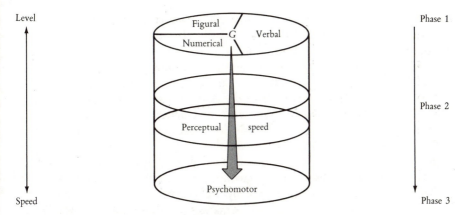

Phase 2

Speed

Phase 3

Figure 5-2 A modified radex-based model of cognitive abilities. Complexity is represented as in the Marshalek et al. model. However, the dimension of level-speed is added to provide for perceptual speed and psychomotor abilities (from Ackerman, 1988). Copyright 1988 by American Psychological Association. Reprinted by permission.

centric sections represent the basic cognitive ability groups, with increasing demands on speededness. With this structure as background, a straightforward specification of ability-performance relationships during the course of skill acquisition can be offered.

The veridicality of the Marshalek et al. radex structure of abilities can be defended partly because of the logical identification of the radex structure with a hierarchical factor structure of abilities (see Marshalek et al., 1983). Further support for the radex structure has been derived from examination of nonmetric multidimensional scaling reanalyses of intercorrelations of large ability test batteries (such as that of Thurstone and Thurstone, 1941; see Snow et al., 1984). Snow et al. demonstrate that a two-dimensional representation of such data yields general agreement with the complexity and content classifications specified by their model.

The overlap between the Snow et al. model and the modified structure just proposed (see also Ackerman, 1988) provides for agreement between the models only when there is minimal or moderate sampling of speeded tests. The divergence occurs when sufficient perceptual speed and psychomotor measures are included in the test battery.

Initial justification of this modified structure comes from the logical distinction between level-speed and complexity-specificity. These arguments can be supplemented with empirical data, given that a sample includes sufficient numbers of tests ranging from simple to complex and from level to highly speeded test format. Most of the test batteries reanalyzed by Snow et al. (1984)

were limited in the sense that few psychomotor measures were included in the batteries. One data set investigated by Snow et al.—the battery constructed by Allison (1960)—does contain a sufficient sampling of moderately and highly speeded measures (such as the perceptual speed and psychomotor domains) along with reference measures differing in content and complexity.

In performing their reanalysis of the Allison data, Snow et al. found that "the results of these scaling analyses were interpretable but complicated . . ." (p. 77). As a result, Snow et al. proceeded to create composites for three general ability factors in order to further discuss their model and learning task-ability factor correlations. The scaling solution to the Allison battery was not reported.

Given that the Allison battery satisfies the test sampling requirements of the modified structure hypothesized by Ackerman (1988), it is relevant to present a multidimensional scaling reanalysis of those data for validation purposes.

Allison Data Reanalysis

The study by Allison (1960) remains one of a sparse set of large-scale ability-learning studies in the literature. Allison used a sophisticated form of analysis (multi-battery factor analysis) to compare factors underlying learning and reference intellectual ability factors. In addition to a large set of learning measures, a reference test battery of thirty-seven measures was administered during the study. Data on the ability test and learning tasks were collected on a sample of 315 naval recruits. For present purposes, the multiple measure learning task data were excluded from the analysis. (For relevant discussion of the learning data, the reader should consult Allison, 1960; Cronbach and Snow, 1977; and Snow et al., 1984.)

In an effort to investigate the ability structure underlying the Allison reference tests, the present author recently performed two sets of multidimensional scaling reanalyses. The analyses mirrored those by Snow et al. for other ability batteries (namely, nonmetric multidimensional scaling of the correlation matrix via the KYST algorithm). The first analysis included all thirty-seven ability test variables in a three-dimensional solution. The results from this analysis were in general agreement with the modified ability structure presented here.

In order to clarify the structure, six variables were excluded from the analysis: these measures were the four memory tests, along with cubes and steadiness tests. The memory tests were excluded because it was not clear how speeded such tests were (given a speeded presentation but a longer free-response period). The cubes and steadiness tests were excluded as a result of extremely low communality estimates, which forced these items to the periphery of the ability space (but, otherwise these tests had no substantive impact on the solution). The remaining thirty-one variables were submitted to the same analytic procedure, again specifying a three-dimensional solution. The multidimensional scaling results were rotated to principal components, and *no* attempt was made to maximize fit of the data to the proposed model. Nonetheless, the results clearly support the modified model. A listing of the reference tests, the dimension loadings, and Allison's hypothesized factors underlying each test are presented in Table 5-2. Figures 5-3 and 5-4 present plots of dimension 1 and dimension 2 versus dimension 3 for a visual comparison with the hypothesized ability structure.

Dimension 1 (see Figure 5-3) is obviously a contrast between level and speed. Power tests such as letter sets and reasoning provide the anchors for the level tests; moderately speeded tests (that is, perceptual speed tests) such as word checking, addition, and clerical aptitude define the middle portion of the dimension; and highly speeded tests (psychomotor ability tests) such as turning, placing, and writing x's define the speed anchors of the dimensions.[1]

Dimensions 2 and 3 (see Figure 5-4) also support the complexity-content radex postulated by Marshalek et al. (1983) and Snow et al. (1984), which is incorporated into the present model. Highly complex tests that define general intelligence (G) are located in the center of the structure, with content abilities (here numerical, verbal, figural, and mechanical) in the surrounding quadrants.

Together these results offer convincing evidence in support of the proposed model of reference abilities for skill acquisition. Scaling reanalyses of selected data from a more extensive reference test battery (the Army – Air Force Sheppard Field Battery, with sixty-five variables) are also consistent with the model and the Allison data, but are not reported here in light of space considerations.

In summary, the available data are consistent with this modification of the Marshalek et al. model. Clearly, as with other efforts to test structure of abilities models, the ability sampling of any particular battery will affect whether the level-speed dimension is revealed through scaling analysis.

PRINCIPLES OF AN INTEGRATIVE THEORY OF INDIVIDUAL DIFFERENCES AND SKILL ACQUISITION

With this structure of abilities as a foundation, a proposed linkage between theories of skill acquisition and the ability structure is offered by outlining three fundamental principles. These theoretical principles, in turn, provide (a) a

---

[1]It is interesting that in the full test battery analysis, the memory tests were found to load quite highly on the speed part of the level-speed dimension. While this was a serendipitous finding, it is consistent with the fact that speed is a critical component of two of these tests given that memory items were presented to the subjects at a rapid rate for this subject sample; for example, in the word-number test, twenty associative pairs were to be memorized in 300 seconds.

Table 5-2 Nonmetric Multidimensional Scaling Data

Ref. No.*	Dimension			Test name (description)	Factor†
	1	2	3		
42	-.870	.030	-.343	Sentence completion	(Verbal)
34	-.835	.064	.217	Letter sets	(Induction)
37	-.642	.142	.452	Math aptitude (story problems)	(Reasoning)
41	-.623	.152	-.304	36-item vocabulary	(Verbal)
39	-.590	.665	-.116	Reasoning (meaningful syllogisms)	(Deduction)
38	-.554	.972	-.713	False premises (nonsense syllogisms)	(Deduction)
35	-.519	.352	.084	Arithmetic	(Reasoning)
36	-.518	-.128	-.009	Ship destination (compute distance to port)	(Reasoning)
40	-.460	.041	-.127	General classification test (analogies and sentence completion)	(Verbal)
64	-.459	.076	-.062	Otis self-administering achievement test	(Intelligence)
45	-.452	-.704	.511	Paper folding	(Visualization)
50	-.442	.689	.332	Division (two- or three-digit by one-digit)	(Number facility)
63	-.434	-.290	-.015	Armed Forces Qualification Test (composite score)	(Intelligence)
33	-.429	.276	.346	Number series	(Induction)

65	−.379	−.007	.396	Otis directions test	(Intelligence)
48	−.348	−1.249	−.220	Guilford-Zimmerman mechanical knowledge	(Mechanical knowledge)
47	−.317	−1.028	−.109	Mechanical (knowledge and mechanical comprehension)	(Mechanical knowledge)
46	−.205	−.934	.399	Paper form board	(Visualization)
62	−.133	.230	−.748	Word checking (select words—do not grow, smaller than football)	(Speed of association)
49	−.119	.893	.433	Addition (one- and two-digit)	(Number facility)
61	−.105	.077	−.610	Words associated with unfurnished house (select from list)	(Speed of association)
43	.110	−.962	−.103	Cards	(Spatial relations or orientation)
60	.217	−.147	.146	Picture discrimination (faces comparison)	(Perceptual speed)
59	.574	.524	.516	Clerical aptitude (name/number comparison)	(Perceptual speed)
54	.768	.609	−.074	Writing digits (write digits 1 through 9)	(Motor speed)
56	1.100	−.557	.280	Turning (Minnesota rate of manipulation)	(Motor dexterity)
51	1.149	−.263	.144	Tracing (draw line through pattern)	(Aiming)
55	1.257	−.042	−.716	Tapping (two-plate tapping)	(Motor speed)
57	1.285	−.517	−.427	Placing (Minnesota rate of manipulation)	(Motor dexterity)
53	1.433	.522	−.385	Writing x's	(Motor speed)
52	1.537	.513	.824	Dotting (put dot inside $\frac{1}{16}$-inch circles)	(Aiming)

*Reference variable numbers from Allison (1960), pp. 31–42.
†Factors identified by Allison (1960), pp. 31–42.

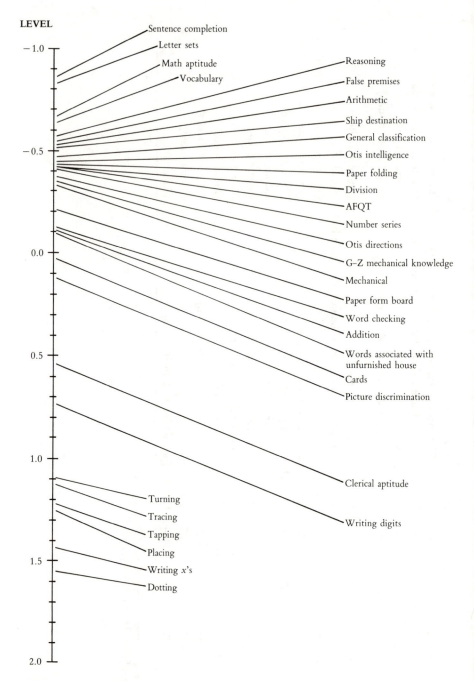

Figure 5-3 Mapping of thirty-one reference test variables on dimension 1, from multi-dimensional scaling reanalysis of Allison (1960) data. The dimension is identified as level versus speed (from Ackerman, 1988). Copyright 1988 by American Psychological Association. Reprinted by permission.

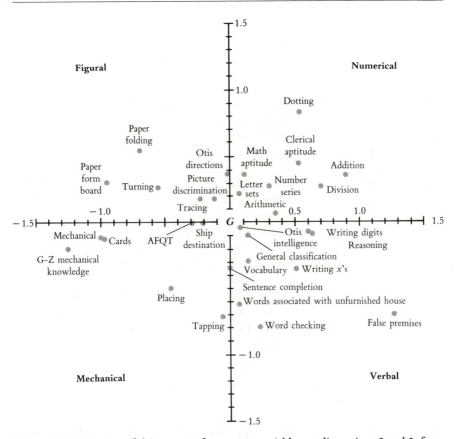

Figure 5-4 Mapping of thirty-one reference test variables on dimensions 2 and 3, from multidimensional scaling reanalysis of Allison (1960) data. Dimensions 2 and 3 identify the radex complexity-content structure as identified by Marshalek et al. (1983) and incorporated into the Ackerman (1988) three-dimensional structure of abilities. Copyright 1988 by American Psychological Association. Reprinted by permission.

framework for empirical evaluation of the experimental-differential linkage and (b) specific predictions for patterns of ability-performance correlations under a variety of skill acquisition conditions. This section describes the theoretical principles and sets the stage for demonstration of empirical investigations of the theory.

Theory Principles

1. Skill acquisition, phase 1 – cognitive corresponds to demands on general and content abilities.

With a mapping of general ability with phase 1, Figure 5-5a gives the theoretical representation of the associations of ability and performance. The standard task for this representation is of moderate complexity and is relatively high in consistency (a typical skill acquisition task). Initial performance individual differences will be moderately associated with the general ability. With practice (as phase 1 makes the transition into phase 2), the ability-performance association will attenuate, reaching an asymptote late in practice (which will be dependent on the actual level of inconsistency of the task).

For novel tasks, initial (that is, in the absence of pretreatment practice) individual differences will be determined by the general ability, as well as by task-appropriate broad content abilities such as verbal abilities for tasks that demand processing of semantic material or spatial abilities for tasks that demand figural processing. The overall magnitude of association between these abilities and performance will depend on task complexity, but also on the adequacy of instruction and, of course, on the subject population under study. With practice, as production systems are formulated to accomplish the *consistent* components of the task, the influence of general and content abilities will diminish.

2. Skill acquisition, phase 2 – associative corresponds to demands on perceptual speed abilities.

If perceptual speed is equated with compilation and tuning of production systems, there will be an inverted U-shaped function which describes ability-performance relationships over practice (see Figure 5-5b). Early in practice, the productions are still being formulated and tested. Thus, compilation and tuning are only involved to the degree that previously learned productions can be readily adapted for successful performance of the current task. There is an initially increasing association between perceptual speed ability and performance once the productions are formulated. The facility and speed of compilation of production systems that determine performance efficiency are the essence of perceptual speed ability. As learners reach their psychophysical limitations of skilled performance, the influence of this variable will attenuate as phase 2 moves to phase 3. Finally, as phase 3 asymptotic performance levels are reached, perceptual speed will further decline to some asymptotic level which is also constrained by the consistency parameters of the task.

3. Skill acquisition, phase 3 – autonomous corresponds to predominantly noncognitive psychomotor abilities.

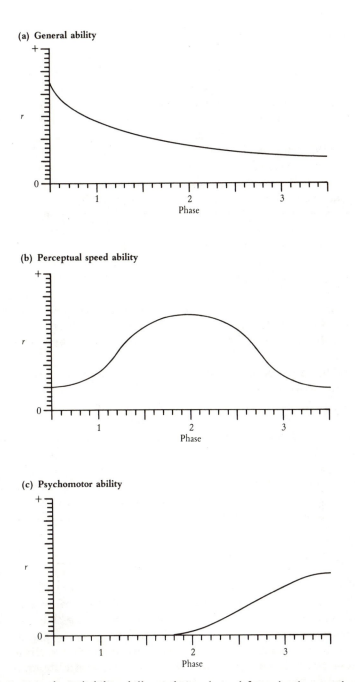

Figure 5-5 Hypothetical ability-skill correlation derived from the theory. The prototypical task is moderately complex and requires predominantly consistent information processing (from Ackerman, 1988). Copyright 1988 by American Psychological Association. Reprinted by permission.

For tasks that allow skilled performance across a wide ability range, individual differences in asymptotic task performance will be more dependent on noncognitive motor abilities than cognitive abilities. As cognitive abilities no longer limit performance, individuals converge on performance asymptotes that are ultimately determined by psychomotor speed differences (as in cigar-rolling [see Crossman, 1959] or choice RT tasks [Newell and Rosenbloom, 1981]). Even so, the actual performance differences between the fastest and slowest learners at this level of skill development are vastly reduced. That is, interindividual performance variability is reduced with consistent practice.

Therefore, as phase 2 gives way to phase 3, psychomotor abilities will increase in association with performance, ultimately stabilizing to a moderate degree of correlation. It follows that the theoretical predictions of psychomotor ability-performance relationships are as illustrated in Figure 5-5c. During phases 1 and 2 of skill acquisition, psychomotor abilities have inconsequential influence on performance. However, as phase 2 makes the transition to phase 3, the information-processing productions have been formulated, compiled, and tuned. Asymptotic performance will be associated with individual differences in psychomotor ability when little or no new information must be processed from trial to trial.

An additional point should be noted. For comparisons of novel tasks, initial correlations between the general abilities with performance and perceptual speed with performance are generally negatively associated. When the load on general abilities is high (a greater number of productions must be formulated or more complex productions must be built), little opportunity for compilation and tuning exists early in practice; that is, the correlations between perceptual speed and performance are attenuated. Conversely, when the load on general abilities is minimal (as with simple tasks), compilation of production systems can proceed early in the process of skill acquisition; this leads to low correlations between performance and general abilities, but higher correlations between performance and perceptual speed.

A Dynamic Representation of Abilities and Skills

This theory of the relationship of ability and skill predicts that novel tasks are located towards the top of the cylinder (in Figure 5-2). Performance on these tasks will have high correlations with general and content abilities, relatively low correlations with perceptual speed abilities, and, thus, negligible correlations with psychomotor speed. As autonomous skills are developed, the task moves downward through the ability structure. At intermediate levels of practice, association with general and content abilities declines and associations with perceptual speed and psychomotor ability increase. When the appropriate production systems are compiled and tuned, the task moves further away from the cognitive ability domain. Ultimately, even associations with perceptual speed decline, as individual differences in asymptotic performance are determined by psychomotor abilities. At this point, the task can be located towards the bottom of the cylinder.

With specification of an ability-performance theory and several task constraints as background, the form of investigation most conducive to assessment of individual differences in skill acquisition will utilize a combination of experimental and differential methods. Specifically, by selecting several task contrasts (along the dimensions of complexity, consistency, and transfer) and by assessing key abilities, one may draw comparisons between abilities and skill development during task practice.

Complexity, Consistency, and Transfer Revisited

As discussed previously, the information-processing parameters of task complexity, consistency, and transfer influence the general skill parameters of initial performance, rate of improvement, and final asymptotic performance. Generalization to the individual differences domain indicates that these factors will moderate the effects of practice on interindividual variability and the relationship of ability and performance. Manipulations of task complexity and transfer thus affect both the initial level of variability and the rate of attenuation with practice. Study of the manipulation of task consistency has demonstrated that performance variability decreases *only* when the information-processing requirements are predominantly consistent. When the task configuration precludes the development of autonomous skills, RT variability remains constant (or actually increases) over practice, even when mean RT decreases.

Similarly, a study reported by Ackerman (1984, 1986b) demonstrated that information-processing *consistency* moderates the relations between particular abilities and performance during skill acquisition. In two within-subject memory search experiments, it was found that tasks that involve smaller degrees of consistency maintain a higher association with the general and broad content abilities. When tasks differ in consistency, general ability-performance correlations are larger for the tasks with less consistency. Thus, an initial parallelism was found: when task factors are introduced that impede development of autonomous skilled performance, the same factors prevent the transition from phase 1 ability determinants of individual differences in performance to phase 3 determinants of performance.

Relevant Previous Research

Until the last few years, few programmatic investigations of individual differences in skill (and knowledge) acquisition have been undertaken. One program in particular, by Pellegrino (1983, 1985), does provide related sources of data that require consideration. Two studies by Pellegrino appear to support aspects of the perspective proposed here. In one investigation (Pellegrino, 1985), performance intercept parameters (asymptotic performance) were found for several consistent cognitive tasks practiced over 500 to 1,000 trials, including perceptual matching (same-different judgments for number pairs), attribute comparison (a word instantiation of the Posner task), perceptual matching II (random polygon stimuli), and visual search (with graphic symbols). In these tasks, the intercept parameters were moderately to strongly correlated with perceptual speed ability (range r = .23 to .64, mean = .49). In contrast, only one of these tasks (fact retrieval) showed significant correlations between intercept parameters and broad quantitative and verbal abilities. As with other tasks discussed here, it is difficult to estimate the exact level of skill acquisition at the end of practice. Also, correlations between the reference abilities and initial task performance are not reported, but the moderate practice obtained by the subjects suggests that the results are nonetheless consistent with the theory predictions for phase 2 task performance.

A second study strikingly illustrates the findings reported earlier for reduction of the magnitude of individual differences (variability) with consistent task practice. Pellegrino (1983) started by task-analyzing the nature of psychometrically defined spatial abilities (at the level of information-processing components). Using an extreme groups design (on the basis of perceptual speed, spatial relations, and spatial visualization test scores), high- and low-ability individuals were given training on the component processes subsumed by these ability measures. To the degree that the productions required for performance of these components are proceduralized (phases 2 and 3 of skill acquisition), and thus free up the general ability (phase 1) system, development of such skills was expected to result in marked improvement in the target broad spatial ability tests. Indeed, subsequent to about 8 hours of training, the original test battery was readministered, with the results of a mean 40 to 50 percent improvement for the low-ability group (well beyond the amount of improvement expected as a result of regression effects), with much smaller gains by the high-ability group.

Pellegrino argues that these results are not situation specific, as the reference tests required substantial generalized transfer from the laboratory tasks. Delayed testing two months after training showed that these gains were not ephemeral. As such, the procedural knowledge transfer of training appeared to enable the processing of the test battery items in a manner that had fewer general ability demands.

Thus, for a sample of simple, consistent tasks, two of the findings by Fleishman et al. (Fleishman, 1972) have been generally substantiated. These are: (a) intellectual abilities appear to correlate markedly with initial task performance, but attenuate as skills are acquired; and (b) some perceptual/motor abilities show small correlations with performance at early trials, but increase in association during practice. These conclusions will be discussed below, in the context of new empirical research.

Previous research on individual differences has provided limited evaluation of how systematic changes in task information-processing requirements affect ability-performance relations during practice. The theory just outlined does allow for specific predictions when comparing tasks differing in levels of transfer, complexity, and consistency (Ackerman, 1988). Two recent studies will be presented that illustrate interactions between the complexity of task information-processing demands and ability-performance associations over practice.

EMPIRICAL EVALUATION OF THE THEORY

Task Complexity and Memory Load

The first study examined how a change in memory load—a complexity manipulation—affects the temporal patterns of performance associations with general and perceptual speed abilities. The strategy of the study was to create two versions of a task with predominantly consistent information-processing requirements—requirements that allow for the development of autonomous skilled performance. The tasks were structured so that the underlying task productions were identical once skilled performance was developed. However, the initial processing demands on working memory differed as a matter of degree.

Briefly, the two tasks were category (word) search procedures. For both tasks, subjects were first presented with a memory set of category labels (such as "animal" or "clothing"). After a short memorization period (5 seconds), the memory display was replaced with a probe display containing three words. Only one word in the probe display was a member of a memory set category. The subjects were to identify and indicate, as quickly as possible with a key response, the position of the probe display item which matched a memory set category (an appropriate probe word might be "cat," which is a member of the "animal" category). Additional details of this type of task can be found in Fisk and Schneider (1983) or Ackerman (1986b).

The distinction between the two experimental tasks was that, in the *high* memory load task, *all three* of the categories comprising the memory set were given on each trial. Thus, the memory set size (M) for the first task version was three items (the task was designated $M = 3$). In contrast, in the *low* memory load task only a subset of two of the three memory set categories was given on each trial. (These categories were randomly sampled on each trial.) The memory set size for this task version was two items ($M = 2$).

In keeping with the Anderson (1982, 1983) and Shiffrin and Schneider (1977) theories, although the subjects in the $M = 2$ condition had to deal with only two of the three categories on any given trial, identical production systems to handle all three categories will eventually be formulated for both tasks. As such, the autonomous processes (or tuned procedural knowledge) developed for these two tasks will be identical, once the cognitive (controlled processing-declarative knowledge) phase of skill acquisition is completed.

The $M = 2$ task is simple and straightforward. The cognitive demands are modest because the categories and exemplars are common and known by the subjects (Battig and Montague, 1969). Thus, subjects can reach phase 2 processing early in practice. However, the cognitive demands of the $M = 3$ task exceed the $M = 2$ task during initial confrontation with the task. Because memory search is serial and error prone at phase 1, the increased processing demands will be reflected in longer average RTs for the $M = 3$ task. Also, the associated increase in cognitive demands will be reflected in an increase in interindividual variability for $M = 3$, as well as an increase in associations between the general ability and task performance. As discussed above, the increased cognitive demands will force an attenuation in associations between $M = 3$ performance and perceptual speed ability.

The parallelism with skill acquisition theory actually goes further here. Previous research and modeling (Schneider, 1985) have indicated that, all other conditions being equal, such an increase in memory load (as long as working-memory capacity is not exceeded) will accelerate the acquisition of autonomous processing. The reason for this is that the learners build productions for all three categories every trial, while in the $M = 2$ condition, productions for only two of the three categories will be under development on each trial. The reduced memory load condition clearly makes fewer demands on the attentional system. Performance is thus easier and phase 2 occurs earlier. Given this situation, an interaction between memory load and practice is expected, with the $M = 3$ condition yielding longer mean RT initially, but shorter RT after practice. However, if practice is carried out far enough (phase 3), the two mean learning curves are expected to asymptote at equal levels.

In summary, the increase in memory load, from a two-item to a three-item memory set, does not result in an enduring increase in task complexity; given that both versions sample from the same three-item set of categories. As with traditional consistent mapping designs, although subjects in the $M = 2$ condition were required to memorize only two items on every trial, once the entire set of categories and exemplars are learned, memory load no longer has an effect on mean performance levels. Category search after practice proceeds nearly fully in parallel (see Fisk and Schneider, 1983). Thus, the increase in memory load is essentially an initial — or front-end — increase in task complexity; that is, the learners must work harder during the early stages of learning, but these demands attenuate rapidly as the categories are learned. Subjects in the $M = 2$ condition can engage in some phase 2 processing earlier (given the reduced cognitive load on any individual trial), but the load on the cognitive system declines more slowly for such subjects than those in the $M = 3$ condition.

This set of conditions was explored within a series of experiments conducted with U.S. Air Force recruits enrolled in basic training. The two conditions were necessarily run with a between-subjects design, with 338 subjects in the $M = 2$ condition, and 216 subjects in the $M = 3$ condition. Task practice was given at individual computer workstations, with twelve blocks of sixty trials per block. Total task practice was completed in a 3-hour period. Ability data were restricted to the Armed Services Vocational Aptitude Battery (ASVAB). While this battery does not allow for determination of psychomotor abilities, orthogonal estimates of general intellectual and perceptual speed abilities are readily found via Schmid-Leiman (1957) hierarchical rotation procedures. Ability-performance relations are derived with the Dwyer (1937) extension procedure, which provides performance loadings on fixed reference ability factors (Ackerman, 1986b, 1988).

In order to assess the veridicality of the theory, predictions were made that contrasted the performance variability and ability-performance data that were expected on the basis of two nearly identical tasks—differing only in the dimension of complexity—as outlined previously.

Predictions

1. In comparison to the baseline $M = 2$ condition, the increase in initial task complexity of the $M = 3$ condition was predicted to yield initially higher correlations with the general ability factor. Given that productions are formed and tested more rapidly in the $M = 3$ condition (this was expected to be reflected in the mean and variability data), an interaction was predicted. That is, with practice, correlations with general ability were expected to attenuate *faster* in the $M = 3$ condition. Finally, correlations with the general ability were expected to asymptote at equivalent levels for the two tasks (see Figure 5-6a).

2. In contrast, the theory predicted that the higher $M = 3$ general ability loadings (phase 1) will come at a cost of reducing the initial association of performance with perceptual speed. With practice, though, as the general ability correlations decline, the perceptual speed correlations should increase. As the cognitive demands reduce, it would become possible for the subjects to begin to compile and tune the production systems. As the $M = 2$ correlations with perceptual speed ability are declining, even early in practice (as phase 2 moves on to phase 3), perceptual speed correlations with $M = 3$ performance were expected to increase, level off, and then decrease during skill development. The expectation then was for an opposite interaction of correlations to also be

(a) General

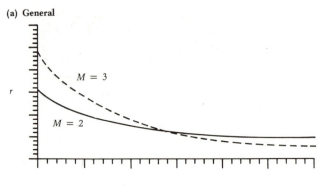

Practice

(b) Perceptual speed

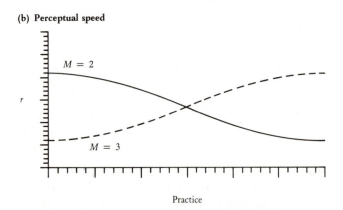

Practice

Figure 5-6 Predictions of correlations of general ability and performance (a) and correlations of perceptual speed ability and performance (b) over practice derived from the theory.

found in the $M = 2$ versus $M = 3$ contrasts for perceptual speed (see Figure 5-6b).

Results   The mean and standard deviation results for the two tasks are presented in Figure 5-7. Although the $M = 3$ mean performance level at session 1 is 84 milliseconds slower than the $M = 2$ mean, these tasks show convergence of mean RT at session 4 (Figure 5-7a). The standard deviations (session 1:404 milliseconds for the $M = 3$ condition, 271 milliseconds for the $M = 3$ condition) show convergence at session 5, and stabilize at equivalent levels in later sessions (Figure 5-7b).

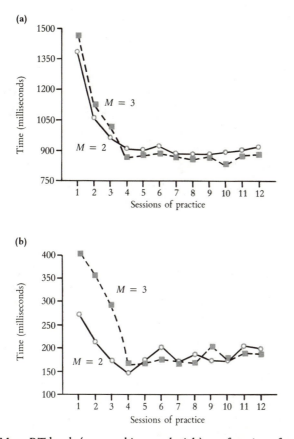

Figure 5-7 a. Mean RT levels (across subjects and trials) as a function of practice for two conditions differing in level of front-end complexity. b. Between-subject standard deviations as a function of practice. $M = 2$ is a memory set size of two items; $M = 3$ is a memory set size of three items. Each session of practice contained sixty trials (from Ackerman, 1988). Copyright 1988 by American Psychological Association. Reprinted by permission.

The interactions of the ability-performance correlations over practice are also found as predicted. Figure 5-8a shows the comparison for the general ability correlations. For this ability, $M = 3$ starts off with a higher correlation with general ability, but by session 7, the $M = 3$ steeper slope of attenuation shows the expected interaction, with $M = 2$ having moderately higher correlations. A test for the difference between regression slopes (McNemar, 1962) was performed towards confirming this result. With $df = 20$, the test statistic ($t =$

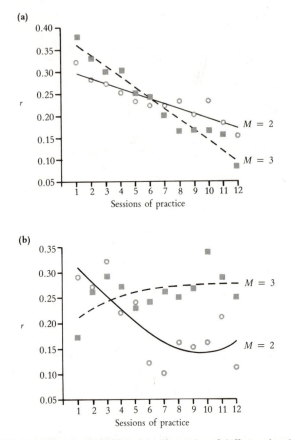

Figure 5-8 Ability-performance relationships for tasks of differing levels of front-end complexity. a. Correlations between derived general ability and task performance. Lines indicate linear regression of G loading over practice. b. Correlations between derived perceptual speed ability and task performance. Lines indicate polynomial (cubic) regression of ability loading over practice (from Ackerman, 1988). Copyright 1988 by American Psychological Association. Reprinted by permission.

5.45) was found to be significant ($p<.001$). The data are less regular for the perceptual speed correlations (depicted in Figure 5-8b), but the interaction is apparent ($t[df= 20] = -3.82$, $p<.01$), even if the exact crossover point is unclear. Nonetheless, the general pattern of results is consistent with the theoretical predictions.

Discussion   These data point to the fact that relatively small changes in the complexity of information-processing tasks markedly alter the initial values and time course of ability-performance correlations during skill acquisition. When a task demands a greater amount of cognitive (phase 1) processing, initial compilation of production systems appear to be impaired. On the other hand, when a task has reduced cognitive demands (at the individual trial level), the perceptual speed abilities that determine compilation efficacy are associated with performance earlier in the course of skill acquisition.

Complexity in a Discrimination Reaction Time Study

In order to directly manipulate the ability-performance correlations in a single within-subject paradigm, a subsequent experiment utilized two variants of a nine-choice discrimination reaction time task. An initial simple, consistent, stimulus-response–compatible task was used in the training segment. In this condition, subjects were presented a single digit between 1 and 9 and responded with a corresponding key press (on a separate numeric keypad).

A transfer segment was created for evaluating the predicted changes in general and perceptual speed ability-performance relationships when a novel but consistent task component is added to a well-practiced task (as information-processing demands shift from phase 2 back to phase 1). In this transfer segment, the additional task component required subjects to first encode and translate a two-letter abbreviation for the number stimulus (rather than the number itself, as in the training segment). With the exception of this additional requirement, the training and transfer tasks — the response components — were identical.

In the training segment of the experiment, stimuli were digits 1 through 9 displayed on the computer screen. In the transfer segment, the digits were replaced with two-letter abbreviations for the location of the number key on the keyboard. The first letter in the abbreviation represented "lower row," "middle row," or "upper row" (L, M, or U) — namely, the vertical position of the key. The second letter in the abbreviation represented "left," "middle," or "right" (L, M, or R) — the horizontal position of the key. The key mapping is represented below.

UL	UM	UR
7	8	9
ML	MM	MR
4	5	6
LL	LM	LR
1	2	3

As with the previous experiment, this study used Air Force recruits as subjects. A total of 334 subjects participated in this experiment, which was also completed in a 3-hour session. Given the faster RTs in the easier initial task, though, it was possible to complete more trials in this experiment. The training segment involved 360 task trials (six trial blocks of sixty trials per block). The transfer segment involved 450 task trials (nine trial blocks of sixty trials per block).

Predictions   Given that the training and transfer task segments differ in terms of information-processing complexity, the situation portrayed in this experiment is roughly analogous to the experiment described earlier. With the substitution of the training segment for the low memory ($M = 2$) task condition, and similarly the transfer segment for the high memory ($M = 3$) condition, and with the qualification that the transfer segment follows the training segment (in this within-subject procedure), the predictions for ability-performance relationships are otherwise analogous (as in Figure 5-6).

1. For the training task, initial loadings of general ability were predicted to be modest, given the inherent simplicity of the training task (equivalent to a very brief phase 1 of skill acquisition). Further, given that early performance would be dominated by phase 2 skill levels, perceptual speed was predicted to have high correlations with performance, which decline as phase 3 skill levels were reached.

2. When the transfer condition is imposed, novel productions must be formulated to successfully perform the task (in other words, phase 1). Thus, general ability was predicted to increase in correlation with performance, and, by implication, the influence of perceptual speed ability was predicted to attenuate. With practice, as the additional phase 1 productions were built and the subjects move into phase 2, general ability was predicted to attenuate in influence and perceptual speed was predicted to increase in influence.

Means and Standard Deviations   As with other consistent tasks, mean RT declines substantially with practice in both tasks (see Figure 5-9a). The comparative complexity of the transfer segment is well illustrated by the initial 564-millisecond average increase over the training segment final performance level. (This performance decrement is found in spite of the expected positive transfer from one task to the other.) In line with the increased task complexity indicated by the slower mean RT levels, interindividual performance standard deviations doubled from the end of the training segment to the beginning of the transfer segment (from 122 milliseconds to 261 milliseconds — Figure 5-9b). Thus, the mean and *standard deviation* initial levels and changes with practice are consistent

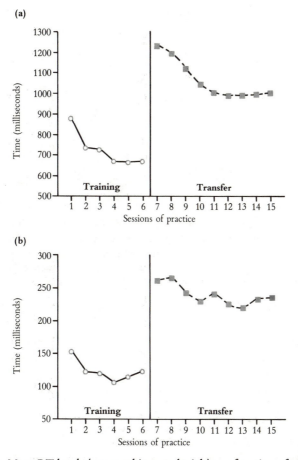

Figure 5-9 a. Mean RT levels (across subjects and trials) as a function of practice for the training and transfer segments. b. Between-subject standard deviations as a function of practice. Each session of practice contained sixty trials (from Ackerman, 1988). Copyright 1988 by American Psychological Association. Reprinted by permission.

with the theoretical expectations regarding a simple, consistent training segment and a more complex but also consistent transfer segment.

Ability-Performance Results   Figure 5-10 presents the correlations between both factors (general and perceptual speed) and performance. As predicted, during the training portion the perceptual speed factor is highly correlated with performance, but shows a decline with practice. The general ability factor shows stable, attenuated correlations with performance. With addition of the

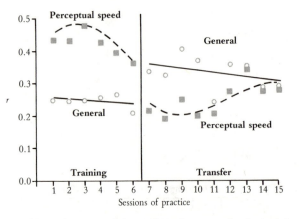

Figure 5-10 Correlations between ability and performance for the training and transfer conditions. Correlations between task performance and derived general and perceptual speed abilities. Lines indicate linear regression of general ability loadings and polynomial (cubic) regression of perceptual speed ability loading over practice (from Ackerman, 1988). Copyright 1988 by American Psychological Association. Reprinted by permission.

translation component (transfer segment), the relative influences of the two factors are reversed, as phase 1 information processing is required. Finally, with practice in the transfer segment, general ability declines in influence (once the new productions are developed) and perceptual speed regains influence, as the new productions are compiled and tuned. While total practice time was short (about 3 hours), the pattern of changes are consistent with the expectation that general ability will ultimately asymptote at a lower level and perceptual speed will ultimately level off and then decline as phase 3 is reached. (While consistent with the theory, the data do not decisively indicate what asymptotic ability-performance correlations would be.)

Discussion The data from the discrimination reaction time tasks illustrate the generalizability of the task complexity predictions. This task did not require the same semantic memory-search information processes, and made use of a training and transfer manipulation rather than the between-subject manipulations discussed in the first experiment. Again, two findings are apparent. First, a relatively modest complexity manipulation brings about marked ability-performance changes for initial performance. Second, the time course of ability-performance relationships follows the changes predicted from the three-stage model of ability determinants of skill acquisition.

IMPLICATIONS FOR PRESENT AND FUTURE RESEARCH

1965 versus 1987

The data discussed in this paper pertain mainly to validation of the theory with respect to phase 1 and phase 2 of skill acquisition. Reanalyses of three of the Fleishman et al. experiments offer supportive evidence relating prediction for phase 3 of skill acquisition (Ackerman, 1987, 1988). As phase 3 skills are developed, further attenuation of correlations of perceptual speed and performance is found, along with an increase in association between psychomotor abilities and performance. Those data also support a thesis that there is an inverse relationship between the initial task loadings on perceptual speed and loadings on psychomotor abilities. Such results take the tradeoff principle of general ability versus perceptual speed one step further. When general ability and perceptual speed loadings are low (which would be associated with abbreviated phase 1 and phase 2 processes), correlations with psychomotor abilities are higher. Conversely, when tasks require substantial phase 2 processing (and thus higher correlations of perceptual speed and performance), the initial associations between psychomotor abilities and performance will be attenuated. In addition, when tasks have inconsistent components, broad ability factors can actually account for more performance variance at the end of practice than at initial performance (Ackerman, 1987).

By this point, it should be clear that Fleishman's notion (1972; Fleishman and Quaintance, 1984) that post-practice individual differences are *specific only to the criterion task* is contradicted by a variety of sources. Reanalysis of the original Fleishman et al. data using modern factor analytic techniques gives results consistent with the theory proposed here (Ackerman, 1987). From all available indications, the major determinants of skilled performance individual differences are in fact tractable.

On the other hand, other broad conclusions about ability-performance relationships by Fleishman et al. have received some qualified support. There *are* systematic changes in the abilities that determine individual differences in performance during the three phases of skill acquisition. General intellectual abilities *do* correlate highly with initial phases of skill acquisition, less so with late phases. While specific abilities like perceptual speed do not uniformly increase in correlations with performance during practice, other specific abilities—such as psychomotor abilities—*do* appear to uniformly increase for tasks which have speeded information-processing demands.

Consequently, the present perspective on individual differences in learning is in a broad sense consistent with many possibilities raised in 1967 (and before). Woodrow's statements notwithstanding, the view offered by Ferguson (1954,

1956) that stable abilities broadly determine learning is supported by the data reviewed in this chapter.

The theory introduced here (and elsewhere—see Ackerman, 1988), however, goes further than the framework offered by Fleishman et al. and others. This theoretical framework delineates the interactions between a structure of abilities for skill acquisition and the critical information-processing task parameters of consistency and complexity that influence general skill acquisition. Where previous research only pointed to general trends in learning and individual differences, the current theory provides a basis for making specific predictions about (a) which abilities will determine performance at various stages of skill acquisition *and* (b) how different task information-processing demands will moderate the ability-performance correlations during initial and well-practiced task performance.

The theory and the underlying determinants of skill acquisition have been considered from a very broad perspective. In spite of these limitations, the data gathered so far have been generally congruent with the theoretical predictions. The two complexity manipulations illustrated above yielded support for the theory. Additional manipulations of the degree of task consistency can be found elsewhere, as can a review of the early Fleishman et al. data (Ackerman, 1987, 1988). These sources illustrate the general agreement between the data and the predicted dynamic ability-performance changes during the course of skill acquisition.

Recurring Issues

Simplex Revisited   In many respects the simplex pattern of intertrial correlations during skill acquisition is a red herring. The first problem in using the simplex pattern as a springboard towards theory of individual differences was the factorial indeterminacy outlined by Corballis (1965). If an infinite number of models are equally sufficient for fitting the data, the fact that a given theory (such as the one outlined in this paper) can predict a simplex structure only results in very weak confirmatory support of the theory (Popper, 1963). The evidence most damning to dependence on these patterns, however, is not psychological at all. As Humphreys (1985) has noted, the simplex pattern of correlations can be found in *any* individual differences data collected over multiple occasions. The pattern is characteristic of repeated measures of intelligence or performance over time, just as it is characteristic of physiological measures of height over occasions. There is nothing particularly special about the simplex patterns found in practice data; the patterns merely represent a general law of flux over time.

Finally, use of two measures taken from within-task intercorrelations—rate of attenuation and stability—fail to directly reflect the task-dependent changes which are clearly indicated in the ability-performance data (Ackerman,

1988). Part of the problem lies with the fact that individual differences variables other than those examined here (such as fatigue and motivation) affect performance over practice. Measures derived from within-task intercorrelations are simply too global to provide more than a rough index of the magnitude of change in *all* performance determinants over task practice.

Intelligence and Skill Acquisition   Does the present approach provide an answer to the perennial question about whether intelligence is equivalent to an ability to learn? If the essence of learning is characterized as representing those processes underlying the phase 1 formulation of production systems that allow a task to be performed, the answer is yes. Earlier discussions (see Zeaman and House, 1967) indicated that intelligence is moderately associated with the speed of learning in simple concept attainment and discrimination learning tasks. The direct assessment of the speed of learning was possible for such tasks because all learners start off with equal performance.

In contrast to concept attainment and discrimination learning tasks, the information-processing tasks reviewed in this chapter showed a substantial spread of performance even on trial 1. These individual differences clearly reflect important determinants of future learning such as task understanding, strategy development, and transfer from previous learning. Nonetheless, the skill learning and abilities data presented here are consistent with the concept attainment data and take the framework further in the sense that these tasks require discriminations and response patterns with higher-order and semantic information processing.

On the other hand, if learning is defined by some achievement index, such as some final, asymptotic performance level attained, a more qualified answer to the question of the intelligence-learning equivalence appears necessary. To the degree that the skill acquisition tasks discussed here are those within the ability repertoire of nearly all members of the subject population (albeit with different levels of initial performance), general intelligence does *not* strongly limit final level of skilled performance. Instead, other abilities determine individual differences at skill phase 3. Thus, for the simple, consistent tasks that are often found in military and industrial settings, it should come as no surprise that individual differences in job performance are only moderately correlated with general intelligence (Brown and Ghiselli, 1952; Ghiselli, 1966).

The theory and data presented here also point to potential solutions to the problems of predicting performance at various stages of task proficiency. An analysis of the major moderating influences of skill acquisition (namely consistency, complexity, and transfer) provides for prediction of what abilities limit performance during training. Coupled with evaluation of interindividual variability levels during training, this information can be further used to provide diagnostic information about (a) why subjects fail during training and (b) what aspects of the training program are preventing (or facilitating) the normal phase transitions of skill acquisition.

Predicting Asymptotic Performance   While many real-world skills are predominantly consistent, consistency is almost never absolute. For example, a secretary collating many copies of a report must always search for the unusual blank or poor-quality pages when assembling a report. Furthermore, conditions such as characteristics of the pages, neatness of the stack, and room humidity require continual modification of the perceptual/motor programs used to quickly perform the task. The general skills of driving a car may be similarly proceduralized, but changes in road conditions, engine temperature, and the like require either the development of new productions or the activation of context-dependent procedural skills. Furthermore, when an initial task is highly complex, even though predominantly consistent in information-processing requirements, many individuals may never reach the stage of processing where proceduralization can take place. Under such conditions, phase 1 or phase 2 abilities (general ability and perceptual speed) are unlikely to completely drop out of the prediction equation.

Other mediators of cognitive performance also are likely to be important determinants of individual differences in asymptotic performance. Variables that appear promising for further study include the presence of environmental stressors, such as heat and noise (see Hancock, 1984). In addition, various conative (motivational) variables seem to increase in influence as skills are acquired. Theories of task-specific motivation (such as the one proposed by Kanfer, 1987) and data collected by Helmreich, Sawin, and Carsrud (1986) are consistent with the notion that individual differences in motivational orientation account for *increasing* portions of performance variance as asymptotic skills are acquired.

Better Methods   Methodology problems have often been at the center of controversy throughout the history of research on individual differences in skill acquisition. Such problems reach far back to the early discussions of individual differences in learning (for example, Kincaid, 1922) and include the uses and misuses of gain scores (Woodrow, 1946; Cronbach and Furby, 1970) and the more recent confusion with respect to the simultaneous factor analysis of learning task and reference ability variables (Ackerman, 1987; Humphreys, 1960).

One critical problem continues to revolve around determination of individual differences in the *amount of learning*. Theorists have occasionally argued that such a variable, even if psychometrically defensible, may be flawed by being logically incomplete (Cronbach and Furby, 1970). When nonzero variance exists on the first task trial, a researcher *must* address how initial differences in performance between individuals are to be handled. Merely using a partial regression technique to statistically adjust post-practice scores is likely to be inappropriate, given different forms of learning curves likely obtained by learners with different starting points.

Ragosa (see, for example, Ragosa and Willett, 1985) discusses a more elaborate perspective on estimating growth (or learning) which requires specification of models of individual growth. It is plausible that a researcher could initially make use of Tucker's (1966) three-mode factor analysis, which is capable of revealing different families of learning curves underlying a particular task and learner sample. With these learning curves as models for individual differences in learning, it may be possible to estimate change (or learning) for the various classes of learners for comparison with reference cognitive abilities. This combination of sophisticated statistical procedures seems to offer an avenue that avoids the artifactual pitfalls associated with simple change scores. In addition, such a technique may further allow the investigator to directly assess the effects of different cognitive styles or strategies during the course of skill acquisition.

Transfer and Abilities Further questions of interest regard the interplay between the acquisition of skills and changes in ability levels (Corballis, 1965; Ferguson, 1956; Alvares and Hulin, 1972). These authors have addressed the particular question of whether the underlying nature of the task changes or abilities of learners change with task practice. From the current perspective on skill acquisition, it is clear that as the learner moves from phase 1 to phase 3, the nature of task information processing undergoes profound changes. How these processing changes feed back to ability changes is less clear.

The current theory indicates that different abilities are involved at each of the three stages of skill acquisition. For example, during phase 3 any potential impact on the general ability will be minimal. Otherwise, ability transfer (that is, increment in the ability in question) is expected to occur in parallel to the current phase of skill acquisition. During phase 1, successful formulations of efficient production systems will result in an increment in general ability. Phase 2 processing will result in increments to perceptual speed, and so on. When task training is given across all phases of skill acquisition, each of these ability classes is expected to show increments. However, given the broad nature of the general ability, increments resulting from acquisition of a single skill may be relatively small. Although decisive experiments that address this issue are not available, cognitive training data, such as those of Pellegrino (1983), are consistent with this inference.

Simple and Choice RT and Intelligence When tasks are simple and consistent, the proposed theory predicts that changing ability-performance relationships will be found over practice. The common methodology of researchers seeking to equate aspects of information processing with cognitive abilities has been to give short administrations, with no attempt made to find stabilized skill levels. Previously, there were a few exceptions to this state of affairs (see Jones, 1980), although such studies have come up short by using very small subject samples. A few investigators (such as, Pellegrino, Alderton, and Regian, 1984) recently have made strides in this domain, and further data can be expected in the future.

One major source of controversy appears when investigators fall into the trap of providing insufficient practice and relying on correlations between general intelligence and performance. For example, research by Jensen (1982; Jensen and Munro, 1979) and others (Vernon, 1983) has repeatedly pointed to marked positive correlations between choice RT task performance and general intelligence as indicative of some basic information-processing speed component of intelligence. The present theory makes an important prediction regarding whether such conclusions are defensible. Recall that the theory predicts that early in task practice (even for relatively simple, consistent tasks), learners are in the cognitive phase of skill acquisition. As Figure 5-5 illustrates, phase 1 performance is at least moderately determined by general and broad content abilities. However, if sufficient task practice is given to insure development of phase 3 — autonomous skilled performance — these correlations between general ability and performance will substantially attenuate (unless an extremely wide range of ability is sampled; under such conditions, some subjects may *never* capture the consistency of the task, and thus fail to proceed past phase 1 processing).

Therefore, *correlations based on initial performance levels will overestimate relationships between general ability and performance once asymptotic skills have been developed.* Less directly implied is that unless perceptual speed and psychomotor abilities are partialled out of general intelligence estimates, the common variance shared by the three ability families may be attributed to general intelligence. As a result, greater spurious communality between choice RT and general intelligence will be found. Clearly, other methodological problems have limited the usefulness of the comparisons offered by those authors (see Longstreth, 1984; Welford, 1986), but the current considerations indicate that when tasks are consistent, practice is a necessary condition to establishing associations between *stable* information-processing task components and cognitive-intellectual abilities.

In contrast, when tasks mostly involve continuous demands on phase 1 (cognitive processing), as with some analogy tasks (Sternberg, 1977), the proposed theory indicates that practice is much less likely to result in marked changes in ability-performance correlations. Attention to these underlying task requirements may allow for much greater clarification of correlations between information processing and ability — outside of the skill acquisition domain.

Complex Tasks   For logistic and theoretical reasons, highly complex tasks were not considered here. The logistic reasons pertained to the need for training times within the 3 hours allowed for the subject samples. Generalization to tasks that, for example, require 20 or more hours for a transition between skill acquisition phases to occur should be straightforward, though other variables may have obscuring effects. Prominent among such variables is motivation. When tasks are simple and training time is short, the demands for perseverance are relatively small. Longer training times will surely exacerbate different effort allocations to performance improvement and maintenance, especially under attention-intensive controlled processing conditions (see Kanfer, 1987, or Thomas, 1983, for a discussion of some of these effects).

As briefly mentioned before, when tasks become complex enough to preclude initially successful performance among all members of the subject sample, Pearson product-moment correlations become increasingly inefficient measures for describing ability-performance associations, given discontinuity in the distribution of performance. In such cases, one can contrast the subjects who can at least do the task, albeit slowly, versus those subjects who cannot do the task correctly at all early in skill acquisition. Furthermore, a greater variety of information-processing strategies are capable of further moderating performance levels, and quite probably, ability-performance correlations as well. Theories of skill have made substantial inroads into tasks as complex as chess (Chase and Simon, 1973), extended digit-span memory (Chase and Ericsson, 1981), solution of college-level physics problems (Chi, Glaser, and Rees, 1982), and so on. It is expected that the current theoretical strategy of linking broad abilities and skills can be used as a springboard to include both specific abilities and other classes of information-processing parameters.

A Related Issue   One of the most interesting questions that follows from this research on individual differences in skill acquisition concerns the nature and developmental patterns of sex differences in cognitive processing. Numerous studies have been conducted to assess the degree of sex differences in a variety of ability content domains—verbal, numerical, and spatial (see Anastasi, 1982; Maccoby and Jacklin, 1974; Hyde, 1981). We have recently begun to investigate hypotheses concerning the experiential development of these sex differences, specifically with respect to spatial information processing. Several investigators (Chance and Goldstein, 1971; Connor, Serbin, and Schackman, 1977) have suggested that sex differences in spatial processing can be remediated by training on test items. The current theoretical framework suggests that *general* (not sex-related) individual differences attenuate with training, thus the results in the literature are not decisive in showing an experiential determinant of these sex differences. Future research will be devoted to considering remediation of sex differences for tasks with both consistent and inconsistent information-processing demands.

Finally, the vast literature pertaining to age-related changes in general, perceptual speed, and psychomotor abilities point to functional distinctions that will allow for other tests of the bases for skill acquisition and learning (Horn, 1965, 1967, 1968). Other differences, such as race and ethnic contrasts, provide even more important sources of data for those researchers interested in remedial skill training (see Frederiksen, Warren, and Rosebery, 1985). On a different level, linkages between differential and experimental approaches to these issues appear capable of making good on the promise of progress from the unification of the "two disciplines of scientific psychology" (Cronbach, 1957), which, after all, constituted the purpose of the 1965 conference on learning and individual differences and remains the goal of this research program.

ACKNOWLEDGMENT

Preparation of this chapter was supported by funds from the Office of Naval Research, Personnel and Training Contract N00014-86-K-0478.

REFERENCES

Ackerman, P. L. (1984). *A theoretical and empirical investigation of individual differences in learning: A synthesis of cognitive ability and information processing perspectives.* Unpublished doctoral dissertation, University of Illinois, Urbana.

Ackerman, P. L. (1986a). Skill acquisition, individual differences and human abilities. *Proceedings of the 30th Annual Meeting of the Human Factors Society.*

Ackerman, P. L. (1986b). Individual differences in information processing: An investigation of intellectual abilities and task performance during practice. *Intelligence,* 10:109–139.

Ackerman, P. L. (1987). Individual differences in skill learning: An integration of psychometric and information processing perspectives. *Psychological Bulletin,* 102:3–27.

Ackerman, P. L. (1988). Determinants of individual differences during skill acquisition: A theory of cognitive abilities and information processing. *Journal of Experimental Psychology: General,* 117:299–329.

Ackerman, P. L. (in press). Within-task intercorrelations of skilled performance: Implications for predicting individual differences? *Journal of Applied Psychology.*

Adams, J. A. (1987). Historical review and appraisal of research on the learning, retention, and transfer of human motor skills. *Psychological Bulletin,* 101:41–74.

Allison, R. B. (1960). *Learning parameters and human abilities.* Office of Naval Research technical report. Princeton, N.J.: Educational Testing Service.

Alvares, K. M., and Hulin, C. L. (1972). Two explanations of temporal changes in ability-skill relationships: A literature review and a theoretical analysis. *Human Factors,* 14:293–308.

Anastasi, A. (1934). Practice and variability: A study in psychological method. *Psychological Monographs,* 45, No. 204.

Anastasi, A. (1982). *Psychological testing,* 5th ed. New York: Macmillan.

Anderson, J. R. (1982). Acquisition of cognitive skill. *Psychological Review,* 89:369–406.

Anderson, J. R. (1983). *The architecture of cognition.* Cambridge, Mass.: Harvard University Press.

Anderson, R. C. (1967). Individual differences and problem solving. In R. M. Gagné (Ed.), *Learning and individual differences.* Columbus, Ohio: Merrill.

Battig, W. F., and Montague, W. E. (1969). Category norms for verbal items in 56 categories: A replication and extension of the Connecticut category norms. *Journal of Experimental Psychology Monograph,* 80 3, Part 2.

Brown, C. W., and Ghiselli, E. E. (1952). The relationship between the predictive power of aptitude tests for trainability and for job proficiency. *Journal of Applied Psychology,* 36:370–372.

Bryan, W. L., and Harter, N. (1899). Studies on the telegraphic language: The acquisition of a hierarchy of habits. *Psychological Review,* 6:345–375.

Carroll, J. B. (1980). *Individual difference relations in psychometric and experimental cognitive tasks.* (Technical report no. 163). Chapel Hill: University of North Carolina, The L. L. Thurstone Psychometric Laboratory.

Chance, J. E., and Goldstein, A. G. (1971). Internal-external control of reinforcement and embedded-figures performance. *Perception and Psychophysics,* 9:33–34.

Chase, W. G., and Ericsson, K. A. (1981). Skilled memory. In J. R. Anderson (Ed.), *Cognitive skills and their acquisition.* Hillsdale, N.J.: Erlbaum.

Chase, W. G., and Simon, H. A. (1973). Perception in chess. *Cognitive Psychology,* 4:55–81.

Chi, M. T. H., Glaser, R., and Rees, E. (1982). Expertise in problem solving. In R. J. Sternberg (Ed.), *Advances in the psychology of human intelligence,* Vol. 1. Hillsdale, N.J.: Erlbaum.

Connor, J. M., Serbin, L. A., and Schackman, M. (1977). Sex differences in children's response to training on a visual-spatial task. *Developmental Psychology,* 13:293–294.

Corballis, M. C. (1965). Practice and the simplex. *Psychological Review,* 72:399–406.

Cronbach, L. J. (1957). The two disciplines of scientific psychology. *American Psychologist,* 12:671–684.

Cronbach, L. J., and Furby, L. (1970). How we should measure "change"—or should we? *Psychological Bulletin,* 70:68–80.

Cronbach, L. J., and Snow, R. E. (1977). *Aptitudes and instructional methods.* New York: Irvington.

Crossman, E. R. F. W. (1959). A theory of the acquisition of speed-skill. *Ergonomics,* 2:153–166.

DuBois, P. H., Manning, W. H., and Spies, C. J. (Eds.) (1959). *Factor analysis and related techniques in the study of learning.* Technical report no. 7. Naval Air Technical Training, Washington University, Saint Louis, Mo.

Dwyer, P. S. (1937). The determination of the factor loading of a given test from the known factor loadings of other tests. *Psychometrika,* 2:173–178.

Ekstrom, R. B., French, J. W., Harman, H. H., and Dermen, D. (1976). *Kit of factor-referenced cognitive tests.* Princeton, N.J.: Educational Testing Service.

Ferguson, G. A. (1954). On learning and human ability. *Canadian Journal of Psychology,* 8:95–112.

Ferguson, G. A. (1956). On transfer and the abilities of man. *Canadian Journal of Psychology,* 10:121–131.

Fisk, A. D., and Schneider, W. (1983). Category and word search: Generalizing search principles to complex processing. *Journal of Experimental Psychology: Learning, Memory, and Cognition,* 10:181–197.

Fitts, P. (1964). Perceptual-motor skill learning. In A. W. Melton (Ed.), *Categories of human learning.* New York: Academic Press.

Fitts, P., and Posner, M. I. (1967). *Human performance.* Belmont, Calif.: Brooks/Cole.

Fleishman, E. A. (1954). Dimensional analysis of psychomotor abilities. *Journal of Experimental Psychology,* 48:437–454.

Fleishman, E. A. (1967a). Human abilities and verbal learning. In R. M. Gagné (Ed.), *Learning and individual differences.* Columbus, Ohio: Merrill.

Fleishman, E. A. (1967b). Individual differences in motor learning. In R. M. Gagné (Ed.), *Learning and individual differences.* Columbus, Ohio: Merrill.

Fleishman, E. A. (1972). On the relation between abilities, learning, and human performance. *American Psychologist,* 27:1017–1032.

Fleishman, E. A., and Quaintance, M. K. (1984). *Taxonomies of human performance.* Orlando, Fla.: Academic Press.

Frederiksen, J. R., Warren, B. M., and Rosebery, A. S. (1985). A componential approach to training reading skills: Part I. Perceptual units training. *Cognition and Instruction,* 2:91–130.

Gagné, R. M. (Ed.) (1967). *Learning and individual differences.* Columbus, Ohio: Merrill.

Ghiselli, E. E. (1966). *The validity of occupational aptitude tests.* New York: Wiley.

Glanzer, M. (1967). Individual performance, R-R theory and perception. In R. M. Gagné (Ed.), *Learning and individual differences.* Columbus, Ohio: Merrill.

Glaser, R. (1967). Some implications of previous work on learning and individual differences. In R. M. Gagné (Ed.), *Learning and individual differences.* Columbus, Ohio: Merrill.

Guttman, L. (1954). A new approach to factor analysis: The radex. In P. F. Lazersfeld (Ed.), *Mathematical thinking in the social sciences.* Glencoe, Ill.: Free Press.

Hancock, P. A. (1984). Environmental stressors. In J. Warm (Ed.), *Sustained attention in human performance.* New York: Wiley.

Helmreich, R. L., Sawin, L. L., and Carsrud, A. L. (1986). The honeymoon effect in job performance: Temporal increases in the predictive power of achievement motivation. *Journal of Applied Psychology,* 71:185–188.

Henry, R. A., and Hulin, C. L. (1987). Stability of skilled performance across time: Some generalizations and limitations on utilities. *Journal of Applied Psychology,* 72:457–462.

Horn, J. L. (1965). *Fluid and crystallized intelligence: A factor analytic study of the structure among primary mental abilities.* Unpublished doctoral dissertation, University of Illinois, Urbana.

Horn, J. L. (1967). Intelligence—Why it grows, why it declines. *Trans-Action,* 5:23–31.

Horn, J. L. (1968). Organization of abilities and the development of intelligence. *Psychological Review*, 75:242–259.

House, B. J., and Zeaman, D. (1960). Visual discrimination learning and intelligence in defectives of low mental age. *American Journal of Mental Deficiency*, 65:51–58.

Humphreys, L. G. (1960). Investigation of the simplex. *Psychometrika*, 25:313–323.

Humphreys, L. G. (1979). The construct of general intelligence. *Intelligence*, 3:105–120.

Humphreys, L. G. (1985). General intelligence: An integration of factor, test, and simplex theory. In B. B. Wolman (Ed.), *Handbook of intelligence*. New York: Wiley.

Hyde, J. S. (1981). How large are cognitive gender differences? A meta-analysis using w^2 and d'. *American Psychologist*, 36:892–901.

James, W. (1890). *Principles of psychology*. New York: Holt.

Jensen, A. R. (1982). Reaction time and psychometric g. In H. J. Eysenck (Ed.), *A model for intelligence*. Heidelberg: Springer-Verlag

Jensen, A. R., and Munro, E. (1979). Reaction time, movement time, and intelligence. *Intelligence*, 3:121–126.

Jones, M. B. (1962). Practice as a process of simplification. *Psychological Review*, 69:274–294.

Jones, M. B. (1970a). A two process theory of individual differences in motor learning. *Psychological Review*, 77:353–360.

Jones, M. B. (1970b). Rate and terminal processes in skill acquisition. *American Journal of Psychology*, 83:222–236.

Jones, M. B. (1980, October). *Convergence-divergence with extended practice: Three applications*. Paper presented at the meeting of the Human Factors Society, Los Angeles.

Kanfer, R. (1987). Task-specific motivation: An integrative approach to issues of measurement, mechanisms, processes, and determinants. *Journal of Social and Clinical Psychology*, 5:237–264.

Kincaid, M. (1922). *An experimental study of variability in learning*. Unpublished doctoral dissertation. University of Minnesota, Minneapolis.

Kincaid, M. (1925). A study of individual differences in learning. *Psychological Review*, 32:34–53.

Longstreth, L. E. (1984). Jensen's reaction-time investigations of intelligence: A critique. *Intelligence*, 8:139–160.

Lohman, D. (1979). *Spatial ability: A review and reanalysis of the correlational literature.* (Technical report no. 8). Aptitude Research Project, Stanford University, School of Education, Stanford, Calif.

Lord, F. M. (1956). A study of speed factors in tests and academic grades. *Psychometrika*, 21:31–50.

Lord, F. M. (1963). Elementary models for measuring change. In C. W. Harris (Ed.), *Problems in measuring change*. Madison, Wis.: University of Wisconsin Press.

Maccoby, E. E., and Jacklin, C. N. (1974). *The psychology of sex differences*. Stanford, Calif.: Stanford University Press.

Marshalek, B., Lohman, D. F., and Snow, R. E. (1983). The complexity continuum in the radex and hierarchical models of intelligence. *Intelligence*, 7:107–127.

McNemar, Q. (1962). *Psychological Statistics*, 3d ed. New York: Wiley.

Miles, T. R. (1957). Contributions to intelligence testing and the theory of intelligence. *British Journal of Educational Psychology,* 27:153–165.

Newell, A., and Rosenbloom, P. S. (1981). Mechanisms of skill acquisition and the law of practice. In J. R. Anderson (Ed.), *Cognitive skills and their acquisition.* Hillsdale, N.J.: Erlbaum.

Nissen, M. J., and Bullemer, P. (1987). Attentional requirements of learning: Evidence from performance measures. *Cognitive Psychology,* 19:1–32.

Pellegrino, J. W. (1983, April). *Individual differences in spatial ability: The effects of practice on components of processing and reference test scores.* Paper presented at American Educational Research Association Meetings, Montreal, Canada.

Pellegrino, J. W. (1985). *Individual differences in skill acquisition: Information processing efficiency and development of automaticity.* Unpublished AFHRL progress report.

Pellegrino, J. W., Alderton, D. L., and Regian, J. W. (1984, December). *Components of spatial ability.* Paper presented at NATO Advanced Study Institute in Cognition and Motivation, Athens, Greece.

Popper, K. R. (1963). *Conjectures and refutation.* London: Routledge and Kegan Paul.

Ragosa, D. R., and Willett, J. B. (1985). Understanding correlates of change by modeling individual diifferences in growth. *Psychometrika,* 50:203–228.

Reed, H. B. (1931). The influence of training on changes in variability in achievement. *Psychological Monographs,* 41, No. 185.

Reynolds, B. (1952a). Correlations between two psychomotor tasks as a function of distribution of practice on the first. *Journal of Experimental Psychology,* 43:341–348.

Reynolds, B. (1952b). The effect of learning on the predictability of psychomotor performance. *Journal of Experimental Psychology,* 44:189–198.

Robinson, R. (1950). *Definition.* Oxford: Oxford University Press.

Roff, M. (1952). A factorial study of tests in the perceptual area. *Psychometric Monographs,* 8.

Schmid, J., and Leiman, J. M. (1957). The development of hierarchical factor solutions. *Psychometrika,* 22:53–61.

Schneider, W. (1985). Toward a model of attention and the development of automatic processing. In M. I. Posner and O. S. M. Marin (Eds.), *Attention and performance,* XI. Hillsdale, N.J.: Erlbaum.

Schneider, W., and Fisk, A. D. (1982a). Dual task automatic and control processing, can it be done without cost? *Journal of Experimental Psychology: Learning, Memory, and Cognition,* 8:261–278.

Schneider, W., and Fisk, A. D. (1982b). Degree of consistent training: Improvements in search performance and automatic process development. *Perception and Psychophysics,* 31:160–168.

Schneider, W., and Shiffrin, R. M. (1977). Controlled and automatic human information processing: I. Detection, search, and attention. *Psychological Review,* 84:1–66.

Shiffrin, R. M., and Schneider, W. (1977). Controlled and automatic human information processing: II. Perceptual learning, automatic attending, and a general theory. *Psychological Review,* 84:127–190.

Simrall, D. V. (1946). *The effects of practice on the factorial equations for perceptual and visual-spatial tests.* Unpublished doctoral dissertation, University of Illinois, Urbana.

Snow, R. E., Kyllonen, P. C., and Marshalek, B. (1984). The topography of ability and learning correlations. In R. J. Sternberg (Ed.), *Advances in the psychology of human intelligence,* Vol. 2. Hillsdale, N.J.: Erlbaum.

Spearman, C. (1927). *The abilities of man.* New York: Macmillan.

Sternberg, R. J. (1977). *Intelligence, information processing, and analogical reasoning: The componential analysis of human abilities.* Hillsdale, N.J.: Erlbaum.

Sternberg, R. J. (1985). *Beyond IQ: A triarchic theory of human intelligence.* Cambridge: Cambridge University Press.

Sternberg, S. (1969). The discovery of processing changes: Extensions of Donders' method. *Acta Psychologica,* 30:276–315.

Stoddard, G. D. (1943). *The meaning of intelligence.* New York: Macmillan.

Terman, L. M. (1921). Intelligence and its measurement: A symposium. *Journal of Educational Psychology,* 12:127–133.

Thomas, E. A. C. (1983). Notes on effort and achievement-oriented behavior. *Psychological Review,* 90:1–20.

Thorndike, E. L. (1908). The effect of practice in the case of a purely intellectual function, *American Journal of Psychology,* 19:374–384.

Thorndike, E. L. (1914). *Educational Psychology,* Vol. III. New York: Teachers College, Columbia University.

Thurstone, L. L. (1944). A factorial study of perception. *Psychometric Monographs,* 4.

Thurstone, L. L., and Thurstone, T. G. (1941). Factorial studies of intelligence. *Psychometric Monographs,* 2.

Tucker, L. R. (1966). Learning theory and multivariate experiments: Illustration by determination of generalized learning curves. In R. B. Cattell (Ed.), *Handbook of Multivariate Experimental Psychology.* Chicago: Rand McNally.

Vernon, P. A. (1983). Speed of information processing and general intelligence. *Intelligence,* 7:53–70.

Vernon, P. E. (1961). *The structure of human abilities.* New York: Wiley.

Wechsler, D. (1955). *Manual for the Wechsler Adult Intelligence Scale.* New York: Psychological Corporation.

Welford, A. T. (1986). Longstreth versus Jensen and Vernon on reaction time and IQ: An outsider's view. *Intelligence,* 10:193–195.

Werdelin, I., and Stjernberg, G. (1969). On the nature of the perceptual speed factor. *Scandinavian Journal of Psychology,* 10:185–192.

Woodrow, H. (1938). The effect of practice on groups of different initial ability. *Journal of Educational Psychology,* 29:268–278.

Woodrow, H. (1946). The ability to learn. *Psychological Review,* 53:147–158.

Woodworth, R. S. (1938). *Experimental psychology.* New York: Holt.

Yeh, Y.-Y., and Schneider, W. (1985, August). *Designing a part-task training strategy for complex skills.* Paper presented at the annual meeting of the American Psychological Association, Los Angeles.

Zeaman, D., and House, B. J. (1967). The relation of IQ and learning. In R. M. Gagné (Ed.), *Learning and individual differences.* Columbus, Ohio: Merrill.

6

Individual Differences in Children's Strategy Choices

ROBERT S. SIEGLER *Carnegie-Mellon University*

JAMIE CAMPBELL *University of Western Ontario*

At the first LRDC Conference on learning and individual differences, Melton (1967), concluded: "What is needed is that we frame our hypotheses about individual difference variables in terms of the process constructs of the contemporary theories of learning and performance" (p. 239). He went on to describe characteristics that would make process models especially useful for understanding individual differences. One was that the models be detailed; another was that they be applicable across a range of task domains. While such a prescription seems uncontroversial today, it was quite bold at the time it was formulated. Recall that this was a time when Neisser's revolutionary volume *Cognitive Psychology* was still hot from the presses and terms like *cognitive* and *mechanism* often appeared in quotation marks.

In the past twenty years some things have changed: but others have remained the same. Unlike twenty years ago, there is general agreement today that precise models of cognitive processes are critical for understanding individual differences across tasks. Like twenty years ago, however, few demonstrations of the usefulness of cognitive models for understanding individual differences are available (although see Just and Carpenter, 1985; Pellegrino and Glaser, 1982; and Sternberg, 1977, for exceptions).

There are two main reasons for the scarcity of analyses of individual differences that are closely linked to cognitive models. First, individual differences have failed to capture the interest of many cognitive researchers; the emphasis has been on capturing the typical process rather than variation in the process. Second, it has proven surprisingly difficult to specify cognitive process variables that strongly discriminate individuals across tasks. It often is difficult to know even whether a process used on one task is the same process used on a different task, much less to establish that individual differences in execution of the process in the two contexts are highly correlated.

Despite these difficulties, Melton's (1967) charge continues to strike a resonant chord. Understanding the performance of individuals is ultimately what psychological research is all about. For cognitive models to advance understanding of individual differences, they must explain what performance on diverse tasks has in common as well as how it differs. Once such common processes are identified, we can begin to understand why they differ among individuals.

One process that may be quite general across tasks — the one that will be of central concern here — is the process by which people decide whether to use retrieval or a backup strategy to solve a problem. This strategy choice needs to be made in a large variety of situations. Consider a few of the choices of this type made by young children in the classroom. When solving addition and subtraction problems they must decide whether to state a retrieved answer or use the backup strategy of counting on their fingers. On multiplication problems they must decide whether to state a retrieved answer or use the backup strategy of repeatedly adding one multiplicand the number of times indicated by the other. When reading they must decide whether to state a retrieved identity of a word or sound out the word's pronunciation. Spelling requires that they decide whether to state a retrieved sequence of letters or look in a dictionary. Telling time on an analog clock requires that they decide whether to retrieve the time or count from the hour.

How wisely children (and adults) make such strategy choices has important consequences for their cognitive functioning. In general, backup strategies such as counting on fingers and sounding out words are slower than retrieval. However, they also tend to be more accurate on items that are in the process of being learned. Overly heavy reliance on retrieval will produce fast but inaccurate performance on such items, whereas overly heavy reliance on backup strategies will produce unnecessarily slow, albeit correct, performance. Ideally one should rely on retrieval when it can yield accurate performance and use backup strategies when only they can do so. This prescription is not just an abstract ideal. As will be described below, even young children's strategy choices have been found to follow such a pattern in domains as diverse as addition, telling time, and reading (Siegler, 1986; Siegler and McGilly, in press; Siegler and Shrager, 1984).

The way in which children choose strategies also has important implications for cognitive and developmental theory. How cognition is governed is a central issue in the study of cognitive development. Such classic constructs as Piaget's (1976) reflective abstraction, Bruner's (1973) autonomous regulation, Flavell and Wellman's (1977) metacognition, Sternberg's (1985) metacomponents, and Case's (1985) executive processes all were motivated by this issue.

Although these constructs address an important problem, they have become the target of considerable criticism. The criticisms have focused on both the theoretical vagueness of the constructs and the lack of strong empirical connections between them and cognitive activities (Brown and Reeve, 1986; Cavanaugh and Perlmutter, 1982; Sternberg and Powell, 1983).

The model of strategy choice offered in this chapter is an alternative to these top-down approaches. It is based on the assumption that people make at least some of their strategy choices without reflection about, or even knowledge of, cognitive capacities, available strategies, and problem characteristics. Rather than any explicit reflective or metacognitive ability directing cognitive activity, the model assumes that basic cognitive processes are organized in such a way that they yield adaptive strategy use without any direct governmental process.

This chapter's goal is to demonstrate the usefulness of this approach for the understanding of individual differences. In particular, we will examine individual differences in young children's strategy choices in three domains — addition, subtraction, and reading — and interpret the differences in terms of the present strategy choice model.

The description of the research is organized into four sections. First, we discuss the general issue of how people choose strategies. Next, we describe the strategy choice model and present evidence concerning its applicability to several tasks. We then present an experiment on individual differences in first graders' addition, subtraction, and reading, interpret the results in terms of the model, and relate the results to the children's standardized test performance. Finally, in the concluding section, we consider the model's implications for understanding individual differences in performance on standardized tests, for understanding classic psychological trait constructs such as impulsivity-reflectivity, and for understanding relationships between trait-level and process-level analyses of individual differences.

THE DIVERSITY OF STRATEGY USE
AND THE ISSUE OF STRATEGY CHOICE

Older and younger children, people more and less knowledgeable in a domain, and people with different ability profiles often vary in the strategies they use. Differences in the strategies of older and younger children are especially well documented. Whether the task involves hypothesis testing (Gholson and Beilin, 1979), memory for serial sequences (Naus, Ornstein, and Aivano, 1977), conservation problems (Case, 1985), or arithmetic facts (Ilg and Ames, 1951), children of different ages use different strategies. People of a single age but different knowledge show similar strategy differences. Experts and novices in physics (Simon and Simon, 1978; Chi, Feltovich, and Glaser, 1981), chess (de Groot, 1965; Chase and Simon, 1973), and medical diagnosis (Clancy, in press; Pople, 1982) often differ profoundly in their problem-solving strategies. Ability differences on standard psychometric variables are a third source of strategy differences. For example, people high and low in spatial abilities differ in their strategies for solving transitive inference problems (Sternberg and Weil, 1980), sentence verification problems (MacLeod, Hunt, and Mathews, 1978), and mental rotation problems (Cooper and Regan, 1982).

Recognizing that strategies vary with age, knowledge, and ability is a useful step toward describing individual differences, but only that. It is true not only that the strategies of individuals vary with age, knowledge, and ability, but also that a single individual — by definition of a particular age, amount of knowledge, and level of ability — will often use different strategies on different occasions close in time. For example, Siegler (1987) presented to five- and six-year-olds a set of subtraction problems twice within a one week period. The same child used visibly different strategies on 34 percent of the pairs of trials. Individual children have been observed to use multiple strategies on a wide variety of tasks, including addition, subtraction, and multiplication (Bisanz et al., 1984; Leal, Burney, and Johnson, 1985; Siegler and Robinson, 1982; Siegler and Shrager, 1984), causal inference tasks (Shultz et al., 1986), spatial reasoning tasks (Ohlsson, 1984), referential communication tasks (Kahan and Richards, 1986), and numerical estimation tasks (Newman, Friedman, and Gockley, 1985).

All these studies indicate that a single individual presented with similar material in closely spaced problem-solving episodes will often use different strategies. They therefore raise the further questions of what functions this use of diverse strategies serves and how a child decides which strategy to use on a given occasion. These were the questions that motivated the present model of strategy choice.

The Distribution of Associations Model of Strategy Choice

Siegler and Shrager (1984) developed the distribution of associations model to account for strategy choices by four- and five-year-olds on simple addition problems. The model has subsequently been applied to subtraction by five- and six-year-olds, reading by six-year-olds, multiplication and telling time by eight- and nine-year-olds, and performance by ten- to fourteen-year-olds with a balance scale (Siegler, 1986, 1987, in press; Siegler and McGilly, in press; Siegler and Taraban, 1986). In principle, the model applies to any task for which an individual has both (a) acquired one or more procedural strategies for generating answers and (b) built up item-specific associations that make possible the use of retrieval on at least some trials.

The model is based on four general assumptions. The first assumption is that on many tasks children use multiple strategies. This is believed to be true for a single child attempting a single problem on two occasions close in time, as well as for different children attempting different problems at different times. Thus, there is intraindividual as well as interindividual variability in strategy use.

The second assumption is that children's strategy choices are adaptive in the sense that they allow children to adapt to varying task and situational demands. Children are assumed to use strategies that they can execute quickly and easily when use of such strategies enables them to succeed, and to employ slower and less-easy-to-execute strategies when these strategies offer the only likely road to successful performance. Thus, children's strategy choice procedures are believed to be organized in a way that will yield performance that is both fast and accurate.

The third assumption is that adaptive strategy choices can arise through use of procedural knowledge that is not accessible to introspection. The present model follows the suggestion of Brown et al. (1983) that the issue of how people regulate their cognitive activities should be separated from the assumption that people use conscious, factual knowledge about capacities, strategies, and task demands to accomplish the self-regulation. Indeed, the model explicitly illustrates a way in which self-regulation can be accomplished without recourse to such knowledge.

The fourth assumption is that children's use of multiple strategies shapes their learning. Problem difficulty is relative to the strategy being used; a problem that is difficult when one strategy is used may be easy when another is used. For example, finding the answer to 12 + 3 is difficult if the strategy is to count from 1, but easy if the strategy is to count from 12. To the extent that children associate the answers they state with the problems on which they state them, the particular strategies that they use will influence their learning as well as their performance.

Organization of the Model

Figure 6-1 is a diagram of the model's basic structure. The two main parts are a representation of knowledge about particular problems and a process that operates on the representation to produce answers. The answers, in turn, reshape the knowledge in the representation; the model learns by doing. Thus, factors that influence which answers are generated on a particular trial also determine the contents of the knowledge representation. Characteristics of backup strategies, of knowledge of related problems, and of presentation rates of different problems all contribute to development through their influence on performance. We first describe how the representation and process produce performance at any given time, and then describe how they lead to changes in performance over time.

Representation

It is hypothesized that children represent information about specific problems —such as 5 + 2—in an associative network. The network's main feature is associations between each problem and possible answers, both correct and

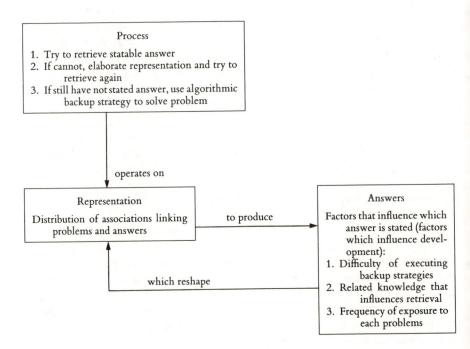

Figure 6-1 Basic structure of model.

incorrect. Representations of problems can be classified along a dimension of the peakedness of their distribution of associations. In a *peaked distribution,* such as that on the left in Figure 6-2, most of the associative strength is concentrated in a single answer, ordinarily the correct answer. At the other extreme, in a *flat distribution,* such as that on the right in Figure 6-2, associative strength is dispersed among several answers with no one of them forming a strong peak. As we will discuss in detail, the peakedness of a problem's distribution is hypothesized to be a key determinant of its percentage of errors, length of solution times, and the strategies that are used on it.

Process

The process that operates on this representation involves three sequential phases, any one of which can produce an answer and thus terminate the process: retrievable, elaboration of the representation, and application of an algorithm. The existence of the three phases is constant across all distribution of associations models, although the particular elaborations and algorithms are task specific.

The hypothesized retrieval procedure is similar to those proposed in several recent models of memory (e.g., Anderson, 1983; Gillund and Shiffrin, 1984).

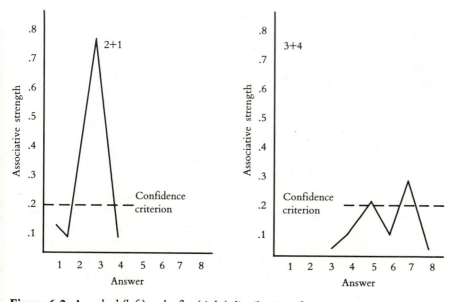

Figure 6-2 A peaked (left) and a flat (right) distribution of associations in preschoolers' addition.

As shown in Figure 6-3, at the outset of the retrieval phase two parameters are set: a confidence criterion and a search length. The confidence criterion is a threshold that must be exceeded by the associative strength of a retrieved answer for the child to state that answer. The search length indicates the maximum number of retrieval efforts the child will make. On each trial, the confidence criterion and search length are chosen through a random process, so that they are independent of each other and independent of their values on previous trials.

Once these two parameters are set, the child retrieves an answer. The probability of any given answer being retrieved on a particular effort is proportional to the associative strength of that answer relative to the associative strengths of all answers to the problem. Thus, in the Figure 6-2 example, the probability of retrieving 3 as the answer to $2 + 1$ would be .80, since the associative strength connecting $2 + 1$ and 3 is .80 and the associative strengths for all answers to $2 + 1$ total 1.00.

If the associative strength of the retrieved answer exceeds the confidence criterion, the child states that answer. Otherwise, if the number of searches that has been conducted on the trial is within the permissible search length, the child again retrieves an answer, compares it to the confidence criterion, and advances it as the solution if its associative strength exceeds the criterion. Retrieval efforts continue as long as the associative strength of each retrieved answer is below the confidence criterion and the number of searches does not exceed the search length.

If no answer has been stated and the maximum number of searches has been attempted, the child proceeds to use a backup strategy. In simple addition and subtraction, some of the backup strategies used by young children are counting on fingers, putting up fingers but answering without any evident counting, and counting without any obvious external referent. In reading (identification of individual words) the main backup procedure is sounding out. All of these backup strategies serve the same function: to provide means for generating answers when no retrieved answer has sufficient associative strength to exceed the confidence criterion and be stated.

How Development Occurs

Why do some problems develop peaked distributions and other flat distributions? The basic assumption of the model regarding acquisition of the distributions is that people associate whatever answer they state, correct or incorrect, with the problem on which they state it. This assumption reduces the issue of what factors lead children to develop a particular distribution of associations on each problem to the issue of what factors lead them to state particular answers on each problem.

Three factors that are hypothesized to influence the likelihood of stating correct answers are relative difficulty of executing backup strategies on different

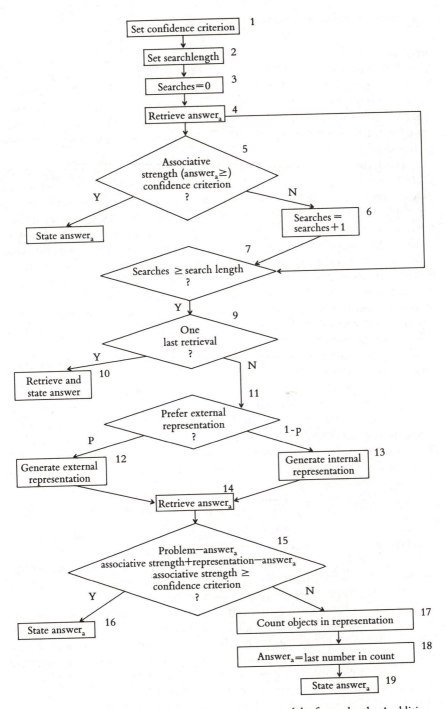

Figure 6-3 Process for distribution of associations model of preschoolers' addition.

problems, relative presentation rates of the problems, and influences of related knowledge on each problem. First consider relative difficulty of executing backup strategies. The more operations and the more difficult the operations needed to use a backup strategy on a particular problem, the more likely the child will err when using it. For example, solving the problem 3 + 4 through counting fingers is more likely to produce erroneous answers than solving 2 + 1 in the same way.

The second factor believed to affect the acquisition process is knowledge of related problems and operations. The influences include both helpful and harmful effects. As an example of a helpful effect, Siegler (1986) found that the better known an addition problem (for example, 2 + 4 = 6), the easier it is to learn the inverse subtraction problem (6 − 4 = 2). As an example of a harmful effect, Siegler and Shrager (1984) found that preschoolers' most frequent erroneous answer on addition problems where the second addend is greater than the first (for example, 3 + 4; 3 + 5) is consistently the number that is one greater than the second addend (3 + 4 = 5; 3 + 5 = 6). Such errors may be a result of preschoolers confusing addition with the related and (to them) better known operation of counting and therefore saying the next number in the counting string as the answer.

The third factor hypothesized to influence acquisition is frequency of presentation. Parents, teachers, and textbooks present some problems more often than others; this may make these problems easier to learn. Consistent with this view, Ashcraft (1987), Siegler and Shrager (1984), and Siegler (in press) found that considering frequency of presentation of addition and multiplication problems by parents and textbooks helped to account for some phenomena that otherwise were difficult to explain. In particular, it helped to explain why tie problems (for example, 6 + 6; 6 × 6) were easier than otherwise might have been expected.

Evidence for the Applicability of the Strategy Choice Model

Evidence has been found for each of the four assumptions underlying the model. As noted previously, children have been found to use diverse strategies on a large variety of problems. The variability in strategy use exists even within a single child performing the identical problem on two occasions close in time (Siegler, 1986; Siegler and McGilly, in press).

The studies have also yielded evidence for the adaptiveness of children's strategy choices. As shown in Figure 6-4, the more difficult the problem, defined in terms of percentage of errors, the more often children use backup strategies. Further, children use backup strategies most often on the problems where doing so yields the greatest difference between percent correct produced by backup strategies and percent correct produced by retrieval (Siegler and Robinson, 1982).

Evidence for the third assumption—that adaptive strategy choices can arise through use of procedural knowledge that is not accessible to introspection—comes from both empirical studies and from computer simulations based on the present model. Empirically, children's judgments of problem difficulty have been found to be only moderately correlated with their strategy choices in a domain, addition, where actual problem difficulty is much more highly correlated with strategy use (Siegler and Shrager, 1984). This suggests that, at least in addition, strategy choices are made on some basis other than judgments of problem difficulty. Theoretically, computer simulations have been generated that model children's strategy choices in addition, subtraction, and multiplication (Siegler, 1987, in press; Siegler and Shrager, 1984). These simulations have no metacognitive knowledge, yet they produce adaptive strategy choices and ones that closely parallel the choices that children make. Thus, the simulations represent a sufficiency proof that metacognitive knowledge of cognitive capacities, available strategies, and task demands is not necessary for adaptive strategy choices.

The fourth assumption underlying the model is that children's use of multiple strategies influences their learning. One type of evidence of this involves parallels between the specific errors produced by backup strategies early in development and the errors produced later by retrieval. For example, in multiplication the two most common errors that children make when using repeated addition are multiplicand-related errors, such as $7 \times 4 = 24$, and close-miss errors, such as $7 \times 4 = 27$ (Siegler, in press). When placed under speed pressure, adults make similar errors (Miller, Perlmutter, and Keating, 1984). Adults also are relatively slow to reject such multiplication errors as false when the problems are presented within a verification paradigm (Campbell and Graham, 1985). A straightforward explanation for a variety of aspects of adults' performance that are otherwise difficult to account for may be that performance produced by early backup strategies has a lasting impact (Siegler, in press).

In addition to this evidence for the assumptions underlying the model, evidence also has been found for the model's usefulness in predicting *when* children use different strategies. The model predicts high correlations among percentage of backup strategies on a problem, percentage of errors on the problem, and mean solution time on the problem. Within the model, all three of these dependent variables are functions of the same independent variable: the peakedness of the distribution of associations. The more peaked the distribution, the higher the probability of retrieval. (This is because the more peaked the distribution, the higher the probability that the answer with greatest associative strength will be retrieved and the higher the probability that once retrieved it will exceed the confidence criterion and be stated.) Because the correct answer is usually the strongest associate, problems with the most peaked distributions also yield the highest percentages of correct retrievals. In such peaked distributions,

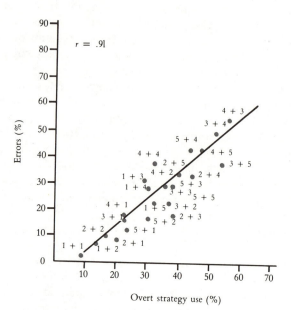

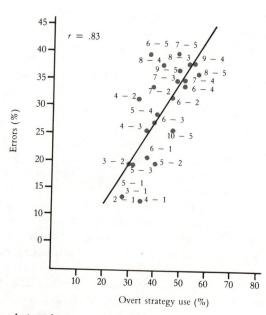

Figure 6-4 Correlations between percent correct and percent use of overt strategy in addition, subtraction, multiplication, and reading.

(c) Multiplication

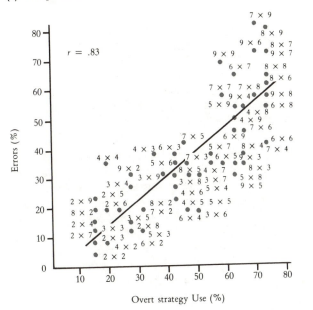

(d) Reading

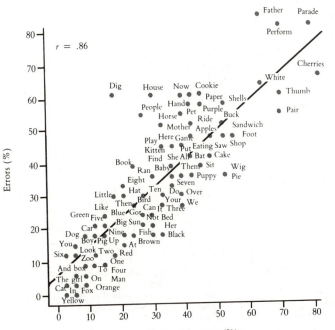

the correct answer both will be retrieved on a higher percentage of searches and will be stated on a higher percentage of searches when it is retrieved. Further, the greater the concentration of strength in one answer, the more likely that retrieval times will be fast, because the probability of sampling an answer greater than the confidence criterion increases with peakedness. Therefore, fewer searches, on average, will take place before a statable answer is retrieved. The high correlations in Table 6-1 among percentage errors, mean solution time, and percent overt strategy use in addition, subtraction, multiplication, and reading (word identification) attest to the presence of the predicted relations.

This first prediction might be expected on general grounds; more difficult problems elicit greater use of backup strategies, as well as more errors and longer solution times. A second prediction is more specific to the model; indeed, it is nonintuitive. The primary source of the correlations among each problem's percent backup strategy use, percent errors, and length of solution times on each problem should be parallels between backup strategy use and patterns of errors and solution times on *retrieval trials* on the problem. Percent backup strategy use on a problem, percent errors on retrieval trials on that problem, and length of solution times on retrieval trials on the problem all are hypothesized to depend

Table 6-1 Source of Correlations of Overt Strategy Use with Errors and Solution Times

	Errors		Solution times	
	Retrieval trials	Overt strategy trials	Retrieval trials	Overt strategy trials
Zero-order correlations				
Addition	.83*	.51	.79*	.42
Subtraction	.83*	.25	.83	.73
Multiplication	.82*	.58	.72	.78
Reading	.69*	.32	.50*	−.12
Partial Correlations†				
Addition	.67	.42	.75*	.10
Subtraction	.72*	.00	.62*	.25
Multiplication	.43*	.11	.58*	.02
Reading	.59*	.27	.34	.10

Note: Numbers in the table indicate correlations of percentage of overt strategy use on each problem with the variable specified in the table. For example, the top left value of .83 indicates a raw correlation of $r = .83$ between percentage of errors on retrieval trials on each problem and percentage of overt strategy use on that problem for addition. Asterisks indicate differences between dependent correlations are significant, $p < .05$, Hotelling t test.
†The variables partialed out were: in addition, the sum; in subtraction, the size of the larger number; in multiplication, the product; in reading, the number of letters in the word.

entirely on the peakedness of the problem's distribution of associations. Because all three depend on the same underlying variable, they should correlate highly. This should be true even when the common influence of problem size is partialed out, because other factors that influence the peakedness of distributions (such as problem presentation rates) would contribute additional shared variance.

In contrast, percent errors and length of solution times on backup strategy trials should not depend on the peakedness of the distribution of associations; they should depend on the difficulty of executing the backup strategy. For example, in preschoolers' addition, difficulty of executing the main backup strategy, counting the fingers, would presumably depend on the number of fingers to be counted—that is on the sum. In older children's multiplication, the difficulty of executing repeated addition, which is the main backup strategy there, would depend on the amount of adding to be done—that is on the product. In word identification, the difficulty of the main backup strategy, sounding out, would depend at least in part on word length. In all of these cases, percentage of errors and lengths of solution times on backup strategy trials should be less highly correlated with percent use of backup strategies. Moreover, partialing out the common relation to the hypothesized source of difficulty on backup strategy trials should reduce the relation to a greater degree for the correlations involving errors and solution times on backup strategies.

As shown in Table 6-1, data have consistently confirmed these predictions. In fifteen of the sixteen comparisons, the pattern of overt strategy use more closely paralleled the pattern of errors and solution times on retrieval trials than the pattern of errors and solution times on overt backup strategy trials. In twelve of the sixteen cases, the differences were significantly in the predicted direction, and in none of the cases was it significantly in the other direction.

The strongest evidence of the model's sufficiency to produce strategy choices much like those of children comes from computer simulations. These have been developed for the domains of addition, subtraction, and multiplication. The simulations produce performance that resembles that of children in many ways. They generate the same strategies, the same relative speed of the strategies, many of the same particular errors, and the same developmental trend from greater use of backup strategies to greater use of retrieval (Siegler, 1986, in press; Siegler and Shrager, 1984).

Perhaps most important, the simulations, like the children, produce high correlations among percent use of backup strategies, percent errors, and mean solution times on each problem. These correlations appear both within the simulation's output (such as the simulations's percentage of errors on each problem and its mean solution time on that problem) and in parallels between the simulation's and the children's performance (such as the simulation's percentage of errors on each problem and the children's percentage of errors on that problem). The within-simulation correlations equaled or exceeded $r = .90$ for each of the three measures in all three simulations. The simulation-child correlations equaled or exceeded $r = .80$ on all three measures in all three simulations. This output of the simulations confirms that the processes hypothesized by the model are sufficient to produce patterns of strategy use, errors, and response times very similar to those produced by children.

Explaining Individual Differences in Terms of the Model

The preceding sections described how the distribution-of-associations model explains relations among percentage of backup strategies, percentage of errors, and mean solution times on different *items*. The model also may help explain relations among these variables for different *individuals*.

Two factors that may be especially important sources of individual differences in strategy choices are peakedness of distributions and stringency of confidence criteria. Intuitively, peakedness of distributions corresponds to degree of knowledge about problems, whereas stringency of confidence criteria refers to how motivated children are to do well on a task: the higher (more stringent) the confidence criteria, the more likely that children will need to use the relatively time-consuming and effortful backup strategies rather than retrieval. Table 6-2 shows how differences in these parameters would influence percent use of backup strategies, percent errors on retrieval trials, and length of solution times on retrieval trials. The table contrasts the effects of high and low values on the two parameters. Dashes indicate cases where the model does not generate any direct prediction of effects of parametric variations on a particular dependent variable.

Table 6-2 Effects of Variations in Model Parameters on Strategy Use, Errors, and Solution Times

Variable	Value	Use of retrieval (%)	Errors on retrieval trials (%)	Solution times on retrieval trials
Distribution of associations				
	Peaked	High	Low	Low
	Flat	Low	High	High
Confidence criteria				
	High	Low	Low	—
	Low	High	High	—

We earlier described the effects of the peakedness of the distributions. Peaked distributions lead to frequent use of retrieval, low error rates on retrieval trials, and short solution times on retrieval trials. Flat distributions lead to the opposite values on each variable.

Variations in confidence criteria affect these three measures differently. High confidence criteria result in a high percentage of backup strategies but a low percentage of errors on retrieval trials. The high percentage of backup strategies is a result of there being few distributions including answers with sufficient associative strength to exceed the high confidence criteria. The low percentages of errors on retrieval trials is attributable to only answers with a great deal of associative strength (almost exclusively correct answers) being statable when confidence criteria are high. With regard to the third variable, solution times on retrieval trials, testing of the mathematical model described in Siegler and Shrager (1984) has shown that variation in confidence criteria has little if any systematic effect.

A STUDY OF INDIVIDUAL DIFFERENCES

To examine individual differences in strategy choices, first graders were tested on addition, subtraction, and reading (word identification) problems. Of particular interest was the degree of consistency in individual children's frequency of use of backup strategies, accuracy and solution times on retrieval trials, and accuracy and solution times on backup strategy trials on the three tasks.

The particular three tasks were chosen because the relations among individual differences in strategy choices on them are potentially very revealing. Strategy choices in addition and subtraction would be expected to be most closely related. These tasks are hypothesized to share a common strategy choice procedure and also numerous other features. The backup strategies children use for adding and subtracting are very similar: drawing on knowledge of the base ten system, counting skills, and the use of fingers and other external means for representing problems. Addition and subtraction also are usually taught by the same teacher using the same textbook. This is likely to contribute commonalities in teaching methods, organization of instruction, and pupils' motivation. Further, Siegler (1986) found that associative strengths linking addition problems and their answers are highly correlated with associative strengths on the inverse subtraction problem (for example, the peakedness of $3 + 5 = 8$ is closely related to the peakedness of $8 - 5 = 3$). Knowledge of the inverse addition problem may activate the correct answer on the corresponding subtraction problem, thus causally linking knowledge of the two operations.

Strategy choices in word identification might or might not be related to those in the two arithmetic domains. Previous research on word identification suggests that it involves the same basic strategy choice procedure as addition and subtraction (Jorm and Share, 1983; Siegler, in preparation). In all cases, the nature of the retrieval mechanism determines when backup strategies are used. Certain parameters within the model might also be similar across these and other domains. For example, a child may set stringent confidence criteria for all tasks to ensure a high level of retrieval accuracy. This would also produce a tendency to rely heavily on backup strategies in many domains. However, beyond these potential sources of similarity, numerous possible sources of differences also exist. Backup strategies and instructional methods differ substantially, and the causal connections between individual differences in arithmetic and reading are unclear.

In sum, four general patterns might relate individual differences in strategy choices in addition, subtraction, and word identification.

1. Strategy choices are similar on all three tasks.

2. Strategy choices in addition and subtraction are closely related, but strategy choices in word identification are only modestly related to those on the arithmetic tasks.

3. Strategy choices in addition and subtraction are closely related, but choices on the reading tasks are completely unrelated to choices on the other two tasks.

4. Strategy choices are unrelated on the three tasks.

One purpose of the experiment was to distinguish among these alternatives.

A second issue concerned relations between stringency of children's confidence criteria and peakedness of their distributions of associations. The model suggests that children who set more stringent (higher) confidence criteria will come to have more peaked distributions. The reasoning is straightforward. More stringent confidence criteria will lead to more frequent use of backup strategies (because fewer retrieved answers will have sufficient associative strength to exceed the higher criteria). Since backup strategies are usually more accurate than retrieval, the greater use of backup strategies will lead to more accurate performance. This more accurate performance will lead to more peaked distributions, since children learn the answers they state. Thus, stringent confidence criteria should be associated with peaked distributions. The experiment reported below produced data relevant to the issue of relations between individual children's confidence criteria and peakedness of distributions, as well as to the more global issue of how individuals differ in strategy choices.

Method

Participants The participating children were thirty-six first graders attending a middle-class suburban public school in the Pittsburgh area. Their chronological age at the time of testing was 81 months (standard deviation = 3.5 months). The experimenter was a thirty-year-old woman research assistant.

Problems The addition problems were fourteen items with sums ranging from 3 to 18 and smaller addends ranging from 1 to 6. The subtraction problems were the fourteen inverse problems from those presented in addition. The reading items were fifty words ranging from two to eight letters. Each word was printed in lower case on a 4-by-6-inch index card. The words and arithmetic problems were sampled from those in the children's textbooks (Addison-Wesley series in arithmetic; Scott-Foresman series in reading). Approximately 70 percent of the words and problems had appeared in lessons that the children had already completed before the time of testing; the remaining items were in lessons that had not yet been encountered. Figure 6-5 shows all of the items used on the three tasks.

Procedure Each child was brought individually from the classroom to a vacant room within the school. The child was seated at a table directly across from the experimenter. Before each session, the child was told what that day's task would be: adding, subtracting, or reading. (A child performed only one task on a given day.) Equal numbers of children were presented each of the three tasks in each of the six possible orders. The three tasks were presented on three consecutive days whenever possible, although at times weekend days or absences intervened.

The task instructions emphasized that children could do anything they wanted to get the right answer: recall the answer from memory, count on their fingers, sound out words, and so on. The only thing that was important was that the children try as hard as they could to be correct. Each child's behavior was videorecorded so that strategies could be analyzed in detail. To supplement the videocassettes the experimenter made notes about the child's observable behavior on each problem where such behavior was detected.

Addition items: $3 + 2$, $7 + 4$, $15 + 3$, $1 + 2$, $5 + 5$, $11 + 4$, $10 + 6$, $5 + 8$, $2 + 2$, $3 + 4$, $9 + 3$, $12 + 6$, $13 + 4$, $8 + 3$

Subtraction items: $5 - 2$, $11 - 4$, $18 - 3$, $3 - 2$, $10 - 5$, $15 - 4$, $16 - 6$, $13 - 8$, $4 - 2$, $7 - 4$, $12 - 3$, $18 - 6$, $17 - 4$, $11 - 3$

Reading items: And, sun, in, car, play, bird, box, yellow, ten, ran, cake, thumb, she, white, kitten, game, sit, pig, seven, shop, hat, zoo, man, look, the, your, all, six, sandwich, baby, then, parade, mother, duck, shells, eating, do, cookie, bed, ride, apples, little, purple, like, bat, nine, perform, to, them, girl

---

Figure 6-5 Items used on the three tasks in a study of individual differences in strategy choices among first graders.

Results

Strategies Used   Analysis of the videocassettes indicated that children used a variety of strategies on each task. For the arithmetic tasks, the strategies used were the same as those observed in other studies involving young children (Siegler and Shrager, 1984; Siegler, 1986). These included counting fingers, putting up fingers but answering without any apparent counting, counting aloud without any apparent external referent, and retrieval. For the reading task, the children also used both retrieval and overt strategies. The overt strategies on the reading task involved either sounding out the letters in the word one at a time before stating an answer or pronouncing a part of the word before offering a pronounciation of the entire word.

For our present purposes we need only be concerned with a two-way classification of strategies: retrieval versus overt backup strategies. A trial was classified as a retrieval trial when children simply stated the answer following presentation of the item. When there was any visible or audible evidence of mediating computations such as counting in the arithmetic tasks or sounding out parts of the words in the reading task, the trial was classified as an overt strategy trial.[1] Two independent raters agreed on 93 percent of their classifications; the remaining 7 percent of cases were classified through review of the videocassettes and discussion.

Performance on the Three Tasks   Before we examine the pattern of individual differences on the tasks, let us describe in general terms children's performance on them. Table 6-3 summarizes the results. Means and standard deviations are presented for a variety of measures involving speed, accuracy, and strategy use. Across all trials, and specifically on retrieval trials, performance on the reading task was fastest, most accurate, least variable, and most frequently generated by retrieval. Performance on the subtraction task was slowest, least accurate, most variable, and most frequently generated by backup strategies.

Although the amount of variability differed on the three tasks, there was nonetheless considerable variability on each of them. Below we consider the degree to which this variability was a result of individual children behaving similarly across the three tasks.

Individual Differences across Tasks   To examine the consistency of individual differences across tasks, we computed correlations between individuals' performance on each of the seven measures shown in Table 6-4 for each of the three possible pairs of tasks. The results of these analyses can be summarized

---

[1] This classification procedure may underestimate the use of backup strategies by classifying covertly executed backup strategies as retrieval. To the extent that such misclassifications occurred, however, they would only undermine the patterns of differences between the types of strategies.

Table 6-3 Descriptive Data on Accuracy and Speed on Each Task

Task	Retrieval (%)	Correct (%)	Median RT	Correct overt retrieval trials (%)	Correct overt strategy trials (%)	Median RT retrieval trials (%)	Median RT overt strategy trials
Addition	61 (27)	76 (24)	9.9 (19.4)	82 (24)	75 (28)	4.2 (2.9)	19.4 (31.4)
Subtraction	54 (32)	64 (27)	11.6 (19.1)	69 (31)	61 (29)	6.1 (4.4)	22.4 (31.2)
Reading	74 (20)	80 (18)	2.5 (1.3)	89 (17)	49 (21)	1.8 (0.1)	20.9 (34.5)

Note: The numbers within parentheses are standard deviations. Solution times are means of medians for each child. Speed and accuracy data for retrieval trials and for overt strategy trials are for children who used each type of approach on at least three trials on the task.

quite simply. Individual children's performance on the two arithmetic tasks was strongly related on all dependent measures. Their performance on the reading task was related on some measures to performance on the two arithmetic tasks, but the relationship was less consistent and less strong.

The correlations between addition and subtraction performance were substantial, both when performance on all trials was considered and when performance on retrieval and overt strategy trials were analyzed separately. The children

Table 6-4 Correlations of Individual Children's Performance in Addition, Subtraction, and Reading

Measure	Addition-subtraction	Addition-reading	Subtraction-reading
Retrieval (%)	.72	.03	.02
Correct (%)	.60	.36	.43
Mean RT	.98	−.09	−.03
Correct—retrieval trials (%)	.48	.59	.61
Correct—overt strategy trials (%)	.70	.31	.27
Mean RT—retrieval trials	.63	.21	.31
Mean RT—overt strategy trials	.88	−.04	.03

Note: All correlations are Pearson product-moment rs. With $df = 34$, $rs > .33$ are significant for $p < .05$.

who used retrieval most often for addition also used it most often for subtraction. The children who answered accurately in addition tended also to be those who answered accurately in subtraction. The children who produced the fastest response times in addition also tended to produce the fastest response times in subtraction. Similarities in children's addition and subtraction were somewhat stronger for overt strategy trials than for retrieval trials. This held true both for the correlations involving percent correct ($r = .70$ versus $r = .48$) and for median solution times ($r = .88$ versus $r = .63$). However, similarities were present on all measures.

The correlations between reading and the two arithmetic tasks were more variable. On some measures there was no significant correlation between reading performance and performance on the arithmetic tasks, on other measures there were moderately strong correlations, and on one measure the correlations between reading and each of the arithmetic tasks were stronger than that between addition and subtraction. The relations between reading and the two arithmetic tasks tended to be stronger on retrieval than on overt strategy trials. This makes sense from the perspective of the present model. Within the model, the retrieval process is similar in all domains. In contrast, there are obvious differences between the overt strategies used in reading and those used in addition and subtraction (for example, sounding out as opposed to counting fingers).

Good Students, Not-so-good Students, and Perfectionists   The most revealing analysis of the data was a cluster analysis conducted to indicate whether children's performance fell into characteristic patterns. The input to the cluster analysis was percent use of retrieval, percent correct retrieval trials, and percent correct on overt strategy trials on each of the three tasks. Thus, the input for each child involved nine data points. On the basis on this input, the clustering program (PKM) divided children into three groups with twelve, nine, and fifteen children, respectively. The performance of the three groups differed significantly on seven of the nine comparisons ($F < .05$). The only two comparisons on which significant differences were absent were those involving percent use of retrieval on the reading task and percent correct on retrieval trials on the reading task.

To provide convergent validation for the groupings that emerged from the cluster analysis, the three groups yielded by it were also contrasted on two measures that were not used as input to the original analysis: solution times on retrieval trials and solution times on backup strategy trials. Again, the three groups differed significantly on most measures (four of six); they also were extremely close to differing significantly on a fifth measure ($p = .06$).

Perhaps most important, the differences among the three groups' performance were readily interpretable. For reasons that should become evident, we will refer to the three groups as the "good students," the "not-so-good students," and the "perfectionists." The differences among the three groups are along two dimensions that intuitively seem likely to contribute to individual differences in cognition: differences in knowledge and differences in motivation. To get a bit ahead of our story, the perfectionists seemed to be children who were both very knowledgeable and very highly motivated to be correct, the good students seemed to be children who were almost as knowledgeable but less highly motivated to be correct, and the not-so-good students seemed to be considerably lower on both dimensions.

The contrast between the good and not-so-good students was evident along all of the dimensions that might be expected from the names. As shown in Figure 6-6, the good students were correct more often on both retrieval and nonretrieval trials on all three tasks. They also used retrieval more often on both addition and subtraction; the two groups were virtually identical in their frequency of retrieval in reading. The good students were also faster in executing the overt strategies on all three tasks and were faster in retrieving answers on addition and subtraction problems.

The relationship of the performance of the perfectionists to that of children in the other two groups was more complex. Despite their being by all measures the equals, and by most measures the superiors, of the good students in terms of both speed and accuracy, they used retrieval even less than the not-so-good students. As shown in Figure 6-6, the perfectionists used retrieval much less often than either the good or the not-so-good students on the addition and subtraction tasks; the three groups were indistinguishable in their percentage of retrieval in reading. When the perfectionists did use retrieval, however, they were the most accurate of the three groups on all three tasks, and were also the fastest on all three (although by only a small amount in reading).

One possible explanation of the perfectionists' superior speed and accuracy on retrieval trials was that they used retrieval on easier problems than children in the other two groups. Both the strategy choice model and common sense indicate that children use retrieval most often on the easiest problems. If this is the case, the fact that the perfectionists used retrieval less often may have meant that they focused their use of it more exclusively on the easiest problems. This alone might account for their greater speed and accuracy on retrieval trials.

To examine the effects of problem difficulty on the retrieval performance of children in the three groups, we developed a formula for calculating the expected percentage of correct answers for children in group j on the problems where they used retrieval.

$$\text{expected percentage correct for group}_j = \frac{\sum_{i=1}^{I} R_{ij} D_i}{\sum R_{ij}}$$

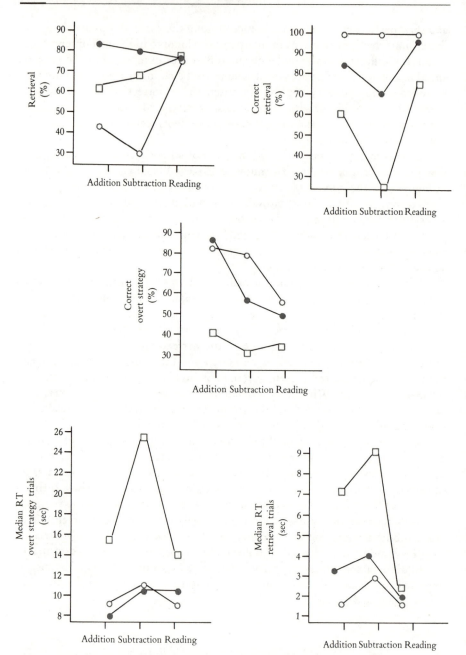

Figure 6-6 Perfectionists' (O——O), good students' (●——●), and not-so-good students' (□——□) strategy use, percent errors, and length of solution times.

where

I = number of problems

R_{ij} = percentage of retrievals on problem "i" by children in group "j"

D_i = percentage of correct answers on problem "i" across all groups

The numerator of this equation multiplies the entire sample's percent correct for an item by the frequency with which children in the group under consideration used retrieval on that item, and sums the results across items. Dividing this sum by the frequency of use of retrieval on all problems by children in the group (the denominator of the equation) gives the percent correct on retrieval trials that would have resulted had children in the group answered correctly on the same percentage of trials on each problem as the group as a whole, but used retrieval on each problem at the rate that they actually did. If each item constituted the same percentage of each group's retrievals, the results of the equation would be identical for all three groups regardless of whether the absolute number of retrievals was equal for the groups. However, if a higher *proportion* of a given group's retrievals came on the easiest problems, the formula would yield a higher expected percentage of correct answers for that group.

The results of the analysis indicated that problems on which children in the three groups used retrieval differed in difficulty. On the addition task, the expected percent correct for the problems on which the perfectionists used retrieval was 86 percent, for the good students 77 percent, and for the not-so-good students 78 percent. Thus, the perfectionists did use retrieval on easier problems. However, the actual percentages correct on retrieval trials — 98 percent for the perfectionists, 80 percent for the good students, and 58 percent for the not-so-good students — showed a greater difference than the expected percentages. Since the difference between the perfectionists and the good students expected on the basis of problem difficulty was nine percent, and since the observed difference was eighteen percent, half of the difference between the two groups in percent correct on retrieval trials could be attributed to the perfectionists using retrieval on easier problems. Only 20 percent (8%/40%) of the difference between the perfectionists and the not-so-good students could be explained in this way.

A similar picture emerged in subtraction. There the expected percent correct for perfectionists, good students, and not-so-good students was 75 percent, 58 percent, and 57 percent, respectively. The observed percent correct was 97 percent, 72 percent, and 26 percent, respectively. Thus, of the 25 percent difference between the observed percent correct for perfectionists and good students, 17 percent would have been expected on the basis of differences in the problems on which retrieval was used. Of the 71 percent difference between perfectionists and not-so-good students, 17 percent could be explained in this way. To summarize, the problems on which the three groups of students used retrieval differed in difficulty, but their differences in problem difficulty only partially explained the differences in the three groups' percent correct on retrieval trials. This implied that the three groups must also differ in how well they knew the problems (the peakedness of their distributions of associations).

Correlations of Experimental Findings and Standardized Test Performance Four months after the experiment was run, all children in the school were given the Otis-Lennon School Aptitude Inventory (Form R, 1979 revision) and the Metropolitan Achievement Test (Form L, 1985 revision). The Otis-Lennon test yields a measure comparable to an IQ score. The Metropolitan test included six achievement test scores that seemed relevant to the present experiment: total mathematics, mathematics computation, mathematics problem solving, total reading, word recognition, and reading comprehension. Of these, the mathematics computation and word recognition tests seemed the closest to the skills that were measured in the experiment, the mathematics problem solving and the reading comprehension tests seemed to have the least overlap with the specific skills tested in the experiments, and the overall mathematics and reading scores included both the specific skills tested in the experiment and a number of others.

The differences on the standardized test scores between perfectionists and good students on the one hand and not-so-good students on the other echoed those in the experimental setting. As shown in Table 6-5, the perfectionists and the good students both scored 20 points higher than the not-so-good students

Table 6-5 Aptitude and Achievement Test Scores of Perfectionists, Good Students, and Not-so-good Students

Measure	Perfectionists	Good students	Not-so-good students
Otis-Lennon			
School Aptitude Inventory	119	120	98
Total math	86	81	37
Math computation	84	68	22
Math problem solving	80	80	38
Total reading	81	83	52
Word recognition	79	84	54
Reading comprehension	76	83	57

Note: Otis-Lennon School Aptitude Inventory measure is an absolute score, comparable to an IQ score. Six Metropolitan Achievement Test scores indicate percentiles according to national norms.

on the aptitude test (means of 120 and 119 versus 98). Similar differences showed up on all of the mathematics and reading achievement scores that were examined. Across the six tests, the perfectionists' average scores were at the 81st percentile, the good students' average scores were at the 80th percentile, and the not-so-good students' average scores were at the 43d percentile.

The three groups' achievement test scores also paralleled their performance in the experiment in several more specific ways. In the experimental data, the difference between the perfectionists and the good students was greater on the addition and subtraction tasks than on the reading task, as was the difference between each of these groups and the not-so-good students. Achievement test performance followed the same pattern. The perfectionists averaged 16 percentiles higher than the good students on the math computation test, exactly as high on the math problem-solving task, and 5 percentiles higher on the overall math test. In contrast, they scored 5 percentiles lower on the word recognition reading test, 7 percentiles lower on the reading comprehension test, and 2 percentiles lower on the overall reading test (there were other subtests on both the math and reading sections of the test that were not analyzed).

With regard to the difference between the not-so-good students and children in the other two groups, the difference between the average of the other two groups and the not-so-good students was 56 percentiles in the total math achievement score, 55 percentiles on the math computation score, and 42 percentiles on the math problem-solving score. These were all considerably more than the differences of 30 percentiles in the total reading achievement score, 28 percentiles in the word recognition test score, and 22 percentiles on the reading comprehension test. Thus, the aptitude and achievement test performance of the perfectionists, good students, and not-so-good students differed in several of the same ways as did their experimental performance.

Interpreting the Pattern of Individual Differences   How can these differences among the perfectionists, good students, and not-so-good students be explained? At a general level, it seems likely that two types of differences are involved: differences in knowledge and differences in motivation. In the specific terms of the model, the two types of differences involve differences in peakedness of distributions and differences in confidence criteria. The pattern of results on the five dependent measures suggests that perfectionists are children who set very stringent confidence criteria and have highly peaked distributions, that the good students are children who set somewhat less stringent confidence criteria and also have highly peaked distributions; and that the not-so-good students set less stringent confidence criteria and have less peaked distributions than children in the other two groups.

First consider the hypothesis that the perfectionists set more stringent confidence criteria than children in the other two groups. If confidence criteria are equal, more peaked distributions of associations lead to a higher percentage of use of retrieval, a higher percentage correct when retrieval is used, and shorter solution times when retrieval is used. The perfectionists defied this pattern, however. Of the three groups, they were most frequently correct on retrieval trials on all three tasks and also the fastest on retrieval trials on all three tasks. However, they were the least likely of the three groups to use retrieval on both addition and subtraction, and no more likely than the other two groups to use it in reading. Such infrequent use of retrieval would be expected if the perfectionists set higher confidence criteria than children in the other two groups.

In addition to setting higher confidence criteria, the perfectionists also appear to have had more peaked distributions of associations than the children in the other two groups. Although they used retrieval on somewhat easier problems (the results of their more stringent confidence criteria), the difference in the degree of difficulty was less than the difference in the percent correct on retrieval trials.

A possible mechanism by which differences in peakedness could arise was also apparent—the accuracy of execution of backup strategies. Recall that within the strategy choice model, the more accurately that backup strategies are executed, the more peaked distributions of associations become. Supporting this assumption, on all three tasks in the present experiment, a child's accuracy in executing backup strategies was significantly correlated with the child's accuracy in using retrieval. For addition, the correlation was $r = .43$; for subtraction, it was $r = .55$; for reading, it was $r = .57$. The perfectionists were the most accurate of the three groups in executing the backup strategies (Figure 6-6). Such accurate execution of the backup strategies provides a means by which the perfectionists could develop more peaked distributions than the other groups.

In sum, the combination of high confidence criteria and highly peaked distributions would be expected to yield the quick, accurate, and infrequent use of retrieval that characterized the perfectionists. Further, their accurate use of backup strategies provided a mechanism that could lead to their possessing more peaked distributions than other children.

The not-so-good students appeared to have less peaked distributions than either of the other two groups and also to set less stringent confidence criteria. First consider evidence that their distributions were less peaked. On all three tasks, their performance on retrieval trials was both slower and less accurate than that of children in the other two groups. A mechanism by which these less peaked distributions could have evolved was these children's less accurate use of backup strategies. On all three tasks, their use of backup strategies was much less accurate than that of children in the other two groups. Again, this lower accuracy on the backup strategies provides a mechanism through which the less peaked distributions of these students may have come to be.

Now consider the interpretation that the not-so-good students set lower confidence criteria than children in the other two groups. The not-so-good students clearly set lower confidence criteria than the perfectionists. Despite their distributions of associations being less peaked, they used retrieval considerably more often on two of the three tasks and as often on the third. The only way that this combination of less accurate yet more frequent retrieval could occur within the model is if one group set much lower confidence criteria than the other.

At first glance, all of the differences between the not-so-good students and the good students might seem attributable to differences in the peakedness of their distributions. As would be expected from the distributions of the not-so-good students being less peaked, they used retrieval on a lower percentage of trials and used it more slowly and less accurately. However, the magnitudes of the differences suggested that they also may have set lower confidence criteria. The good students used retrieval on 10 percent more trials than the not-so-good students. However, they were correct on 28 percent more of retrieval trials, and their solution times on retrieval trials were less than half as long. The combination of much less peaked distributions and somewhat lower confidence criteria would produce these relations.

This analysis allows an ordering of the three groups along the dimensions of peakedness of distributions and stringency of confidence criteria. With respect to the peakedness of distributions of associations across the three tasks, the perfectionists possessed distributions whose peakedness is somewhat greater than those of the good students. Both the perfectionists and the good students have much more peaked distributions than the not-so-good students. With respect to the confidence criteria, the perfectionists set criteria considerably more stringent than those of children in either of the other groups. The criteria of the good students also appear to have been somewhat more stringent than those of the not-so-good students.

Note that these correlations between stringency of confidence criteria and peakedness of the distributions are consistently positive. Perfectionists set the most stringent criteria and had the most peaked distributions, not-so-good students set the least stringent criteria and had the least peaked distributions, and good students were somewhere in the middle on each variable. This fits the model's prediction that setting more stringent confidence criteria would lead to more peaked distributions. Recall that the logic was that setting more stringent criteria for stating correct answers would lead to more frequent use of backup strategies; this would allow greater opportunity to associate the correct answer with the problem and less opportunity to associate incorrect answers with it. The perfectionists' setting of more stringent confidence criteria may, in the short run, have slowed their performance by leading to greater use of backup strategies. In the long run, however, setting of such stringent criteria may have contributed to their superior accuracy.[2]

CONCLUSIONS

The study just described indicates that clear individual differences exist in children's strategy choices. These individual differences were evident both in the children's experimental performance and in their performance on standardized aptitude and achievement tests. Our model of the strategy choice process allowed identification of two sources of the individual differences: peakedness of distributions of associations and confidence criteria for stating retrieved answers. The analysis of individual differences in strategy choice may also be useful for several more general purposes: getting inside the process of taking standardized tests to understand how children achieve the scores they do, deepening our understanding of trait constructs such as reflectivity-impulsivity, and clarifying the relationship between trait-level and process-level analyses of individual differences.

First consider an implication of the analysis of individual differences for understanding why children achieve the standardized test scores that they do. The perfectionists, who set very high confidence criteria, and the good students, who set fairly high ones, achieved the highest standardized test scores; the not-so-good students, who seemed to set the lowest criteria, scored substantially lower on the standardized tests.. This possible relationship between stringency of confidence criteria and standardized test scores suggests that standardized tests may measure more than children's intellect. They may also reflect the fit between children's approaches to the test and the test's requirements. A child's score on an aptitude or achievement test is determined jointly by the number of test items completed and the percentage of those items answered correctly. On speeded tests, at least, a child's ability to efficiently balance time to complete an item against the probability of answering the item correctly will influence the number of correct answers.. This is not necessarily a fault of such tests. Indeed,

---

[2]This conclusion depends on the assumption that backup strategies yield a higher percent correct than would retrieval on those trials where the backup strategies are used. There are two reasons for making this assumption, one theoretical, the other empirical. Theoretically, it is unclear why children would use backup strategies that take longer than retrieval and appear to require more effort to execute unless they were rewarded with superior accuracy. Empirically, use of backup strategies has been shown to lead to better performance. The relevant experiments are ones where children were presented identical sets of problems under two conditions: one where they were required to use retrieval on all trials, and one where they also could use backup strategies. Use of backup strategies as well as retrieval led to greater accuracy in both task domains where the experiment has been run: addition (Siegler and Shrager, 1984) and subtraction (Siegler, 1987).

part of the tests' usefulness as predictive instruments may be precisely that they tap the same types of time-allocation skills that are useful in school.

To illustrate this influence, consider a child who knows that carefully executing backup algorithms almost certainly will lead to a correct answer on certain mathematics problems. The child may also know, however, that use of such procedures is much more time consuming than stating a retrieved answer, and that attempting to maximize accuracy on some items by using the backup algorithms may result in a low score on the test overall if time runs out before all items are tried. The fit between the confidence criteria that the child sets for stating retrieved answers and the speed demands of the test can lead to the child proceeding too slowly and not completing all items or to the child proceeding too quickly and reaching the end of the test with time to spare but without the option of returning to items on earlier pages (a feature of many standardized tests).

Such scenarios might have different impacts on the subgroups of children identified in the present study. The perfectionists, who at least in the experimental situation set stringent confidence criteria, might fall prey to the first type of difficulty on a speeded test. Their very stringent confidence criteria might lead to their not completing all items because they used backup strategies too often. In contrast, the not-so-good students, who in the experiment set less stringent confidence criteria, might fall prey to the second difficulty on a nonspeeded test. Their less stringent confidence criteria might leave them regretting that they had not spent more time on earlier items where they were unsure of answers. Of course, it is possible that the perfectionists might overcome the potential problems of a speeded test if told that speed was important or that the not-so-good students would overcome their potential problem on a nonspeeded test if told that accuracy was all that mattered. We hope in the near future to determine the extent to which children adjust their confidence criteria to such task demands, and also the extent to which the setting of relatively more or less stringent confidence criteria persists across task demands.

A second issue raised by the present analysis of individual differences concerns its relationship to classic individual-difference constructs other than intelligence. Another construct that intuitively seems related to the present analysis is reflectivity-impulsivity (Kagan et al., 1964). Kogan's (1983) definition of reflectivity-impulsivity as "the extent to which a child delays a response in the course of searching for the correct alternative" (p. 672) clearly can be projected into the context of whether to state a particular retrieved answer. Reflective children would resemble the perfectionists of the present study in setting high criteria for stating retrieved answers. Impulsive children would resemble the not-so-good students in setting lower criteria for stating retrieved answers. This equation seems consistent with performance on the Matching

Familiar Figures Test (MFFT), where reflective children proceed slowly but accurately and impulsive children proceed rapidly but inaccurately (Kagan et al., 1964). Slow, accurate performance would follow from setting high confidence criteria; fast, inaccurate performance would result from setting low confidence criteria.

How might the present analysis advance understanding of reflectivity-impulsivity? The greatest benefit would seem to lie in its explicitness concerning mechanisms that result in children acting in reflective or impulsive ways. The strategy choice procedure would produce reflective behavior if confidence criteria were high; it would produce impulsive behavior if confidence criteria were low. However, the model is silent on a critical issue for understanding reflective and impulsive actions: how differences in confidence criteria come about. Given the seemingly large differences in the criteria that people adopt, it seems worthwhile to speculate about factors that could influence the criterion-setting process.

One potentially important factor in setting confidence criteria is knowledge of the consequences of using different strategies. Children may know (consciously or unconsciously) the accuracy and speed of each strategy. If a child has found that backup strategies yield consistently accurate performance, the child may set high confidence criteria. On the other hand, if the child has found that backup strategies are relatively inaccurate as well as slow, the child might set low confidence criteria which would lead to infrequent use of the backup strategies. This interpretation is consistent with the pattern of differences among the three groups in the study. It also suggests that one step that might help make children less impulsive would be to teach them to execute backup strategies more accurately. The larger difference between the accuracy of backup strategies and retrieval that would result from such instruction might persuade the children to use the relatively time-consuming backup strategies more often.

A final question concerns how the present analysis of individual differences relates to Melton's (1967) prescription for research in the area. In one sense, the research seems to fit Melton's recommendations quite precisely. Hypotheses about individual differences have been framed in terms of the process constructs of a cognitive psychological theory. Our ability to describe differences in the experimental performance of perfectionists, good students, and not-so-good students in terms of these constructs attests to the model's usefulness. The external validation provided by the parallel individual differences in standardized test performance increases our optimism that this is a useful level of analysis for understanding individual differences.

Yet the study also suggests that the formulation of process analyses of individual differences does not signal the death knell of more global trait-level analyses. Rather, the more specific and more global analyses may enter into a mutually beneficial relationship with each other. To develop the most useful models, it seems critical to alternate between trying to develop detailed process-oriented models and stepping back to reflect on what global considerations are missing from the models. The global considerations, often summarized by trait and dispositional terms, may then be translated into more specific processes, and the whole model may become broader, more precise, and more useful.

Consider how such a cycle might work in the present area of individual differences in strategy choices. As noted previously, the construct of reflectivity-impulsivity can be conceptualized within the present model in terms of differences in peakedness of distributions of associations and stringency of confidence criteria. However, the general construct of reflectivity-impulsivity clearly indicates that the silence of the model on the question of why children set different confidence criteria is a serious impediment to understanding individual differences in strategy choices. This realization suggests ideas about why different children might set different confidence criteria and how more effective strategy choices (less impulsive behavior) might be promoted by teaching children to execute backup strategies more effectively. In sum, going back and forth between specific analyses of processes and global analyses of traits may be the most effective means for progressing to Melton's and our own goal: detailed and general analyses of individual differences in cognition.

ACKNOWLEDGMENTS

This research was supported in part by grant #HD-19011 from the National Institutes of Health, in part by a grant from the Spencer Foundation, and in part by grant #83-0050 from the National Institute of Education. Thanks are due to Miss Hawkins, Miss Perry, and the teachers and students of University Park Elementary of Monroeville, Pennsylvania, who made the research possible.

REFERENCES

Anderson, J. R. (1983). *The architecture of cognition.* Cambridge, Mass.: Harvard University Press.

Ashcraft, M. H. (1987). Children's knowledge of simple arithmetic: A developmental model and simulation. In J. Bisanz, C. J. Brainerd, and R. Kail (Eds.), *Formal methods in developmental psychology.* New York: Springer-Verlag.

Bisanz, J., Lefevre, J., Scott, C., and Champion, M. A. (1984). Developmental changes in the use of heuristics in simple arithmetic problems. Paper presented at the annual meeting of the American Educational Research Association, New Orleans.

Brown, A. L., Bransford, J. D., Ferrara, R. A., and Campione, J. C. (1983). Learning, remembering, and understanding. In P. H. Mussen (Ed.), *Handbook of child psychology: Cognitive development,* Vol. III. New York: Wiley.

Brown, A. L., and Reeve, R. A. (1986). Reflections on the growth of reflection in children. *Cognitive Development,* 1: 405–416.

Bruner, J. S. (1973). *Beyond the information given: Studies in the psychology of knowing.* New York: Norton.

Campbell, J. I. D., and Graham, D. J. (1985). Mental multiplication skill: Structure, process, and acquisition. *Canadian Journal of Psychology,* 39: 338–366.

Case, R. (1985). *Intellectual development: Birth to adulthood.* Orlando, Fla.: Academic Press.

Cavanaugh, J. C., and Perlmutter, M. (1982). Metamemory: A critical examination. *Child Development,* 53; 11–28.

Chase, W. G., and Simon, H. A. (1973). The mind's eye in chess. In W. G. Chase (Ed.), *Visual information processing.* New York: Academic Press.

Chi, M. T. H., Feltovich, P. J., and Glaser, R. (1981). Categorization and representation of physics problems by experts and novices. *Cognitive Science,* 5: 121–152.

Clancy, W. J. (In press). Heuristic classification. *Journal of Artificial Intelligence.*

Cooper, L. A., and Regan, D. (1982). Attention, perception, and intelligence. In R. Sternberg (Ed.), *Handbook of human intelligence.* New York: Cambridge University Press.

de Groot, A. (1965). *Thought and choice in chess.* The Hague, the Netherlands: Mouton.

Flavell, J. H., and Wellman, H. M. (1977). Metamemory. In R. V. Kail, Jr., and J. W. Hagen (Ed.), *Perspectives on the development of memory and cognition.* Hillsdale, N.J.: Erlbaum.

Gholson, B., and Beilin, H. (1979). A developmental model of human learning. In H. W. Reese and L. P. Lipsitt (Eds.), *Advances in child development and behavior,* Vol. 13. New York: Academic Press.

Gillund, G., and Shiffrin, R. M. (1984). A retrieval model for both recognition and recall. *Psychological Review,* 91: 1–67.

Ilg, F., and Ames, L. B. (1951). Developmental trends in arithmetic. *Journal of Genetic Psychology,* 79: 3–28.

Jorm, A. F., and Share, D. L. (1983). Phonological recoding and reading acquisition. *Applied Psycholinguistics,* 4: 103–147.

Just, M. A., and Carpenter, P. A. (1985). Cognitive coordinate systems: Accounts of mental rotation and individual differences in spatial ability. *Psychological Review,* 92: 137–172.

Kagan, J., Rosman, B. L., Day. D., Albert, J., and Phillips, W. (1964). Significance of analytic and reflective attitudes. *Psychological Monographs,* Vol. 78.

Kahan, L. D., and Richards, D. D. (1986). The effects of context on children's referential communication strategies. *Child Development,* 57: 1130–1141.

Kogan, N. (1983). Stylistic variation in childhood and adolescence: Creativity, metaphor, and cognitive style. In P. H. Mussen (Ed.), *Handbook of child psychology: Cognitive development,* Vol. III. New York: Wiley.

Leal, L., Burney, L., and Johnson, T. D. (1985). Children's strategic behavior and metaknowledge for solving arithmetic problems. Paper presented at the meeting of the Society for Research in Child Development, Toronto, April.

MacLeod, C. M., Hunt, E. B., and Mathews, N. N. (1978). Individual differences in the verification of sentence-picture relationships. *Journal of Verbal Learning and Verbal Behavior,* 17: 493–507.

Melton, A. W. (1967). Individual differences and theoretical process variables: General comments on the conference. In R. M. Gagné (Ed.), *Learning and individual differences.* Columbus, Ohio: Merrill.

Miller, K., Perlmutter, M., and Keating, D. (1984). Cognitive arithmetic: Comparison of operations. *Journal of Experimental Psychology: Learning, Memory, and Cognition,* 10: 46–60.

Naus, M. J., Ornstein, P. A., and Aivano, S. (1977). Developmental changes in memory: The effects of processing time and rehearsal instructions. *Journal of Experimental Child Psychology,* 23: 237–251.

Newman, R. S., Friedman, C. A., and Gockley, D. R. (April 1985). Children's numerosity judgments: Adaptation to task factors. Paper presented at the meeting of the Society for Research in Child Development, Toronto.

Ohlsson, S. (1984). Induced strategy shifts in spatial reasoning. *Acta Psychologica,* 57: 47–67.

Pellegrino, J. W., and Glaser, R. (1982). Analyzing aptitudes for learning: Inductive reasoning. In R. Glaser (Ed.), *Advances in instructional psychology,* Vol. 2. Hillsdale, N.J.: Erlbaum.

Piaget, J. (1976). *The grasp of consciousness: Action and concept in the young child.* Cambridge: Harvard University Press.

Pople, H. (1982). Heuristic methods for imposing structure on ill-structured problems: The structuring of medical diagnostics. In P. Szolovits (Ed.), *Artificial intelligence in medicine.* Westview Prell.

Shultz, T. R., Fisher, G. W., Pratt, C. C., and Rulf, S. (1986). Selection of causal rules. *Child Development,* 57: 143–152.

Siegler, R. S. (1986). Unities across domains in children's strategy choices. In M. Perlmutter (Ed.), *Minnesota symposium on child development,* Hillsdale, N.J.: Erlbaum.

Siegler, R. S. (1987). Strategy choices in subtraction. In J. A. Sloboda and D. Rogers (Eds.), *Cognitive process in mathematics.* Oxford: Clarendon Press.

Siegler, R. S. (In press). Strategy choice procedures and the development of multiplication skill. *Journal of Experimental Psychology: General.*

Siegler, R. S. (In preparation). Strategy choices in beginning reading.

Siegler, R. S., and McGilly, K. (In press). Strategy choices in time telling. In I. Levin and D. Zakay (Eds.), *Psychological time: A life span perspective.*

Siegler, R. S., and Robinson, M. (1982). The development of numerical understandings. In H. Reese and L. P. Lipsitt (Eds.), *Advances in child development and behavior,* Vol. 16. New York: Academic Press.

Siegler, R. S., and Shrager, J. (1984). Strategy choices in addition and subtraction. In C. Sophian (Ed.), *Origins of cognitive skills.* Hillsdale, N.J.: Erlbaum.

Siegler, R. S., and Taraban, R. (1986). Conditions of applicability of a strategy choice model. *Cognitive Development,* 1: 31–51.

Simon, D. P., and Simon, H. A. (1978). Individual differences in solving physics problems. In R. S. Siegler (Ed.), *Children's thinking: What develops?* Hillsdale, N.J.: Erlbaum.

Sternberg, R. J. (1977). Component processes in analogical reasoning. *Psychologicl Review*, 84: 353–378.

Sternberg, R. J. (1985). *Beyond IQ: A triarchic theory of human intelligence.* New York: Cambridge University Press.

Sternberg, R. J., and Powell, J. S. (1983). The development of intelligence. In J. H. Flavell and E. M. Markman (Eds.), *Handbook of child psychology*, Vol. III. New York: Wiley.

Sternberg, R. J., and Weil, E. M. (1980). An aptitude × strategy interaction in linear syllogistic reasoning. *Journal of Educational Psychology*, 72: 226–239.

7

Individual Differences in Practical Knowledge and Its Acquisition

ROBERT J. STERNBERG *Yale University*

RICHARD K. WAGNER *Florida State University*

Thousands of studies have examined learning and knowledge representation. An enormous inventory of studies exists on learning and representation of nonsense syllables, word lists, number strings, geometry, physics, mathematics, chemistry, and so on. From some points of view, this list would seem to be diverse. However, from one point of view, it is not: almost all of the studies that have been done on learning and knowledge representation have dealt with academic rather than practical knowledge. Yet much if not most of the knowledge with which we need to deal in our everyday lives is practical rather than academic. Indeed, beyond the first twenty-two or so years of life, many people need to deal with academic knowledge hardly at all. Our focus in this chapter is on the understudied side of the academic-practical distinction, namely, on the practical side.

The chapter discusses many aspects of practical knowledge, including its nature and representation, comparison to other forms of knowledge, its acquisition and use, and experiments. We discuss the implications of these different aspects for understanding individual differences across people. We also suggest directions for future research on practical knowledge.

THE NATURE OF PRACTICAL KNOWLEDGE

Practical knowledge is defined as procedural information that is useful in one's everyday life (Sternberg and Caruso, 1985). This definition poses two major constraints on the nature of practical knowledge. First, it requires that practical knowledge be procedural. Practical knowledge is viewed as procedural because it is viewed as knowledge of and for use. For example, what kinds of suit patterns go with what kinds of tie patterns is practical knowledge: it is procedural in the sense that it specifies what to wear with what. Second, practical knowledge is required to be relevant to one's everyday life. It would include knowledge learned in school that one can use outside as well as inside school settings.

The actual content of practical knowledge will differ from one person to another as a function of the second constraint. What is practical for one person may be academic for another. So, for example, knowledge about accounting procedures that may be academic for a mail carrier may be practical for an accountant or bookkeeper. In contrast, knowing how to deliver mail might be academic for the accountant but practical for the mail carrier. Similarly, knowledge about how to design experiments is very practical for a scientist but is probably academic for a literary critic. In sum, there exists no organized body of knowledge that could be designated "practical knowledge" for everyone. Rather, what constitutes practical knowledge can differ interindividually.

The corpus of practical knowledge can also differ intraindividually. What is academic at one point in a person's life may become practical at another point. For example, what one learns in a high school shop class may be academic until one actually attempts to build something, such as a piece of furniture. What one learns in a college statistics class may be academic until one actually uses this knowledge to analyze experimental data. Our position is that a major function of schooling should be to render the academic practical. Too often knowledge is taught in such a way that the learner is not able to see how the academic can be translated into the practical. Schooling should help students to make the bridge between the world inside the school and the world outside.

THE REPRESENTATION OF PRACTICAL KNOWLEDGE

Because of its procedural nature, practical knowledge is likely to be stored in the form of productions, also called condition-action sequences (Sternberg and

Caruso, 1985). If a certain condition is met, then a certain action is performed. Sequences of productions constitute production systems. The notion of a script (Schank and Abelson, 1977) is useful for understanding the utilization of practical knowledge. Scripts may be seen as comprising one or more production systems.

Although it seems likely that all people represent practical knowledge in the form of productions embedded within production systems that are in turn embedded in scripts, the content of the productions, production systems, and scripts will vary widely across people with the degree of variation depending on the particular situation to which the practical knowledge needs to be applied. For example, people's standard restaurant scripts may be quite similar to one another, but the productions they have available for situations when things are amiss may not be. Consider, for example, the options when, after what seems a substantial amount of time, no waiter or waitress has come to take an order. Some people might just walk out. Others might go looking for a waiter or waitress before they walk out. Others might continue waiting still longer, not wanting to impose themselves on a busy food server. Still others might go looking for the manager. Similarly, when two college students go out on a date, they may well have a standard script for how to act. But if one violates the notion of the other of what constitutes an appropriate script, individuals may differ widely in their response. For example, if a man is perceived as overly aggressive, some women may submit, others may chastise the date verbally, others may withdraw physically, and so on. Thus, the most interesting information about a person may not be in what his or her standard scripts are but in how he or she reacts to departures from those scripts.

A COMPARISON BETWEEN PRACTICAL KNOWLEDGE AND OTHER FORMS OF KNOWLEDGE

The nature and representation of practical knowledge can be further illustrated by comparing it with some other forms of knowledge. Consider some examples.

Probably the most obvious comparison is with *academic knowledge.* Academic knowledge can be either procedural or declarative. However, if it is procedural, then it is procedural knowledge that is not relevant to one's everyday life.

Consider the grid shown in Figure 7-1. The grid of types of knowledge crosses procedural and declarative knowledge on the one hand with everyday relevant and irrelevant information on the other. In this framework (Sternberg and Caruso, 1985), information is classified either as academic or practical, with academic information taking up three cells of the two-by-two grid and practical knowledge taking up the fourth. What differentiates practical from academic knowledge is the necessity for practical knowledge having both real-world

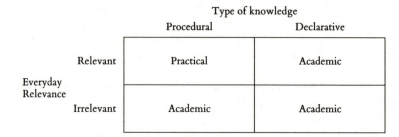

Figure 7-1 Practical knowledge is both procedural and relevant to a person's everyday life. Knowledge that is declarative or irrelevant to everyday life is academic knowledge.

relevance and procedural (action) consequences, whether immediate or more distal. Information that does not satisfy these two constraints is viewed as academic.

Other kinds of knowledge can be either academic or practical depending upon the content of the knowledge and the context in which it is used. In other words, other classifications of knowledge are orthogonal to the practical-academic distinction and hence can be crossed, conceptually, with this distinction. Scientific knowledge, for example, can be practical or academic depending upon whether one can use it in one's everyday life. For example, the knowledge that "if my child whines, I should not reinforce his behavior by paying attention to it" is scientific in nature, following from reinforcement theory, but at the same time is very practical. The knowledge that "if I push someone too hard toward intimacy, they may back off from me" is also scientific in nature, following from some research on interpersonal relationships (Sternberg and Barnes, 1985), but it is also highly practical. Similarly, intuitive knowledge may be quite practical if one can put it to use, but academic if its use does not extend outside of the classroom. A parent's intuitive knowledge of how to handle his or her children when they cry is practical, but a psychologist's intuitive knowledge about the inscrutable Ivan in *The Brothers Karamazov* does not prove to be of much use in everyday life.

Because people live according to different life styles and work in different occupations, the relationship between practical and academic knowledge and other kinds of knowledge will differ across people. For example, scientific knowledge about designing experiments is eminently practical for one who does research, but for undergraduate psychology majors who later pursue law this knowledge is likely to be just academic. Intuitive knowledge about integrating mathematical expressions is academic for a psychologist, but may be practically relevant for a mathematician. Moreover, what is academic at one point may become practical at another, so that the relationships among one's various forms of knowledge may change over time. For example, someone who has never prepared a tax return before but then decides to do it himself or herself may need to garner all those intuitions that previously may have been academic but now can be applied to saving money.

ACQUISITION OF PRACTICAL KNOWLEDGE

According to the triarchic theory of human intelligence (Sternberg, 1985), knowledge acquisition occurs through three basic processes: selective encoding, selective combination, and selective comparison. These processes apply without regard to the type of knowledge involved. *Selective encoding* involves separating, in an array of inputs, information that is relevant for one's purposes in learning from information that is irrelevant. *Selective combination* involves putting this information together so as to form an integrative cognitive structure. *Selective comparison* involves properly relating the new information in the cognitive structure to old information in previously formed cognitive structures so as fully to integrate the new knowledge with knowledge already acquired.

Consider, for example, the task confronting a new entry-level manager in a steel company. The manager is interested in finding out what he will need to do in order to attain promotion as quickly as possible. Although he knows some basic information about the company, the literature he has been given says little about what leads to promotions. On the present view, the new manager engages in at least three processes of knowledge acquisition in order to learn what is likely to lead to promotion. First, he seeks out what information is relevant to promotion within the particular company. Does the company care about dress, the effectiveness with which one manages one's subordinates, the extent to which one goes along or questions higher-level management, the amount of revenue one produces, or whether one attends social functions? Second, the manager draws upon his past experience in deciding what is likely to be relevant. If this is not the manager's first job, then he might relate promotion practices in his previous employment setting to what he anticipates they will be in the present one. This selective comparison will be successful to the extent that the promotion requirements in the new firm match those in the old firm. Finally, the new manager must selectively combine the information he has selectively encoded and compared. Selective combination is not always straightforward. For example, it is possible that certain cues lead the manager to believe that one practice is more likely to lead to promotion, whereas other cues will lead him to believe that the reverse is true.

Children use the processes of selective encoding, selective combination, and selective comparison in their learning of practical knowledge just as adults do. For example, children may have developed a set of strategies to employ when they want to get a toy. They have learned through selective encoding and comparison, for example, what kinds of behavior are likely to steer their parents in their favor: they have learned to be insistent but not to nag, to emphasize the educational value of the toy, to point out how long a period of time has passed since they got their last toy (unless they recently got a toy, in which case they will go to pains *not* to point out when their last toy was purchased), and so on. They not only know which kinds of behavior are relevant, but they know how to combine them in a given situation so as to maximize the effectiveness of their plea.

Our research suggests that people differ widely in the effectiveness with which they use the processes of selective encoding, selective combination, and selective comparison (Davidson and Sternberg, 1984; Sternberg and Davidson, 1982; Sternberg and Powell, 1983). Davidson and Sternberg, for example, found that children identified as gifted are considerably more effective in all three processes of knowledge acquisition than are children who are not identified as gifted. Sternberg and Powell (1983) found that more effective utilizers of these processes are better able to apply them to the acquisition of vocabulary. The general point is that individuals differ fairly widely in their effectiveness in knowledge acquisition, both for practical and academic knowledge. The processes of selective encoding, combination, and comparison are believed to be used in a wide variety of domains. However, the effectiveness with which they are employed by a given individual can vary widely across domains as a function of the mental representation of information within a given domain (linguistic, imagistic, symbolic), the prior knowledge base that one brings to bear upon learning in a given domain, and one's motivation to learn within the given domain. In other words, intraindividual as well as interindividual differences can be expected in the effectiveness of the application of the three processes. For example, a person with a pattern of abilities that renders him or her effective in the verbal domain but not in the spatial domain might find it much easier to selectively encode, combine, and compare information in reading a text than in reading a diagram or a map.

USE OF PRACTICAL KNOWLEDGE

According to the triarchic theory of intelligence (Sternberg, 1985), practical knowledge serves three main functions in a person's interactions with the environment: adaptation to existing environments, selection of new environments, and shaping of old environments into new environments.

Adaptation refers to the process of accommodating oneself to the demands of the environment, however these demands may be imposed. One adjusts oneself to situations as they arise, attempting to gain the best possible fit between the self and these situations. Note that the term *adaptation* is used here in the narrow sense of accommodating oneself to the environment rather than in the broad sense of any action that fits in the environment.

In a new situation one generally tries adaptation as a first application of practical knowledge. For example, one tries to adapt to a new job or to a new intimate relationship. Early on, the individual is so busy trying to figure out the situation that he or she is unlikely to have the mental or emotional resources to try more active forms of environmental interaction. On one's first day at college, for example, one is scarcely able to change the rules of the college, and it would probably be inadvisable to decide so early on that the college is the wrong place to be.

Selection is involved when one decides that the environment in which one is living or working is simply not satisfactory. One therefore decides to deselect that environment and to select another one instead. Changing jobs, changing colleges, changing spouses, and changing places of residence all involve forms of environmental selection.

A lower-level manager, for example, may first try to adapt to the demands of the new job. She learns everything she can about the environment, and she does her best in trying to fit into it. After awhile she comes to the conclusion that promotion to a higher position is more a function of ingratiation toward one's superiors than it is a function of effective performance. If the manager perceives herself as competent but not willing or able to ingratiate herself with superiors, then she may decide to seek a new job where her talents are better rewarded.

In some instances, adaptation proves to be inadequate to the demands of oneself, others, or the task one confronts, but selection may be either impossible or undesirable. For example, changing jobs may not be possible in a one-company town if one is in fact stuck in that town for one reason or another; changing colleges may not be practical if the college one attends is the only college willing to give one a scholarship. In such cases people have a third option, namely, shaping the environment to themselves. This option may be difficult, or even impossible in some cases, to implement, but the opportunity, nevertheless, potentially exists. The college student who finds that a course she would like to take is unavailable may petition for that course to be taught; the wife who tires of her husband's excessive drinking may attempt to help him to reduce his drinking; the manager in a corrupt firm may try to blow the whistle on those whom he perceives as corrupt. In each case, practical knowledge about how to attain a certain goal is put to use through the function of shaping the environment.

People differ in the balance they apply in implementing adaptation, selection, and shaping in their lives. Some people, for example, seem primarily to be adapters, whereas others appear primarily to be shapers. The balance with which the three functions are applied probably depends at least as much on personality as upon cognitive variables. Sternberg (in press) has suggested that the balance of the three functions will depend in part upon what he refers to as intellectual styles, or ways in which one utilizes one's intelligence. For example, he describes legislative, executive, and judicial styles. Legislators tend to be creators of rules and systems, executives to be implementers of rules and systems, and judges to be evaluators of rules and systems. The legislative style is probably more likely to lead to shaping of environments because shaping requires creation of a new environment, whereas the executive style is probably more likely to lead to adaptation which involves actions on an already specified environment.

EXPERIMENTAL DATA

With our collaborators, we have done a series of studies investigating the role of practical knowledge in various kinds of real-world performance. Our motivation is quite straightforward. Traditional ability tests have not proven to be nearly as predictive of performance outside of academic situations as inside, and we hoped to construct new measures that would be more predictive of performance in practical situations.

We will describe here three sets of studies designed to explore individual differences in practical knowledge and its acquisition as a basis for individual differences in real-world performance. The studies differed primarily in the ages of the target populations. The first set of studies (Wagner, 1987; Wagner and Sternberg, 1985, 1986) investigated practical knowledge in adults pursuing either of two careers, academic psychology or business management. The second set of studies, done in collaboration with Wendy Williams (Williams, Sternberg, and Wagner, in preparation), investigated practical knowledge in college students. The last set of experiments, done by Cynthia Berg as her dissertation under Sternberg's supervision (Berg, 1986), investigated practical knowledge in primary and secondary school students.

Experiment with Adults

We interviewed both business managers and university professors of psychology who had been named as highly successful in their chosen occupations (Wagner and Sternberg, 1985). Although there were some minor disagreements among them, the various interviewees agreed on at least three points.

First, intelligence as it is measured by standard tests of intellectual ability is not very important to adaptation in real-world occupational environments. There seem to be many individuals with high IQs who do not perform particularly well on the job, at the same time that there are those with lower IQs who perform quite well. Obviously, this observation applies within a restricted range of IQs. If the IQs ranged from, say, 40 to 140, the effect of IQ would be more pronounced. But within the range of IQs normally found within one or the other of the occupations we studied, IQ was seen as being not very important. The data on job performance confirm this observation of the interviewed individuals (Ghiselli, 1966; Wigdor and Garner, 1982).

Second, our informants agreed that what one learns in graduate school (for the university professors) or business school (for the business executives) is also not very important. School learning seems to exhibit minimal transfer to on-the-job settings. In one respect this finding was somewhat of an embarrassment for one author (Sternberg) because when we did the studies the coauthor (Wagner) was his graduate student. At the same time, we recognized the validity of what the interviewees were saying. For example, with respect to the training of a research psychologist, much of what was learned in graduate school becomes not wrong but irrelevant. The necessary knowledge for success in one's first year on the job is not what was taught in graduate school. What one needs to know is how to write a grant proposal, how to decide on a journal to which to submit an article, how to acquire resources from a department that does not give of its resources munificently, and so on. These are not things learned in graduate school; rather, they are things one must pick up on the job.

Third, they agreed that what was perhaps most important to on-the-job success was what we labeled "tacit knowledge," that is, what one needs to know in order to succeed in a given environment but that one is never explicitly taught and that might not even be verbalized. For example, knowing how to write a grant proposal, knowing how to acquire departmental resources, or knowing how to interest students in one's work are all examples of tacit knowledge. We therefore decided to pursue prediction of real-world performance through the understanding and measurement of individual differences in levels of tacit knowledge. This tacit knowledge is a form of practical knowledge, as discussed in this chapter.

Studies of Academic Psychologists   One set of studies looked at tacit knowledge of people in the profession of academic psychology. In a first experiment, 187 subjects, varying in amounts of experience and formal training in the field of academic psychology, served as subjects. The faculty group consisted of fifty-four members of twenty psychology departments, including individuals both in highly-rated departments and in departments that were not highly rated (Roose and Andersen, 1970). A total of 104 graduate students in comparable psychology departments and twenty-nine Yale undergraduates also participated in the experiments.

Tacit knowledge important for success in academic psychology was measured by presenting subjects with a series of twelve work-related situations, each of which was associated with from six to twenty response items. Subjects rated the importance of response items on a scale of 1 (not important) to 7 (extremely important). An example of a typical work-related situation and associated response items follows.

It is your second year as an assistant professor in a prestigious psychology department. This past year you published two unrelated empirical articles in established journals. You don't, however, believe there is yet a research area that can be identified as your own. You believe yourself to be about as productive as others. The feedback about your first year of teaching has been generally good. You have as yet to serve on a university committee. There is one graduate student who has chosen to work with you. You have no external source of funding, nor have you applied for funding.

Your goals are to become one of the top people in your field and get tenure in your department. The following is a list of things you are considering doing in the next two months. You obviously cannot do them all. Rate the importance of each by its priority as a means of reaching your goals.

_____ a. improve the quality of your teaching

_____ b. write a grant proposal

_____ c. begin long-term research that may lead to a major theoretical article

_____ d. concentrate on recruiting more students

_____ e. serve on a committee studying university-community relations

_____ f. begin several related short-term research projects, each of which may lead to an empirical article

_____ g. participate in a series of panel discussions to be shown on the local public television station

_____ h. write a paper for presentation to an upcoming American Psychological Association convention

_____ i. adjust your work habits to increase your productivity

_____ j. write an integrative literature review chapter in a soon to be published book (due in six weeks)

_____ k. accept an invitation to be on an American Psychological Association task force on ethics in psychological experiments

_____ l. ask for comments from senior members of the department on future papers

_____m. write a paper for possible publication in a general circulation magazine.

_____ n. become more involved in local public-service organizations

_____ o. volunteer to be chairperson of the undergraduate curriculum committee.

Tacit knowledge was theorized to be of three basic kinds: knowledge about managing oneself, knowledge about managing others, and knowledge about managing career. Separate scores were obtained for each of these areas, and a total score was obtained as well. Scoring was done by selecting items that distinguished statistically among the professional, graduate student, and under-graduate groups. For details, see Wagner and Sternberg (1985).

In a second experiment (Wagner, 1987), 212 individuals drawn from the same population as in the first experiment participated. The experiment differed in three major respects from the first experiment. First, the classification scheme for items was changed somewhat. In this experiment, scoring was done sepa-rately for managing oneself, managing others, and managing careers, with each of these scores computed separately for short-range versus long-range planning. Items were chosen so that there would be sufficient representation for each of the subscores. Second, scoring was done in a way different from in the first experiment. In particular, scores were computed using a prototype method whereby an expert group of highly successful individuals served as the proto-type. Scores were computed on the basis of statistical distance from this proto-type group. Third, subjects were asked to fill out the questionnaire not only for their actual department but also for an ideal department in which the way things work would be the way they should work in a department that is perceived as "perfect."

Studies of Business Executives   The studies of business executives were gener-ally comparable to those for academic psychologists. Indeed, many of the classrooms were parallel to those for the academic psychologists but rendered appropriate for business management settings. Consider, for example, the fol-lowing question.

It is your second year as a mid-level manager in a company in the commu-nications industry. You head a department of about thirty people. The evaluation of your first year on the job has been generally favorable. Performance ratings for your department are at least as good as they were before you took over, and perhaps even a little better. You have two assistants. One is quite capable. The other seems only to go through the motions and to be of little real help. You believe that although you are well liked, there is little that would distinguish you in the eyes of your superiors from the nine other managers at a comparable level in the company.

Your goal is rapid promotion to the top of the company. The following is a list of things you are considering doing in the next two months. You obviously cannot do them all. Rate the importance of each by its priority as a means of reaching your goal.

_____ a. find a way to get rid of the "dead wood," meaning the less helpful assistant and three or four others

_____ b. participate in a series of panel discussions to be shown on the local public television station

_____ c. find ways to make sure your superiors are aware of your important accomplishments

_____ d. make an effort to better match the work to be done with the strengths and weaknesses of individual employees

_____ e. become involved in local public-service organizations

_____ f. as a means of being noticed, propose a solution to a problem outside the scope of your immediate department that you would be willing to take charge of

_____ g. when making decisions, give a great deal of weight to the way your superior likes things to be done

_____ h. accept a friend's invitation to join the exclusive country club to which many higher-level executives belong

_____ i. accept a position of responsibility in the upcoming United Fund drive

_____ j. ask for comments from superiors about important decisions you need to make

_____ k. transfer many employees to get some "new blood" in the department

_____ l. become involved in the local chamber of commerce and junior achievement organizations

_____m. adjust your work habits to increase your productivity

_____ n. write an article on productivity for the company newsletter

In the first study, fifty-four managers, fifty-one graduate students, and twenty-two Yale undergraduates participated. The managers were either from companies in the top twenty of the Fortune 500 list or from companies that were not listed in the Fortune 500 and that were not particularly large. The business graduate students were either from schools ranked highly in prestige or from schools not so ranked. The second study consisted of a cross-validation of the business questionnaire involving twenty-nine managers from offices of the local bank. The officers were roughly at the level of branch manager for the bank. The third study with business managers involved 149 subjects drawn from the same populations as in the preceding experiment, and the design was basically parallel to that of the second experiment with the psychologists. Thus, the new item classification system, scoring system, and ideal ratings were used to supplement the earlier studies. Although a number of findings emerged from these studies, the basic results can be summarized succinctly.

First, on the average, level of tacit knowledge increases with amount of experience in the field whether the field be academic psychology or business. In other words, scores generally increased with level of advancement. However, there is an important caveat to this finding. Scores did not always increase with level of advancement. Some individuals who had advanced quite far had relatively low tacit knowledge scores, whereas other individuals who had not advanced as far had higher scores. Thus, we can infer that what matters is not how much experience one has had but how much one has learned from this experience. In terms of the process model proposed earlier, what matters is the success with which one applies selective encoding, combination, and comparison in order to form production systems for procedural knowledge when on the job. Some people do not apply these processes successfully to their job, regardless of how well they may apply them in other kinds of settings.

Second, scores on the tacit knowledge inventories were unrelated to IQ. The correlations were generally near zero and nonsignificant. This result demonstrates that the measures of tacit knowledge are not merely a fancy form of IQ test. Rather, they measure skills that are distinct from IQ, at least within the range of ability that we are dealing with here. The range is of course restricted, especially in view of the fact that we were able to give a verbal IQ test only to the undergraduates. Nevertheless, studies with comparable undergraduates have yielded high correlations with cognitive measures, reaching into the .70s and beyond (Sternberg, 1985). Thus, the low correlations were not due solely to restriction of range.

Third, tacit knowledge correlates about twice as highly with selected criterion measures for success as does IQ. For example, in the Wagner and Sternberg (1986) studies, the correlations of total score with productivity and number of conferences attended by the professors were in the mid-.30s, and the correlation with level of school was at the .40 level. For the graduate students, correlation with level of school was at the .50 level. For the business managers in the first study with managers, the correlation with level of company was .34, and the correlation with salary was .46. In the replication study with the bank managers, the correlation with merit salary increases was .48. Not all the correlations were this high, but correlations in the .30 to .50 range were typical. Fourth, Wagner (1986) found in his dissertation studies that scores on the various subscales correlate fairly highly with each other (almost all are significant) and that they correlate equally well with the criterion measures. Thus, it appears that there is a sort of G or general factor for the various kinds of tacit knowledge, but that this G is not the same as that found on conventional IQ tests (because tacit-knowledge measures do not correlate with IQ). Exactly what this G is remains to be determined.

Fifth, one might argue that the measures of tacit knowledge assess a kind of "sell-out" ability — that the reason that they correlate with the external criterion is that both assess the extent to which a person has sold out. Contradicting this interpretation of the data is the fact that when scores from the "ideal-ratings" condition were correlated with the criteria, the correlations actually went up slightly from those in the "actual-ratings" condition. It therefore appears that we are not just measuring sell-out potential.

The study thus concludes that the measures of tacit knowledge do appear to measure acquisition of practical knowledge as it pertains to real-world job success.

Experiments with College Students

In a separate series of studies, now underway in collaboration with Wendy Williams, we asked fifty-three Yale College students to write a response to the question: "What does it take to succeed at Yale that you don't learn from textbooks?" We analyzed the responses by content, sorted them into categories, and used the results of our analysis as the basis for formulating an inventory of tacit knowledge for college students.

The student group comprised eighteen men and thirty-five women with a mean age of 19.8 years. Our intention was to skew our sample toward freshmen (new students) and seniors (old students), and, in fact, our sample comprised eighteen freshmen, three sophomores, nine juniors, and twenty-three seniors.

The inventory contained fourteen items, each of which had a set of response options associated with it. Each response option was to be rated on a scale of 1 to 9. The labels associated with the response items differed from one item to another. Some sample items and a subset of their response items follow.

1. You are enrolled in a large introductory lecture course. Requirements consist of three term-time exams and a final. Please indicate how characteristic it is of *your behavior* to spend time doing the following if your goal is getting an A in the course. [1 = not at all characteristic, to 9 = extremely characteristic]

_____a. attending class regularly

_____b. attending optional weekly review sections with the teaching fellow

_____c. reading assigned text chapters thoroughly

_____d. taking comprehensive class notes

_____e. speaking with the professor after class and during office hours

4. Please indicate how much *you* believe *professors* value the following aspects of a paper when they grade it. Choose a number from the scale below. [1 = no value at all, to 9 = extreme value]

_____a. no typographical errors

_____b. no grammatical errors

_____c. clear, direct writing style

_____d. good organization of thoughts and ideas

_____e. creative or unusual ideas

_____f. brings in outside interests or material

_____g. accurately and thoroughly referenced

5. Please indicated how important *you* believe the *average professor* considers the following attributes in a student to be, using the scale below. [1 = not at all important, to 9 = extremely important]

_____a. making an effort to speak with the professor before or after class

_____b. meeting with the professor during office hours

_____c. completing work ahead of schedule — handing work in early

_____d. attending class regularly and arriving on time

_____e. writing especially creative and unusual papers

_____f. getting high grades on exams

_____g. getting high grades on papers

In addition to the tacit knowledge inventory, we also included in the experimental materials a biographical questionnaire. The questionnaire asked some background questions and also some specific questions dealing with objective and subjective aspects of performance. The objective aspects were high school average, grade point average in college, Scholastic Aptitude Test scores, and College Entrance Examination Board achievement test scores. The subjective questions dealt with how happy the student had been in college to date, how successful the student had felt in college to date, how successful the student felt himself or herself to be dealing with situations such as the ones presented in the questionnaire, the extent to which the student felt he or she would benefit from training in the areas of the questionnaire, and the closeness of the school attended to the ideal college. The objective measures were combined into an overall index of academic performance, and the subjective measures were combined into an overall index of adjustment to college.

We found that the academic performance and adjustment measures were statistically independent ($r = -.09$). We also found that although the academic performance measure was constant across the years of college (as would be expected), adjustment decreased over time: The correlation between academic year at Yale and the adjustment index was $-.43$. We also analyzed the particular items that were correlated with higher scores on the academic performance and adjustment indices.

Some items significantly correlated with overall scores on the academic performance index were: perceived importance to the student of maintaining a high grade point average, doing extra reading and school work not specifically assigned, not attending optional weekly review sections with the teaching fellow, not skimming the required reading during the morning before class, not preparing a brief outline of points to raise in class discussion, not helping friends with their assignments, not behaving consistently from situation to situation, finding it uncharacteristic to accept pressure and stress as parts of life, finding it uncharacteristic to stand up for oneself, and finding it uncharacteristic to play a sport or exercise regularly.

Some items significantly correlated with overall scores on the adjustment index were the belief that professors value a clear, direct writing style, good organization of thoughts and ideas, and creative or unusual ideas; the belief that professors value papers that bring in outside interests or material; the belief that it is important sometimes to take on too many responsibilities at once; seeking advice from several faculty in addition to one's own professors; taking classes that permit occasional absences; being positive and looking on the bright side of life; not being intimidated; being flexible; maintaining a strong sense of confidence and independence; not worrying unnecessarily or destructively; knowing how to make oneself happy; and not letting small disappointments affect long-term goals.

We also found some sex differences in our research. For example, men are more likely than women to believe that professors value funny and entertaining papers, to downplay the seriousness of their actions when caught committing an academic dishonesty, and to worry less. Women are more likely than men to take comprehensive class notes, to believe that professors value papers that express special interest and enthusiasm for the material, to try to figure out what will make them happy, to think about what they are able to do best, to try to discover and understand their limitations, and to cultivate a sense of responsibility and commitment.

Finally, there were some significant differences between freshmen and seniors in their responses. Freshmen are more likely to believe that professors value papers that have no typographical or grammatical errors, creative and unusual ideas, mention of outside interests, accurate and thorough references, and a demonstration of effort and motivation. Freshmen make more of an effort to speak with professors before and after class, derive more reward from getting to know their professors and teaching fellows and from making progress as the term goes on. Freshmen are more likely to choose courses with professors who are well known and well respected by students and peers and to place more emphasis on their friends' opinions of both courses and teachers. They are also more likely to choose teachers who reportedly give students a lot of personal attention, choose courses with flexible requirements, choose majors likely to lead to lucrative jobs, be positive and look on the bright side of life, not be intimidated, look for good in difficult situations, behave consistently from situation to situation, work at caring about and supporting others whom they value, laugh at themselves, accept stress and pressure, know their strengths and weaknesses, worry less, try to make other people happy, and not let small disappointments affect long-term goals. Freshmen also spend more time playing sports, having a good social life, keeping in touch with old friends, maintaining their personal appearance, helping friends or classmates with school work, and exercising regularly. In contrast, their ratings indicate that seniors are more likely than freshmen to believe that professors value students who get high grades on papers and exams, more likely to ask directly for forgiveness when caught committing an academic dishonesty, and more likely to participate in clubs or organizations.

We attempted to predict both the academic and adjustment indices using stepwise multiple regression of these indices on items from the tacit knowledge inventory. Using four variables, we accounted for 43 percent of the variance in the academic index. The items that entered into the final stepwise regression were: not preparing an outline of points to raise in class discussion, maintaining a high grade-point average, not helping friends with assignments, and not playing a varsity or intramural sport. Using six variables, we were able to account for 63 percent of the variance in the adjustment index. The six variables were: believing that professors value a clear and direct writing style, maintaining a strong sense of confidence and independence, standing up for oneself, sometimes taking on too many responsibilities at once, seeking advice from other faculty in addition to the instructor of the course, and taking classes that permit occasional absences.

The studies of tacit knowledge in college students are still in progress. For example, we are now examining the results from our questionnaire when administered to students at a college less selective in its admissions procedures than is Yale. But the results gathered to date indicate that tacit knowledge is an important part of student life and that it is predictive both of academic perform- ance and of adjustment to college life. In other words, practical knowledge matters in academic life. Hard academic indices of performance and subjectively perceived adjustment are uncorrelated with each other, but both are moderately predictable from selected responses to our inventory of tacit knowledge.

Personal adjustment seems to decline from the freshman to senior years, although this decline may be due in part to the anxieties associated with acceptance to a graduate or professional program or to uncertainties about what life in the future holds in general. The freshmen have their lives for the next four years more or less cut out for them, whereas the seniors face tremendous uncertainties. Moreover, the seniors are probably somewhat jaded by their fourth year in college, and more aware of the limitations of their college or any other.

We also found sex differences in our results, differences that in many cases were stereotypical of sex-typed distinctions. Women seemed to be more in- wardly turned and reflective than men and more concerned with pleasing others. It is possible, of course, that the differences between the sexes that were obtained are in some sense adaptive: what works for women may actually differ somewhat from what works for men.

The results obtained to date are consistent with the notion that tacit knowledge is not something that becomes important only when one takes a job; it is important in the college years as well. The importance of tacit knowledge to students raises the question of whether it should be dealt with more explicitly than it is now. At present, college students are left pretty much on their own to acquire the tacit knowledge required to succeed—and adjust—in college. Our experience is that students differ substantially in the extent to which they acquire tacit knowledge, and as well in the extent to which they are able to use the tacit knowledge they acquire. Some students probably fail to make it in college not because of a lack of academic ability, but because they are unable to incorporate the tacit knowledge they need to succeed in the college environ- ment. Students coming from secondary school backgrounds that do not prepare them well for college life would seem to be especially at risk: unless they acquire the needed tacit knowledge rather quickly, they may fall progressively further behind the other students.

At Yale, experience has shown that students who come from private preparatory schools tend to attain better grades in their initial year or two, and then to lose their advantage by the second or third year. This pattern of achievement suggests that the private school students are indeed better prepared, at least for the Yale environment, than are the public school students but that, on the average, the public school students catch up before too long. The system might be made fairer to everyone if all students were given more of an orientation to college life right at the beginning so that they would be more nearly equated in tacit knowledge as they start their college careers.

Experiments with Grade-school Students

In her dissertation, Cynthia Berg has investigated practical knowledge and problem-solving skills in grade school children. The subjects in Berg's dissertation experiment were 217 fifth-, eighth-, and eleventh-grade students from six public schools in southeastern Connecticut. Mean ages were 11.5, 14, and 17.5.

Children received three main kinds of materials.

1. *Self-assessments questionnaire.* This questionnaire required subjects to rate themselves on practical-intellectual skills such as getting along with teachers, decision making, flexibility in problem solving, and organization. Ratings were on a scale of 1 (much worse than most people of my age) to 7 (much better than most people of my age). A total of twenty-four different skills were rated.

2. *Problem-solving questionnaire.* This questionnaire consisted of twenty practical problems. Half of the students received a questionnaire that presented the twenty problems in a school context; the other half of the students received a questionnaire presenting twenty problems that occurred outside of a school environment.

Problems in both questionnaires were followed by six answer choices which students were asked to rate on a scale from 1 (very bad) to 7 (very good) in terms of each option's suitability for use. The six options were preclassified so as to fall into six general categories.

1. Plan to solve the problem at some later point in time.

2. Seek more information about the problem before actually solving the problem.

3. Change one's perception of the problem.

4. Change one's behavior to be more compatible with the demand present in the problem.

5. Change aspects in the environment so that they are more compatible with one's own needs and goals.

6. Select out of the present situation in which the problem occurred.

Consider an example of each of the two kinds of problems, school and everyday.

Example 1. Your teacher believes in working on projects in groups. You have been put in charge of a group that is to work on a project about different types of fossils. Fossils are things that you know nothing about, and you think the topic is boring. Your friends tell you that your teacher thinks that fossils are very interesting. Rate how good each answer is in *helping you deal with working on this project.*

a. Plan how other members of the group who know more about your topic can help you in running this group.

b. Go to the library and check out books on fossils.

c. Decide that this group project is something you just have to do.

d. Decide for each member of the group what task they will do on the project (such as make posters, write the report, look up books, and so on).

e. Persuade the group to see the project as a game.

f. Talk to the teacher to see if you can be switched to a group that is working on a more interesting topic.

Example 2. Your parents have become more strict about what time you must be home at night. On Friday and Saturday nights you have to be home by 10:30. You and your friends wish to go out to a movie on Friday night that will not be over until 11:00, and thus you won't be home until 11:30. You find out from the movie theater that the movie will be showing at your local movie theater for another week. Rate how good each of the answers is in *allowing you to see the movie and be home by 10:30.*

a. Ask your friends if they have a strict time that they must be home at night.

b. Decide that seeing the movie is really not worth causing problems with your parents.

c. Wait to see the movie on Saturday afternoon.

d. Persuade your parents that the new rule is unfair.

e. Spend Friday night at the house of a friend that does not have to be home so early.

f. Plan how you could both see the movie and be home by 10:30.

An additional feature of the experiment was that subjects were later asked to re-rate their answers, given either an added constraint or a relaxed constraint. For example, in the first (school) problem above, the relaxed constraint was that the teacher really thinks that fossils are not interesting. In the second (everyday) problem, the added constraint was that Friday night is the last time the movie will be showing at the local theater. Thus, subjects were asked to re-rate options in accordance with the new set of constraints in addition to having rated the problems in their original form.

3. *Experiential questionnaire.* Subjects were asked to rate on a scale 1 (never) to 7 (all of the time) how often they had experienced each of the twenty specific problems presented in their problem-solving questionnaire.

Teachers were also asked to rate the problems on the everyday intellectual skills that the students rated themselves on. In this way, it was possible to compare teacher versus student ratings.

In sum, the main independent variables in the experiment were (a) the two ways in which the constraints present in the problem were manipulated (additional constraint problems versus relaxed constraint problems), (b) the six categories of response modes or problem-solving strategies (plan to take action, seek more information, change perception of the problem, adapt to the problem, shape the environment, select another environment), (c) time of ratings (before receiving the additional information versus after receiving the additional information), (d) grade level (fifth, eighth, or eleventh), (e) gender, (f) domain of problems (school versus nonschool), and (g) form of the questionnaire (a versus b). The first three independent variables were within subjects, the last three were between subjects. The major dependent variable of interest was the rating each subject assigned to each of the problem-solving options posed for the various problems.

The main result of interest was the rank-ordering of the various answer options for the problem-solving questionnaire. The two most preferred options were changing one's behavior to be more compatible with the demand present in the problem (adaptation) and seek more information about the problem before actually solving the problem (seek). The next most preferred option was plan to solve the problem at some later point in time (plan). Next on the list was change aspects of the environment so that they are more compatible with one's own needs and goals (shape). Then came change one's perception of the problem (change). Finally came select out of the present situation in which the problem occurred (select). This rank-ordering of response modes was constant across grades and sex and questionnaire type, suggesting that it is quite robust with respect to situational changes. Thus, the school children tend to prefer solutions that require adaptation to an existing environment or delaying solutions until a later time. They least prefer solutions involving selection of a new environment, but this reduced preference may reflect the reality of their situation: children are least in a position to select new environments as a response to their problems.

It was also found that ratings on the school problem-solving questionnaire were significantly higher than those on the everyday problem-solving questionnaire, indicating that the school problems were seen as more easily soluble through the options given than were the everyday problems.

In addition, it was found that the older the student, the more their ratings of the effectiveness of options corresponded to ratings of effectiveness by teachers. Moreover, ratings of girls were more consistent with ratings of the teachers than were ratings of boys. It was also found that the younger the students, the more their ratings were affected by adding and relaxing constraints.

Various kinds of correlations were also computed in order further to elucidate the data. It was found that correlations between problem-solving scores (computed using the teacher's patterns of responses as a prototype) and achievement test scores decreased with grade level. In other words, academic and everyday measures of competence for the eighth and eleventh graders showed only a very weak relationship. There was less differentiation between the two kinds of measures at the fifth-grade level.

Berg's dissertation demonstrates that it is possible to construct a practical problem-solving questionnaire for use with school-aged children and that such a questionnaire has properties that resemble those for questionnaires used for older children. In particular, there is a modest to moderate correlation between practical problem-solving skills and school achievement, but it is clear that the practical skills are tapping an aspect of behavior that is not merely a proxy for achievement. Rather, these skills need to be measured in their own independent way.

CONCLUSIONS

Research on practical knowledge has been underrepresented in the literature of cognitive psychology compared to research on more formal and academic kinds of knowledge. But much of the problem solving people do in their lives is informal and outside of school situations. We therefore need to understand the uses of practical knowledge in their own right, not just as extensions of the uses of academic knowledge. Our research program on practical knowledge is a first step toward correcting the imbalance in research on academic versus practical knowledge.

We believe there are a number of plausible directions for future research on practical knowledge, but we view four of them as paramount. The first two are basic, the latter two applied. The first direction is toward a better understanding of the processes involved in the *acquisition* of practical knowledge. For example, how does a person decide just what features of the environment are relevant to his or her purpose? The second direction is toward a better understanding of how people *utilize* and ultimately *transfer* practical knowledge. In a new job, for example, how does one decide which strategies to carry over from one's last job and which strategies not to carry over? Acquisition, utilization, and transfer would seem to be three of the most interesting loci of individual differences in practical knowledge that we could study. The third direction is toward better *testing.* We have made a start, as have others, but we need to sustain and augment our efforts to measure practical knowledge as separate from academic knowledge. Finally, the fourth direction is toward *teaching* practical knowledge. After all, what more practical use is there of our information about practical knowledge than teaching it?

ACKNOWLEDGMENT

Preparation of this chapter was supported by Contract MDA90385K0305 from the Army Research Institute.

REFERENCES

Berg, C. A. (1986). Everyday problem solving during the school-aged years. Unpublished doctoral dissertation.

Davidson, J. E., and Sternberg, R. J. (1984). The role of insight in intellectual giftedness. *Gifted Child Quarterly,* 28: 58–64.

Ghiselli, E. (1966). *The validity of occupational aptitude tests.* New York: Wiley.

Roose, K. D., and Andersen, C. J. (1970). *A rating of graduate programs.* Washington, D.C.: American Council on Education.

Schank, R., and Abelson, R. (1977). *Scripts, plans, goals, and understanding.* Hillsdale, N.J.: Erlbaum.

Sternberg, R. J. (1985). *Beyond IQ: A triarchic theory of human intelligence.* New York: Cambridge University Press.

Sternberg, R. J. (In press). Mental self-government: A theory of intellectual styles and their development. *Human Development.*

Sternberg, R. J., and Barnes, M. (1985). Real and ideal others in romantic relationships: Is four a crowd? *Journal of Personality and Social Psychology,* 49: 1589–1596.

Sternberg, R. J., and Caruso, D. (1985). Practical modes of knowing. In E. Eisner (Ed.), *Learning the ways of knowing.* Chicago: Chicago University Press.

Sternberg, R. J., and Davidson, J. E. (1982). The mind of the puzzler. *Psychology Today,* 16: June, 37–44.

8

Inference and Discovery in an Exploratory Laboratory

VALERIE J. SHUTE[1]

ROBERT GLASER

KALYANI RAGHAVAN *LDRC, University of Pittsburgh*

Formulating and testing hypotheses using observations and empirical findings is central not only to scientific work, but to the acquisition of knowledge in general. As individuals obtain new information they infer hypotheses which serve as a basis for confirming or refuting perceived regularities and lawful relationships. In the research described here we employ a computer laboratory, which we call an intelligent discovery world, to study the strategies students use to explore this environment. Our interest focuses on the study of individual differences in strategies of inference and discovery including comparative studies of successful and less successful learners. We are also investigating the impact of tutorial assistance on discovery skills.

Central to the process of induction and hypothesis formation is carrying out cognitive performances that ensure that inferences drawn are plausible and

[1] Currently at Air Force Human Resources Laboratory, Brooks Air Force Base, Texas.

relevant to the world or system being observed. One determines the plausibility of inductions and stated hypotheses by referring to knowledge obtained about the system. Thus the students' process of inference depends on the application of observation, experimentation, and data organization that enable the specification and testing of the knowledge obtained through experiments, hypotheses, and confirmations. As Holland et al. (1986) wrote, "The study of induction, then, is the study of how knowledge is modified through its use" (p. 5).

The kind of learning that we are considering has a long research history in experimental psychology, mostly in the context of laboratory and knowledge-lean tasks. In recent years, investigators have undertaken studies set in more complex situations, studies of machine learning, experimental studies, and computer simulation of problem solving and discovery tasks (Klahr and Dunbar, 1988; Kuhn and Phelps, 1982; Langley et al., 1987). Still, relatively few studies have investigated the domains taught in schools or other forms of formal education. Some exceptions are studies of microworlds in physics (Champagne and Klopfer, 1982; diSessa, 1982; White, 1984; White and Horowitz, 1987).

As we have indicated, the environment presents inductive problem-solving information, and the problem solver must attempt to find a general principle or structure that is consistent with this information. An important example is scientific induction. In medical and technical diagnosis a set of symptoms is presented from which one must induce the fault or cause. To paraphrase Greeno and Simon's (1984) description: Solving an induction problem can proceed in two ways, and in most tasks a combination of the methods is used. A top-down method involves generating hypotheses about the structure and evaluating them with information about the observed instances. A bottom-up method involves storing information about observations and events and making judgments about new events on the basis of similarity or analogy to the stored information. To perform the top-down method, the problem solver requires a procedure that generates or selects hypotheses, a procedure for evaluating hypotheses, and then a way of using the hypothesis generator to modify or replace hypotheses that are found to be incorrect. To use the bottom-up method, the problem solver needs a method of extrapolating from stored information, either by judging similarity of new stimuli to stimuli stored in memory or by forming analogical correspondences with stored information.

To a large extent, classic studies of induction have focused on inducing a rule or classifying relatively abstract stimuli into categories on the basis of feedback about classification errors and other information (see Pellegrino and Glaser, 1980; Smith and Medin, 1981). Given our concern for exploratory environments, we perceive this large literature as pertaining, for the most part, to *passive* induction in which the learners induce rules, make hypotheses, and classify and taxonomize observations on the basis of sets of predetermined instances designed by the experimenter. However, a more *active* process is apparent when the learner can select variables, design instances, and interrogate his or her existing knowledge and memory for recent events. In the latter form of induction, we need a research paradigm that allows us to examine active experimentation in which learners explore and generate new data and test hypotheses with the data they have accumulated in the course of their investigations. Recent experimental technology and computer modeling have made this type of experimentation feasible (Bonar, Cunningham, and Schultz, 1986; Michalski, 1986; Yazdani, 1986).

In our research program we have been investigating the learning of topics in elementary physics, basic electronics, and economics. In this chapter, we report on the results of an empirical study conducted using a computer program called *Smithtown,* for learning economics. The environments that we design enable us to investigate a range of inductive or discovery learning, from learning in purely discovery environments to more guided discovery worlds. What we are learning from our work is that as students explore phenomena they can be guided and coached in the interrogation of a subject matter, analyzing their own understandings and misunderstandings, assessing progress toward their goals, and revising their problem-solving and learning strategies.

Our exploratory systems are designed to record, structure, and play back to students their own problem-solving processes. Such systems have been developed in algebra and geometry in which they provide a structured "trace" of problem solutions so that students can see the alternative paths that they have tried (Anderson et al. 1984; Brown, 1983). Previous papers report early work on the design and implementation of some intelligent discovery world environments (Reimann, 1986; Shute and Glaser, in press), and this paper describes an initial study of individual differences in exploration, data collection, and hypothesis formation in an exploratory world of microeconomic laws.

Smithtown is a computer program that provides a discovery environment for learning elementary microeconomics. An ideal sequence of iterative behaviors in *Smithtown* would include: exploring the world (informally), developing a plan for investigation (more formally), choosing on-line tools or techniques for executing the plan, collecting and recording data from the experiment, organizing the results, seeing if the data confirm or negate prior beliefs, constructing a problem representation, modifying the problem based on discrepant results, refining the problem based on additional information, recognizing discrepancies between the result and expectations, testing out findings in additional realms, and, finally, generalizing a principle or law.

The focus of the study we are discussing is students' inductive inquiry skills, which in this context refers to the students' effectiveness in collecting, organizing, and understanding data, concepts, and relationships in a new domain. This system has been implemented on Xerox 1108/1186 LISP machines, allowing self-paced, individualized, and interactive instruction in a rich data source (see Shute and Glaser, in press, for an overview of the system).

We hypothesize that discovery learning can contribute to a rich understanding of domain information by enabling the student to access and organize information. Furthermore, a proposition to be evaluated in this work is that effective interrogative skills are teachable if the particular skills involved can be articulated and practiced under circumstances which require them to be used.

Intelligent tutorial guidance, in conjunction with a discovery world environment, has the potential to transform a student's problem-solving performance into efficient learning procedures rooted in an individual's own actions and hypotheses. In such experiential learning, students are introduced to new subject matter and are given the opportunity to compare their observations with their current beliefs and theories, which they may reject, accept, modify, or replace (see Glaser, 1984). As they develop this knowledge, students ask questions, make predictions, make inferences, and generate hypotheses about why certain events occur with systematic regularity. Significant experience of this kind in discovering principles in a field of knowledge should affect the relationship learners perceive between themselves and the knowledge and their way of behaving when they forget a solution procedure or encounter an unprecedented problem (Cronbach, 1966).

KNOWLEDGE BASES IN *SMITHTOWN*

The primary purpose of the system is to help students become more methodical and scientific in learning a new domain. The first knowledge base — or "expert" — that we will discuss is concerned with efficacious inquiry skills.

The First Knowledge Base: Inductive Inquiry Skills

An earlier study conducted with *Smithtown* yielded information about more and less effective behaviors for interrogating and inducing information from a new domain (reported in Shute and Glaser, in press). This information was subsequently coded into rules that the system monitors in conjunction with a learner's actual behaviors. Thus, the system knows of sequences of good behaviors and also sequences of ineffective — "buggy" — behaviors.

The system leaves a student alone if she or he is performing adequately in the environment. However, if the system determines that a student is floundering or demonstrating buggy behaviors, the computer "coach" will intervene and offer assistance on the specific problematic behavior(s). For instance, if a student persists in changing many variables at one time without first collecting baseline data into the on-line notebook, the rule that would be invoked would look like the following.

If The student changes more than two variables at a time prior to collecting baseline data for a given market, *and* it is early in the session where the experiment number is less than four,

Then Increment the 'Multiple Variable Changes' bug count by 1 and pass the list to the coach for possible assistance.

If this rule does get fired and the number of times it has been invoked has surpassed some threshold value (for instance, four times), then the coach would appear and say, "I see that you're changing several variables at the same time. A better strategy would be to enter a market, see what the data look like before any variables have been changed, then just change one variable while holding all the others constant."

In addition to the rules monitored by the system, we developed a list of performance measures, called *learning indicators,* that enable us to determine what type of actions or behaviors yield better performance in this type of environment. We created a range of learning indicators, from low-level, simple counts of actions (for example, total number of activities taken within *Smithtown*) to higher-level, complex behaviors (for example, number of times a manipulation to an independent variable was made that showed an obvious change in the dependent variables). These indicators will be discussed in a later section and serve as one data source for our study on individual differences in learning in *Smithtown*.

The Second Knowledge Base: Economic Concepts in *Smithtown*

The second knowledge base, or expert, in the system knows about the functional relationships among economic variables which comprise valid economic concepts and laws. The system has a defined instructional domain which is decomposed into key concepts that are organized in a bottom-up manner (that is, from simpler to more complex ideas). An understanding of these concepts should result from the student's experiments in the microworld. The hierarchy of domain knowledge was developed by first reviewing six introductory microeconomics textbooks and determining the presentation order of information, and then discussing the optimal ordering of these concepts for student learning in the classroom with a college instructor of economics.

Although a student is not required to learn the concepts in any prescribed order, the hierarchy shown in Figure 8-1 provides the system with information about where the student is likely to be with regard to his or her knowledge acquisition. For example, the student can more readily understand the concept of equilibrium having first learned the laws of supply and demand. For the reader unfamiliar with this domain, we will now describe the basic concepts in microeconomics that can be learned using *Smithtown*.

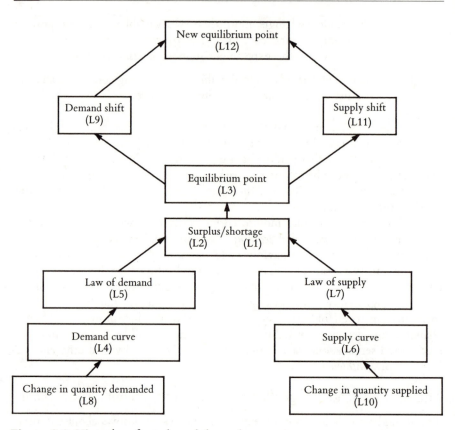

Figure 8-1 Hierarchy of supply and demand concepts.

Supply and Demand   The buyer's side of the market is called *demand*. The law of demand states that the quantity of a product which consumers would be willing and able to purchase during some period of time is inversely related to the price of the product. If the price of gasoline goes up, consumers will demand a smaller quantity of gasoline; if the price goes down, consumers will demand larger quantities. If we graph this relationship, we get what is called a *demand curve* (see Figure 8-2) showing how the quantity demanded of a product will change as the price of that product changes, holding all other factors constant.

The seller's side of the market is called *supply*. The law of supply is that the quantity of a product which producers would be willing and able to produce and sell is related to the price of the product by a positive function. If the price of color televisions goes up, producers will tend to offer more television sets for sale. If the price of color television sets goes down, producers will reduce the number of television sets they put on the market. If we graph this relationship,

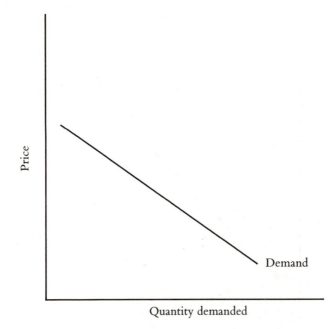

Figure 8-2 Graph of a typical demand curve.

we get what is called a *supply curve* (see Figure 8-3). A supply curve is a graph showing how the quantity supplied of some commodity will change as the price of that commodity changes, holding all other factors constant.

Equilibrium, Surplus, and Shortage There are many factors that influence the price of a given product, but when a price is reached at which the quantity that sellers want to sell is equal to the quantity that buyers want to buy, we say that the market is at a point of *equilibrium* (see Figure 8-4). Competitive markets always tend toward points of equilibrium. If the market price is higher than the equilibrium price, buyers will demand smaller quantities than sellers are supplying. This will create a *surplus*. Surpluses of unsold goods will convince sellers to lower their price down toward the equilibrium level. If, for some reason, the market price is lower than the equilibrium price, buyers will demand larger quantities than sellers are supplying, thus creating a *shortage*. Shortages will lead to price increases, and the price will rise toward the equilibrium level.

Changes in Supply and Demand A change in the price of a good will influence the quantities demanded and supplied and cause movement along a fixed curve. A change to variables other than price will cause the entire curve (demand or supply) to shift depending on which variable is changed and the

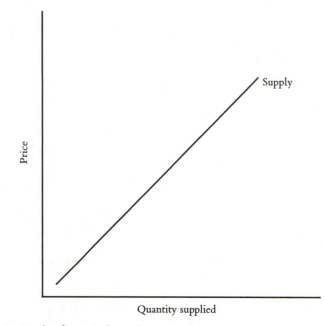

Figure 8-3 Graph of a typical supply curve.

magnitude of the adjustment. We refer to the variables in *Smithtown* that can be manipulated as *town factors;* they include per capita income, population, interest rates, weather, consumer preferences, labor costs, number of suppliers, and the price of substitute and complementary goods. For instance, if the population of *Smithtown* were increased from 10,000 to 25,000 persons, then the demand for automobiles would increase, resulting in a shift to the right of the demand curve for cars. Alternatively, if the number of suppliers of a particular good were to decrease, this would affect the supply curve for that commodity, resulting in a shift to the left. These shifts are depicted in Figures 8-5 and 8-6.

New Equilibrium Point   Competitive markets tend to converge toward equilibrium points. Equilibrium, once established, can be disturbed by changes in demand or supply or both. If demand or supply change, a surplus or shortage will result at the original price, and the price will move toward a new equilibrium. A shortage at the original price will cause the old price to rise to the new level and cause changes in the quantities supplied and demanded. A new equilibrium will be established at the second price and the second quantity, and may be seen in Figure 8-7.

In addition to these economic concepts there are at least two more that can be extracted from the discovery world, although they are not explicitly recog-

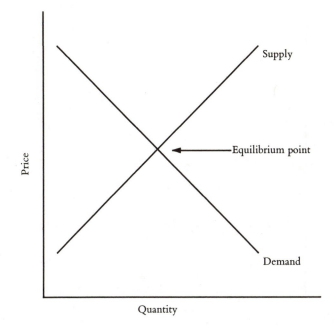

Figure 8-4 Graph of demand and supply curves intersecting to form an equilibrium point.

nized by the system: cross elasticity of demand and supply. Cross elasticity of demand indicates how a change in one market affects the demand in a related market, whereas cross elasticity of supply indicates how a change in one market affects the supply in a related market.

MANEUVERING THROUGH *SMITHTOWN*

Students can discover regularities in the market by manipulating variables, observing effects, and using tools to organize the information in an effective way. The on-line tools for scientific investigations in *Smithtown* include a notebook for collecting data, a table to organize data from the notebook, a graph utility to plot data, and a hypothesis menu to formulate relationships among variables. Three history windows allow the students to see a chronological listing of actions, data, and concepts learned.

First, a student selects a market to investigate from the "Goods Menu" and informs the system of his or her experimental intentions by choosing variables she or he is interested in from the "Planning Menu." For each new experiment, the system asks the student if he or she would like to make a prediction

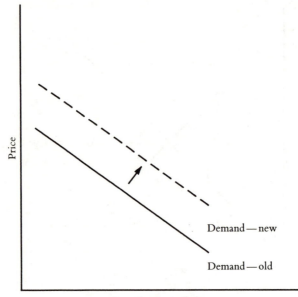

Figure 8-5 Graph of a demand curve shift (an increase).

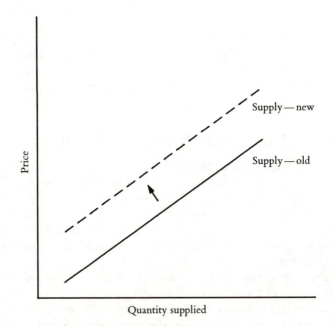

Figure 8-6 Graph of a supply curve shift (a decrease).

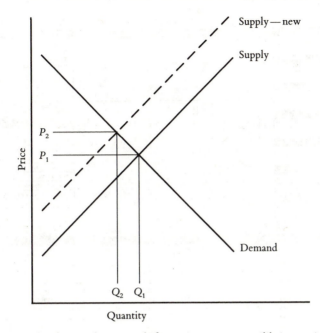

Figure 8-7 Graph of a supply curve shift causing a new equilibrium price.

regarding the planned experiment. If the student chooses "No," the next menu of options is the "Things To Do Menu." If the student responds "Yes," a window appears where specific statements can be entered about predicted outcomes to a planned manipulation. For example, if the student's experiment was to increase the price of gasoline in order to see the repercussions in the market place, one prediction might be, *"The quantity demanded [of gasoline] will decrease."* Explorations and experiments are directed from the "Things To Do Menu" which provides ten options. Seven of the ten options are listed here. There are also three *experimental frameworks*, which are options 8 through 10.

1. *See market sales information.* This window displays information on the current state of the market.

2. *Computer adjust price.* The computer will increase or decrease the price, whichever brings the current market closer to equilibrium.

3. *Self adjust price.* This option provides the student with an on-line calculator and allows the price of the particular good to be changed.

4. *Make a notebook entry.* The student selects variables to record, and the current values are automatically put into the notebook (see Figure 8-8).

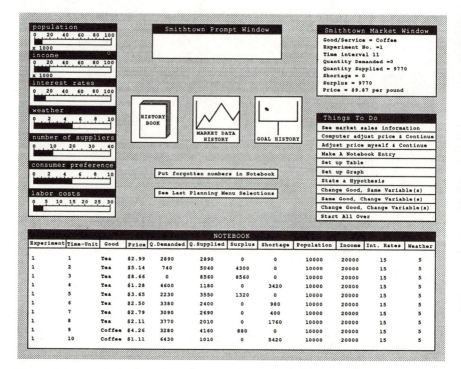

Figure 8-8 Screen display of *Smithtown* with notebook entries made.

5. *Set up table.* The table package allows the student to select variables of interest from the notebook, put them together in a table, and sort on any selected variable by ascending or descending order (see Figure 8-9).

6. *Set up graph.* The graph utility allows a student to plot data collected from his or her explorations and experiments. This provides an alternative way of viewing relations between variables (see Figure 8-10).

7. *Make a hypothesis.* The hypothesis menu allows students to make inductions or generalizations from relationships in the data they have collected and organized. There are actually four interconnected menus of words and phrases comprising the hypothesis menu (see Figure 8-11). First, the "Connector Menu" includes the items "if," "then," "as," "when," "and," and "the." Next, the "Object Menu" contains the economic indicator variables used by the system. The "Verb Menu" describes the types of change, like "decreases," "increases," "shifts as a result of," and so on. Finally, the "Direct Object Menu" allows for more precise specification of concepts such as "over time," "along the demand curve," "changes other than price." As students combine words or

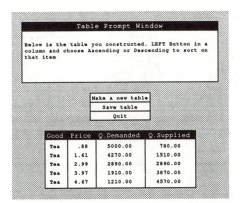

Figure 8-9 Screen display of the table package with four variables represented (ordered on price in ascending order).

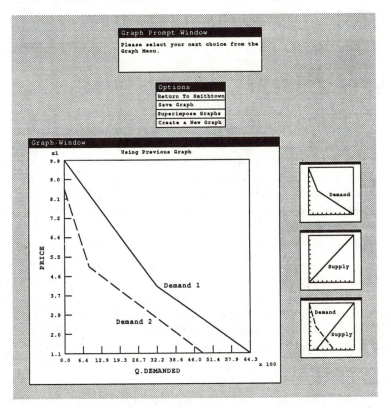

Figure 8-10 Screen display of the graph package with supply and demand curves superimposed.

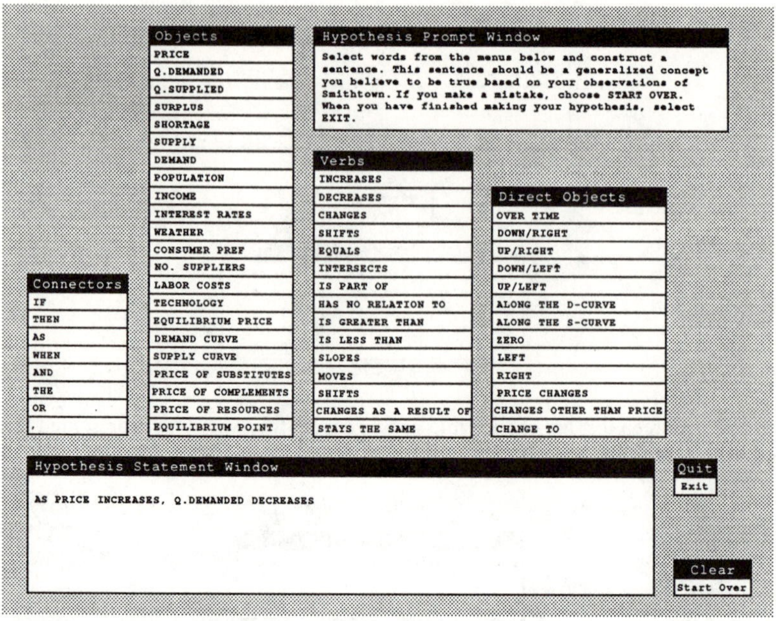

Objects		Hypothesis Prompt Window
PRICE		Select words from the menus below and construct a
Q.DEMANDED		sentence. This sentence should be a generalized concept
Q.SUPPLIED		you believe to be true based on your observations of
SURPLUS		Smithtown. If you make a mistake, choose START OVER.
SHORTAGE		When you have finished making your hypothesis, select
SUPPLY		EXIT.
DEMAND		Verbs
POPULATION		INCREASES
INCOME		DECREASES	Direct Objects
INTEREST RATES		CHANGES	OVER TIME
WEATHER		SHIFTS	DOWN/RIGHT
CONSUMER PREF		EQUALS	UP/RIGHT
NO. SUPPLIERS		INTERSECTS	DOWN/LEFT
Connectors	LABOR COSTS	IS PART OF	UP/LEFT
IF	TECHNOLOGY	HAS NO RELATION TO	ALONG THE D-CURVE
THEN	EQUILIBRIUM PRICE	IS GREATER THAN	ALONG THE S-CURVE
AS	DEMAND CURVE	IS LESS THAN	ZERO
WHEN	SUPPLY CURVE	SLOPES	LEFT
AND	PRICE OF SUBSTITUTES	MOVES	RIGHT
THE	PRICE OF COMPLEMENTS	SHIFTS	PRICE CHANGES
OR	PRICE OF RESOURCES	CHANGES AS A RESULT OF	CHANGES OTHER THAN PRICE
,	EQUILIBRIUM POINT	STAYS THE SAME	CHANGE TO

Hypothesis Statement Window

AS PRICE INCREASES, Q.DEMANDED DECREASES

Quit Exit

Clear Start Over

Figure 8-11 Screen display of the hypothesis menu with the law of demand stated.

phrases from these menus, the resultant statement appears in a window below. A pattern matcher analyzes key words from the input and checks whether this matches stored relationships for each targeted concept. For instance, if the student stated "As price increases, quantity demanded decreases," the system would match that to the law of demand which it understands to be the inverse relationship between price and quantity demanded.

Experimental Frameworks

The three experimental frameworks, options 8, 9, and 10, provide the student with easy maneuvering within and between experiments. These include: "Change good, same variable(s)"; "Same good, change variable(s)"; and "Change good, change variable(s)." They are used to change to a new market while holding the independent variables the same, change town factor(s) within the current market, or to change the town factor(s) and the market.

History Windows

Three history windows are included in the system which are accessible by both the students and the system. As students continue to interact with *Smithtown*, histories accumulate that delineate the various actions resulting from different explorations and experiments. This summary is maintained in the "Student History Window." The "Market History Window" keeps a record of all variables and associated values that the student has manipulated. Finally, there is the "Goal History Window." This provides a representation of what the student has successfully learned in terms of concepts targeted by the system.

LEARNING AND INDIVIDUAL DIFFERENCES

In this section we describe an exploratory study of learning and individual differences in performance in this intelligent discovery world environment. The system was able to categorize sequences of student actions as being more or less effective and intervened with a hint at times when the student was floundering.

This study was undertaken with two main goals in mind. One goal was to evaluate *Smithtown* to see if individuals interacting with it actually acquired any of the economic concepts embedded in the environment, such as the law of demand, equilibrium point, and so on. The second goal was to determine the performance characteristics of those individuals who were more successful in learning in this type of environment as compared to those less successful. Another implicit goal was to examine the computer architecture and interface features that facilitated or overly constrained an exploratory environment.

The kind of inference-discovery task that we are studying has been interpreted within a problem-solving framework by Klahr and Dunbar (1988) who conceived of the interplay between hypothesis formation and experimental design phases of the discovery process as a search between two problem spaces — a hypothesis space of rules and an experimental space of instances.

> This means that, first, we need to account for the identification of relevant attributes, for, unlike the conventional concept-formation studies, our situation does not present the subject with a highly constrained attribute space for hypotheses. Second, we need a more complex treatment of the instance generator, because in our context it consists of an experiment, its predicted outcome, and the observation of the actual outcome (p. 7).

Klahr and Dunbar placed their subjects in a discovery context by first teaching them how to use an electronic device — a computer-controlled robot tank called BigTrak — and then asked them to discover how a particular function works. They formulated a general model of scientific discovery as dual search that shows how search in the two problem spaces shapes hypothesis generation, experimental design, and the evaluation of hypotheses. Strategy differences among subjects were a consequence of the efficiency of search in the hypothesis space. Successful subjects were classified as theorists and those who abandoned hypothesis testing in order to search the experiment space were classified as experimenters.

We also take a problem-solving perspective in our investigation and are guided in our search for individual differences by certain general findings in problem-solving performance. For example, Sternberg (1981) makes a distinction between two forms of metacognitive performance: global planning and local planning. Global planning refers to a strategy that applies to a set of problems instead of focusing on the characteristics of a particular problem; global planning refers attention to the context or overall characteristics of the group of problems. Local planning refers to a strategy that is sufficient for solving a particular problem within a given set; local planning is less sensitive to general context and focuses more on the difficulty of carrying out the specific operations of a problem-solving task. Sternberg finds that better reasoners spend relatively more time in global planning of a strategy for problem solution and relatively less time in local planning. Such a distinction is also evident in studies of expert versus novice problem solving. In studies of writing, Hayes and Flower (1986) point out that experts attend more to global problems than do novices. Experts and novices attend to different aspects of a text. Novices focus on the conventions and rules of writing; experts make more changes that affect the text's meaning. The perceptions of the novices are more local or shallow whereas those of the expert are more global and have more overall meaning. The strategies used by novices are local strategies concerned with the deletion and addition of words and phrases whereas experienced writers are concerned more with strategies that involve changes in content and structure. In physics (Larkin et al., 1980; Simon and Simon, 1978), differences in problem solving between novices and experts also relate to surface and deep problem representations. The novice's representation of a problem results in a local form of problem solving in which they work with equations to solve the unknown. Experts, in contrast, work in a more top-down manner indicating that a general solution plan is in place before they begin the manipulation of specific equations.

The findings just outlined direct our attention to conceivable differences between good and poor inductive problem solvers in terms of the global and local aspects of their performance or their attention to specific versus more general features of the problem-solving task. In a discovery situation, taking a lead from Klahr and Dunbar, we translate this distinction to data-driven performance in contrast to behavior which is more rule or hypothesis driven. In our task, an individual starts out with attention to computer-generated observations or to subject-designed experiments. On the basis of these data, he or she induces generalizations or hypotheses which drive further data collection, data organization, and experimentation. Based on the studies on problem solving we have described, we can anticipate that good reasoners might display rule-driven performance earlier in their discovery activity and use rules as a performance goal rather than more sustained attention to data collection, although the latter is necessary at certain points in the course of discovery.

Furthermore, in addition to behaviors at a general level, we must also look at more direct performance components. We refer to specific performance heuristics manifested by good reasoners that may not be available to others. A good example in discovery performance is the heuristic of identifying one variable as a dimension of examination and holding all other variables constant while the chosen one is varied systematically. Lawler (1982), in discussing computer-based microworlds that use LOGO language, refers to this as variable stepping. He points out that Piaget judged variable stepping to be an essential component of formal operational thought—a powerful idea because it is universally useful and crucial to the process of scientific investigation. In this regard we look for individual differences in our discovery worlds that relate to such performance procedures.

As a general caveat in the work reported here, we must point out that scientific discovery involves a whole array of processes including observing and gathering data, finding regularities that describe the data, formulating and testing the generalizability and limitations of these regularities, and formulating and testing explanatory theories. In this study we are primarily concerned with a subset of these processes, principally with discovery that starts with a data set that can be investigated and that derives descriptive rules, laws, or regularities from them. As has been pointed out (Bradshaw, Langley, and Simon, 1983), "the generation of data, and even the invention of instruments to produce new kinds of data, are also important aspects of scientific discovery. And in many cases, existing theory, as well as data, steer the course of discovery" (p. 971). We consider in this chapter the path from data to descriptive laws about data (not necessarily explanatory theories). This subset of scientific work is important in discovery and in our concern with individual differences in induction from data and the process by which inductive discovery is carried out. Also to be kept in mind is the fact that data-driven induction is not completely "pure." Individuals come with previous conceptions of regularities in the data, and they manipulate data and experiment on the basis of hypotheses they generate. So the discovery process that we study here will involve some combination of data-driven induction and hypotheses-generated data which guide performance.

Subjects

Three groups of subjects were involved in the experiment: (1) students who received traditional classroom instruction in introductory economics, (2) a control group which received no economics instruction, and (3) students interacting with *Smithtown*. There were ten subjects in each group. All subjects were from the University of Pittsburgh, and none had any formal economics training or previous economics courses. The *economics group* were students who volunteered to participate in an experiment and who were enrolled in an introductory microeconomics course. About half of the *control group* consisted of psychology students who took the tests for class credit; the other half consisted of students selected from those who responded to ads placed around the campus for subjects who had no economics background. They took the tests and received payment for their time. The *experimental group* were individuals who similarly responded to ads placed around the University of Pittsburgh campus. They were paid for their participation. It should be noted that the chapters covered by the economics class during the testing interval corresponded to the identical material covered by *Smithtown* (that is, the same introductory economic principles involving the laws of supply and demand in a competitive market). All subjects were debriefed about the purpose of the experiment at its conclusion.

Test Materials

The test battery on microeconomics was developed by an economics instructor at the University of Pittsburgh. The tests were initially piloted by individuals who provided feedback about the tests as to the clarity of instructions, the timing of the tests, and the general level of difficulty. The battery consisted of two tests, multiple choice and short answer. After test development, the batteries were reviewed by an independent economics instructor for content validity —that is, completeness and accuracy.

Multiple-Choice Test Two alternate forms were created for the pretest and posttest. This involved knowledge of various concepts and principles of microeconomics. Subjects were to circle the best answer from the four alternatives given. An example of a pretest item from the test is:

> The supply curve of houses would probably shift to the left (decrease) if:
>
> a) construction workers' wages increased
> b) cheaper methods of prefabrication were developed
> c) the demand for houses showed a marked increase
> d) the population increased

A corresponding posttest item was constructed for each of the pretest items. The counterpart to the above question is:

> Which of the following is likely to move a supply curve for beef to the right (an increase)?
>
> a) a rise in the price of beef

b) a decrease in the price of cattle feed

c) an increase in the wages of farm laborers

d) a decrease in the price of raw hides

Short-answer Test   This test involved the same concepts to be defined by the subject for both the pretests and the posttests. Elaborated knowledge was required to define different concepts, come up with instances of a given concept, or draw a curve on a labeled but empty grid. Two examples from the short answer test include:

1.   What is market equilibrium?

2.   List as many important factors as you can causing the demand curve for a good or service to shift over to the left or right.

Each answer on the short answer test was scored with reference to a list of necessary and sufficient elements.

Procedures

Subjects from the economics group were administered a pretest battery in their class prior to the lectures and readings on the laws of supply and demand. They received about two and one-half weeks of instruction on this part of the curriculum after which they were retested in the classroom with the posttest battery.

The control group completed the pretest battery and then returned in about two weeks for the posttests. This interval corresponded to the pretest and posttest intervals for the other two groups.

The experimental group took the pretest battery individually then signed up for three additional 2-hour sessions. This translated to a total of 5 hours on the computer (session 1 = pretest battery plus demonstration of the system; session 2 = 2 hours on the computer; session 3 = 2 hours on the computer; and session 4 = 1 hour on the computer and 1 hour for the posttest battery). The sessions were spread out over a two-week period to correspond to the same time frame as the economics group and the control group. Prior to the first real learning session with the system, students were given a *Guide to Smithtown* in session 1. This guide informed them of their goal — to discover principles and laws of economics — and told them that the best way to achieve that goal is to imagine themselves as scientists, gathering data and forming and testing hypotheses about emerging economic principles and laws. The guide overviewed some of the on-line tools available in *Smithtown* with examples provided on how to use them. Finally, the guide emphasized that the individual would probably make errors or get stuck, but should try to learn from the mistakes. A glossary of terms concluded the guide, and the students were free to take it home with them between sessions.

RESULTS

The first question addressed whether the three groups were *initially comparable* on their scores on the pretest battery of multiple-choice and short-answer problems. Table 8-1 shows the summary statistics for the raw data; the mean percentage scores for the pretest battery and for the posttest battery, collapsed across multiple choice and short answer, are plotted in Figure 8-12.

As shown in Table 8-1 and Figure 8-12, the three groups *are* initially comparable whereas on the posttest both the economics group and the experimental group surpass the control group. First we computed an ANOVA, a repeated measures design where the grouping factor was *treatment group* and the trial factors were *test type* and *pretest* versus *posttest* condition. The most important interaction that we were interested in was pretests and posttests by treatment group, collapsed across tests, $F_{2,27} = 2.99$, $p = .067$. This shows that the three groups did differ in terms of their pretest to posttest changes in scores. We then computed a Hotelling T^2 test, contrasting all three pairwise combinations of groups on the pretest battery, yielding the following nonsignificant T^2 values:

Economics by control group $T^2 = .03$, $p = .77$
Control by experimental group $T^2 = .11$, $p = .42$
Economics by experimental group $T^3 = .03$, $p = .80$

Table 8-1 Summary Statistics: Means and Standard Deviations

	Control group		Economics group		Experimental group	
	MC	SA	MC	SA	MC	SA
Pretest						
M=	11.50	16.20	11.70	15.00	12.00	14.10
SD=	2.88	5.77	2.31	3.83	2.87	3.93
Posttest						
M=	13.70	17.90	16.00	25.70	15.20	25.30
SD=	3.65	5.17	2.36	2.54	2.90	1.89

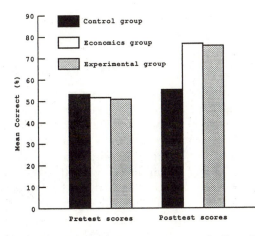

Figure 8-12 Pretest and posttest scores by treatment group (collapsed multiple choice and short answer test data).

After their respective interventions the groups differed; however the economics group and the experimental group ended up with equivalent posttest scores. It is important to note that students in the experimental group spent only five hours interacting with the discovery world compared to 2.5 weeks (or about 11 hours) of classroom lectures and recitation covering identical curricular information.

Hotelling's T^2 analysis allows us to see particular differences between independent groups on their test scores. The mean vectors for each group can be extracted from the summary statistics. First, we compare the posttest scores of economics students and the control group: $T^2 = 1.02$, $p = .003$. As expected, these two groups differed overall in their test scores. Individual t-tests on the data showed that the difference is primarily associated with the responses on the short answer posttest. The economics students had much more complete and articulate responses than the control group ($t = 4.28$, $p = .0005$). Second, the results from this analysis revealed that the economics group and the experimental group performed the same not only on their pretest scores but on their posttest scores as well: $T^2 = .031$, $p = .774$. The experimental group, with significantly less time on task, performed comparably with the students in the traditional classroom environment. No differences were found between any of the individual tests. Third, we compared the control and the experimental groups. We expected that there would be a difference between these two groups in their test composites given the experimental group's interaction with the system. This comparison also showed a significant difference between the posttests: $T^2 = 1.24$, $p = .001$. Individual t-tests were generated for each of the tests, and the short-answer posttest, again, was the major reason for the differences ($t = 4.25$, $p = .0005$). The experimental group had much more complete responses than the control group.

Individual Differences in the Experimental Group

The results from the between-group analyses suggest that, overall, *Smithtown was* effective in teaching a targeted set of microeconomic concepts comparable to a traditional classroom environment. We now further examined the experimental group data to see how differential interaction with this exploratory world affected subsequent learning. In other words, some individuals learned more than others from the system, and we wanted to know what it was that the more successful individuals did compared to the less successful persons in extracting and understanding new knowledge. "Successful," in this context, refers to someone who started out with a low pretest score on the battery of economics tests and, after interacting with the system, ended up with a high posttest score. Thus the two interesting comparisons are between those scoring (1) low on the pretest and low on the posttest, and (2) low on the pretest but high on the posttest. We were not interested in those who scored high on both the pretest and the posttests as they seemed to have started out with some domain-related knowledge. Table 8-2 lists each of the ten experimental subjects with their associated pretest and posttest scores (percent correct).

We are interested in comparing individuals who scored above the mean gain score with those below it. Thus there is a pool of five subjects having large

Table 8-2 Subjects' Scores on the Economic Tests (percent correct)

Subject	Pretest	Posttest	Gain
BW	53.7	89.9	36.2
JS	54.2	75.4	21.2
SS	53.3	75.4	22.1
ML	54.2	84.4	30.2
HT	43.1	56.8	13.7
CR	77.8	84.4	6.6
JH	42.7	73.9	31.2
CF	40.2	83.4	43.2
OY	51.7	69.4	17.7
CS	42.7	70.4	27.7
Mean	51	76	25
Standard deviation	12	10	11

gains and five subjects with small gains. These subjects will be discussed after the presentation of the learning indicators.

Table 8-3 lists the performance measures or learning indicators that were computed for each individual across sessions. For this exploratory study we collapsed data from the sessions into a single index for each indicator; we will look at changes over time later on. Two data sources were used in computing these values: (1) detailed computer history lists of all student actions, and (2) verbal protocols from each student about justifications for each action, what they expected to see after a particular action, and what their plans were for further experimentation.

Comparison of Subjects

Subjects BW, CF, HT, and OY all began the experiment at about the same level of knowledge as measured by pretest scores, but after the sessions with *Smithtown*, subjects BW and CF (more successful) greatly surpassed subjects HT and OY (less successful) on the posttest battery. In terms of gain scores (that is, posttest score minus pretest score), BW and CF scored over one standard deviation above the average gain score whereas HT and OY scored about one standard deviation below it.

	Pretest	Posttest
BW and CF	47.0	86.7
HT and OY	47.4	63.1

The question reduces to: What did BW and CF do, in terms of the indicators, that HT and OY did not do? Table 8-4 summarizes the standardized scores for these two pairs of subjects. The largest differences (ordered) between these two groups are for the following ten indicators: 22, 6, 24, 29, 9, 20, 16, 23, 28, and 13. The difference scores for all of these indicators exceeds .90 standardized units.

The first observation is that the majority of these indicators are from the most cognitively complex set of behaviors delineated, in other words, those in the thinking and planning category with six of the difference scores greater than .90. Next, there are three main differences between the two groups in the data management category. Finally, only one significant difference score is from the activity/exploration category. The progression of behaviors across these three categories goes from simply being active in the environment (activity/exploration) to being efficient (data management) to, finally, being effective (thinking and planning).

Table 8-3 Learning Indicators

Activity level
1. Total number of actions.
2. Total number of experiments.
3. Number of changes to the price of the good.

Exploratory behaviors
4. Number of markets investigated.
5. Number of independent variables changed.
6. Number of computer-adjusted prices.
7. Number of times market sales information was viewed.
8. Number of baseline data observations of market in equilibrium.

Data recording
9. Total number of notebook entries.
10. Number of baseline data entries of market in equilibrium.
11. Entry of changed independent variables.
12. Number of reinsertions of changed independent variables.

Efficient tool usage
13. Number of relevant notebook entries divided by total number of notebook entries where relevant refers to those variables specified in the planning menu.
14. Number of times the table package was used correctly divided by the total number of times the table was used, where "correctly" means fewer than six variables tabulated, and sorting was done on variables with differing values.
15. Number of times the graph package was used correctly divided by the total number of times the graph was used, where "correctly" means plotting relevant variables, saving graphs, and superimposing graphs with a shared axis.

Use of evidence
16. Number of specific predictions made divided by the number of general hypotheses made.
17. Number of correct hypotheses divided by the total number of hypotheses made.

Consistent behaviors
18. Number of notebook entries of planning menu items.
19. Number of times notebook entries of planning menu items were made divided by the number of planning opportunities the subject had.
20. Number of times variables were changed that had been specified beforehand in the planning menu.

Effective generalization
21. Number of times an experiment was replicated.
22. Number of times a concept was generalized across unrelated goods.
23. Number of times a concept was generalized across related goods.

Table 8-3 Learning Indicators (*continued*)

24. Number of times the student had sufficient data for a generalization (that is, at least three data points in the notebook before using the hypothesis menu).

Effective experimental behaviors

25. Number of times a change to an independent variable was sufficiently large enough (greater than 10 percent of the possible range).

26. Number of times one of the experimental frames was selected (that is, chose "same good, change variable," "change good, same variable," or "change good, change variable").

27. Number of times the prediction menu was used to specify a particular outcome to an event.

28. Number of variables changed per experiment. (In the initial sessions, a low number indicates effectiveness, whereas in the later sessions a higher number indicates effectiveness since the domain knowledge increases and the student can deal with interrelationships among variables.)

29. Average number of actions per experiment. This should be an increasing function over sessions.

30. Number of economic concepts learned per session.

We will now discuss each of these ten indicators in their relation to individual differences in performing in this type of environment. We will illustrate the between-subjects' differences in each of the three relevant categories with excerpts from their verbal protocols and student procedure graphs developed to depict student solution paths.

Thinking and Planning Discriminating Indicators

This category represents the more complex learning indicators relating to experimental behaviors. First, the data show that the subcategory of effective generalizations was a very good discriminator between these subjects. Overall, BW and CF attempted to generalize findings across markets (indicators 22 and 23) to see if developing beliefs extended beyond the current market. This included both generalizing to related markets (for example, investigating the effects of a manipulation on substitute or complementary goods) or testing beliefs in unrelated markets to see the limits and extent of a particular concept. To illustrate, BW (more successful) was careful to try out his developing ideas in different markets to test his hypotheses. In the first session he was investigating the tea market, testing the idea that increasing the population caused an increase in the quantity demanded (it actually shifts the demand curve). BW increased the population and then said:

Table 8-4 Z-scores for Subjects on Each Indicator

Indicator/group	BW and CF	HT and OY	Difference
General activity/exploration levels			
Activity level			
1.	0.32	0.73	0.41
2.	−0.11	−0.29	0.18
3.	0.19	0.55	0.36
Exploratory behaviors			
4.	0.17	−0.32	0.49
5.	0.42	0.13	0.29
6.	1.09	−0.70	1.79*
7.	0.69	0.80	0.11
8.	0.22	−0.21	0.43
Data management skills			
Data recording			
9.	1.17	−0.01	1.18*
10.	0.21	−0.31	0.52
11.	0.48	0.90	0.42
12.	−0.37	0.33	0.70
Efficient tool use			
13.	0.70	−0.20	0.90*
14.	−0.67	0.10	0.77
15.	0.67	−0.06	0.73
Use of evidence			
16.	1.29	0.17	1.12*
17.	0.91	0.64	0.27
Thinking and planning skills			
Consistent behaviors			
18.	0.02	0.87	0.85
19.	0.88	0.00	0.88
20.	−0.13	1.01	1.14*
Effective generalizations			
21.	1.26	0.93	0.33
22.	1.88	−0.59	2.47*
23.	0.50	−0.50	1.00*
24.	1.52	−0.02	1.54*
Effective experimental behaviors			
25.	0.77	−0.01	0.78
26.	0.50	0.07	0.43

global planning and local planning, isolated from a complex reasoning task. In a study of planning behavior in problem solving he found that more intelligent persons scoring high on reasoning tests tended to spend relatively more time than low-scoring persons on global (higher-order) planning and relatively less time on local (lower-order) planning. Poorer reasoners, however, seemed to emphasize local rather than global planning relative to the better reasoners. Similarly, Anderson (1987) investigated individual differences in students' solutions to LISP programming problems and found that the poorer students tended to plan less in their problem-solving activities. These findings are similar to those of our study: individuals who engage in planning an experiment are more successful (measured by our gain scores criterion) than those who do not. To illustrate, CF (more successful) decided to test the effects of weather on the demand for ice cream (where weather can range from 1 — cold and wet — to 10 — warm and dry). From the planning menu she chose the variables to investigate: price, quantity demanded, quantity supplied, surplus, shortage, and weather. After changing the weather index from a medium default value of 5 to a value of 10, she said, "OK, then that means, I think, there should be an increased demand for ice cream." She collected and recorded the data, observed that, indeed, the quantity demanded of ice cream went up, and chose the framework "same good, change independent variable" so that she could stay in the ice cream market and manipulate the weather variable further. From the new planning menu she selected the same variables as before, then changed the weather: "I'm gonna make the weather really bad. I'll put it at 1. . . . I think there'll be a surplus now, at the other extreme." This prediction was confirmed by her data. The other two subjects that were less successful evidenced much less front end (higher-order) planning of an experiment and typically only selected a few (or irrelevant) variables from the planning menu. Often changing an independent variable has effects on certain other variables, and a given experiment should focus on those. That is, a population increase could have an effect on the *demand* of a good and, in the long run, on the *price* of that good.

The next discriminating indicator (indicator 29) reflects the richness and tenacity of an individual's actions within an experiment as measured by the average number of actions taken per experimental episode. A thorough, systematic investigation of a concept is indicated by more connected actions within an experiment while more aimless behavior is seen by fewer connected actions. If a person were to move around randomly in this environment, making changes, moving on to new things, with little or no thread of consistency, then each experiment would have a small number of actions taken within a given market. Subjects BW and CF were not random movers. Their method of investigation was to choose a market and do many things within that market, always observing the effects of their manipulations and recording them in the on-line notebook. Thus, the average number of actions within their experiments was much greater than for subjects HT and OY. In addition, across three sessions the more successful subjects' number of actions per experiment *increased,* showing that their experiments became more complex as they gained additional domain knowledge. The less successful subjects did not demonstrate a similar increase in complexity of experiments over time; rather, their average number of actions went up and down across sessions.

Relevant to these results, Sternberg and Davidson (1982; see also Sternberg, 1985) looked at individual differences in the solution to insight problems where individuals were free to spend as long as they liked in the solution process. They computed a correlation of .62 between the time spent and the score on the insight problems; thus, persistence and involvement in the problems was significantly correlated with success in solution. They argue that more intelligent persons do not give up, nor do they fall for the obvious, often incorrect, solutions.

This activity is captured in *student procedure graphs;* we constructed these for subjects based on the idea of the problem behavior graphs of Newell and Simon (1972) showing student actions and the resulting state of knowledge. A state of knowledge is represented by a node, and the application of an operator is represented by an arrow pointing to the right. The result of the operation is the node at the head of the arrow. Vertical lines connecting nodes indicate a return to a previous state of knowledge because no new information was supplied. The operators and their symbols used for our purposes are listed below. Each operator is recorded above or below a horizontal arrow; an operator below the arrow indicates that the variable was changed back to its original default or baseline value. Most of the nodes (rectangles) contain symbols representing the resulting operation, also listed below.

Operators and variables		Operations	
P	Price	R	Notebook recording
G	Good	S	Supply curve
H	Hypothesis	D	Demand curve
FD	Town factor (demand shifts)	/	Superimposed curves (e.g., S/D)
FS	Town factor (supply shifts)		
GR	Graph	X	Error
T	Table		

Learning goals, meaning economic concepts that can be discovered, are indicated by symbols beginning with the letter "L" followed by a number—for example, the law of demand is L5. Their meaning can be seen in Figure 8-1.

Following are two examples of how the student procedure graphs are used to visually illustrate the flow of problem-solving activity in more and less efficient individuals (in relation to indicator 29).

Figures 8-13 and 8-14 exhibit obvious differences in experimental behavior using data from BW and another subject showing below average gain (subject SS) whose performance illustrates well the contrast between focused and fragmented search. The horizontal movement depicted in the graph of BW's performance (see Figure 8-13) shows much more focused and connected persistent behavior than the vertical, less relevant movement in SS's experimental

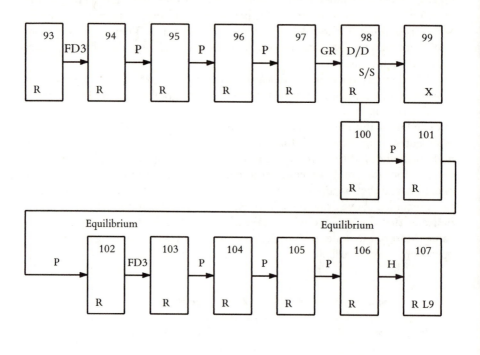

P	Price	X	Incorrect attempt at demand shift
R	Records data	L9	Demand shift
H	Hypothesis	D/D	Superimposes two demand curves
GR	Graph	S/S	Superimposes two supply curves
FD3	Income		

Figure 8-13 Student procedure graph of a more successful subject where horizontal movement of the graph indicates market investigation prior to the second hypothesis.

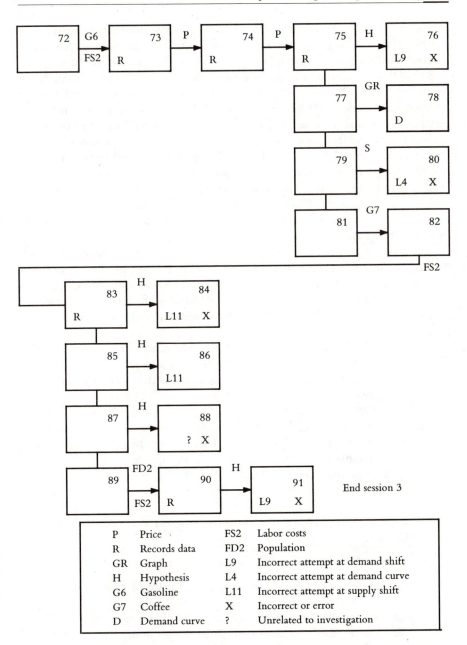

Figure 8-14 Student procedure graph of a less successful subject where vertical movement of the graph indicates a lack of experimentation.

behavior, as seen in Figure 8-14. In Figure 8-13, BW (more successful) began investigating the large car market by collecting data for the market when income was $20,000. At nodes 94 through 97 he changed the average income to $30,000 and collected additional data by changing price three times. Next, he plotted a demand curve (node 98) with income at $20,000 and then at $30,000, and at node 99 he made a hypothesis that when income increased quantity demanded increased and the demand curve would move to the right. During the period from nodes 100 to 102 he had the computer adjust the price back to equilibrium. From 103 to 106, he changed income to $40,000 and again had the computer adjust the price back to equilibrium. The subject said, "It's only if you change something other than price that you get a new demand curve." Finally, at node 107 he hypothesized correctly that demand curves shift as a result of changes other than price (that is, one characterization or description of what causes demand curves to shift).

In contrast to the systematic, persistent performance evidenced by BW, subject SS (less successful) spent a considerable amount of time generating hypotheses that were unrelated to the current experiment. Although both subjects were attempting to characterize a demand shift, Figure 8-14 and the following summary of actions clearly demonstrate an ineffective experimental procedure.

At node 73, SS entered the market for gasoline, and from nodes 74 to 75 she changed the price from $1.18 a gallon to $1.00 a gallon and then down to $0.75 a gallon. At node 76 she hypothesized that "as the price of complementary goods decrease, the quantity demanded increases." This was incorrect. She then tried to graph a demand curve (77 to 78) but was unsuccessful. During the period involving the nodes 79 to 80 she hypothesized that as price increases the demand curve shifts down and to the left. This was incorrect. The subject then entered the coffee market suddenly and without any apparent reason (82). At 83 she changed labor costs from $4.00 an hour to $20.00 an hour followed by three more incorrect hypotheses (84 to 88):

- As labor costs increase, the quantity supplied decreases and shortage increases.

- Quantity demanded has no relation to labor costs.

- Quantity demanded has no relation to the price of resources.

During 89 and 90 she decided to change the population from 10,000 to 50,000 and then returned the labor costs to $4.00 per hour. Finally, at 91, she again attempted a hypothesis that as population increases quantity demanded increases and quantity supplied increases. This, too, was not quite right.

A major difference in experimental behavior illustrated here seems to be one of staying with a problem until it is solved. Subject BW, when his initial hypothesis turned out to be incorrect, did more experimenting to understand more precisely the nature of the problem. In contrast, subject SS, who apparently was motivated by just getting a hypothesis correct, tried different hypotheses, some of which were wild guesses since there was no relation between the stated hypotheses and the experiments actually conducted.

The next indicator to discriminate between more or less effective performance was indicator 28: changing only a limited number of variables per experiment in which the fewer variables that are changed the better the subsequent performance. BW and CF (more successful) were very conscientious in changing only one variable at a time per experiment. Given the freedom of the environment, the temptation was often to make changes to multiple variables concurrently; however, the ensuing results were obscured as to what was actually responsible for the state of current market affairs. Subjects HT and OY (less successful) often fell prey to this temptation of making multiple changes. For example, while investigating the market for large cars, OY, when asked what he was going to do, responded, "I want to just go back and change some stuff." He then proceeded to change interest rates from 15 percent to 6.7 percent, number of suppliers (that is, large car dealerships) from ten to twenty, consumer preference (meaning the popularity of large cars) from 5 (medium) to 10 (very high) and then back to 5, per capita income from $20,000 to $25,000, and then interest rates from 6.7 percent to 9 percent. He did this all at once without collecting any data between the changes. When asked about what he would predict as a result of all of the changes, he said, "I think they'll still buy the cars, because the income is higher now . . . but the interest rates are higher . . . but since they're making more income, then I think they can afford it." OY's working memory capacity has obviously been overloaded at this point, and he fails to even consider the effects of the number of suppliers, consumer preference, or any of the potential interactions. Upon inspecting the market data, he sees that, in fact, there is an overall surplus of large cars. This he views as confirmation of his prediction, but it obviously is confounded by the fact that he had raised the number of large car dealerships in *Smithtown* as well as the per capita income. These last two actions actually have opposing effects: increasing the number of dealers would result in a surplus of cars but increasing the income would cause a shortage of cars.

The last indicator falling under the thinking and planning category involves collecting sufficient amounts of data before making a hypothesis of any of the economic concepts (indicator 24). Good scientific methodology involves generalizing a concept based on enough examples or instances of a phenomenon rather than inadequate data which may include elements of chance, confounding variables, or other things. BW (more successful) investigated the concept of surplus and its relationship to price, quantity demanded, and quantity supplied. In the following protocol, it is apparent that he investigated the concept from many angles, collecting more than enough data before rendering a hypothesis. BW has just had the computer adjust the price of hamburger buns (raising the price):

> The price went up a lot, and there's a big surplus. . . . Well, as I found out before, as price goes up, the quantity demanded goes down, quantity supplied goes up. So, by now the quantity demanded has gone below the quantity supplied, and there's a surplus. So, the next time around I think the price should go back down 'cause there's a lot of hamburger buns around here. They'll go on sale.

He watched the price slowly converge on equilibrium, interrupting the computer adjustments with price adjustments himself until he found the equilibrium price where, "at $1.55 it came out right . . . no surplus and no shortage." BW speculated,

> OK, so I found out when there's no surplus and no shortage the price won't change. I could phrase that into a hypothesis also. When there's a surplus, price decreases, and when there's a shortage, price increases. . . . If surplus is greater than zero, then the price decreases.

When asked if he could characterize surplus any other way, he responded,

> Well, it's just quantity supplied minus quantity demanded. I can state that. *I've got enough examples!* There's a surplus when the quantity supplied is greater than the quantity demanded.

He then used the hypothesis menu and formalized the above statement into a successful specification of "surplus." Immediately afterwards, he used the same data and logic to characterize "shortage."

In contrast, HT (less successful) was content to make predictions and hypotheses based on single events and nonreplicated experiments. This was a poor strategy for this subject to follow since her data management skills were neither efficient nor consistent. Moreover, sometimes she forgot or misconstrued what the previous data were, not bothering to go back and retrieve the omitted data. For instance, after spending a long time in the final session trying to determine the influence of population changes on some of the dependent variables, she conducted an experiment which involved decreasing the population of *Smithtown* from 10,000 to 5,000. At that time, she was investigating the doughnut market, and the experimenter asked what she expected to see as the result of this population decrease.

HT: So, less people will eat [doughnuts].

EXPERIMENTER: What about quantity supplied and price?

HT: When population decreases, demand . . . quantity demanded decreases, and quantity supplied decreases . . . price increases.

The market actually depicted the price and the quantity supplied remaining the same while the only change was in the quantity demanded, which changed as a function of the demand curve shift. Next, HT's actions centered around price changes to get an equilibrium price for the doughnut market in the smaller sized town. She did not replicate the experiment with the population change, and later, when attempting to articulate a hypothesis, she remembered erroneous results and showed little understanding of cause and effect among the variables:

HT: OK, so, I think when population decreased, the price decreased. That's why there is changes between quantity supplied and quantity demanded.

EXPERIMENTER: What was the first thing that happened?

HT: I think quantity demanded decreased . . . and when quantity demanded decreased, price decreased. Quantity supplied . . . let's see, population decreased . . . quantity supplied decreased.

Data Management Discriminating Indicators

Our more successful subjects, BW and CF, generally exhibited very good data management skills, using their notebooks efficiently and consistently. They typically made notebook entries following variable changes and included variables in their notebooks that had been specified beforehand in the planning menu. In contrast, the less successful subjects (HT and OY) never became fully automatic in entering data to their notebooks. They continued to forget to record important information throughout the three sessions and had to rely on the history window to insert forgotten data. They also excluded variables whose values were changed or that were listed in the planning menu. In addition, they continued to omit baseline data. This latter omission was a major problem when attempting to attribute causes to market conditions.

Indicator 9 concerns the total number of notebook entries and indicator 13 the number of relevant notebook entries made. With regard to just the total number of notebook entries, the more entries, the better the performance. As to the *type* of notebook entries, the more relevant notebook entries that were made overall, the better the performance, where relevant variables are those specified in the planning menu as the variables the subject was interested in exploring and collecting data on. This measure indicates whether the individual used the notebook efficiently for recording important information.

To illustrate the contrast in types of data recording skills, Figures 8-15 and 8-16 show examples of students with better and worse recording skills. In Figure 8-15, BW (more successful) entered the tea market and, prior to changing any variables, decided "to see what the initial conditions are." He followed the observation with a notebook entry of the baseline data, seen in nodes 1 and 2. At node 3 he increased the price of tea from $1.83 a box to $2.50 a box "to see if there's a relation between price and quantity demanded and quantity supplied." This price change was also duly recorded in the notebook. During nodes 4 and 5 BW continued to investigate this relationship by decreasing the price twice more, following each change with a notebook entry. He then

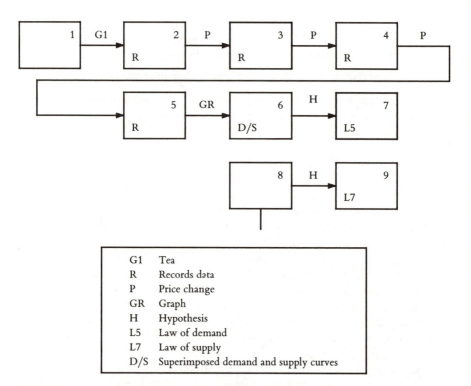

Figure 8-15 Student procedure graph of a more successful subject showing good data recording skills.

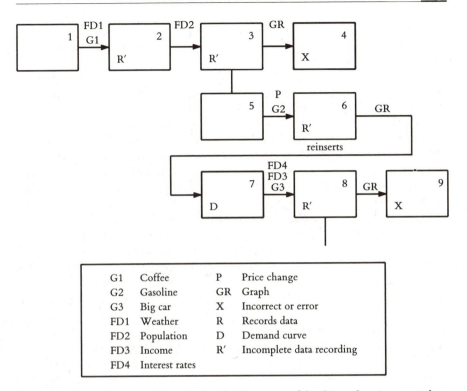

G1	Coffee	P	Price change
G2	Gasoline	GR	Graph
G3	Big car	X	Incorrect or error
FD1	Weather	R	Records data
FD2	Population	D	Demand curve
FD3	Income	R′	Incomplete data recording
FD4	Interest rates		

Figure 8-16 Student procedure graph of a less successful subject showing poor data recording skills.

graphed a demand curve (6) and successfully superimposed a supply curve, saving the graph for future reference. This systematic performance led to the correct induction of the laws of demand and supply (7 through 9):

- As price increases, the quantity demanded decreases.
- When price increases, quantity supplied increases.

Our less successful subject, HT, demonstrated inefficient data recording skills (see Figure 8-16). She rather haphazardly entered data into the notebook and failed to systematically record variable changes. Figure 8-16 illustrates some of the multiple variable changes and subsequent failure to record sufficient data into the on-line notebook. In Figure 8-16, the subject started out in the coffee market and changed the weather conditions from a mediocre value of 5 to a slightly less pleasant value of 3 to see if that would affect the demand for coffee, seen in nodes 1 and 2. She predicted that if the weather decreased (became worse), then the price of coffee would increase. However, since she had failed to record any baseline data for the coffee market, she was unable to make the appropriate comparisons.

She then decided to ignore the weather influences, and at 3 changed the population from 10,000 to 4,000 persons. She predicted that if the population decreased, then a surplus would result. But, as with the above situation, she had failed to record the baseline data for when the population was 10,000, so she reinserted the necessary data from the past experiments. Next, HT tried to graph some data at node 4: price by quantity demanded and price by population. However, in each case there was only one data point per variable and thus no line could be drawn. She then switched to the market for gasoline (5 and 6) and raised the price from \$1.50 a gallon to \$4.00 a gallon. Since she again had failed to record the data from the market when gasoline was \$1.50 a gallon, she had to reinsert this information into the notebook. With these additional data she tried to graph it again, and at 7 she successfully plotted a demand curve. At node 8 she entered the market for large cars. Her first action there was *not* to record the baseline data, but to change income from \$20,000 to \$30,000. She predicted that "if the income increases, people will have more money to buy large cars, so the price of the cars will increase, and the quantity demanded will increase, the quantity supplied will decrease, and there will be a shortage." When she saw the data resulting from her increase to the per capita income, however, price and quantity supplied actually stayed the same while the quantity demanded did, in fact, go up. Since she did not have the baseline data, she was unable to tell whether or not her prediction was confirmed since "increase" and "decrease" have to be interpreted relative to some other data. Finally, at node 9, she changed interest rates from 15 percent to 10 percent, predicting that if interest rates decrease then price will decrease and quantity demanded will increase and quantity supplied will decrease. She stated that she believed her prediction was confirmed, but later realized that price had stayed the same. Her last action in this segment shows how she tried to graph price against interest rates, but she did not have enough data.

Indicator 16 is the last major discriminating index in the data management category and deals with the number of specific predictions made by an individual in relation to the number of general hypotheses. In this case, the higher the ratio, the better the overall performance. Studies that have investigated individual differences between novices and experts in solving physics problems have found that an important distinction between the two groups is that whereas the experts used a "working-forward" strategy, the novices used a "working-backward" strategy (Simon and Simon, 1978; Larkin et al., 1980; Chi, Glaser, and Rees, 1982). These studies suggest that the novices may be more data driven whereas experts may be schema driven in the sense that their representation of a problem accesses a repertoire of solution methods. Thus, the novices' limitations are derived from their inability to infer further knowledge from the literal cues in the problem statement. In contrast, these inferences necessarily are generated in the context of the relevant knowledge structures that experts possess. Predictions in *Smithtown* serve as a foundation or stepping stones to more general abstract principles and laws of economics. Our more successful subjects seemed to be able to work forward toward a goal—that is, they knew where they were going—in contrast to our less successful subjects who often got stuck at the more superficial or data level of investigation. To illustrate, CF (more successful) was interested in looking at the relationship between the coffee and tea markets, "because they are similar." First she increased the price of coffee and collected data on the resulting decreased quantity demanded and increased quantity supplied. Next, she chose the framework "change good, keep independent variables the same," changing to the tea market. Since the price of coffee had been increased, more people had shifted to drinking tea; thus the tea market came up with an initial shortage, confirming her initial prediction that "If the price of coffee increases, then the quantity demanded of tea will increase." She remained in these two markets and went on to investigate the concept of a new equilibrium point and demand shifts. She continued making predictions, observing the data, then proceeded on to successfully articulate the rules underlying the higher-level concepts. The less successful subjects skipped among markets, failing to make sufficient predictions in order to test developing hypotheses that would have led ultimately to the discovery of more economic concepts.

Activity/Exploration Discriminating Indicator

This last category concerns the number of times the subject had the computer make a price adjustment toward equilibrium (indicator 6). From the beginning sessions, our better subjects immediately grasped the utility of letting the computer make price adjustments while both the pattern of the changes it made and the effects on the market condition were observed. After his first computer change of the price, subject BW (more successful), when asked if the change was in accord with his expectations, said

> Well, yes, I thought so. Quantity demanded for hamburger buns was very high, and there were very few hamburger buns, so, it seems that suppliers would be able to get more for them. So, the price went up and there's still a shortage of hamburger buns. If I let the computer adjust the price again, the price will probably go up again.

He demonstrated an understanding that when the computer changed the price, it provided him an opportunity for observing systematic changes and relationships. Although he did not have enough data to conceptualize "equilibrium point," he had started to understand that when shortages exist, prices go up. Our less successful subjects tried to use the option "computer adjust price," but they did not really grasp its purpose. It was revealed in the second session that subject HT (less successful) had no idea what was going on:

HT: Just now I had the "Computer Adjust Price."

EXPERIMENTER: Yes. Do you understand what's going on?

HT: No, I have no idea about that.

EXPERIMENTER: What happened when you chose that? How did it adjust the price?

HT: So, the price now increased from $1.70 to $1.90, and the quantity demanded decreased, decreased just a little bit. The quantity supplied increased a little bit too. No surplus, and the shortage is 6. Population is the same. So the price increased.

EXPERIMENTER: What would happen if you let the computer adjust the price again? Would it go up, down, or stay the same?

HT: I don't know much about the "Computer Adjust Price." It can increase or decrease, reduce the price.

The subject continued to have difficulty with this throughout the first two sessions (or 80 percent of the entire time with *Smithtown*), not realizing the benefits of observing the computer make price adjustments toward equilibrium.

Performance differences between our two groups were probably a function of the interaction of all of the aforementioned performance indicators. The behaviors that differentiated the subjects consisted of generalizing concepts across markets where the generalizations were a result of well thought out and executed plans, having sufficient data collected prior to the generalization, engaging in more complex experiments within a given market and not moving randomly among markets (that is, staying in an experiment long enough to extract valuable information), changing variables in a parsimonious and systematic fashion, recording important data in the notebook from different experiments, and generating and testing predictions that could lead to the induction of economic principles and laws.

GENERAL DISCUSSION

The comparisons between the economics classroom and the experimental group in their pretest and posttest results suggest that learning in the exploratory world is at least as effective as traditional classroom learning. In fact, when learning time is compared, the students interacting with *Smithtown* spent less than half the amount of time formally learning economics compared to the length of time spent by the students in the economics classroom. It is possible that a group receiving classroom instruction *and* the intelligent discovery world could do even better. This remains an empirical question.

Our second, more compelling concern, was with the experimental group. In particular, we wanted to know how individuals learn or do not learn in this type of environment and on what measures the better and poorer learners differ. We illustrated that the contrasting pairs of subjects differed mostly on measures related to thinking and planning skills (that is, effective experimental behaviors) with fewer but significant differences in data management skills. The behaviors that differentiated the subjects were the following:

1. *Generalizing concepts across markets.* The better subjects would try out economic concepts in different markets to see if they were supported whereas the less effective subjects would not bother to extend an experiment across markets.

2. *Engaging in more complex experiments within a given market and not moving randomly among markets.* Typically, the better subjects had many more actions within a given experiment and investigated fewer markets overall compared to the less effective subjects.

3. *Changing only one variable at a time and holding all others constant.* The biggest problem for the poorer subjects was that they persisted in changing multiple variables simultaneously. The better subjects changed fewer variables at a time, typically just single variables.

4. *Basing generalizations on sufficient data.* We set as our criteria having at least three related rows of notebook entries before using the hypothesis menu. The more successful subjects did not attempt to make general hypotheses prior to collecting enough data on a given concept whereas the less successful subjects were content to make careless and impulsive generalizations based on inadequate data.

5. *Conducting an experiment based on a planned manipulation or set of manipulations.* The planning and inferencing abilities of the better subjects allowed them to set up an experiment and execute it thoroughly, whereas the less successful subjects rarely evidenced advance (higher-level) planning throughout the experimental sessions.

6. *Generating and testing experimental predictions.* The better subjects tended to be more hypothesis or rule driven (working forward towards a goal), whereas the less efficient subjects were more data driven in experimentation. When

evidence does not confirm a hypothesis, further experimentation is required to modify the hypothesis. The better subjects generally recognized and implemented this approach, whereas others engaged in less systematic activities.

7. *Entering data into the on-line notebook.* Better subjects had more notebook entries overall compared to the less effective subjects. In addition, those entries tended to be more consistent with, and relevant to, the focus of their investigation.

8. *Using the computer to make price adjustments of a good towards equilibrium.*

We obtained demographic information from all subjects along with the pretest battery; two questions asked were (1) what science courses the subject had taken since high school, and (2) what the subject's major was. Subject BW (more effective) had taken just two science courses (physics I and II), and he was a sophomore, majoring in math. Subject CF (more effective) had taken three science courses (physics I, II, and III) and was also a sophomore, majoring in electrical engineering. In our less effective group, subject HT had five science courses (physics, two semesters of calculus, Fortran, and chemistry), and she was a freshman, majoring in pharmacy; subject OY had taken three science courses (chemistry, biology, and physics) and was a sophomore majoring in electrical engineering. These pairs could have differed in their scientific investigative behaviors as a function of past academic courses or variables relating to learning style differences. Thus, according to a hypothesis that different backgrounds were a cause of the observed differences, we would have expected the less scientific subjects to have taken fewer science courses. This was not the case. In fact, the less successful group had an average of four prior science courses while our more successful group had an average of 2.5 science courses since high school. In addition, each of the subjects was a science major. Of the original ten subjects in our experimental group, this same pattern was found. Dividing the subjects into two groups of five each based on their gain score, the two groups had the same number of declared science majors in each (three per group). However, the less successful group had taken considerably more science courses since high school (total of twenty-seven) compared to the more successful group (total of eight). Thus the idea of differential exposure to science training seems not to be a major factor in determining who will demonstrate better scientific behaviors.

Although this study focused on contrasting subjects in a descriptive and exploratory sense, the question arises as to whether the findings generalize to the population at large. As part of the Learning Abilities Measurement Program (LAMP) at the Air Force Human Resources Laboratory, the first author tested a large group of subjects — 527 basic recruits at Lackland Air Force Base, Texas

—with a modified version of the system which included forty-four perform-ance indicators automatically tallied in real time and summarized by the com-puter at the end of a 3.5-hour session. Using a measure of general intelligence as the dependent variable (the AFQT, a composite score derived from the Armed Services Vocational Aptitude Battery), we list the results of a correlational analysis of the indicators with AFQT score. Following are the indicators which significantly correlated with the AFQT score at $p < .001$:

1. Engaging in more complex experiments within a given market was tallied by the average number of actions per experiment. This indicator had a significant correlation with AFQT score; therefore the more connected actions taken in an experiment was associated with a higher AFQT score. Related to the *nature* of the experimentation, we also tallied the total number of markets investigated. A stepwise regression analysis was run on the data with AFQT score as the dependent variable. "Number of markets" was one of the five most predictive variables with an inverse relationship to AFQT. That is, the fewer the number of markets investigated, the more predictive of higher AFQT score.

2. The average number of independent variables changed at one time (that is, per experiment) had a significant negative correlation to AFQT score, implying that the fewer variables changed at a time, the better the performance.

3. Making hypotheses based on sufficient data was estimated by the indicator computing if the subject had at least three rows of related notebook entries before using the hypothesis menu. This correlated with AFQT score in our larger sample. Thus the better subjects relied on more data before formulat-ing general principles and laws.

4. When a subject specifies his or her intentions for an experiment via a contrived manipulation on a variable or set of variables in the planning menu and actually conducts the experiment with those variables, this indicator is incremented. There was a significant correlation between planned performance and AFQT score. This implies that the more intelligent persons tended to engage in more higher-level, advance planning of an experiment.

5. Making and testing predictions of experimental outcomes and then observing the results for confirmation or negation of the prediction is effective interrogative behavior and tallied by this indicator. In the larger study, the overall number of predictions that a subject made was correlated with AFQT score.

6. The quantity and quality of on-line notebook entries were two signifi-cant indicators discriminating among subjects. First, the total number of entries in the notebook was significantly correlated with AFQT score; therefore the

higher AFQT scores were associated with more notebook entries overall. Variables entered into the notebook that had been specified in the planning menu was the second indicator, correlating with AFQT score. This implies that higher AFQT scores are associated with consistent behaviors, meaning formulating a planned set of variables to investigate and reliably entering those variables into the notebook.

Other indicators from the larger study that significantly correlated with AFQT score included the total number of actions taken in the experimental sessions, total number of economic concepts learned, and the number of experimental frameworks utilized by the subject. The total number of actions taken in the experimental sessions correlated with AFQT score, implying that the more intelligent persons were more active overall than the less intelligent persons. This must be viewed in light of the other indicators relating to the quality of performance, however, since it is not a matter of simply being "busy" in the environment but of being active in a connected, directed, systematic sense. For total number of economic concepts learned, the higher AFQT scores were associated with learning more concepts in the 3.5-hour session. Finally, the number of experimental frameworks utilized by the subjects correlated with AFQT score, implying that the experimental frameworks were employed more by the successful individuals as a planning procedure than the less successful persons.

Thus, the larger study seems to corroborate many of the findings from the descriptive analyses, extending and more precisely delineating individual differences in learning from this type of environment.

A limitation of the present study was the collapsing of data across sessions for this initial investigation. This can result in a loss of information that is valuable for examining individual differences and changes in knowledge and skills over time. Another limitation was that the use of difference scores on the economic tests as the measure of success was not ideal. That is because our primary focus for *Smithtown* was on the learning of good inquiry skills and only secondarily on the acquisition of economic knowledge. The ideal criterion (and data we plan to collect) should be the transfer of skills across domains; that is, how well students perform in a new environment with a similar structure or architecture but which differs in content from *Smithtown*. Currently there are several other systems being developed that fit these criteria, and further studies are planned which will investigate transfer of learning of these inquiry skills to new domains.

In general, it appears that in the rather complex task involved in this study many of the behaviors that differentiated successful and less successful subjects are similar to those identified in previous studies with both laboratory and more realistic tasks. Individual differences in performance in our exploratory environment involved the following dimensions: generalization, goal setting and planning, more or less structured search, specific performance heuristics, and memory management.

Better subjects tended to think in terms of generalizing their hypotheses and explorations beyond the specific experiment or market they were working on. They conceived of a lawful regularity as a general principle and as a description of a class of events rather than a local description. Better reasoners were more sensitive to the existence of deeper explanatory principles in addition to local data descriptions; they appeared to realize that discovery was not only a function of data, but that they needed to generate some rule that could provide them with a goal for their actions. In this sense they tended to be more rule or hypothesis driven than the less successful subjects.

Better reasoners also engaged in more connected actions — structured search. They conceived of a particular market as a rich environment in which many actions needed to be taken in order to develop a structured understanding; disconnected probes did not assist them in their attempt at understanding. Less successful subjects, on the other hand, moved more frequently between markets. Their behavior was more fragmented and displayed a breadth of exploration, in contrast to a more in-depth search, in their attempt to establish meaning in a particular context.

Planning behaviors differentiated individuals whereby successful subjects planned their manipulations and experiments. Given the opportunity, successful subjects would structure a plan and then carry it out with specific information. The immediacy of carrying out some action was more desirable to the less successful subjects, comparable to jumping to solving equations in physics problems.

The successful individuals in our study employed more powerful heuristics compared to the less successful individuals. They manipulated fewer variables, holding variables constant while one variable was systematically explored. Less successful subjects did not seem to realize the power of this heuristic, and for them it was a less desirable activity. Successful subjects took their time to generate sufficient evidence before coming to a conclusion, whereas the less successful subjects were more impulsive and attempted to induce generalizations based on inadequate information.

The necessity to manage memory was evident in the performance of the better subjects. They realized that they needed to store and display the information they had collected. Their data management performance was goal driven in the sense that the data collected were relevant to the current focus of their investigation. This contrasts with the poorer subjects' data management behaviors which were mostly inconsistent and often unrelated to an overall goal in their experimentation.

With regard to inductive problem solving, as Klahr and Dunbar (1988; see also Greeno and Simon, 1984) describe the interplay between rules and instances, the best learning strategy is a combination of bottom-up and top-down processing. In our subjects, this seemed to be the case: the better subjects would predict variable relationships and then test those hypotheses while concurrently exploring and collecting data which led to further generalizations. Our less effective subjects seemed to be limited to a more data-driven (or bottom-up) approach, often falling short of grasping the larger picture. This is in accord with findings investigating differences between novice and expert in problem solving (Larkin et al., 1980).

Furthermore, the importance of higher-level planning in this inductive discovery environment is in agreement with studies of individual differences in reasoning tasks (Sternberg, 1985). Better subjects consistently planned an experiment and then executed it to completion according to plan, in sharp contrast to the more haphazard, less planned approach applied by less successful subjects in their experimental methodologies.

This, then, is our initial study of individual differences in learning from an exploratory environment where students had the opportunity to engage in active discovery learning of economic concepts by manipulating variables in a hypothetical town and observing the repercussions. Overall, the system worked as we had hoped: tutoring on the scientific inquiry skills resulted in learning the domain knowledge as evidenced by the performance on the posttest battery.

We have begun to delineate those skills and behaviors which are important to scientific discovery. Although there is currently very little research being conducted in this area, the behaviors we have identified in this chapter fit in with the findings from related research (Klahr and Dunbar, 1988; Langley et al., 1987). In addition, these specific behaviors relate to individual differences found in general studies on problem solving, concept formation, and so on. From an instructional perspective, the behaviors we have denoted can consequently serve as a focal point for relevant intervention studies.

ACKNOWLEDGMENTS

The authors wish to acknowledge the many persons whose contributions have been invaluable to this project: Jeff Blais, Jeff Bonar, Kathleen Katterman, Alan Lesgold, Paul Resnick, and Jamie Schultz.

The Center for the Study of Learning is funded by the Office of Educational Research and Improvement of the U.S. Department of Education. Support for computer equipment and software development was provided by the Cognitive Science Program of the Office of Naval Research. Additional support for the current large-scale testing and analyses was provided by the Air Force Human Resources Laboratory. The opinions expressed do not necessarily reflect the position or policy of either NIE, ONR, or AFHRL, and no official endorsement should be inferred.

REFERENCES

Anderson, J. R. (1987, July). Using intelligent tutoring systems to analyze data. Paper presented at the Cognitive Science Society Conference, Seattle, Wash.

Anderson, J., Boyle, C., Farrell, R., and Reiser, B. (1984). *Cognitive principles in the design of computer tutors.* Technical report, Advanced Computer Tutoring Project, Carnegie Mellon University, Pittsburgh.

Bonar, J. G., Cunningham, R., and Schultz, J. N. (1986, September). An object oriented architecture for intelligent tutoring. In *Proceedings of the ACM conference on object oriented programming systems, languages, and application.*

Bradshaw, G. F., Langley, P. W., and Simon, H. A. (1983). Studying scientific discovery by computer simulation. *Science,* 222(4627): 971–975.

Brown, J. S. (1983). Learning by doing revised for electronic learning environments. In M. A. White (Ed.), *The future of electronic learning.* Hillsdale, N.J.: Erlbaum.

Champagne, A., and Klopfer, L. (1982). *Laws of motion: Computer-simulated experiments in mechanics. Teachers Guide.* New Rochelle, N.Y.: Educational Materials and Equipment Co.

Chi, M. T. H., Glaser, R., and Rees, E. (1982). Expertise in problem solving. In R. J. Sternberg (Ed.), *Advances in the psychology of human intelligence,* Vol. 1. Hillsdale, N.J.: Erlbaum.

Cronbach, L. J. (1966). The logic of experiments on discovery. In L. S. Shulman and E. R. Keisler (Eds.), *Learning by discovery.* Chicago: Rand McNally.

diSessa, A. (1982). Unlearning Aristotelian physics; A study of knowledge-based learning. *Cognitive Science,* 6(1): 37–75.

Glaser, R. (1984). Education and thinking: The role of knowledge. *American Psychologist,* 39:93–104.

Greeno, J. G., and Simon, H. A. (1984). *Problem solving and reasoning* (Tech. Rep. No. UPITT/LRDC/ONR/APS-14). Pittsburgh: University of Pittsburgh, Learning Research and Development Center. To appear in R. C. Atkinson, R. Herrnstein, G. Lindzey, and R. D. Luce (Eds.), *Stevens' handbook of experimental psychology* (rev. ed.). New York: Wiley.

Hayes, J. R., and Flower, L. S. (1986). Writing research and the writer. *American Psychologist,* 41(10): 1106–1113.

Holland, J. H., Holyoak, K. J., Nisbett, R. E., and Thagard, P. R. (1986). *Induction: Processes of inference, learning, and discovery.* Cambridge, Mass.: MIT Press.

Klahr, D., and Dunbar, K. (1988). Dual space search during scientific reasoning. *Cognitive Science,* 12: 1–48.

Kuhn, D., and Phelps, D. (1982). The development of problem-solving strategies. In H. W. Reese (Ed.), *Advances in child development and behavior* Vol. 17. New York: Academic Press.

Langley, P., Simon, H. A., Bradshaw, G. L., and Zytkow, J. M. (1987). *Scientific discovery: Computational explorations of the creative process.* Cambridge, Mass.: MIT Press.

Larkin, J., McDermott, J., Simon, D. P., and Simon, H. A. (1980). Models of competence in solving physics problems. *Cognitive Science*, 4: 317–345.

Lawler, R. W. (1982). Designing computer-based microworlds. *Byte*, 7(8): 138–160.

Michalski, R. S. (1986). Understanding the nature of learning: Issues and research directions. In R. S. Michalski, J. G. Carbonell, and T. M. Mitchell (Eds.), *Machine learning: An artificial intelligence approach*, Vol. II. Los Altos, Calif.: Morgan Kaufmann.

Newell, A., and Simon, H. A. (1972). *Human problem solving*. Englewood Cliffs, N.J.: Prentice-Hall.

Pellegrino, J. W., and Glaser, R. (1980). Components of inductive reasoning. In R. Snow, P. Federico, and W. Montague (Eds.), *Aptitude, learning and instruction*, Vol. I. Hillsdale, N.J.: Erlbaum.

Reimann, P. (1986). *REFRACT: A microworld for geometrical optics*. Unpublished manuscript, LRDC, University of Pittsburgh.

Shute, V. J., and Glaser, R. (In press). An intelligent tutoring system for exploring principles of economics. In R. Snow and D. Wiley (Eds.), *Straight thinking*. San Francisco: Jossey Bass.

Simon, D. P., and Simon, H. A. (1978). Individual differences in solving physics problems. In R. Siegler (Ed.), *Children's thinking: What develops?* Hillsdale, N.J.: Erlbaum.

Smith, E. E., and Medin, D. L. (Eds.) (1981). *Categories and concepts*. Cambridge, Mass.: Harvard University Press.

Sternberg, R. J. (1981). Intelligence and nonentrenchment. *Journal of Educational Psychology*, 73(1): 1–16.

Sternberg, R. J. (1985). *Beyond IQ: A triarchic theory of human intelligence*. Cambridge, England: Cambridge University Press.

Sternberg, R. J., and Davidson, J. (1982). The mind of the puzzler. *Psychology Today*, 16 (June): 37–44.

Yazdani, M. (1986). Intelligent tutoring systems survey. *Artificial Intelligence Review*, 1: 43–52.

White, B. Y. (1984). Designing computer activities to help physics students understand Newton's laws of motion. *Cognition and Instruction*, 1: 69–108.

White, B. Y., and Horowitz, P. (1987). *Thinker tools: Enabling children to understand physical laws*. (Report No. 6470). Cambridge, Mass.: Bolt, Beranek, and Newman.

Name Index

Page numbers for references are in *italics*.

Subject Index

Page numbers for definitions are in *italics*.

About the Editors

PHILLIP L. ACKERMAN is McKnight-Land Grant Professor of Psychology at the University of Minnesota. His research concerns ability determinants of skill acquisition and the integration of information processing and intellectual ability theories. He has published widely in the areas of intelligence, information processing, and human factors.

ROBERT J. STERNBERG is IBM Professor of Psychology and Education at Yale University. He has published extensively on all aspects of human intelligence, thinking, and intellectual development, and he is the editor of *Human Abilities: An Information Processing Approach* and *Mechanisms of Cognitive Development*.

ROBERT GLASER is University Professor of Psychology and Education and Director of the Learning Research and Development Center at the University of Pittsburgh. His research in the area of individual differences has ranged from cognitive analyses of aptitude and expertise to studies of adaptive machine and classroom instruction. He is editor of the series *Advances in Instructional Psychology* and, in the 1989 *Annual Review of Psychology*, he examines the status of learning theory.